PERSONAL FINANCIAL PLANNING

How to Plan for Your
Financial Freedom

PERSONAL FINANCIAL PLANNING

How to Plan for Your Financial Freedom

G. Victor Hallman, Ph.D., CPCU, CLU

*Director of Examinations, American Institute for
Property and Liability Underwriters
and
Adjunct Professor, School of Business
Administration, Temple University*

Jerry S. Rosenbloom, Ph.D., CPCU, CLU

*Executive Director, S. S. Huebner Foundation
and
Associate Professor, Wharton School
University of Pennsylvania*

McGraw-Hill Book Company

*New York   St. Louis   San Francisco
Auckland   Düsseldorf   Johannesburg
Kuala Lumpur   London   Mexico   Montreal
New Delhi   Panama   Paris   São Paulo
Singapore   Sydney   Tokyo   Toronto*

Library of Congress Cataloging in Publication Data:

Hallman, G Victor.
Personal financial planning.

Includes index.
1. Finance, Personal.   I. Rosenbloom, Jerry S.,
joint author.   II. Title.
HG179.H24   332'.024   75-4552
ISBN 0-07-025639-X

1234567890   KPKP   784321098765

The editors for this book were W. Hodson
Mogan and Patricia A. Allen, the designer
was Elliot Epstein, and the production super-
visor was George E. Oechsner. It was set in
Caledonia by University Graphics, Inc.

It was printed and bound by The Kingsport
Press.

to Susan and Victor
and
to Lynn, Debra, Heather, and Amy

CONTENTS

PREFACE

WHAT PERSONAL FINANCIAL PLANNING IS ALL ABOUT

Consumerism has been a rising tide during the 1960s and early 1970s. This is a natural and logical development because consumers always want to get the most for their money and, in addition, people generally are becoming increasingly sophisticated and understanding in financial matters. Furthermore, our economy since the end of World War II has developed an almost unheard-of level of affluence which has made financial planning important for more and more people. This has been true also because of the increasing role of women in the executive and professional work force and the rapid growth of multi-income-earner families. At the same time, however, the economic uncertainties of inflation and growing unemployment have made prudent personal financial planning all the more important.

Personal financial planning really is consumerism applied to your financial affairs. It involves coordinated, realistic planning in the areas of buying insurance, accumulating capital (including handling investments), retirement planning, tax planning, and estate planning. The aim is to help you meet your objectives in these vital areas as fully as possible and at the lowest practicable cost.

HOW YOU CAN USE PERSONAL FINANCIAL PLANNING

Personal financial planning can help you arrange your affairs in a coordinated way to meet your and your family's total financial objectives. So often, people do not look at the whole, but rather consider only one or a few particular aspects of their planning at any one time.

In this book, we consider personal financial planning as the process of determining your total financial objectives, considering alternative plans or methods for meeting those objectives, selecting the plans and methods that are best suited for you in your circumstances, implementing the plans, and then periodically reviewing the personal financial plan and making necessary changes. Interestingly enough, this is virtually the same process that business firms follow in planning for their own risks, referred to as "risk management." This technique is just as valuable for individuals and families as it is for business firms. To aid the reader in applying this process in a coordinated fashion, the book includes a "Personal Financial Planning Checklist for Decision Making" and "Personal Financial Planning Review Forms." The points and questions in this "Checklist" and much of the information called for in the "Review Forms" are cross-referenced to the appropriate chapters or pages of the book where the particular subjects are discussed. The Checklist and Review Forms can be used by the reader in several ways. They can be employed as a reference guide or review technique after reading the book, or the reader can start by going through them to review his or her own affairs and then read those sections of the book relating to the particular subjects in which he or she is most interested at that time. The book, of course, can always serve as a reference guide when other questions or problems come up on personal financial planning.

WHO CAN USE THIS BOOK

The book can be useful to a great many people. Its subject matter really applies to almost everyone. Thus, consumers will find it valuable in planning their own financial affairs. Also, as we said above, the Personal Financial Planning Checklist and Review Forms provide valuable tools to aid consumers in doing this. Consumers also will find the book helpful in aiding them to know what questions to ask of their professional or business advisors in these fields and to help them understand better the advice they receive.

Practitioners and professionals in the various fields covered by the book—lawyers, accountants, life insurance agents, bankers and trust officers, general insurance agents and brokers, stockbrokers, mutual fund representatives, investment advisors, and others—also will find the book useful. It will aid them in applying their specialties to the total financial planning process. It will give them information on how the specialties of other practitioners relate to their clients' or customers' total financial well-being. And it will aid them in explaining technical questions and problems to their clients or customers.

Naturally, however, the book does not cover all aspects of these subjects in great depth. That is not its purpose and would be an impossible task in any event. Thus, it is obvious that the knowledge, experience, and judgment of professionals and practitioners in these fields are vital in advising the public properly and in applying personal financial planning to the public's needs.

G. Victor Hallman
Jerry S. Rosenbloom

PERSONAL FINANCIAL PLANNING

How to Plan for Your
Financial Freedom

PART ONE
COORDINATED FINANCIAL PLANNING

1
PERSONAL FINANCIAL PLANNING—THE PROCESS

Most people are in great need of personal financial planning. They usually have certain basic financial goals they want to attain, but such objectives usually are not precisely defined. Furthermore, a bewildering array of investments, insurance coverages, savings plans, tax-saving devices, and the like is constantly being offered to us, often in a piecemeal fashion. But we are faced with a dilemma because the very affluence of our society, coupled with improving educational levels, helps create a situation in which more and more people can benefit from the more sophisticated financial planning techniques.

WHAT IS PERSONAL FINANCIAL PLANNING?

Personal financial planning is the development and implementation of total, coordinated plans for the achievement of one's overall financial objectives. The essential elements of this concept are the development of *coordinated* plans for a person's *overall* financial affairs based upon his or her *total financial objectives*. The idea is to focus on the individual's objectives as the starting point in financial planning, rather than emphasizing the use of one or more financial instruments to solve only *some* financial problems.

Most people, in fact, use a variety of financial instruments before they can achieve all their objectives. Thus, such basic financial tools as insurance, mutual funds, common stocks, bonds, fixed and variable annuities, savings accounts, personal trusts, and real estate are essential elements of many, if not most, soundly conceived financial plans.

Also involved in the planning process is the development of *personal financial policies* to guide your financial operations. Examples of such policies in investments would be deciding what percentage of your investment portfolio is to go into bonds (or other so-called "fixed-dollar" securities) and what percentage into common stocks (or other "equity"-type investments), or deciding to invest primarily in "growth" type common stocks to be held for the long pull, or deciding to invest your "equity" money primarily in real estate. In the insurance area, you might decide to buy property and liability insurance and health insurance with the largest deductibles you can afford in order to save on premiums and thereby avoid the disadvantage of "trading dollars with the insurance company." You might also decide to buy the highest limits of liability insurance available to protect yourself against potential catastrophic losses—the ones that can destroy you financially. When it comes to buying life insurance, you may want to purchase mainly cash value life insurance, or you may decide to buy mostly term life insurance—which is just pure protection—and place your savings dollars elsewhere. There are many other such financial policy decisions that could be mentioned.

Unfortunately, many people do not follow any consistent policy in making these decisions, but rather make them as each day-to-day problem comes up or as a result of some sales presentation. The more completely you can formulate the financial policies that make sense for you and your family, the more rational your financial decisions will be and the less likely you are to be unduly influenced by others.

In financial planning, people consciously or unconsciously make some assumptions about the current economic climate and what the economy holds for the future. A commonly held view, for example, has been that the United States economy generally will experience consistent, real long-term growth, accompanied by persistent price inflation, for the indefinite future. Such an assumption has clear implications for personal financial policies and planning. On the other hand, some people fear that economic conditions will deteriorate into a prolonged recession or even depression, and they plan their financial policies accordingly.

FOCUS ON OBJECTIVES

Each person's financial objectives differ in terms of his or her individual circumstances, goals, attitudes, and needs. However, the total objectives of most people can be classified as follows:

1. Protection against the personal risks of
   a. Premature death
   b. Disability income losses
   c. Medical care expenses
   d. Property and liability losses
   e. Unemployment
2. Capital accumulation for
   a. Emergency fund
   b. Family purposes
   c. General investment portfolio
3. Provision for retirement income

4. Reduction of the tax burden

   a. During lifetime

   b. At death

5. Planning for your heirs (estate planning)

6. Investment and property management

This overall view of personal financial planning encompasses the work of several specialized fields. Tax planning, for example, involves planning for the reduction, shifting, and postponement of the tax bite and cuts across several specialties. Estate planning is concerned primarily with planning for the disposition of one's property to his or her heirs (during one's lifetime as well as at death) in such a way as to accomplish the person's objectives with minimum overall shrinkage in the estate. Life underwriting traditionally has involved all the uses of life insurance, health insurance, and annuities to meet your financial objectives. Now, many life insurance agents also have at their disposal various equity products, such as mutual funds and variable annuities, to help meet your investment needs. Similarly, the personal insurance survey deals primarily with your exposures to property and liability losses. Investment planning is concerned largely with your accumulation of capital and the management of your investment portfolio.

Lawyers, accountants, bankers and trust officers, investment advisors, insurance agents and brokers, and others all may serve the public toward meeting these financial objectives. In fact you frequently must deal with several practitioners to receive all the expert advice you need. This makes coordination of effort among these experts all the more important. What is needed might be termed a "systems approach" toward meeting your financial goals by integrating the basic principles of each of these specialties into a cohesive whole that is approached from the consumer's point of view.

NEED FOR PERSONAL FINANCIAL PLANNING

Who Should Plan?

Most people find themselves in need of financial planning to some degree. Some of the more sophisticated techniques tend to be used by those with higher incomes and larger property or business interests, but partly this is so because many persons of more modest circumstances lack information about financial planning. If they knew of the techniques, they would use them more. In fact, less affluent people actually may need such planning more than those with greater wealth because each dollar of income or capital means relatively more to them.

Interestingly, our economic growth, the tax structure, and the changes that have taken place in our social framework have increased tremendously the need for and complexity of financial planning. One product of our "affluent society" is the large number of people who now have enough income, assets, and/or possibilities of gifts and inheritances within their families to find themselves, as never before, with a real need for investment, tax, insurance, and estate planning services. For example, it is quite easy today for people who would not consider themselves wealthy to have a potential estate large enough to be subject to federal estate tax as well as state death taxes. For this and other reasons, they would be logical candidates for estate planning.

As an illustration of this, take the fairly typical case of a rising young middle-management executive—George Able. George is 33, has a wife, Mary, and three children, and earns about $20,000 per year in base salary. He and his wife jointly own their home, now worth about $50,000, with a $20,000 mortgage; $2,000 in mutual fund shares; and $2,000 in savings and checking accounts. George owns in his own name about $6,000 in common stocks. He also owns the family autos and other personal property worth about $20,000 on which there are installment credit and other personal debts outstanding of $4,000. George owns individual life insurance on his life with total death benefits of about $80,000. This insurance is payable to Mary as beneficiary. At work, George has group life insurance equal to two times his base salary ($40,000) and a deferred profit-sharing plan with about $12,000 currently credited to George's account; the benefits of both plans are payable to George's estate at his death. George's will leaves everything outright to Mary, if she survives him; otherwise, outright to his children in equal shares.

Mary owns no property in her own name, but her parents in their wills have left their farm, presently worth about $150,000, to Mary and her two brothers in equal shares. Mary has no will.

From these facts, if George were to die today, his estate tax picture would look like this:[1]

Gross estate for federal estate tax purposes		$212,000
Less: George's debts	$24,000	
Less: Estimated funeral and estate administration expenses	8,000	
Less: Federal estate tax marital deduction (maximum)	90,000	
Less: George's personal exemption	60,000	−182,000
Taxable estate		$ 30,000
Federal estate tax (on $30,000)		$ 3,000

Clearly, George and his family could benefit from estate planning services right now, and it seems likely that his estate will increase markedly in value as he rises in the business world in the years to come. In addition, George

[1]The computation of the federal estate tax in this illustration assumes a knowledge of tax principles that are covered later (see Chapters 15 and 16). The illustration is presented at this point only to show the need for estate planning even in what might be called "modest" estates. For purposes of simplicity, income taxes and state death taxes have been ignored in this example.

undoubtedly has investment, insurance, retirement, and income tax planning needs that we have not yet considered. The point is that planning services which some may believe are only for the wealthy really have broad applicability in our society today.

It is important to plan for both husband and wife.[2] This is true for many reasons, particularly today. First, the wife will usually be the key person in managing the family in the event of the husband's death or disability. Second, several important tax-saving devices, such as the federal estate tax marital deduction, split gifts for gift tax purposes, and joint income tax returns, depend upon marital status. Moreover, today many wives are employed and receive good incomes, have an opportunity to acquire property and investments, and are entitled to various employee benefits in their own right. Some women also have an interest in their own or their husband's business. Finally, a wife often will acquire substantial property upon her husband's death and may be the beneficiary of an inheritance from other sources.

In our hypothetical case of the Ables, for example, Mary can expect to receive a net amount of about $177,000 from all sources in the event of George's death. She also expects an inheritance of about $50,000 from her parents. This would give her an estate of about $227,000, with all the resulting property management and investment problems. Also, at Mary's subsequent death, her estate's tax burden would have increased considerably, as shown below.[3]

Gross estate for federal estate tax purposes		$227,000
Less: Estimated funeral and estate administration expenses	$10,000	
Less: Mary's personal exemption	60,000	−70,000
Taxable estate		$157,000
Federal estate tax (on $157,000), ignoring any possible credits		$ 37,800

Thus, assuming only the current values in the Ables' estates, when taken together they have a potential federal estate tax liability of $40,800 ($3,000 at his death and $37,800 at hers). Proper planning of both estates could substantially reduce this sizable tax drain as well as accomplish other objectives. (See Chapters 15 and 16 for specific planning ideas.)

[2]It is desirable to plan for the whole family, and this may be possible. However, as a practical matter, it may be difficult in some cases to have coordinated planning beyond the immediate family of husband, wife, and their children. For example, in some cases grown, self-supporting children may find it difficult emotionally to coordinate their planning with that of their aged parents from whom they might expect an inheritance. But where this can be done, everyone normally benefits.

[3]This assumes Mary does not remarry prior to her death and thus does not have the marital deduction available to her estate. It also assumes that the unpaid mortgage and installment loans were paid off following George's death.

Why Planning May Be Neglected

People fail to plan for a host of reasons. They often feel they do not have sufficient assets or income to need planning, or that their affairs already are in good order. Both these assumptions frequently are wrong. There also is the natural human tendency for busy people to procrastinate with respect to planning. Some persons actually may fear planning, since part of it involves consideration of unpleasant events such as death, disability, unemployment, and property losses. Finally, people may be deterred by what they consider the high cost of planning services. Actually, the real cost of planning may be lower than people believe.

A knowledgeable consumer can secure some valuable planning services without additional cost to him or her. For example, stockbrokers, trust officers, insurance agents and brokers, and others stand ready to give valuable advice in the areas of their specialties without extra cost to the consumer beyond that already built into the overall cost of their products or services. The consumer must pay this cost in any event, whether he or she uses their planning services or not. Of course, a consumer must evaluate carefully the advice he or she receives in light of the advisor's experience, knowledge of the field, and objectivity. The trick is for the knowledgeable and discerning consumer to have the benefit of the knowledge and experience of these advisors and yet reserve for himself the final decision as to what advice to accept and act upon and what advice to ignore.

Remember, too, that the fees charged for some planning services are deductible for federal income tax purposes. The tax law permits the deduction of expenses incurred for the management, conservation, or maintenance of property held for the production of income, except to the extent such expenses are incurred in earning tax-exempt interest or income. Thus, investment counsel and advisory fees, trustees' fees, custodian fees, legal fees for advice concerning the arrangement and conservation of income-producing property, and similar expenses incurred in connection with investments are deductible on the income tax return of the person receiving or entitled to receive the income from the investments.[4] An income tax deduction can also be taken for expenses incurred in connection with the determination, collection, or refund of any tax (including gift and estate taxes).

Costs of Failure to Plan

While there may be understandable human reasons why people neglect to plan, the costs of failing to do so can be high indeed. Your family may be

[4]Except to the extent such expenses relate to rents and royalties, they are deductible only from adjusted gross income to arrive at taxable income. Expenses incurred to earn rents and royalties are deductible from gross income to arrive at adjusted gross income. See Chapter 14 for more ideas on income tax planning.

unprotected or inadequately protected in the event of personal catastrophes such as death, disability, serious illness, an automobile accident, prolonged unemployment, or similar risks of life. There may not be enough money set aside for education and retirement, necessitating painful compromises when such predictable needs actually arise. On the other hand, some of these risks may be covered more than adequately, resulting in a waste of family resources.

Failure to plan can result in higher than necessary income, estate, and perhaps gift taxation. It can also cause larger estate settlement costs in general. The case of the Ables illustrates these results.

When there is a closely held business interest in the family, failure to plan for the future disposition of this interest can result in severe problems in the event of the death, disability, or retirement of one of the owners. This can cause severe business losses as well as bitter disputes within the family as to who will control the business. In the same vein, failure to engage in proper estate planning can not only result in higher-than-necessary death taxation and estate settlement costs, but, perhaps more importantly, also cause disputes and harsh discord within the family, resulting in unhappiness for the very persons the estate owner wishes to benefit. In an unplanned estate, for example, the bereaved and perhaps inexperienced widow may find herself faced with a multitude of unexpected and complex problems in managing property and investing money at the very time she is least capable emotionally to do so. At the same time, in the wings all too frequently wait those who are anxious to advise her but not always for *her and her children's benefit.* In many cases, these human problems of an unplanned estate can be more costly than higher taxes and estate settlement costs.

Last but not least, a very important cost of the failure to plan is that your own personal objectives in life may not be realized. You may not be able to achieve the degree of financial independence you want. It is sad indeed when a person is tied to an employer or a job because "he can't afford to move." Yet this can happen even in our "affluent" society because so much of our personal financial security can be tied to a particular employer. It stands to reason that a properly planned personal investment and insurance program, within the control of the individual, can go a long way toward providing the individual and his or her family with a desirable degree of personal independence. Such a planned program will also enable the person and his or her family to achieve their financial objectives in life on an organized basis. Nothing is more common than the person who intends to "get my financial house in order" but never does. Planning is the first step toward achieving this.

STEPS IN THE PLANNING PROCESS

The financial planning process basically involves the translation of personal objectives into specific plans and finally into financial arrangements to implement those plans. To this end, the following are logical steps in the process. These steps are covered in greater detail throughout the book. The following is a brief overview of the whole process.

Gathering Information and Preparation of Personal Financial Statements

You cannot plan well without certain basic information. Also, most experts with whom you deal need some basic facts before they can really help you. Therefore, the first step in the planning process is getting together useful information about your financial situation to help you develop intelligent plans.

The kinds of information you need vary with your situation, but they usually include information about your *investments;* the *life, health, and property and liability insurance policies* you carry; your *retirement and other employee benefits;* your *tax situation*—income, estate, and perhaps gift taxes; *wills, trusts, and other estate planning documents;* and similar pertinent financial documents and information. You probably have many of these documents and much of this information in your own possession now, and normally you can easily get more information about them from other sources, such as your stockbroker, insurance agents, employer, lawyer, accountant, trust officer or banker, and the like. Of course, not everyone will have all of these advisors, but most people have at least some of them to go to for further information if they need it.

In summarizing your present financial position, it may be helpful to prepare some simplified personal financial statements, much like those business concerns use. These can include a *personal balance sheet,* a *personal income statement,* and other financial statements you feel would be helpful. A sample Family Balance Sheet (Statement 1-1) and a sample Family Income Statement (Statement 1-2) are given at the end of this chapter. Of course, these can be changed or simplified as you wish for your own purposes. They are meant only as examples. Many people are surprised how much they are "worth" when everything is considered. As an illustration of how these statements can be used, the sample balance sheet and income statement are filled out for the Ables, whom we met earlier in this chapter.

In addition, many financial concerns, like banks, insurance companies, and stockbrokers, have or use forms and reports that you may find useful in the areas of their particular specialties.

This information-gathering step does not have to be overly extensive or burdensome. It is surprising how much can be done with relatively little additional information if you know what to look for. Of course, normally, the more information you have, the better you can plan. Again, outside sources can be helpful in this regard if you use them properly.

Identification of Objectives

The next step is the identification and setting of your objectives, as outlined previously in this chapter. This is such an important step that the next chapter is devoted to it.

Analysis of Present Position and Consideration of Alternatives

The third step in the process is an analysis of your present position in relation to your objectives and then considering alternative ways of remedying any deficiencies found in your present situation. There almost always are problems to solve in meeting at least some of your objectives. And sometimes a person actually will be overprepared in one area but seriously lacking in others. Thus, balancing the plan is important.

Therefore, at this stage, and under the guidance of your advisors, you would consider the various alternatives available to meet your objectives, given your financial position, personal situation, and investment constraints. Depending on the circumstances and complexity of your situation, these alternatives may be relatively few and not difficult to accomplish or they may be numerous and quite complex.

Development and Implementation of the Plan

Given the facts of the case, your objectives, an analysis of your present financial position, and consideration of alternatives, recommendations can be made for a financial plan to meet your objectives. Naturally, reasonable people may differ on the specific recommendations that should be made for any such plan. It also goes almost without saying that you can reject those parts of a plan with which you do not agree or feel you cannot afford.

Periodic Review and Revision

No plan, once developed and implemented, should be considered as "engraved in bronze." Circumstances change, and so should financial plans. There are births, marriages, divorces, deaths, job changes, different economic conditions, and a host of other factors too numerous to mention that may make revisions in financial plans desirable or even necessary. Therefore, the final step in the process is adopting a procedure for periodic review and needed revision of your personal financial plan.

PERSONAL FINANCIAL PLANNING CHECKLIST FOR DECISION MAKING AND REVIEW FORMS

To aid the reader in applying this process to his or her own situation, a *personal financial planning checklist* and *personal financial planning review forms* have been prepared for use with this book and will be found at the end. The Checklist and Review Forms are cross-referenced to the appropriate sections of the book so that you can review your own situation in an organized manner and perhaps get some worthwhile, money-saving ideas. *It must be emphasized, however, that such materials can never be regarded as a substitute for sound professional advice in the areas where such advice is necessary.* Naturally, the authors do not intend them as such a substitute. In fact, the checklist and review forms may simply help you formulate in your mind the right questions to ask your advisors.

STATEMENT 1-1
YOUR FAMILY BALANCE SHEET (as of present date)

ASSETS

Liquid Assets

Cash and checking account(s)	$ 200	
Savings account(s)	1,800	
Life insurance cash values	3,000	
United States savings bonds	-0-	
Brokerage accounts	-0-	
Other	-0-	
Total liquid assets		$ 5,000

Marketable Investments

Common stocks	6,000	
Mutual funds	2,000	
Bonds (corporate, municipal, etc.)	-0-	
Other	-0-	
Total marketable investments		8,000

"Nonmarketable" Investments

Business interests	-0-	
Investment real estate	-0-	
Pension, profit-sharing, etc., accounts	12,000	
Tax-sheltered investments	-0-	
Other	-0-	
Total "nonmarketable" investments		12,000

Personal Real Estate

Residence	50,000	
Vacation home	-0-	
Total personal real estate		50,000

Other Personal Assets

Auto(s)	4,000	

Boat(s)	-0-	
Furs and jewelry	-0-	
Collections, hobbies, etc.	-0-	
Furniture and household accessories	14,000	
Other personal property	2,000	
Total other personal assets		20,000
Total assets		$95,000

LIABILITIES AND NET WORTH

Current Liabilities

Charge accounts, credit card charges, and other bills payable	$ 200	
Installment credit and other short-term loans	3,800	
Unusual tax liabilities	-0-	
Total current liabilities		$ 4,000

Long-term Liabilities

Mortgage(s) on personal real estate	20,000	
Mortgage(s) on investment real estate	-0-	
Bank loans	-0-	
Margin loans	-0-	
Life insurance policy loans	-0-	
Other	-0-	
Total long-term liabilities		20,000
Total liabilities		$24,000
Family net worth		$71,000
Total liabilities and family net worth		$95,000

STATEMENT 1-2
YOUR FAMILY INCOME STATEMENT (for the most recent year)

INCOME

Salary(ies):

You	$20,000	
Your spouse	-0-	
Others	-0-	
Total salaries		$20,000

Investment Income:

Interest (taxable)	100
Interest (nontaxable)	-0-
Dividends	280
Real estate	-0-

Realized capital gains	40	
Other investment income	-0-	
Total investment income		420
Bonuses, Profit-Sharing Payments, Etc.		-0-
Other Income		-0-
Total income		$20,420

EXPENSES AND FIXED OBLIGATIONS

Ordinary Living Expenses		$ 9,000

Interest Expenses:

Consumer loans	$ 280	
Bank loans	-0-	
Mortgage(s)	1,300	
Insurance policy loans	-0-	
Other interest	-0-	
Total interest expenses		1,580

Debt Amortization (mortgages, consumer debt, etc.)		1,600

Insurance Premiums:

Life insurance	850	
Health insurance	400	
Property and liability insurance	670	
Total insurance premiums		1,920

Charitable Contributions		500

Taxes:

Federal income tax	2,200	
State (and city) income tax(es)	500	
Social security tax(es)	825	
Local property taxes	1,200	
Other taxes	-0-	
Total taxes		4,725
Total expenses and fixed obligations		19,325

BALANCE AVAILABLE FOR DISCRETIONARY INVESTMENT		$ 1,095

2
SETTING YOUR OBJECTIVES

Since personal financial planning is concerned primarily with helping people meet their objectives, the nature of those objectives and the ways they can be met are of critical importance in the planning process. A problem defined and broken down into its component parts frequently is half-solved. In this chapter, we shall analyze the financial objectives common to most people and outline briefly the sources available to help meet these objectives.

IMPORTANCE OF SETTING OBJECTIVES

As a general principle, it is desirable to formulate and then state your objectives as *explicitly* as possible. This can have several advantages. *First,* it forces you to think through exactly what your financial objectives are. *Second,* by doing this you are less likely to overlook some objectives while concentrating unduly on others. *Third,* when you carefully define your objectives, you may see solutions that had been overlooked before. You also are less likely to be sidetracked by persuasive sales presentations into actions that run counter to your long-range planning. *Finally,* the explicit determination of your financial objectives establishes a rational basis for you to take appropriate action to realize those objectives.

Once established, a person's financial objectives do not remain static. What may be entirely appropriate for a young married man with small children may prove quite inappropriate for an executive with college-age children or for a husband and wife approaching retirement.

HOW TO ORGANIZE YOUR OBJECTIVES

While the emphasis on particular objectives will change over a family's life cycle, the following classification system of personal financial objectives provides a systematic way for identifying your specific objectives and needs. It is used throughout the book as a framework for total financial planning.

Protection against Personal Risks

This category recognizes the desire of most people to protect themselves and their families against the risks they face in everyday life. These risks can arise from the possibility of premature death, disability, large medical expenses, loss of their property from various perils, liability they may have to others, and unemployment.

Premature Death. A major objective of most people is to protect their dependents from the financial consequences of their deaths. Some people also are concerned with the impact of their deaths on their business affairs. At this point, let us briefly note the various financial losses that may result from a person's death.

Loss of the deceased's future earning power that would have been available for the benefit of his or her surviving dependents. Most families live on the earned income of the husband or husband and wife combined. The death of an income earner results in the loss of his or her future earnings from the date of death until he or she would have retired or otherwise left the labor force. For most families, this represents a potentially catastrophic loss and usually is the most important financial loss arising out of a person's premature death. The so-called "needs approach" to valuing this potential loss of future earnings for insurance purposes is illustrated in Chapter 4.

Costs and other obligations arising at death. Certain obligations are either created or tend to come due at a person's death. Perhaps the most important of these are funeral and burial expenses, cost of settlement and administration of the deceased's estate, and any federal estate and/or state death taxes that may be due. The deceased's estate also owes the federal income tax on his or her income during the year of his or her death.

In addition to the costs created by death itself, there often are obligations that tend to come due at death. Most people have balances on charge accounts, credit cards, and other personal debts that their estate must pay in the event of their death. In addition, many people have larger debts outstanding that they may want to be paid at their death. Perhaps the most typical would be the balance due on any mortgages on their homes. While there may be valid reasons why a family would decide not to pay off such a mortgage debt after a breadwinner's death, many persons in planning their affairs like to think that their families at least would be able to pay off all their debts and thus would not "inherit a mortgage."

Increased expenses for the family. The death of certain family members, especially the wife and mother, results in increased expenses for the family to replace the economic functions she performed as homemaker. This potential loss is frequently overlooked, and yet it can be considerable (one source, for example, estimated this loss at $12,140 in a fairly typical case). Also, in a great many families today, the wife is an important income earner, and her premature death results in the loss of her present or future earning power in the outside job market.

Loss of tax advantages. In some cases, the death of a family member can result in substantially increased taxation for the survivors. This results largely from the loss of income, estate, and gift tax advantages accorded to married persons under our tax laws. Generally, the tax benefit most discussed in this regard is the potential loss of the federal estate tax marital deduction on a spouse's death (see Chapter 16).

Loss of business values because of an owner's or key person's death. When the owner or one of the owners of a business that can be called "closely held" (i.e., a sole proprietor, a partner in most partnerships, or a stockholder in many smaller corporations with only a few stockholders who actively run the business) dies, the business may die with him or suffer considerable loss in value. These potential losses in business values are directly related to the owners' personal financial planning because such closely held business interests frequently constitute the major part of the owners' estates. Planning for such business interests is covered in Chapter 18.

Many businesses also have certain key employees, whether owners or not, whose premature death can cause considerable financial loss to the business until they can be replaced.

Sources of Protection against Premature Death. Various kinds of death benefits may be available to a deceased person's family. While each is described in greater detail in later chapters, they are shown here in outline form to give an overview of the planning devices that may be available to meet this important risk.

1. Life insurance
   a. Individual life insurance purchased by the insured, his or her family, or others
   b. Group life insurance
      (1) Through the insured's employer or business
      (2) Through an association group plan provided through a professional association, fraternal association, or similar group
   c. Credit life insurance payable to a creditor of the insured person to pay off a debt
2. Social Security survivors' benefits
3. Other government benefits
4. Death benefits under private pension plans
5. Death benefits under deferred profit-sharing plans
6. Death benefits under tax-sheltered annuity (TSA) plans, plans for the self-employed (HR-10 plans), nonqualified deferred compensation plans, personal annuity contracts, and the like
7. Informal employer death benefits or salary-continuation plans
8. Proceeds from the sale of business interests under insured buy-sell agreements or otherwise
9. All other assets and income available to the family after a person's death

Disability Income Losses. Another major objective of most people should be to protect themselves and their dependents from financial losses arising out of their disability, either total and temporary or total and permanent. Disability, particularly total and permanent disability, is a serious risk faced by almost everyone. Yet, surprisingly, it is often neglected in financial planning.

Actually, the probability that someone will suffer a reasonably long-term disability (90 days or more) prior to age 65 is considerably greater than the probability of death at those ages. For example, the data below show that the probability of such a long-term disability at age 32 is about 6½ times the probability of death at that age. This is something for the young family man and woman to think about.

Attained Age	Probability of Disability of 90 Days or More per 1,000 Lives	Probability of Death per 1,000 Lives	Probability of Disability as a Multiple of Probability of Death
22	6.64	0.89	7.46
32	7.78	1.18	6.59
42	12.57	2.95	4.26
52	22.39	8.21	2.73
62	44.27	21.12	2.10

The financial losses from disability generally parallel those resulting from death. An important difference from the consumer's viewpoint, however, is that there is a wide range of possible durations of total disability—from only a week or so to the ultimate, personal catastrophe of total and permanent disability. Thus, a person must recognize in personal financial planning that he or she could become disabled for a variety of durations—from a few days to the rest of his or her life. Virtually all experts agree, however, that the consumer should give greatest planning attention to protecting himself or herself against long-term and total and permanent disability rather than being unduly concerned with disabilities that last only a few weeks. For example, depending on individual circumstances and resources, it often is much more economical for a family to rely upon their emergency investment fund for shorter-term disabilities than to buy disability income insurance to cover such disabilities.

The total and permanent disability of a family breadwinner actually is a much greater catastrophe than his or her premature death because the fact, total and permanent disability has been graphically characterized as increase because of the disability, and because other family members must devote at least some of their time to caring for him or her, and, of course, his or her spouse is not free to remarry as long as the disabled spouse is alive. In fact, total and permanent disability has been graphically characterized as the "wheelchair death."

One final point about the disability risk is in order. The disability of someone who owns property may give rise to particular property management problems because the disabled person might be in such a physical or mental state that he or she is unable to manage his or her affairs effectively. Advance planning is desirable to provide a means for handling this unhappy contingency. (See Chapter 17 for the possible use of revocable trusts to help meet this problem.)

Sources of Protection against Disability Income Losses. As was done in the case of premature death, the various sources of protection against disability income losses are outlined below. They will be described in greater detail later.

1. Health insurance
    a. Individual disability income insurance purchased by the insured, his or her family, or others
    b. Group disability income insurance
       (1) Through the insured's employer or business
       (2) Through an association group plan
    c. Credit disability income insurance payable to a creditor of the insured person to pay off a debt
2. Disability benefits under life insurance policies
    a. Disability income riders added to some individual life insurance policies
    b. Waiver of premium benefits included with, or added to, most individual life insurance policies
    c. Disability benefits under group life insurance
3. Social Security disability benefits
4. Workmen's compensation disability benefits
5. Other government benefits
6. Disability benefits under private pension, profit-sharing, and nonqualified deferred compensation plans
7. Noninsured employer salary-continuation (sick-pay) plans
8. All other income, investment or otherwise, available to the family

This outline, and that for premature death, show that there often are more sources of protection available than many people may think. The problem is to recognize these sources and use them efficiently to meet your and your family's needs.

Medical Care Expenses. There is little need to convince most people of the need to protect themselves and their family against medical care costs. Mounting medical care costs have become a national problem, and they are no less so for you and your family.

For your personal financial planning, it may be helpful to divide family medical care costs into three categories, as follows.

"Normal" or budgetable expenses. These are the medical expenses the family more or less expects to pay out of its regular monthly budget, such as routine visits to physicians, routine outpatient laboratory tests and x-rays, expenses of minor illnesses, and small drug purchases. Just what expenses are "normal" or budgetable depends a great deal on the needs, other resources, and desires of the individual or family. The federal income tax law seems to imply that about 3 percent of your income is considered "normal" medical expense for tax purposes because medical expenses of less than this amount cannot be taken as itemized deductions for income tax purposes. But as a general principle, the larger the amount of annual expenses a family can afford to assume, the lower will be its overall costs. This is true because buying insurance against relatively small potential losses results in what is called "trading dollars with the insurance company," which usually is an uneconomical practice for the insured (see Chapter 3 for a more complete explanation). Also, to the extent an emergency fund is established to meet unexpected expenses and losses (of all kinds), the investment earnings on this fund would be available to the consumer.

"Larger than normal" expenses. These are medical expenses that exceed those that are expected or budgetable. If they occur, they probably cannot be met out of the family's regular income. To meet such expenses, most people need insurance. The cutoff point between "normal" and "larger than normal" expenses depends upon the family's circumstances.

Catastrophic medical expenses. These are expenses so large as to cause severe financial strain on a family. They are important to plan for because they are potentially so damaging. Again, the dividing line between "larger than normal losses" and "catastrophic losses" depends on individual circumstances. One family, for example, may feel that uninsured medical expenses of over $500 in a year would be a severe financial strain. Another family, however, with a larger income and an emergency fund, may feel that uninsured medical expenses of several thousand dollars could be tolerated, provided the annual cost savings were significant enough for the family to assume this much risk. The significance of the dividing line lies in the fact that insurance generally is necessary to protect the family against truly catastrophic medical expenses, while the family may elect to assume at least some of the larger than normal expenses. In many cases, however, this decision is, in effect, taken away from the individual because his or her employer provides group medical expense insurance which the employee must either accept or, in rare cases, reject.

The traditional approach for protecting your family against catastrophic medical expenses is coverage under so-called "major medical expense" insurance. But even major medical expense insurance, as it is presently written, may prove inadequate to meet some of the really large medical bills that are possible today. As an example, *The Wall Street Journal* reported the case of a 2½-year-old girl suffering from nephrosis (a kidney disease) whose father (a corporate executive) had incurred medical expenses on her behalf of $57,794 over a 21-month period and still expected at least four more years of treatment. The father's group major medical expense insurance reimbursed only $13,082 of these expenses before its benefits were exhausted.[1] While such instances are relatively infrequent, they nevertheless point up the need for planning to meet this risk.

There really is no way for you to know in advance just how large catastrophic medical expenses might be. Since they could be *very* large, you should plan for that possibility.

Sources of Protection against Medical Care Expenses. The following are the major sources to which consumers may look for coverage of medical care costs.

1. Health insurance
    a. Individual medical expense insurance
    b. Group medical expense insurance
2. Medical payments coverage under liability insurance policies and "no-fault" automobile coverages
3. Social Security medical benefits (Medicare)
4. Workmen's compensation medical benefits
5. Other government benefits
6. Employer medical reimbursement benefits under a noninsured plan
7. Other assets available to the family

Property and Liability Losses. All families are exposed to the risk of property and/or liability losses. For planning purposes, it is helpful to consider property exposures and liability exposures separately because somewhat different approaches may be used for each.

Property losses. Ownership of property brings with it the risk of loss to the property itself, or *direct losses*, and the risk of indirect losses arising out of loss or damage to the property, called *consequential losses*. Direct and consequential losses to property can result from a wide variety of perils, some of which, such as fire, theft, windstorm, and automobile collision, are common, while others, such as earthquake and flood, are rather rare except in certain geographical areas.

Some of the kinds of property owned by individuals and families that may be exposed to direct loss include:

Residence

Summer home

Investment real estate

Furniture, clothing, and other personal property

[1]"The Cost of Illness: Medical Bills Burden Even Affluent Families," *The Wall Street Journal,* May 7, 1970, p. 1.

Automobiles

Boats (and aircraft)

Furs, jewelry, and fine art works

Securities, accounts, credit cards, cash, and the like

Professional equipment

Assets held as an executor, trustee, or guardian and assets in which the person has a beneficial interest

Some of the consequential losses that may arise out of a direct loss to such property are as follows:

Loss of use of the damaged property (including additional living expenses while a residence is being rebuilt, rental of a substitute automobile while a car is being repaired, etc.)

Loss of rental income from damaged property

Depreciation losses (or the difference between the cost to replace damaged property with new property and the depreciated value, called "actual cash value," of the damaged property)

Cost of debris removal

Many property losses are comparatively small in size, but some are of major importance. As with disability income losses and medical care expenses, what constitutes a "small" loss depends upon the resources and attitudes of those involved. Also, like disability income and medical expense exposures, a financial planning decision needs to be made as to how much of your property loss exposure should be assumed and how much insured. Another decision is what property to insure against what perils.

Liability losses. By virtue of almost everything you do, you are exposed to possible liability claims made by others. Such liability claims can arise out of your own negligent acts; the negligent acts of others for whom you may be held legally responsible; liability you may have assumed under contract (such as a lease); and liability imposed on you by statute (such as workmen's compensation laws).

Some of the exposures that may result in a liability claim are:

Ownership of property (e.g., residence premises, summer home)

Rental of property (e.g., vacation home)

Ownership, rental, or use of automobiles

Ownership, rental, or use of boats, aircraft, snowmobiles, etc.

Hiring of employees (e.g., domestic and casual)

Other personal activities

Professional and business activities (including officerships and directorships)

Any contractual or contingent liability

Most people realize the financial consequences that could occur as a result of liability claims against them. However, they may not recognize all the liability exposures they have and may not protect themselves against the possibility of *very* large claims. Like medical expenses, there really is no way you can know in advance just how large a liability loss you may suffer. Judgments and settlements for $1 million and more are not unheard of by any means. Therefore, prudent financial planning calls for the assumption that the worst can happen and providing for it.

Sources of Protection against Property and Liability Losses. For most persons, the main source of protection against property and liability losses is insurance. This insurance generally is available under individually marketed property and liability policies, but increasingly it also may be available under so-called "mass (or collective) merchandised" plans. In some cases, it may be possible for some individuals to protect themselves by not assuming liability under contract or by transferring a liability risk to others by contract. But this really is not feasible for most people.

Capital Accumulation

Many people and families do not spend all their disposable income, and thus they have an investible surplus; many also have various semiautomatic plans, such as profit-sharing plans, that help them build up capital; and some receive gifts and/or inheritances that must be invested. Thus, in one way or another, an important and desirable financial objective for many is to accumulate and invest capital.

There are a number of reasons why people want to accumulate capital. Some of the more important are for an *emergency fund,* for the *education of their children,* for *retirement purposes,* and for a *general investment fund* to provide them with capital and additional income for their own financial security. In other words, people want to accumulate capital to promote their own personal financial freedom. People also save with certain consumption goals in mind, such as the purchase of a new car or taking an extended trip or vacation.

The relative importance of these reasons naturally varies with individual circumstances and attitudes. A woman in her fifties may be primarily interested in preparing for retirement, while a younger family man or woman may be more concerned with educating his or her children or the capital growth of a general investment fund.

Emergency Fund. An emergency fund may be needed to meet unexpected expenses that are not planned for in the family budget; to pay for the "smaller" disability losses, medical expenses, and property losses that purposely are not covered by insurance; and to provide a financial cushion against such personal problems as prolonged unemployment.

This need for an emergency unemployment fund has received greater attention in recent years as many capable persons have lost their jobs because of economic dislocations. A reasonable emergency fund can help prevent the problem of temporary unemployment from becoming a crisis by giving the affected family time to adjust without having to change drastically their living standards or disturb their other investments.

The size of the needed emergency fund varies greatly and depends upon such factors as family income, number of income earners, stability of employment, assets, debts, insurance deductibles and uncovered health and property insurance exposures, and the family's general attitudes toward risk and security. The size of the emergency fund can be expressed as so many months of family income—such as three to six months.

By its very nature, the emergency fund should be invested conservatively. There should be almost complete security of principal, marketability, and liquidity. Within these investment constraints, the fund should be invested so as to secure a reasonable yield, given the primary investment objective of safety of principal. Logical investment outlets for the emergency fund include:

Bank savings accounts (regular accounts)

Savings and loan association accounts (regular accounts)

United States savings bonds

Life insurance cash values

Short-term United States Treasury securities

The careful person also may want to have some ready cash available for emergencies, even if it is non-interest-earning.

Education Needs. The cost of higher education has increased dramatically, particularly at private colleges and universities. For example, it may cost $5,000 or more per year in tuition, fees, and room and board only for a student to attend some private colleges. This can result in a tremendous financial drain for a family with college-age children, and yet it is a predictable drain that can be prepared for.

The size of the fund obviously depends upon the number of children, their ages, their educational plans, any scholarships and student loans that may be available to them, and the size of the family income. It also depends upon the attitudes of the family toward education. Some people feel they should provide their children with all the education they can profit from and want. Others, however, feel that children should help earn at least a part of their educational expenses themselves. There is also the idea in some cases that older children should help send their younger brothers and sisters through school after their parents have helped them. What types of schools the children plan to attend also have a considerable bearing on the costs involved.

An investment fund for educational needs often is a relatively long-term objective, and it is set up with the hope that the fund will not be needed in the meantime. Therefore, wider investment latitude seems justified than in the case of the emergency fund to secure a more attractive investment yield. All that is really necessary is for the principal to be there by the time each child is ready for school.

Retirement Needs. This is a very important objective for many people in accumulating capital. They want to make sure they can live independently and decently during their retired years. Because of the importance and unique characteristics of retirement planning, it is dealt with as a separate objective later in this chapter.

General Investment Fund. People often accumulate capital for general investment purposes. They may want a better standard of living in the future, a second income in addition to the earnings from their employment or profession, greater financial security or a sense of personal financial freedom, the ability to retire early or to "take it easier" in their work in the future, or a capital fund to pass on to their children or grandchildren; or they may simply enjoy the investment process. In any event, people normally invest money for the purpose of *maximizing their after-tax returns,* consistent with their objectives and the investment constraints under which they must operate.

The size of a person's investment fund depends upon how much capital there originally was to invest, how much the person can save each year, any other sources of capital, and how successful the person or his or her advisors are. There are, of course, wide variations in how much different people have to invest. However, one investment advisory organization has estimated that there are 10 million people in the United States who have $5,000 or more available for investment.

There are a number of ways people can accumulate capital and many possible investment policies they might follow. However, in terms of the objective of capital accumulation, an individual basically has the following factors to consider: (1) an estimate of how much capital will be needed at various times in the future (your financial objectives); (2) the amount of funds available to invest; (3) an estimate of how much will be saved each year in the future; (4) the amount of time left to meet your objectives; (5) the general investment constraints under which you must operate in terms of security of principal, stability of income, tax status, and the like; and (6) the adoption of an investment program that will give the best chance of achieving as many of your financial objectives as possible, within the limitations of the investment constraints.

Tables 2-1 and 2-2 give some growth rates for capital at assumed rates of return over various time periods. Table 2-1 shows how much an investment fund of $1,000 would grow to at certain assumed rates of return for the number of years indicated.

The dramatic effect of compound rates of return over a number of years can be seen from Table 2-1. Suppose you are age 35 and have $10,000 to

TABLE 2-1
VALUES OF A $1,000 INVESTMENT FUND INVESTED FOR SPECIFIED NUMBERS OF YEARS AT VARIOUS RATES OF RETURN

Annual Net Rate of Return (Compounded)	Number of Years the $1,000 Is Invested							
	5	8	10	12	15	20	25	30
3%	$1,159	$1,267	$1,344	$1,426	$1,558	$ 1,806	$ 2,094	$ 2,427
4%	1,217	1,369	1,480	1,601	1,801	2,191	2,666	3,243
5%	1,276	1,478	1,629	1,796	2,079	2,653	3,386	4,322
6%	1,338	1,594	1,791	2,012	2,397	3,207	4,292	5,744
8%	1,469	1,851	2,159	2,518	3,172	4,661	6,848	10,064
10%	1,611	2,144	2,594	3,138	4,177	6,727	10,835	17,449
15%	2,011	3,059	4,046	5,350	8,137	16,367	32,919	66,212

invest. If you receive a *net* rate of return (after investment expenses and income taxes) of only 4 percent, you can accumulate $14,800 by the time you are age 45, $21,191 by the time you are 55, and $32,430 when you reach 65. But if you can increase this *net* rate of return to 6 percent, you can accumulate $17,910 by 45, $32,070 by 55, and $57,440 by age 65. And if you could possibly increase this *net* return to 8 percent, the comparable figures would be $21,590 by 45, $46,610 by 55, and $100,640 by age 65.

Approached in a somewhat different manner, if a man, aged 35, with a $10,000 investment fund feels he needs approximately $20,000 in 12 years for his children's education, he can see from Table 2-1 that he will have to earn a net rate of return of about 6 percent on the money to accomplish his goal ($10,000 at 6 percent per year for 12 years = $20,120).

You also may want to know to how much a certain amount saved each year will accumulate in a specified period. This can be determined from Table

TABLE 2-2
VALUES OF A PERIODIC INVESTMENT OF $100 PER YEAR AT THE END OF SPECIFIED NUMBERS OF YEARS AT VARIOUS RATES OF RETURN

Annual Net Rate of Return (Compounded)	Number of Years at $100 per Year							
	5	8	10	12	15	20	25	30
3%	$531	$ 889	$1,146	$1,419	$1,860	$ 2,687	$ 3,646	$ 4,758
4%	542	921	1,201	1,503	2,002	2,978	4,165	5,608
5%	553	955	1,258	1,592	2,158	3,307	4,773	6,644
6%	564	990	1,318	1,687	2,328	3,679	5,486	7,906
8%	587	1,064	1,449	1,898	2,715	4,576	7,311	11,328
10%	611	1,144	1,594	2,138	3,177	5,728	9,835	16,449
15%	674	1,373	2,030	2,900	4,758	10,244	21,279	43,474

2-2, which shows to how much $100 per year would grow at certain assumed rates of return for the number of years indicated. Now assume you are 35 and can save $1,200 per year (about $100 per month). If you receive a *net* rate of return of 5 percent on the money, you can accumulate $15,096 by the time you are 45 ($1,258 × 12), $39,684 by the time you are 55, and $79,728 by the time you reach age 65.

It often is helpful to combine the results of Tables 2-1 and 2-2. People frequently have an investment fund and also are saving so much each year. Suppose, for example, you are age 35 and have $10,000 to invest now and expect to save about $1,200 per year that you can invest in the future. If you can invest these amounts at a *net* annual rate of return of 5 percent, you will accumulate $31,386 by age 45 ($16,290 from Table 2-1 and $15,096 from Table 2-2), $66,214 by age 55, and $146,168 by age 65. You can see from the tables that substantially higher accumulations could be achieved by securing a net rate of return even 1 or 2 percentage points higher than the 5 percent assumed above. It also is clear that consistent saving and investment can produce rather startling results.

Investment Instruments for Capital Accumulation. There is a wide variety of possible investment instruments (or media) that you can use as investment outlets. These are discussed in detail in Part Three, "Accumulating Capital," but they are outlined briefly below. The instruments are classified as "fixed-dollar" and "variable-dollar" (or "equity") investments. *Fixed-dollar* investments mean those whose principal and/or income are contractually set in advance in terms of a specified or determinable number of dollars. *Variable-dollar* (or *equity*) investments are those where neither the principal nor the income is contractually set in advance in terms of dollars. In other words, both the value and income of variable dollar investments can change in dollar amount, either up or down, with changes in economic conditions.

1. Fixed-dollar investments

    a. Bonds

    b. Savings accounts and certificates

    c. Certificates of deposit, treasury bills and notes, and other short-term investments

    d. Preferred stock

    e. Life insurance cash values

2. Variable-dollar investments

    a. Common stock (individually purchased by the investor)

    b. Mutual funds (stock and balanced funds)

    c. Real estate

    d. Variable annuities

    e. Tax-sheltered investments

    f. Ownership of business interests

    g. Commodities

    h. Fine arts, precious metals, and other miscellaneous assets

Provision for Retirement Income

We noted above that a basic personal objective is to provide a retirement income for an individual and also for his or her spouse. This objective has become increasingly important in modern times because of changes in our socioeconomic institutions and because most people now can anticipate living to enjoy their retirement years. As you can see from the figures below, the life expectancy at all these ages exceeds the typical retirement age in the United States of 65. Also, at all these ages the probability of survival to age 65 considerably exceeds the probability of death before age 65.

Age	Life Expectancy in Years*	Probability of Death before Age 65*	Probability of Survival to Age 65 (1 − Probability of Death)
25	46	0.29	0.71
30	41	0.28	0.72
35	37	0.27	0.73
40	32	0.26	0.74
45	28	0.25	0.75
50	24	0.22	0.78
55	20	0.18	0.82
60	16	0.12	0.88
65	13	—	—

*Computed from the 1958 Commissioners Standard Ordinary Mortality Table.

Today, there are many ways a person can plan for retirement—some involve government programs while others rely primarily on private insurance, and some involve tax advantages while others do not. The following is a brief outline of these sources.

1. Social Security retirement benefits

2. Other government benefits

3. Private pension plans

    a. Employer-provided pension plans

    b. Retirement plans for the self-employed (HR-10 plans)

    c. Individual retirement accounts and annuities (IRA plans)

    d. Tax-sheltered annuity (TSA) plans

4. Deferred profit-sharing and other employee benefit plans

5. Nonqualified deferred compensation plans

6. Individually purchased annuities

7. Life insurance cash values

8. Investments and other assets owned by the individual

Many of these instruments for providing retirement income offer substantial tax advantages to the individual if the plan meets the requirements of the tax laws. The nature of these plans, the tax benefits afforded, and the requirements that must be met to secure them will be discussed in detail in Part Four, "Planning for Your Retirement."

Because many persons today do have a variety of retirement benefits available to them, coordination of these benefits becomes increasingly important. It does not make sense to either underprovide or overprovide for retirement income.

Reducing the Tax Burden

In many ways, we have a tax-oriented economy in the United States. Most people have the legitimate objective of reducing their tax burden as much as legally possible, consistent with their nontax objectives. Also, the tax implications of most transactions at least must be considered, and some transactions are entered into because of their tax advantages. Thus, tax planning has an important role in personal financial planning.

People are subject to many different taxes. These include sales taxes, real estate taxes, social security taxes, federal income taxes, state and/or local income taxes, federal estate tax, state inheritance and/or estate taxes, and federal gift taxes. The relative importance of these taxes varies considerably among families, depending upon their circumstances and income levels. When engaging in tax planning, however, most people are concerned primarily with income taxes, death taxes, and perhaps gift taxes.

There is a wide variety of specific tax-saving plans being used or proposed today. In general, however, they fall under one or more of the following *basic tax-saving techniques:* (1) tax elimination or reduction, (2) shifting the tax burden to others who are in lower brackets, (3) taking returns as long-term capital gains rather than ordinary income, and (4) postponing taxation. These techniques, along with many specific tax-saving ideas, are covered in detail in Part Five, "Tax and Estate Planning."

Planning for Your Heirs

This is commonly referred to as "estate planning." An *estate plan* has been defined as "an arrangement for the devolution of one's wealth." For a great many people, such an arrangement can be relatively simple and inexpensive to set up. But for larger estates or estates with special problems, estate plans can become quite complex. Estate planning is a technical and specialized field where such diverse areas of knowledge as wills, trusts, tax law, insurance, investments, and accounting are important. Thus, it frequently is desirable to bring together several professionals or specialists into an estate planning team to develop a well-rounded plan.

Unfortunately, there has developed over the years the impression that estate planning is only for the wealthy. However, as we saw in the hypothetical example of George Able and his family in Chapter 1, many persons who would not regard themselves as wealthy actually do have potential estates large enough to justify the use of estate planning techniques.

The specific objectives of estate planning, the various methods of estate transfer, both lifetime (inter vivos) and at death, and the use of common estate planning techniques are treated in greater detail in Part Five.

Investment and Property Management

Need for Management. The need and desire to obtain outside investment or property management vary greatly among individuals and families. Some people have a keen interest in investments and property management and hence seek little, if any, help in managing their affairs. Others who may be knowledgeable enough to handle their own investment and property management nevertheless prefer to devote their full time and energies to their business or profession and leave the management of their personal financial affairs to professionals in that field. Then, of course, there are those who by temperament or training are not equipped to manage their own financial affairs.

However, the increasing complexity of dealing with investments, insurance, tax problems, and the like generally has increased the need for investment and property management. Also, these complexities tend to increase as personal incomes and wealth increase in our society.

Sources of Aid in Management. There are many such sources now available. They vary considerably in the nature and scope of the aid they offer.

Use of financial intermediaries. Broadly speaking, a *financial intermediary* is a financial institution that invests other people's money and pays them a rate of return on that money. Such institutions serve as conduits for savings into appropriate investments. In effect, then, they take over the investment and money management tasks with respect to those savings. They may also offer subsidiary financial advice, but normally only within their particular areas of interest. The important financial intermediaries as far as most individuals are concerned include:

Commercial banks (offering various types of savings accounts)[2]

Mutual savings banks

Savings and loan associations

[2]Commercial banks also provide trust and investment advisory services that are covered later.

Life insurance companies

Investment companies (mutual funds and closed-end investment companies)

Trusts. One of the basic reasons for establishing trusts is to provide experienced and knowledgeable investment and property management services for the beneficiary(ies) of the trust. The various uses of personal trusts, including the use of revocable living trusts to provide investment and property management services for the person creating the trust, are covered in greater detail in Chapters 15, 16, and particularly 17.

Investment advisory services. There are more than 1,500 investment advisory firms that offer their clients professional investment advice on a fee basis. These firms range from small advisory firms of one or a few persons to large firms handling hundreds or even thousands of clients and having sizable staffs of specialists in various phases of investments. Many banks and some investment banking firms also offer investment advisory services on a fee basis.

The investment advisory services that may be rendered include: (1) analysis of the client's investment needs and objectives, (2) recommendation of an investment program and specific investment policies to achieve the client's objectives, (3) recommendation of specific security issues to implement the policies, and (4) continuous supervision and review of the client's investment portfolio. Banks and some investment advisory firms also provide custody services for their clients, which include safekeeping of securities, handling buy and sell orders with brokers, collection of dividends, dealing with rights under securities, and record keeping, as a part of their advisory services. Banks also provide custody services separately if that is all the customer wants.

In terms of investment decision-making authority, investment advisors may operate in one of three ways: (1) on a strictly *discretionary* basis, under which the advisor actually makes investment decisions and buys and sells securities for the client without prior consultation on the transactions with the client; (2) under an arrangement whereby the advisor basically makes the investment decisions but does consult with the client to inform him or her of the reasons for the decisions before taking action; and (3) an arrangement under which the advisor and client consult extensively before investment decisions are made, but the client reserves the actual decision making for himself. There are advantages and disadvantages for the advisor and client in each of these methods of operation. In the final analysis, however, the worth of any investment advisor basically lies in how good his or her advice turns out to be over the long pull in terms of the client's objectives.

Annual fees charged by investment advisors vary, depending upon such factors as the size of the client's portfolio, the extent of the services rendered, and the kinds of securities (or property) in the portfolio. For example, an annual fee might start at $1/2$ of 1 percent of principal with a minimum annual fee of, say, $250. Unfortunately, the use of investment advisors by smaller investors frequently is made impractical by the relatively large minimum annual fees charged. For an investor with a $10,000 portfolio, for example, the above $250 minimum annual fee would constitute an annual charge of $2^{1}/_{2}$ percent of principal. For this reason, many investment advisors discourage accounts of less than, say, $50,000. Some advisors, however, encourage smaller accounts, but with proportionally higher fees.

Investors, small and large, also can obtain valuable investment advice from account executives and others with stock brokerage firms. Many brokerage houses have active and well-staffed research departments that provide their customers with considerable investment information and often helpful recommendations. It must be pointed out, however, that the relationship between the stockbroker and his customer is not the same as that of the investment advisor and his client. The broker typically is paid commissions based on the transactions in his customers' accounts, while the advisor is paid on an annual-fee basis as described above. However, the professionally minded broker recognizes that his long-term success ultimately depends upon the investment success of his customers and acts accordingly.

Other advisors. There obviously are other important sources from which individuals can secure aid in managing their affairs. Many were mentioned in Chapter 1. Attorneys provide necessary legal and other advice. The old adage, "The man (or woman) who acts as his own lawyer has a fool for a client," still holds true. In the area of estate planning, for example, costly mistakes can be made in the absence of professional advice. Accountants are depended upon by many persons for advice concerning their financial affairs, particularly in the tax area. Life insurance agents can offer valuable advice concerning life insurance, health insurance, and pensions, as well as the other financial products and services their companies may offer. Similarly, property and liability insurance agents and brokers are becoming increasingly important for the advice they can provide on personal risk management, property and liability insurance coverages, and the other financial products and services their companies may offer.

The total-financial-services concept also has fostered the development of a new kind of financial services or financial planning organization. These organizations typically attempt to provide coordinated planning for their clients in such areas as investments, insurance, pensions and other employee benefits, and tax and estate planning. Their goal is to deal with the client's total picture. A few banks, insurance companies, and others now offer this kind of service, but it is not widespread at present.

PART TWO
USING INSURANCE EFFECTIVELY

SAVINGS AND LOAN ASSOCIATION OF FORT WAYNE
719 COURT STREET • FORT WAYNE, INDIANA 46801
PHONE 423-2377

3
BASIC INSURANCE PRINCIPLES

Insurance provides an important means of meeting the financial objectives of most people. To understand how insurance may be useful in meeting your financial objectives, it will be helpful to look first at the broader field of risk management.

RISK MANAGEMENT

The term *risk management* normally means the use of all the alternative methods of dealing with risk. Business firms are becoming increasingly aware of the benefits that can be derived from a well-developed risk management program. Although most people are perhaps less able to implement these techniques in a "personal risk management" situation, the knowledge of this concept can assist you in developing the proper philosophy toward handling the personal risks you face.

Approach to Risk Management

Risk management, in its simplest form, consists of knowledge of the existence of various forms of risk and their magnitude and the management of the various methods for dealing with those risks. The ultimate goal is the recognition and control of risk. The first steps in the risk management process are risk analysis and risk evaluation.

Risk Analysis. The logical start of any risk management program is the recognition of your risk exposures. This may not be as easy as it seems at first glance. For example, if you hire a domestic worker in your home, what liability or workmen's compensation exposures do you have? Also, some losses can be avoided if knowledge of the cause of loss is known in advance.

Risk Evaluation. Once a risk is discovered, it should be evaluated to determine its cause and the probable degree of control you have over it.

Basic Risk Management Techniques

Avoidance of Risk. Risk avoidance is simply the act of eliminating risk by avoiding the causes of risk. As an example, if one does not choose to drive a car, there is little risk from the auto liability peril. Of course, such drastic measures are not necessarily recommended in dealing with risks of this nature. In some cases, however, risk avoidance may be quite logical. One of the factors a family may consider in deciding whether to put a swimming pool in their back yard, for example, is whether they want to be responsible for any accidents.

Risk Reduction (Loss Prevention). Risk reduction is almost synonymous with loss prevention and consists of all activities intended to prevent the occurrence of a loss. Also included are those steps taken to minimize a loss should one occur. An example of the former would be the removal of combustible materials (such as paints, thinners, and gasoline) from a garage or basement and storing them in an outside shed to minimize the risk of fire to the dwelling. An example of the second type of risk reduction would be placing fire extinguishers in certain areas of the house to control a fire should one occur.

Retention (Assumption) of Risk. Risk retention is the conscious act of keeping or assuming a risk rather than transferring it. In some cases, like the risk of loss from war or insurrection, retention is the only practical method of risk handling, since insurance usually cannot be purchased for such risks. In other cases, risk retention may be the most economical alternative. For example, this usually is the case with respect to the use of deductibles, which are discussed later in this chapter.

Transfer of Risk. Risk transfer (including insurance) consists of any measure by which the risk of one party actually is transferred to another. A noninsurance transfer of risk can perhaps best be explained by an example. Suppose Mrs. A volunteers her services to supervise a Girl Scout troop on a hike. However, the Scouts' parents all sign waiver agreements agreeing not to hold Mrs. A liable for any injuries. In this way, Mrs. A's liability risk has been at least partly transferred.

Insurance really is an important type of transfer device and usually is defined as the transferring of risk to a third party (the insurance company) in return for the payment of an amount of money (the premium). For the remainder of this chapter, we shall concentrate on this most popular technique for individuals to use in their personal risk management—*insurance*.

THE INSURANCE PRINCIPLE

Not all risks are insurable. In fact, most of the risks we are exposed to in daily life are insignificant and do not involve serious financial consequences.

However, there are many potentially serious events, such as fire, automobile accidents, robbery, death, and disability, that can cause substantial losses when they occur. These are the risks insurance is all about.

In essence, insurance is a means of eliminating or reducing the financial burden of such risks by dividing the losses they produce among many individuals. For example, assume there are 1,000 individuals aged 35, each of whom needs $10,000 of life insurance protection. Further assume that the chance of a male aged 35 dying during the next year is 0.002, or 2 out of 1,000. To protect the entire group, since each person cannot apply the laws of probability to himself (that is, each individual does not know whether he will be one of the two to die during the year), each of the 1,000 individuals could agree to contribute $20 to a common fund. This fund then will be used to reimburse the families of any individuals who die during the next year. The probability is that two persons will die, and so we would expect the fund to pay out $20,000 in the next year.

Therefore, for a "premium" of $20, each individual in the group will lose no more than $20, while the risk, as far as a major financial loss is concerned, will have been reduced. Of course, under the arrangement just described, each of the 998 individuals who did not die during the year could have saved money by not joining the plan. However, no one knew beforehand which particular individuals would die during the year; therefore, each of them was subject to a serious financial risk before the "insurance" plan was adopted. This risk was reduced when each contributed $20 to the fund. The assurance that his or her family's loss would be limited to $20, rather than as much as $10,000, was the return obtained by the 998 for the small sum ($20) they paid.

Before leaving this illustration, we must note that the overhead expenses of running such an insurance plan would add to the cost of the plan. Thus, the amount each of the 1,000 persons would have to pay must be "loaded" to cover these overhead expenses. These are the costs of running an insurance business.

Insurance Purchase Decisions

Most people must make decisions concerning which risks should be insured and which risks should be handled in other ways. To help you do this, a convenient kind of measure that quickly shows the types of risks that can wipe out an individual or family financially is contained in the following simple formula.

$$\text{Relative value of a risk} = \frac{\text{total amount at stake}}{\text{total wealth}}$$

The greater the result of this formula, the less able an individual is to assume any given risk and the more he or she needs to insure the risk.

To illustrate, suppose an individual has a home worth $40,000 and a total net worth of $60,000. Applying the above formula, we have:

$$\text{Relative value of the loss of the home} = \frac{\$40,000}{\$60,000} = \frac{2}{3}$$

Obviously, the risk of the home being totally destroyed, say by fire, is too great for the individual to bear alone because $\frac{2}{3}$ of his or her net worth could be lost. Thus, this person would be wise to purchase fire insurance.

Now, let us assume the same individual is wondering whether to carry a $100 deductible on the collision insurance covering his or her car. If a covered loss does occur, the insured will have to pay the first $100 as the deductible. According to our formula, we would put the $100 over the individual's total wealth and come up with a value of 0.0016, or about $\frac{1}{7}$ of 1 percent. Thus, use of the deductible seems sound. Any such loss can be handled easily by the individual. Moreover, the administrative expenses of settling such a claim would be high relative to the actual loss itself.

These two examples illustrate that the first principle of insurance buying is to place primary emphasis on those risks that potentially could wipe out or substantially deplete your net worth. This sometimes is called the "large-loss principle." Insurance against such losses is considered as *essential*. Note that the *severity* of a potential loss, not its *frequency*, should be the determining factor.

Some losses cannot be handled out of current income but nevertheless are not large enough to bankrupt the family. However, they may impair the family's accumulated savings or saddle it with unwanted debt. Insurance against these losses is considered *desirable*, provided the family's insurance budget is large enough to provide more than the essential coverages.

The final category is *available* insurance coverages. Included in this class is insurance against small losses that can be paid out of current income or an emergency fund without seriously impairing your financial position. Few families will be able to afford the luxury of insurance simply because it is available to offset some possible financial loss. For most families, premium dollars are needed for insurance necessities.

Use of Deductibles and Other Cost-Sharing Devices

Whenever feasible, an individual should consider the use of deductibles in his financial planning. A deductible requires the insured to pay the first portion, such as the first $100, of a covered loss before the insurance comes into play. Use of deductibles can result in several benefits for the insured. For example, it makes the insurance *less expensive*, since deductibles eliminate small losses and hence the disproportionately high administrative expenses associated with handling small losses. Furthermore, for the same premium as without a deductible, you can purchase much higher benefits. For example, by taking a $100 instead of a $50 deductible on automobile collision insurance, an insured might save enough premium to increase his liability limits from $10,000 and $20,000 to $100,000 and $300,000 for the same premium. Thus, by foregoing an additional $50 recovery on a small collision loss, the insured is able to guard against the possibility of a catastrophic liability loss that could destroy him financially.

Deductibles can take various forms. The use of deductibles in particular lines of insurance is discussed in later chapters. Other cost-sharing devices, such as coinsurance and copayment in medical expense insurance, also are discussed in succeeding chapters.

SELECTION OF INSURANCE COMPANIES, AGENTS, AND BROKERS

A perplexing task facing many people is the selection of appropriate insurance companies and counselors to help them with the insurance aspects of their overall financial plan.

Types of Insurers

A starting point in intelligently selecting an insurer is for the consumer to have a basic understanding of the different types of insurers that offer their wares to the public. The several thousand private insuring organizations in the United States may be broadly categorized as to whether they seek a profit for those who own the organization or whether they are nonprofit in operation. Stock insurance companies comprise the major segment of the profit-seeking insurers, while mutual insurance companies are the most important nonprofit insurers.

Profit is an elusive concept, particularly insurers. It should not be inferred, therefore, that "nonprofit" necessarily means lower operating costs. Any broad classification of insurers sets up an almost endless chain of qualifications that may be halted by a fundamental statement: *The purchaser of insurance can draw no meaningful conclusions about a particular insurer solely on the basis of its legal form of organization.* Later, we shall consider the significant factors to be considered in the choice of an insurer, *but early warning should be sounded against the all-too-common error of generalization, e.g., about the safety of an insurer, the price of its coverage, or the service it provides, based solely on the insurer's legal structure.*

Profit-seeking Insurers. Stock insurance companies are the main type of profit-seeking insurer. They are owned by stockholders who provided the original capital for the company as required by law or who acquired the stock from other shareholders. Stock companies seek to pay dividends to their stockholders after the payment of claims and expenses and the possible provision for additions to surplus.

It has been traditional for stock insurance companies to sell coverage at a fixed price. Thus, until recent decades, most stock insurance companies issued nonparticipating policies; that is, no dividends were paid to policyholders in the event of underwriting (or investment) profits. There is a current tendency, however, for many stock insurers to offer "par" (participating) policies, particularly in the life insurance field. However, contracts with a fixed cost still comprise a major portion of the business of most stock insurers.

Lloyd's of London, one of the best-known insurance organizations in the world, also is considered a profit-seeking insurance operation. The operations of the underwriters at Lloyd's, however, do not directly affect most individual insurance consumers.

Nonprofit Insurers. There are various kinds of nonprofit insurers and comparable organizations from whom you may buy coverage. There really is no uniform pattern among them.

Mutual insurance companies. These companies have no capital stock and, therefore, no stockholders. Technically they are owned by their policyholders. This is the primary difference between mutual insurance companies and stock insurance companies. However, both are organized as corporations. In theory, the policyholders of a mutual exercise control through their right to elect the corporation's board of directors.

Mutual insurers are of one of two basic types—assessable or nonassessable. Many of the early mutual insurers required no payment of premiums at the inception of the protection period. Rather, insureds had to pay their share of each claim as it arose. An insured's share of claims was his or her assessment. Thus, the cost of protection provided by these assessment mutuals was never known prior to the end of the policy period.

Today, however, most insurers have modified or eliminated the assessment concept, and the bulk of insurance coverage currently written by mutual insurance companies is *nonassessable.* This means that the premium the insured pays to the mutual insurer is the most the insured will have to pay for his or her insurance coverage. The insured cannot be assessed further. As a matter of fact, the charters of major mutual insurers generally prohibit assessment. The nonassessable arrangement is made possible by the fact that before mutual insurers can issue nonassessable policies in a particular state, they generally must meet the same financial requirements stipulated for stock insurers. A policy issued by a mutual insurer must indicate on its face whether it is nonassessable. While there may be arguments on the other side, in general an individual consumer should buy only nonassessable insurance, or possibly insurance where the right of assessment is strictly limited.

But even in nonassessable mutuals, the final cost of insurance coverage often is unknown, although insureds never have to pay more than the advance premium. This is because policyholders may receive policy dividends, thus reducing the cost of the coverage. Policy dividends are entirely different from dividends on common stocks. Policy dividends, at least to an important extent, amount to a return of unneeded premium and thus are a cost saving for the policyholder. Therefore, they are not subject to federal income taxation. Dividends on stocks, on the other hand, are a type of investment income and normally are taxable income.

Not all mutual insurance is "participating," that is, entitled to the possible payment of dividends. Some mutual health insurance and property and liability insurance policies, for instance, are nonparticipating. Sometimes mutual property and liability insurers will write insurance at lower initial premiums than otherwise would have been the case, instead of paying dividends at the end of the policy period. With the exception of some annuities, mutual life insurance is almost always participating.

A few insurers in limited geographical areas write "perpetual" property insurance. The *perpetual* approach requires the payment of a relatively large advance premium, which is invested by the insurance company; the investment earnings on the advance premiums are expected to be sufficient to pay claims and expenses. In addition, perpetual companies frequently pay generous dividends to their policyholders along with providing insurance protection. Thus, perpetual insurance combines insurance with investment returns. Normally, the insured may cancel the perpetual contract at any time and get back 90 to 100 percent of the deposit premium, depending on how long the policy has been in force.

Hospital and medical expense associations. Much early hospital, surgical, and medical expense protection was issued by nonprofit associations. A substantial portion still is written by these organizations, which includes Blue Cross and Blue Shield plans.

Most of these associations have been established at the instigation of hospitals, physicians, dentists, or civic groups. Covered persons, called "subscribers," are not the owners of the associations, nor do they generally have a vote in the selection of the board of directors. Technical control of a plan often rests with a "corporation," a body composed of various occupational and civic representatives.

Hospital service associations, of which Blue Cross plans are the most significant, were the first types of nonprofit health care associations to be organized on a wide scale. The hospital associations have sought in most instances to obtain hospital services on a cost basis for subscribers through contractual arrangements with hospitals and possibly other institutions that provide health care services.

Blue Shield plans and other medical service associations (e.g., organizations providing surgical and certain medical benefits) were developed after the hospital service associations. The two types of organizations ordinarily operate under similar rules and often cooperate in performing various functions. The establishment of dental service associations is a recent development.

Reciprocal insurance exchanges. Reciprocal exchanges (also called "interinsurance exchanges") are a type of nonprofit insurer resembling mutual insurance companies in many ways despite organizational, operational, and local differences between the two. In a reciprocal, each insured assumes a proportionate share of every risk being pooled (except his own). Thus, each insured is individually liable for a portion of the risk presented by every other insured in the organization. Reciprocals may operate on an assessable or nonassessable basis. The bulk of the business written by reciprocals is automobile and fire insurance.

Considerations Affecting the Choice of an Insurer

Selection of an insurer or insurers is one of the practical problems you face in buying insurance. For the most part, this problem is resolved either by the selection (or acceptance) of an agent or broker, who then determines the insurer to be used, or by the use of direct insurance-buying facilities (e.g., through the mail or at a counter or booth in a place of business patronized by the individual). Unfortunately, many insureds who have an agent or broker may not be able even to identify the insuring organization with which they are placed. However, more insureds appear to be taking an interest in the actual choice of the insurers through whom they will obtain protection. This interest may be fostered by such factors as rising premiums in some lines of insurance; extensive advertising by insurers and others; consumers' guides issued by some state insurance departments; intense competition among all insurers and between so-called "agency" companies and "direct-writing" organizations in particular; and the general mood of "consumerism" in the country.

We noted above that *no generalization should be made concerning a particular insurer solely on the basis of its legal form of organization.* Instead, insurers should be evaluated on the basis of such aspects of the insured-insurer relationship as the *financial soundness of the insurer,* the extent and quality of the *service it will render the insured,* the *types of coverage and policies the insurer offers,* and the *price* it charges for a particular coverage.

Financial Soundness. The financial soundness of an insurer is of obvious interest to potential insureds. Unfortunately, it is difficult for the average person to assess the financial status of an insurer. This problem arises in part from the specialized accounting methods used by insurers and their practices in setting up reserves. Also, the stability of an insuring organization is affected to a considerable degree by the types and quality of insurance it writes. As a consequence, the asset-liability position of an insurer is not the only indication of its financial soundness.

Nevertheless, one measure of financial soundness that you can use is the policyholders' surplus ratio. This ratio is shown by the formula:

$$\text{Policyholders' surplus ratio} = \frac{\text{insurer net worth (i.e., assets} - \text{liabilities)}}{\text{insurer liabilities}}$$

While this ratio certainly is not the complete answer, it is commonly used in the insurance industry. It can also be easily calculated by the consumer from an insurance company's balance sheet. Note that the policyholders' surplus ratio compares net worth with liabilities, which is logical. Beware of insurance company claims of financial strength based on assets alone. Companies, in effect, may say, "Look how strong we are; we have over x million in assets." However, assets alone mean little in judging an insurer's financial strength.

The individual buyer of insurance can receive some assurance about the strength and stability of insurers through the regulatory procedures of the various states. The financial requirements that insurers must meet vary by states, but there is some indication that an insurer is stable if it is authorized to issue coverage in states that have effective insurance regulation. People often cite New York as an example in this regard. The sources of information dealing with an insurer's financial strength are discussed later in this chapter.

Service. There are many facets to the service an insurer might be expected to offer its customers. *Claims service*—the expeditiousness and fairness with which claims are settled—naturally is a major consideration. An insurer should be expected to provide equitable claims settlement that is neither too low nor too high. An idea of the general reputation of a particular insurer relative to claims settlement sometimes can be gained by asking several of your acquaintances about their experience with the insurer. Some people will always think they have been cheated, whether in connection with insurance claims or in any other business dealings; but by obtaining and evaluating the comments of a number of individuals, you may be able to get an impression of an insurer's claims practices. Then, too, the reputation of the insurance agent or broker in itself may testify to the type of claims service you can expect. In fact, in many instances agents have authority to settle certain claims for an insurer. Even without claim settlement authority, an agent often is in a position to present very effectively an insured's position concerning a claim to the insurer. Thus, an agent or broker of good repute can be expected to render considerable assistance to the insured if a claim arises.

A number of services in addition to claims treatment may be of importance to insureds. For example, *life and health insurance programming and other estate analysis services* in life insurance and *risk analysis and insurance surveys* for property and liability insurance may be of importance. As noted in Chapter 1, such services can be of considerable aid to the consumer in the personal financial planning process.

Types of Coverage. The types of contracts a particular insurer offers in a given area of insurance are a consideration, but they tend to be more significant for large insureds than for insureds with average risks.

Price. It is self-evident that the price charged for a given amount of insurance is of great significance to insurance buyers. It also goes almost without saying that price considerations should never be placed above financial safety, since protection in an unstable organization is a questionable buy at any price. Also, if a particular policy is available at a lower cost because the insurer provides less service of a particular type, such as claims service or evaluating the customer's risk situation, then the customer should evaluate how important the service is to him.

To some extent, the price of a given policy may depend upon the type of sales organization used by the insurer. Here again, the question of which services are important to the customer is a signficant consideration.

It should be noted again in connection with price considerations that the legal form of organization of an insurer gives no direct clue as to the competitiveness of its premiums. For example, it would be incorrect to assume that the coverage of a stock insurance company, which may pay dividends to its stockholders, is necessarily more expensive than mutual insurance. Many stock insurance companies offer participating policies, and the total amount of dividends paid to stockholders in large stock companies generally is but a small fraction of their overall operating expenses. On the other hand, it is equally improper to think that the cost of mutual insurance is erratic. The dividends of most mutuals, for instance, have a tendency to be stable over a period of years, and the final cost of mutual (participating) protection often can be predicted rather closely.

In general, the selection of an insurer presents some of the same kinds of problems as the selection of a doctor or a lawyer or the choice of an important item like a home. In relatively few decisions of this nature is the choice clear-cut; rather, one must weigh relative factors on the basis of information that is not always readily available or easily interpreted.

The existence of several thousand insurers in the United States virtually precludes an insurer-by-insurer comparison. Most individual insureds are limited to a selection from among insurers with sales representatives—agents, brokers, employees, or other sales methods—within their locale. Furthermore, many lines of insurance often are not purchased unless some type of sales effort is made toward prospective insureds. The range of choice then is reduced to those insurers who make themselves available to an individual. However, the more knowledgeable the consumer, the more likely it is that he or she will evaluate such aspects as strength, service, and price in an intelligent manner.

Sources of Information

Several sources of information are available to an insured or prospective insured who wants to know more about an insurer's financial strength, service, and cost. Published sources provide the most detailed information. The sources noted here are illustrative only and are not meant to be exhaustive. The annual reports that insurers must submit to state insurance departments provide extensive information on the financial affairs of the insurer and may be consulted by the public. Sometimes an insurance commissioner will issue a report which condenses much of this information, and many insurers will send interested parties copies of their reports to stockholders or policyholders.

Reporting services, however, are the most frequently consulted sources. In life insurance, illustrative reporting services include: *Best's Life Reports* and *The Spectator Insurance Year Book,* which present the background histories of most insurers, the lines of insurance they write, the states in which they operate, and detailed financial data; *Flitcraft* and *Little Gem Life Chart,* which indicate the principal policy provisions, premium rates and dividend rates (for participating policies), and the settlement option values used by most life insurers; *The Handy Guide,* which reproduces one insurance contract issued by each of the leading insurers and, in addition, presents important premium information; *Settlement Options,* which also contains tables of settlement option values but in addition describes in detail the practices of most insurers with respect to settlement options; *Who Writes What in Life and Health Insurance,* which lists the contracts and underwriting practices of the leading life and health insurers; and *Time Saver,* which analyzes the policies and rates of most health insurers.

In property and liability insurance, *Best's Insurance Reports, Fire and Casualty,* occupies a position similar to *Best's Life Reports* in life insurance. For each insurer, this service describes the history, management, and general underwriting policy of the insurer and presents detailed financial data. An additional feature is the rating of each insurer according to the quality of its underwriting results, the economy of its management, the adequacy of its reserves, the ability of its capital and surplus to absorb unfavorable operating results, and the soundness of its investments. Grades run from A + and A (excellent) to C (fair). Because of the large proportion of insurers receiving high grades, the major value of the grades is the assistance they afford the consumer in detecting questionable insurers. They also prove useful when an individual is approached by an insurer about which he knows little or nothing. *Who Writes What?* is similar for property and liability insurance to *Who Writes What in Life and Health Insurance. Best's Aggregates and Averages* reports important financial data for leading insurers and the industry. *The Fire, Casualty, and Surety Bulletins* provide up-to-date information on property and liability insurance coverages. A few state insurance departments have distributed tables of rates charged by different insurers.

Other sources of information are agents and insurers, who can supply specimen contracts and premium information; other consumers, especially those facing the same problems; and your personal experiences.

Considerations Affecting the Choice of an Agent or Broker

How does an individual go about finding a good insurance agent or broker? What readily visible earmarks are there that will enable the insurance buyer to select an agent or broker wisely from the start? The answer is, practically none—that is, practically none that are readily visible. There are several, however, that the individual buyer should try to evaluate. The consumer can ask pertinent questions, such as: What is the agent's or broker's experience in terms of years and extent of practice? Is he a noted specialist in any certain line? Does he do business mostly with individual households, with business firms, or on a general across-the-board basis? How does he sell insurance? Does he engage in survey selling? Does he present a unified program of coverage based on a careful analysis of exposures? Does he represent a sound company or companies? The answers to all these questions offer some measure of the quality of the agent or broker.

In selecting an insurer, a consumer must pay attention to financial strength, service, and cost. In selecting an agent or broker, the consumer must realize that service and cost are the primary factors to be considered. The agent's or broker's ability to service his insureds depends upon his knowledge of the insurance business, his understanding of special problems, and his ability (in terms of time, interest, analytical skill, markets, and facilities) to help the consumer design and implement, with minimum delay and cost, a proper program of protection. The agent's or broker's task does not terminate, however, with the design and implementation of the original program. Insurance needs constantly change, and the program must be kept up to date. In addition, when losses occur, the agent or broker can render valuable assistance. He also may provide or request additional services, such as appraisals, when desirable or necessary.

Sources of Information

Obtaining information about agents, brokers, and other sales representatives is much more difficult than investigating insurers. The service to be provided is the principal issue, and published sources cannot provide this type of information. Personal or business associates may be able to provide some useful evaluations of agents and brokers as well as insurers, but the most satisfactory source of information probably is personal contact with the agent or broker.

One positive indication of an agent's, broker's, or insurance representative's knowledge and basic professional commitment to his or her career is whether he or she has earned the "Chartered Property Casualty Underwriter" (CPCU) designation or "Chartered Life Underwriter" (CLU) designation. To obtain these designations, a practitioner must have passed a series of examinations covering such diverse fields as insurance, law, economics, social legislation, finance, accounting, taxation, and management. Although it is true that many competent producers do not have either designation, and that designations do not always indicate competence, the consumer should be aware of the existence and meaning of CPCU and CLU.

4

LIFE INSURANCE AND SOCIAL SECURITY

Once it is determined that you need some form of life insurance to protect against the economic risk of premature death, many questions still remain. They include: Should I buy term life insurance and invest the difference? Should I purchase whole life or endowment insurance? Is participating or nonparticipating life insurance best for me? What provisions should I make sure are in my policy? Should I purchase extra coverages like double indemnity, guaranteed insurability, or other supplementary benefits? How does social security affect my life insurance planning? and many similar questions. This chapter responds to such questions concerning the decision factors involved in your life insurance planning.

SOURCES OF LIFE INSURANCE PROTECTION

But before you respond to such questions, you should consider the various sources (and forms) of life insurance available to you. As far as the consumer is concerned, they can conveniently be broken down into (1) individually purchased, (2) employer-sponsored, and (3) government-sponsored life insurance coverages.

Individually Purchased Life Insurance

Individually purchased life insurance is characterized by the sale of life insurance on an individual basis. That is, the individual typically applies for and, if found insurable, is issued an individual contract of life insurance. The various forms of individually purchased life insurance include ordinary life insurance, industrial life insurance, credit life insurance, fraternal life insurance, and savings bank life insurance.

Ordinary Life Insurance. This category of life insurance typically is sold through an agent to the individual. An applicant for ordinary life insurance may obtain any amount he or she wishes, as long as the insurer is willing to write it and the applicant can afford the coverage. Premiums for ordinary life insurance policies usually are paid directly to the insurer on an annual, semiannual, quarterly, or monthly basis. There are three basic types of ordinary life[1] insurance: term, whole life, and endowment. These are discussed later in this chapter.

Industrial Life Insurance. This form of life insurance normally is issued in small amounts, usually not over $500, with premiums payable on a weekly or monthly basis and generally collected at the home of the insured by an agent of the insurance company. In recent years, industrial life insurance in force has decreased. It generally is a high-cost form of life insurance.

Credit Life Insurance. Credit life insurance may be written on either an individual or a group basis, but most of it is written as group insurance. This coverage is issued through a lender or lending agency to cover the payment of a loan, installment purchase, or other obligation in the event of the debtor's death. Credit life insurance protects both the debtor and the creditor against loss as a result of the debtor's death during the term of the loan. The debtor normally pays for this coverage.

Fraternal Life Insurance. This life insurance is available through membership in a lodge or fraternal order, religious group, or the like. In the past, the number of fraternal insurers was large and they operated on an almost pure assessment basis, with uniform assessments regardless of age each time a death occurred. Today, however, fraternal insurers generally operate on a legal-reserve basis as other life insurers do.

Savings Bank Life Insurance. The distinctive feature of savings bank life insurance, sold by mutual savings banks, is that it is transacted on an over-the-counter basis, or by mail, without the use of agents. Currently, only three states permit savings bank life insurance: Massachusetts, New York, and Connecticut. Savings bank life insurance is available only to residents of, or workers in, these states, but, of course, such coverage remains in force if the policyholder should leave the state. The amount of savings bank life insurance obtainable by any one applicant is limited by law.

Association Group Life Insurance. You may become eligible to buy group or wholesale (see below) life insurance by being a member of one or more associations of individuals, such as professional, fraternal, alumni, and community service groups. The life insurance usually is sold to members of the group through the mails, with limited individual selection and with the

---

[1]There often is confusion concerning the term "ordinary" as it pertains to types of life insurance. The word "ordinary" can have two very different meanings. "Ordinary life" can be used to mean that type of insurance on which a minimum of $1,000 of insurance is written on an annual premium basis. It is thus used to distinguish this type of insurance from group insurance and industrial insurance. This is how the term is used here. But "ordinary" also is commonly used to indicate the kind of policy where protection is furnished for the whole of life. In this regard, "ordinary" is used interchangeably with "straight life."

insured person paying the entire cost. Only certain plans and amounts of coverage are normally available. Once insured, you can normally continue your coverage until you reach a certain age, such as 70 or 75, unless you terminate your membership in the association or unless the association group policy itself is terminated.

Life insurance plans of this type are usually sold to association members on the basis of low cost. When deciding whether to buy coverage under an association group plan, however, be sure to compare its cost with that of other life insurance plans on the same basis. Sometimes you must make a few calculations to do this. One association group plan written for the members of a college fraternity, for example, would provide $40,000 of group term life insurance (with waiver of premium) for members aged 35 through 44 at a semiannual premium of about $100. This amounts to an annual premium of $5 per $1,000 ($100 × 2 ÷ 40) for term insurance in that age bracket. With this information, you now can compare the cost of this plan with the cost of other term policies.

Employer-Sponsored Life Insurance

The employer-employee relationship can result in providing you with substantial life insurance protection. The vast bulk of this life insurance is sold as an employee benefit. However, the employment mechanism also sometimes provides a convenient means of purchasing life insurance on an employee-pay-all basis. The various employer-sponsored life insurance programs include: group life insurance, wholesale life insurance, and salary savings life insurance.

Group Life Insurance. Group life insurance generally is available as a fringe benefit through an individual's place of employment, with part or all of the cost being paid by the employer. Group life is generally issued without individual evidence of insurability, while individual life insurance generally requires some evidence of insurability. The amount of group life insurance on individual employees is determined automatically by some type of benefit formula. Because of its importance to most people, group life insurance is discussed in greater detail later in this chapter.

Wholesale Life Insurance. This is a hybrid between individual and group life insurance, utilizing some of the principles of each. Wholesale life insurance is normally used for groups too small to qualify for group life insurance and also for association group cases. Under wholesale life insurance, an individual policy is issued to each person in the group and there is some individual underwriting.

Salary Savings Life Insurance. This plan developed as a means of selling regular forms of individual life insurance to employees under a convenient arrangement with their employer. Its distinguishing characteristics are the collection of premiums on a monthly basis from the employer, who deducts the necessary amounts from the wages of the insured employees; the necessity of individual evidence of insurability; and the issuance of individual life insurance policies to the insured persons.

Federal Government Life Insurance Programs

United States Government Life Insurance (USGLI) and National Service Life Insurance (NSLI) were government life insurance programs enacted during World War I and World War II, respectively. The issuance of new insurance under these plans has since been terminated and replaced with Servicemen's Group Life Insurance (SGLI), which started in 1965. All servicemen and servicewomen on active duty are eligible for up to $15,000 of group term life insurance at a premium of $3 per month (or at a rate of $2.40 per year per $1,000).[2] This group life insurance coverage terminates 120 days after the person is separated from active duty. During this 120-day period, the person can convert this coverage, without evidence of insurability, into one of the standard life insurance contracts (other than term) offered by an insurance company selected by the person from a list of companies participating in the program.

While normally not thought of as life insurance, social security provides survivorship benefits which, in essence, represent life insurance coverage. These survivorship benefits are described later in this chapter.

TYPES OF INDIVIDUAL LIFE INSURANCE CONTRACTS

As indicated earlier, the three basic types of individual life insurance contracts are term, whole life, and endowment. Various kinds of contracts, sometimes with imaginative names, are when analyzed one of, or some combination of, these three basic forms.

Term Insurance

Perhaps no other type of life insurance has generated so much confusion, and sometimes controversy, as term insurance. You may have heard such expressions as, "Buy term and invest the difference," or, "Term insurance is only usable for mortgage protection," or, "There is no insurance like term insurance."

Term life insurance provides financial protection for a limited period. If death should occur during the specified period, the face amount of the policy is paid, with nothing being paid in the event the insured survives the period. Term insurance thus is comparable to most forms of property and liability insurance. Term policies frequently have no cash or loan values. Since term

---

[2]Reservists, national guardsmen, and ROTC members also can secure this coverage on a part-time basis while on active duty.

insurance provides temporary protection, its principal appeal lies in the low premium per $1,000 of protection provided.

The very nature of term insurance suggests how it can be used in meeting your needs for life insurance protection. Term insurance is especially suitable when either the need for protection is temporary or the need is permanent but the insured cannot presently afford the premiums for some type of whole life insurance.

When the need for insurance is temporary, term insurance may supply the whole answer to the protection problem. For example, George Able might want to fulfill a temporary need, such as mortgage insurance, by purchasing a decreasing term life insurance contract (described below). In this way, George can insure his family's ability to pay off the mortgage if he should die before it is completely paid.

The other major use of term insurance is where the need is permanent but the insured temporarily cannot afford the premium for a more permanent type of insurance. As more funds become available, the policyholder may convert some or all of a term policy to more permanent forms of insurance or to some other combination of insurance and investment.

Kinds of Term Insurance

In terms of amount of coverage, there are two main kinds of term insurance you can buy—level term and decreasing term.

Level Term Insurance. This type of contract provides a specified level amount of insurance for the entire period of the contract. For example, a five-year $20,000 level term policy provides $20,000 of protection for the five years.

Decreasing Term Insurance. This type of term insurance provides an amount of insurance that decreases over the period of the contract. It is well suited to those situations where the need for protection decreases over time. Probably the two best examples are with regard to a home mortgage where the mortgage decreases over time, and in situations of growing families where the need for insurance may decrease as the children become self-sufficient.

Whole Life Insurance

Whole life insurance furnishes protection for the whole of life regardless of how many years premiums are paid. Premiums may be paid throughout the insured's lifetime or over a limited period, such as 10, 20, or 30 years; or conceivably they could be paid in one lump sum at the inception of the policy. When the insured is to pay premiums throughout his or her lifetime, the policy is commonly referred to as "ordinary (or straight) life insurance." When the insured is to pay premiums over a specified period, such as for 20 years or to age 65, it is referred to as "limited-payment life insurance."

In addition to permanent protection, the other major distinguishing feature of whole life insurance as compared with term insurance is the combining in an insurance contract of savings (cash value) with insurance. The savings feature arises from the fact that in the early years of a whole life contract, the annual level premium is more than enough to pay the current cost of insurance protection. The excess of premiums in the early years, coupled with the effect of compound interest, makes up for the deficiency of premiums in the later years when the annual level premium is no longer sufficient to pay for the actual cost of insurance. The funds accumulated from the extra premiums in the early years are held by the insurer for the policyholder. This is the savings or investment element (cash value) of a whole life policy.

Endowment Insurance

The endowment life insurance policy offers insurance protection against death for a specified period of time, such as 10, 20, or 30 years, to age 65, and so forth, and then if the insured lives to the end of the specified period (term of the endowment), the contract pays the face amount either in a lump sum or in installments. Endowment life insurance contracts are basically savings plans with an insurance element added.

This stress on the saving feature also is a major limitation of endowment life insurance. If death protection is what you need, a great deal more death protection can be provided through either term or whole life insurance. Your own needs and financial situation should determine what types of life insurance should be purchased.

Special Life Insurance Contracts

There are a great many life insurance policies with all kinds of names sold by insurance companies. However, as we said before, such contracts really boil down to combinations or adaptations of the three major types just discussed. We discuss only the more important types of special life insurance contracts here.

"Modified" Life Insurance Policies. Under this type policy, the premiums are smaller for the first few years than for the remainder of the contract duration. It is typically a whole life contract in which the premiums are redistributed so that they are lower during the first three, five, or even 10 years than they are thereafter. Modified life often is attractive to a young family man who cannot afford to buy enough insurance on a regular whole life basis, but whose income permits him to purchase something more than term insurance.

Family Income-Type Policies. The family income policy or rider is a popular and widely sold special life insurance contract. It goes by many names, such as "income protector," "family security," "family protector," and the like. When you understand the concept underlying this type contract, you will have little trouble in recognizing the "family income" approach regardless of the name used.

Under the traditional family income contract, if the insured dies during the family income period, the proceeds of the whole life insurance are held at interest until the end of the family income period, at which time they are paid to the beneficiary. In the meantime, the interest on the proceeds provides part of the family income payments (which frequently are $10, $15, or even $20 per month for each $1,000 of face amount), and the proceeds from decreasing term insurance provide the rest. Assume, for example, that George Able at age 33 purchased a 20-year, $10,000, $10-per-month family income policy and then died at age 38. In this case, his beneficiary would receive $100 a month for 15 years and then the $10,000 face amount at the end of the 15 years.

Family Maintenance-Type Policies. This type of contract is similar to the family income policy or rider. The traditional family maintenance policy or rider consists of a basic life insurance policy, usually a form of whole life, plus level term insurance (instead of decreasing term, as used in family income policies). The level term insurance provides income for a stated number of years after the insured's death, provided this occurs within the family maintenance period. If, for example, George Able died at age 38 and had a $10,000, 20-year, $10-per-month family maintenance policy, the contract would pay an income of $100 per month to his beneficiary for 20 years, and then the $10,000 face amount would be paid at the end of the 20-year family maintenance period.

Family Policy. This policy includes coverage on all family members in one contract. Most family policies provide whole life insurance on the father, designated as the insured, with the premium based on his age, while term insurance is provided on the wife and children. All living children are covered, even if adopted or born after the policy is issued, until a stated age, such as 21. The children's term insurance usually is convertible to any permanent plan of insurance without evidence of insurability. A unit of coverage may consist of $5,000 whole life insurance on the insured, $1,500 whole life or term insurance on his wife, and $1,000 of term insurance on each child. The premium does not change in the event of the wife's death or the inclusion of additional children.

SOME IMPORTANT LIFE INSURANCE POLICY PROVISIONS

Most people buy individual life insurance contracts as part of their personal financial planning. Thus, an understanding of some important policy provisions will be helpful to you.

Assignment

A life insurance contract is personal property and, as such, is freely transferable (assignable) by the owner in the absence of a policy provision to the contrary. Two *types of assignments* are used in life insurance. One is the *absolute assignment,* under which all ownership rights in the contract are transferred to another. The second type is the *collateral assignment,* whereby only certain rights are transferred to another when the policy is to serve as security for a loan or in other debtor-creditor situations. The right to assign your life insurance policy can be a valuable one in both personal and business transactions.

Grace Period

The grace period, commonly 31 days, is a period after the premium for a life insurance policy is due during which the policy remains in full force even though the premium has not been paid. This provision is designed to protect the policyholder against inadvertent lapse of his or her policy.

Incontestable Clause

This provision states that after a life insurance contract has been in force a certain length of time (called the "contestable period"), which normally is two years, the insurer agrees not to deny a claim because of any error, concealment, or misstatement (generally including even fraud) on the part of the insured. From the standpoint of the insured and the beneficiary, such a clause alleviates the fear of lawsuits, especially at a time, after the insured's death, when it may be very difficult for the beneficiary to combat successfully a charge by the insurer of a violation in securing the contract.

Delay Clause

The delay clause is included in life insurance contracts to permit an insurance company to postpone payment of the cash surrender (or loan) value for a period of six months after requested by the policyholder. Insurers by law must include this provision in their contracts. It is designed to protect the insurer against losses that might develop from excessive demands for cash in times of economic crisis. It is expected that only under the most severe economic circumstances would this clause be invoked by insurers. However, it must be recognized that use of this provision potentially could restrict the liquidity of life insurance cash (or loan) values.

Suicide Clause

Life insurance contracts contain a suicide provision stating that if the insured commits suicide during a certain period of time after the policy is issued, generally two years, the insurer is liable only to return to the beneficiary the premiums paid, either with or without interest. After the two-year period, suicide becomes a covered risk and is treated like any other cause of death.

Reinstatement Clause

The reinstatement provision is designed to help a policyholder who has failed to pay a premium within the time allowed, including the grace period. This clause usually gives the insured the right to reinstate the policy within a specified period, usually three years of any default in premium payment, subject to furnishing evidence of insurability satisfactory to the insurer and the payment of back premiums.

This clause may be helpful to a policyholder for several reasons. For example, it may be advantageous for you to use the reinstatement clause of a current policy, instead of purchasing a new policy, because: a new policy generally will involve a higher premium (because of your higher age); the contestable and suicide periods may have run their course under your current policy; a new contract may have no cash value for one or two years; you, in effect, will have to pay the higher first-year costs of putting a life insurance policy into force again; and some older life insurance policies may have more liberal provisions with regard to policy loan interest rates, settlement options, and the like.

Policy Loan

The policy loan provision in a life insurance contract allows the policyholder to take a loan (technically an "advance" because it does not have to be repaid) on the sole security of the policy up to an amount that, with interest as specified in the contract, will not exceed the cash (loan) value of the policy as of the next policy anniversary. The rate of interest that can be charged on a policy loan is stated in the contract. Policy loans on most existing life insurance policies have a 5 percent interest rate. Some more recently issued policies specify a somewhat higher rate. These low, guaranteed policy loan interest rates can be very advantageous to a policyholder during periods of high interest rates and/or "tight" money. Under these circumstances, policy loans can be a low-cost, readily available source of credit.

The policy loan provision is a valuable right to the policyholder. It enables the policyholder to draw upon policy cash values to meet temporary financial needs without surrendering the contract. The main disadvantage of policy loans is that when a policyholder borrows against his or her life insurance and does not repay the loan, the death proceeds going to the beneficiaries will be reduced by the amount of the loan.

Automatic Premium Loan

Closely akin to the policy loan is the automatic premium loan provision. This provision operates when a policyholder fails to pay a premium when due. In this event, the premium is paid out of the policy loan value. Thus, through use of an automatic premium loan, you can protect your life insurance policy against lapse if you should fail to pay a premium as long as the policy has sufficient loan value to cover the premium payment.

In many companies, the automatic premium loan provision is not included automatically in the policy but can be included at the request of the policyholder. It is a feature you should check for in your policies, since it is possible for anyone to overlook making a premium payment. Also, there is no extra cost to you for the provision.

Beneficiary Designation

A life insurance contract allows the policyholder to select the person or persons (beneficiaries) who will receive the proceeds of the contract in the event of the insured's death. When the owner reserves the right to change the beneficiary, the beneficiary designation is called *revocable*. When the owner does not reserve the right to change the beneficiary, the designation is called *irrevocable*. An irrevocable beneficiary in effect becomes a joint owner of the policy rights. This means his or her signature is necessary for such things as assignments and policy loans. Most people use revocable beneficiary designations.

It usually is advisable to name a second beneficiary to receive life insurance proceeds in case the first (primary) beneficiary predeceases the insured. This contingent or secondary beneficiary can then receive the proceeds directly according to the insured's wishes. If no contingent beneficiary is named in the policy, the proceeds normally would go to the insured's estate if the primary beneficiary predeceases the insured and the insured dies without naming another primary beneficiary.

Aviation Clause or Exclusion

The aviation hazard at one time was either excluded from coverage or subject to an extra premium. Now, however, travel as a passenger in any type of aircraft, except military aircraft, is no longer considered an extra hazard. Additionally, many insurers are ignoring aviation restrictions previously written into existing policies if the insured currently would qualify under the new underwriting rules.

War Clause

Insurers may add so-called "war clauses" to their contracts during periods of war or impending war. This is particularly true of policies issued to young men of draft age. The major purpose of war clauses is to control the possibility of selection by applicants for insurance against the insurer.

CASH VALUES AND NONFORFEITURE OPTIONS

Life insurance companies are required to include certain nonforfeiture options in life insurance contracts. These provisions are designed to protect a policyholder who has accumulated a value in his or her life insurance policy (as the result of the level premium system described previously) but who for one reason or another wishes either to stop paying premiums or to surrender the contract. Nonforfeiture options (values) can take one of three forms: (1) a cash surrender value, (2) reduced paid-up life insurance, or (3) extended term life insurance.

Cash Surrender Value

Under state nonforfeiture laws, a cash value generally is required, at the latest, after premiums have been paid for three years and the policy produces a nonforfeiture value. Many policies today, however, provide for a cash value at the end of the first or second year. When you are considering buying a policy, see how early it will produce a cash value for you.

When the cash value option is elected by a policyholder, life insurance protection ceases and the insurer has no further obligation under the policy. Consequently, although this option provides a ready source of cash for emergencies or other needs, you should give careful consideration to this alternative before you surrender a policy. Essentially the same amount of cash can be obtained through a policy loan (described above), and so you should consider the policy loan alternative before surrendering your policy for cash.

But if you no longer need all the life insurance protection you carry, surrendering some of your policies for cash may be a logical move. Remember, too, that when you surrender a policy for cash, the amount of insurance protection you lose is not the face amount of the policy but rather the so-called "net amount at risk." Generally speaking, this is the face amount less the cash surrender value. Suppose, for example, you have a $10,000 life paid-up-at-age-65 policy with a current cash value of $4,000. If you surrender this policy for cash, your insurance protection will decline by $6,000 ($10,000 face minus the $4,000 cash value). This is so because you now have the $4,000 cash value to invest in some other form and which will go to your heirs in the event of your death.

Reduced Paid-up Insurance

This option permits the policyholder to elect to take the cash value as paid-up insurance of the same type as the original policy but for a reduced face amount. This option would be appropriate where a smaller amount of permanent insurance is satisfactory and it is desirable to discontinue premium payments, such as when the policyholder approaches retirement.

Extended Term Insurance

This nonforfeiture option allows the policyholder to exchange the cash value for paid-up term insurance for the full face amount of the original insurance contract. The duration of the term coverage is that which can be purchased with the net cash value applied as a single premium at the insured's attained age. This option is useful when the need for the full amount of insurance protection continues but the insured cannot, or does not wish to, continue premium payments.

DIVIDEND OPTIONS

Policyholders having participating life insurance contracts, i.e., those under which policyholders are entitled to policy dividends as declared by the insurer, may use such dividends in various ways. The dividend options available to policyholders usually include to: (1) take dividends in cash; (2) apply dividends toward payment of future premiums; (3) leave dividends with the insurance company to accumulate at interest; (4) use dividends to buy additional whole life insurance, called "paid-up additions"; and (5) use dividends to purchase one-year term insurance.

Cash dividends most frequently are taken when a policy is paid up. The use of *dividends toward the payment of future premiums* is a convenient and simple way to handle dividends. In order to afford a reasonably adequate life insurance program, many families depend on policy dividends to help meet their premium obligations.

Dividends also may be left with the insurer *to accumulate at a minimum guaranteed rate of interest (dividend accumulations).* If the insurer earns more than the guaranteed rate, dividend accumulations may participate in the excess earnings. This dividend option essentially is like a savings account held with the insurance company, and dividends left in this way can accumulate to a rather sizable sum over a period of years. If you have such dividend accumulations, you might want to check the interest rate being paid on them by the insurance company to see if you can get a better return with at least equal safety elsewhere.

Another dividend option is *paid-up additions.* This option provides paid-up insurance at net single-premium rates (i.e., no charge for expenses is added to the rate). If an insured wishes to convert accumulated dividends to paid-up additions, he or she might be asked to show evidence of insurability.

One-year term insurance (the so-called "fifth dividend option") is another option offered by many insurance companies. The amount of one-year term insurance that can be purchased with dividends generally is limited to the cash value of the policy. This option provides for the purchase of term insurance at net rates.

SETTLEMENT OPTIONS

Life insurance policies provide that when the proceeds become payable, the insured or the beneficiary may elect to have such proceeds paid in some form other than a lump sum. These forms of settlement, other than lump-sum, are called "settlement options." The various settlement options include the: (1) interest option, (2) fixed amount option, (3) fixed period option, and (4) life income options.

Interest Option

The proceeds of a life insurance policy may be left with the insurer at a guaranteed rate of interest, such as $2\frac{1}{2}$ or 3 percent, for example. In addition to this guaranteed interest rate, most life insurers pay an additional, nonguaranteed rate of interest consistent with the earnings on their investments (called "excess interest"). For example, an insurer may guarantee $2\frac{1}{2}$ per cent but actually be paying 5 percent (i.e., $2\frac{1}{2}$ percent excess interest).

Proceeds left under the interest option may carry a limited or unlimited right of withdrawal by the beneficiary. The beneficiary also may be given the right to change to another option or options. The interest option provides a great deal of flexibility in that the principal can be retained intact until such time as it is needed. In essence, it is like holding the proceeds in a savings account with the insurance company.

Fixed-amount Option

This option provides a stated amount of income each month until the proceeds are exhausted. For example, the insured or beneficiary may desire that the proceeds be paid out at the rate of, say, $500 a month for as long as the proceeds last. Each payment is partly interest and partly a return of principal. Again, the insurer guarantees a minimum rate of interest but actually usually pays a rate closer to that being earned on its investments.

Fixed-period Option

This option is similar to the fixed-amount option except that the period of time over which payments are made is fixed and the amount of each monthly installment varies accordingly. For example, $20,000 of proceeds at $2\frac{1}{2}$ percent interest (guaranteed) payable in 120 monthly installments would be $188.14 per month. Again, most insurers pay a higher rate than that guaranteed, and such excess interest increases the amount of each installment.

Life Income Options

Under a life income option, the insured or beneficiary elects to have the proceeds paid for the rest of his or her life or for the life of one or more beneficiaries. This option amounts to using the proceeds to buy a life annuity of some sort. Several types of life income options are available. They include: (1) pure life income, (2) life income with a period certain, (3) refund life income options, and (4) joint and last survivor life income options.

Pure Life Income. This option permits the policyholder to have the proceeds paid out over the lifetime of the recipient. There are no guarantees as to the return of the insurance proceeds. This option provides the highest monthly income for a given dollar amount of proceeds, primarily because of the absence of any refund feature. But the entire proceeds are considered "used up" at the recipient's death, and therefore people tend to shy away from this option.

Life Income with Period Certain. Under this option, payments are guaranteed for as long as the recipient lives; however, if the recipient should die before the end of a specified period, such as 10 or 20 years, for example, payments continue for the remainder of that period to a second payee. Thus, if Mary Able has been left $40,000 of life insurance proceeds under a life income option with 10 years certain, and she lives for 18 years, she would receive the monthly income for 18 years. However, if Mary should die after 4 years, monthly income payments would continue to a second payee (perhaps her children) for an additional six years.

Refund Life Income Options. This type of option provides a life income with the additional guarantee that in the event the recipient dies before receiving the full amount of the original life insurance proceeds, the difference (original proceeds less the amount paid to date) will be paid to a second payee. The difference can be paid either in a lump sum (cash refund option) or in installments (installment refund option) until the full proceeds are paid.

Joint and Last Survivor Life Income Options. Under these options, the insured may elect to have the proceeds paid during the lifetimes of two or more recipients. For example, a husband and wife may wish to use this type of settlement arrangement. Income can be paid while both live and then continue for the lifetime of the survivor. A joint and last survivor option can be set up to have the same income continue to the second person (joint and survivor option) or the payments can be reduced upon the death of the first payee (such as joint and two-thirds or joint and one-half options). The lower the percentage of income to the survivor, the larger will be the life income payments while both recipients are alive.

Use of Life Income Settlement Options. These options, like annuities, can be used to provide your beneficiary (or yourself) with a secure life income that he or she cannot outlive. The beneficiary also generally cannot "get at" the proceeds once they are placed under a life income settlement arrangement. Thus, the option can be used to protect the beneficiary against himself or herself.

However, whether to use life income options should be considered carefully by the consumer. First of all, once the option begins, it cannot be changed. You have committed your funds once the beneficiary begins to receive the life income payments. Second, use of life income options for relatively young beneficiaries, who have longer life expectancies, often is questionable. The extra income resulting from the annuity aspect (i.e., the scientific using up of principal) may be relatively small for them, particularly in the case of women, who have longer life expectancies than men. Also, you should consider how much the life insurance proceeds could earn in alternative, secure investments, such as savings accounts, savings certificates, high-grade bonds, and the like, where the principal would remain intact, and then decide whether the extra income from a life income option is worth the expending of principal and the loss of flexibility. Naturally, it is normally unwise to elect a life income option for beneficiaries who are in poor health.

RIDERS TO INDIVIDUAL LIFE INSURANCE CONTRACTS

Riders are a way of adding additional amounts and/or types of insurance benefits to a basic life insurance contract. For example, if you have or are buying a $25,000 whole life policy and need additional protection until your children are self-sufficient, you might obtain a $20,000 decreasing term insurance rider added to your whole life contract for increased protection during the child-rearing years.

Decreasing term insurance and some of the forms of special life insurance contracts previously described (i.e., family income and family maintenance benefits) may be provided through riders to basic contracts. In addition, some of the other types of riders frequently purchased include: (1) guaranteed insurability, (2) double indemnity, (3) waiver of premium, and (4) disability income.

Guaranteed Insurability Option

This option, for an additional premium, permits the policyholder to purchase additional amounts of insurance at stated intervals without additional proof of insurability. For example, Mary Smith might purchase a $10,000 whole life policy at age 27 with a guaranteed insurability rider added. The rider might permit her, beginning at age 30, to purchase additional amounts of insurance (up to $10,000) every three years until she is, say, age 40 without any proof of insurability for the subsequent purchases. This rider is commonly used by persons who feel they will have increasing insurance needs in the future.

Double Indemnity

This popular clause or rider, often referred to as an *accidental death benefit,* provides that double (or sometimes triple or more) the face amount of life insurance is payable if the insured's death is caused by accidental means.

From an economic standpoint, there seems little justification for double indemnity. The loss to the insured's dependents is just as great if death is caused by means other than accidental. Furthermore, the risk of death from disease, for most persons, is much greater than the risk of death by accident. The cost of this feature is relatively small, again because the risk is small, but it has appeal to many people—perhaps because of their gambling instincts or because of the *appearance of* a large amount of insurance.

Waiver of Premium

This rider also may be added to life insurance contracts for an extra premium. It provides that in the event the insured becomes totally disabled before a certain age, typically 60 or 65, premiums on the life insurance policy will be waived (i.e., not required to be paid by the insured) during the continuance of disability after six months. In addition, premiums are normally waived retroactively for this six months. The operation of, and values in, the basic life insurance policy continue just as if the disabled insured actually were paying the premiums. Some life insurance companies include waiver of premium automatically in their life insurance contracts and include its cost in their basic rates. Most, however, write it as an extra benefit which the insured must elect and for which the insured must pay an extra premium. Waiver of premium really is disability income insurance where the amount of insurance equals the life insurance premium that would be waived in the event of disability.

Disability Income Rider

Some life insurance companies allow disability income benefits, based on the face amount of life insurance, to be added to permanent life insurance policies for an extra premium. Such disability income riders often provide a disability benefit of 1 percent of the face amount of life insurance per month (or $10 per $1,000 of life insurance). The benefit is payable if the insured becomes totally disabled for a specified elimination (waiting) period, which usually is six months. The disability income rider really is a way of writing disability income insurance in conjunction with life insurance. (See Chapter 5 for more details.)

SUBSTANDARD RISKS

Most applicants who cannot qualify for individual life insurance at standard rates can still obtain insurance through the issuance of life insurance on a so-called substandard ("rated") basis. While a number of factors may cause a person to be classified as "substandard" for life insurance purposes, about 80 percent of these cases concern such physical defects as heart conditions, overweight, albumin in the urine, high blood pressure, and the like. The other 20 percent are accounted for by occupational hazard, moral hazard, extensive foreign travel or residence, and less common medical impairments.

An insured who has been issued insurance on a substandard basis may subsequently learn that he or she is eligible for new insurance at standard rates or at least under better terms than those governing the existing substandard insurance. Such an insured should appeal to the insurer issuing the original insurance for a reconsideration of the original substandard rating. An insurer generally will consider a premium reduction for an insured who demonstrates an improved condition; otherwise, the insured could get insurance from a competing company.

Also, if you have been told you can get insurance only on a rated basis, you may want to check with some other life companies to see what kind of deal you can get from them. Reputable life companies can differ in their underwriting of certain conditions, and so you may be able to get a lower rating or even none at all by shopping around a little.

NONMEDICAL LIFE INSURANCE

Nonmedical insurance typically refers to the issuing of regular life insurance without requiring the applicant to submit to a medical examination. Today, many life insurers will provide up to $30,000 and even more on a nonmedical basis. This nonmedical limit varies by age groups, with the largest amounts being permitted at the younger ages. Additionally, there typically is an age limit, such as 40 or 45, beyond which nonmedical insurance is not available. There is no disadvantage to the insured in buying nonmedical life insurance. The cost is the same as for medically examined business, except that some plans may not be available on a nonmedical basis.

WHAT ACTIONS CAN AN UNINSURABLE PERSON TAKE?

Although only about 3 percent of the applications for ordinary life insurance are rejected entirely, this nevertheless causes a severe problem for this group desiring and needing insurance. The following are some steps an uninsurable person may take. First, he or she can see if it is possible to remove or reduce the reason for the uninsurability. Second, he or she should check with several different insurers. As we said before, underwriting standards can vary, and a person who may be considered uninsurable by one insurer may be regarded as insurable on a substandard basis by another company. Also, the life insurance industry has made considerable progress in making insurance available to previously uninsurable people. Therefore, even if you have been uninsurable, you may be able to get insurance on some basis now.

In addition, look for sources of insurance that do not require you to show evidence of insurability. Group insurance, for example, may be available through your place of employment, and typically no individual evidence of insurability is needed; or you might check other groups or associations to which you belong to see if you can get any insurance through them. Also, nonmedical life insurance may be available on an individual basis. Remember, though, that nonmedical life insurance does involve individual underwriting, and the applicant must answer questions about previous medical history on an application that becomes part of the policy. Also, an insurer can require a medical examination or additional underwriting information in nonmedical cases if it seems warranted.

GROUP LIFE INSURANCE COVERAGES

Most people who are eligible for group life insurance obtain such coverage through their place of employment. From the individual's and his or her family's standpoint, employer-employee group life insurance probably is the most important form of group life insurance available to them. However, as we said at the beginning of this chapter, group life insurance can be provided through other means as well.

Group life insurance may be provided on either a term or a permanent basis. Most, however, is term insurance.

Group Term Life Insurance

Under this type plan, the insurance protection has the same basic characteristics as individual term life insurance. The employee has the insurance protection (with no cash values) while he or she is working for the employer. If the employee leaves the employer, the group term coverage terminates 31 days after his or her employment ceases, subject to the right of the employee to convert the group term insurance to an individual permanent life insurance contract. This conversion privilege is discussed below.

Permanent Forms of Group Life Insurance

Several types of group life plans providing permanent life insurance have been devised and are provided by some employer-employee groups.

Group Paid-up Plans. These plans are basically a combination of accumulating units of single-premium whole life insurance and decreasing amounts of group term life insurance.

Level Premium Group Permanent. Under this type plan, the distinguishing characteristic is that some form of permanent life insurance is purchased on a level premium basis, with premiums payable for life or to a specified age, such as 65. On termination of employment, the employee will have certain cash or paid-up insurance privileges and also may have the option of continuing the full amount of insurance in force by paying the level premium directly to the insurer.

Other Group Plans

Survivor Income Plans. A type of group plan that is gaining a good deal of attention is one designed to provide a monthly income that becomes payable to surviving dependents upon the death of an employee who may be covered under either a pension plan or a group life plan. There generally are three characteristics that distinguish this type plan from other kinds of group life insurance: (1) the benefits are payable only in the form of a monthly income; (2) the covered employee does not name his or her beneficiary, benefits being payable only to specified beneficiaries; and (3) benefits usually are payable only as long as there is a living, surviving beneficiary. (See Chapter 13 for more on survivor income plans.)

Group Credit Life Insurance. This is a special form of group term insurance issued to creditors covering the lives of their debtors in the amount of their outstanding loans.

Elective Group Coverages

Employers may make several group life insurance plans available to their employees. Typically, such arrangements specify that an employee must sign up for the group term life insurance portion of the program to be eligible to elect coverage under one or more of the other group life plans. Such *elective plans* may include: additional levels of group term insurance, group paid-up insurance, or group survivor income plans. An employee should give careful consideration to electing one or more of these plans if provided through his or her employer, as they may be a convenient way of supplementing his or her individual insurance program at moderate cost.

Conversion Rights

An insured employee has the right to convert up to the face amount of his or her group term life insurance to an individual policy of permanent insurance under certain conditions. Typically, the employee may convert, within 31 days after termination of employment, to one of the insurer's regular permanent forms at standard rates for his or her attained age *without evidence of insurability.* For employees who are in poor health or even uninsurable, this can be a very valuable provision, allowing such individuals to obtain life insurance at standard rates.

Group policies also may give a terminating employee the right to continue the amount of his or her group life insurance as term insurance for one year following termination of employment and then to convert to a permanent form of life insurance if the insured so elects. This gives the employee more time to make a final decision.

Coverage after Retirement

In the past, whenever an employee terminated his or her employment, whether for retirement or otherwise, his or her group term life insurance ceased unless the employee exercised a conversion privilege. At advanced ages, however, it is too expensive for most people to utilize the conversion right. Presently, a number of group life plans continue at least some life insurance coverage after retirement.

SOCIAL SECURITY

Some people consider the social security system to be one of the most complex and perplexing concepts designed by man, yet the basic philosophy of the program is quite simple. The basic concept of social security is that during one's working years, employees, employers, and self-employed individuals pay social security taxes (FICA taxes), which are pooled in special trust funds. Then, when you retire, or in the event of your death or disability, monthly benefits are paid to you and/or your dependents to replace part of the earnings lost as a result of these risks.

Part of your contributions to social security go into a separate Hospital Insurance Trust Fund so that when workers and their dependents reach age 65 they will have help in paying their hospital bills. Voluntary medical insurance also is available to persons 65 or over to help pay physicians' bills and other medical expenses. This voluntary program is financed out of premiums shared equally by the covered persons and the federal government. To better understand the social security system, the following sections will analyze the coverage, eligibility, and benefits provided by the system.

Eligibility for Benefits

Eligibility for various benefits under the social security system depends upon the "insured" status of the worker. Eligibility requires that a worker, depending on the benefits sought, be *fully insured* or *currently insured.* The determining yardstick to measure whether a worker is currently or fully insured is a "quarter of coverage." A "quarter of coverage" is a period of three calendar months, ending on certain dates during the year, in which, generally, a worker has at least $50 in wages; or if self-employment income is at least $400 in a given year, the worker is credited with four quarters of coverage.

Fully Insured Status. Although there are many ways in which a worker can achieve fully insured status, two basic ones will be noted here. First, you are considered fully insured if you are credited with 40 quarters of coverage earned at any time since 1936. Second, you can attain fully insured status by earning at least one quarter of coverage for every calendar year elapsing since 1950 (or after the year in which you attain age 21, if later) up to the year in which you reach age 65 (62 for women), die, or become disabled. A minimum of six quarters is required in any case.

Currently Insured. To achieve currently insured status, a worker must be credited with a minimum of six quarters of coverage during the 13-quarter period ending with (1) the quarter in which he or she died, (2) the quarter in which he or she first became eligible for old-age or disability benefits, or (3) the quarter in which he or she actually retired.

Benefits

The basic types of benefits provided by the social security system are retirement, survivorship, disability, and medical.

Retirement Benefits. The basic retirement benefit provides a *monthly income starting at age 65 (or 62 through 64 at reduced benefits) for the retired worker's lifetime.* The amount of the monthly benefit is determined by a formula based on the worker's average monthly wage over his or her working years.

The wife of a retired worker is entitled to a benefit, called the *wife's benefit,* equal to 50 percent of her husband's retirement benefit if she is 65 or over (or 62 through 64 at reduced benefits), or, regardless of her age, if she has under her care a dependent and unmarried child of the worker under age 18, or, regardless of the child's age, if the child is disabled and has been so since age 18 (called the *mother's benefit*).

In addition, each dependent and unmarried child under 18 (or under 22 if a full-time student) is entitled to a benefit, called the *child's benefit,* equal to 50 percent of the retired worker's retirement benefit. Also, a retired worker's *grandchildren* whose parents are dead or disabled and who live with the retired worker and the *dependent husband* of a woman drawing primary retirement benefits are entitled to benefits. However, the total of all retirement benefits is subject to an *overall family maximum.*

To receive retirement benefits for himself or his dependents, a worker must be fully insured. Social security retirement benefits are received income-tax-free and normally are very important in your retirement planning.

Survivorship Benefits. There are several types of social security survivorship benefits. All except the lump-sum death benefit are a percentage of the retirement benefit the deceased worker would have received at age 65. Social security survivorship benefits usually are a very important part of your life insurance planning. The following illustrates the various survivorship benefits available under social security. As with retirement benefits, there is an *overall family maximum.*

SOCIAL SECURITY SURVIVORSHIP BENEFITS

Monthly Payments to Your:

Widow age 65 or over (or 60 through 64 at reduced benefits), or disabled widow age 50 or older

Widow (regardless of age) if caring for your child who is under 18 or disabled and is entitled to benefits

Dependent child

Dependent widower 65 or over (or 60 through 64 at reduced benefits), or disabled dependent widower age 50 or older

Dependent parents at 62 or over

Lump-sum death benefit

Disability Benefits. A disabled worker and his or her eligible dependents may be entitled to monthly cash disability benefits under social security if the disabled worker meets the requirements of the law. These requirements and benefits are explained further in Chapter 5, "Health Insurance."

Health Insurance Benefits. The health insurance portion of the social security system, popularly called "Medicare," comprises two major programs, Hospital Insurance (HI) and Supplementary Medical Insurance (SMI). Both programs are for persons age 65 or over. These programs also are described in greater detail in Chapter 5.

The preceding discussion merely provides a framework of the provisions and various benefits of the social security system. If you have specific questions or desire additional information about your specific entitlement to social security benefits, you should contact an office of the Social Security Administration or consult with your advisors, such as your life insurance agent.

PLANNING AND USING LIFE INSURANCE

Paying Life Insurance Premiums

Premiums on life insurance contracts can be paid at different intervals and in several different ways.

Annual or Fractional Premiums. A policyholder normally may pay life insurance premiums on an annual, semiannual, quarterly, or monthly basis. When paid other than annually, the insurer modifies the annual premium by adding a percentage amount to the annual premium and then dividing the result into the requisite number of parts. It generally is more economical for you to pay life insurance premiums annually if you can.

Preauthorized Check Plans. If a policyholder so desires, he or she generally may authorize the life insurer to collect the premiums as they come due from the policyholder's bank by signing a form authorizing the bank to deduct the premiums from the policyholder's checking account. The advantages of this approach to the policyholder are convenience and paying the premium on an annual basis even if it is paid more frequently by the bank.

Prepayment of Premiums. Subject to certain limitations, most life insurance companies permit policyholders to prepay premiums, either in the form of so-called "premium deposits" or through the discounting of future premiums. Under both arrangements, the prepaid premiums generally are credited with interest at a stipulated rate and, in some instances, also are credited with interest earned by the insurer in excess of the stipulated rate. Some insurers permit withdrawal of premium deposits at any time, while others limit withdrawals to anniversary or premium due dates. A few companies permit withdrawals only in case of surrender or death. Some companies credit no interest or otherwise penalize the policyholder if the funds are withdrawn. If the insured dies, the balance of any prepaid premiums is paid to the insured's estate or designated beneficiary in addition to the face of the policy. If interested, you should check with your own company on its policy toward prepayment of premiums to see if it might be worthwhile for you.

Premiums Graded (Reduced) by Size of Policy. Most life insurers today follow the practice of grading premium rates by size of policy issued. That is, the larger the face amount of the policy, the lower will be the premium rate per $1,000 of insurance.

As a practical matter, another way of giving lower rates per $1,000 for larger policies is by offering certain policies, often called *specials,* only in minimum face amounts, such as $25,000 or $50,000. Such "specials" often have a lower rate per $1,000 of insurance than applies to reasonably comparable coverage of lesser face amounts.

The practical effect of grading premium rates by size of policy is that life insurance has become "cheaper by the dozen." Thus, it is relatively less expensive for you to buy one larger policy than several smaller ones. So in buying life insurance, consider the various ranges at which the cost per $1,000 decreases. Also, look out for the availability of "specials." They may be good buys.

Lower Cost for Women. Women generally have lower mortality rates than men. For many years life insurance rating did not reflect this fact, but today many companies have lower premium rates for women than for men.

Life Insurance Policy Dividends. One of the basic decisions you must make in buying life insurance is whether to buy participating or nonparticipating insurance. Unfortunately, there is no pat answer to this question, but the following information may be helpful to you in making your choice.

Participating life insurance refunds a portion of the gross premium to the policyholder in the form of policy dividends that are based on the insurer's actual mortality experience, investment earnings, and administrative expenses. Such policy dividends cannot be guaranteed by the insurer and depend upon its actual experience.

Nonparticipating (nonpar) policies are sold at definite, fixed premiums that do not provide for any dividends. Thus, the policyholder knows in advance what his or her life insurance cost will be under a nonpar policy, while under a participating contract the final premium will depend upon: (1) the gross premium, and (2) the policy dividends actually paid by the insurer. Of course, depending on the insurer's actual experience under a participating policy, the policyholder's final premium may be lower or higher than under a comparable nonpar contract.

Participating life insurance is sold by both mutual and stock life insurance companies. Nonparticipating policies normally are sold only by stock companies.

For most plans of life insurance, a given dividend scale will produce dividends that generally increase each year with policy duration. This assumes the dividend scale itself does not change. However, an insurer may either increase or decrease its whole dividend scale, depending on its experience and its management policies.

Beneficiary Designations

The right to name a beneficiary or beneficiaries is vested in the policyholder. The insured usually is the owner of a policy, but there are many policies outstanding today that have been applied for and are owned by someone other than the insured or in which ownership has been transferred by the insured to another after the policy was in force. The insured generally reserves the right to designate and change the beneficiary, and the rule prevailing in most states is that the insured can exercise the rights under a policy without a revocable beneficiary's consent.

Consider this beneficiary designation: "Sue Smith, wife of the insured, if living at the death of the insured, otherwise to such of the lawful children of the insured as may be living at the death of the insured." Here Sue Smith is the primary beneficiary and the children are contingent beneficiaries. Also, second contingent beneficiaries may be designated in the event none of the primary or contingent beneficiaries survive the insured. It is considered good practice to designate more than one beneficiary.

Probably the most commonly used designation is one that names the insured's wife or husband as primary beneficiary, with the children as contingent beneficiaries. It is customary to describe the beneficiary by his or her family relationship to the insured, or as a "friend," "business associate," "fiancée," and the like.

The insured may want to designate a group of persons without identifying the individual members of the group. This is known as a "class designation."

For example, in the illustration cited above, the designation "lawful children of the insured" is an example of a class designation. The beneficiaries actually entitled to receive the proceeds in the event of the insured's death will be determined by the members of the class at that time. Such a class designation automatically includes members of the class who may be born or otherwise join the class after the date of the beneficiary designation but before the insured's death.

When you want to name all your children as beneficiaries, usually the safest way is to designate "children of the insured" as a class. If the children are designated by name, such as "John Smith and Doris Smith, children of the insured," then unnamed children or children born after the date of the beneficiary designation will be excluded. If this result is not desired, then "children of the insured," or "children of the insured, including John Smith and Doris Smith," should be used.

If there are children by a former marriage of the insured's wife or husband, these children must be specifically named to be included under the beneficiary designation. This can be done by some designation such as "children of the insured, and George Baker and Carol Baker, children of the insured's wife (husband)."

With regard to adopted children, until the adoption proceedings are completed, such children would not be included in a class designation "children of the insured." To share in the proceeds, their names would have to be specifically included in the beneficiary designation as was done above.

An insured may wish to have the death proceeds of his or her life insurance paid to a trustee, the fund to be administered for the beneficiaries as a trust. A trust may be established under an agreement signed by the insured during his or her lifetime or under the insured's will. A typical lifetime trustee beneficiary designation might read: "The XYZ Trust Company, trustee, or its successor or successors in trust, under trust agreement dated——————." Of course, an individual can be named as trustee or as cotrustee if the insured wishes. (See Chapter 17 for a discussion of the uses of insurance trusts.)

Sometimes insureds name an individual (e.g., wife or husband) as primary beneficiary and a trustee as contingent beneficiary. This is referred to as a "contingent life insurance trust." In this case, the proceeds may be paid to the primary beneficiary in one sum or under one or more of the settlement options discussed earlier.

There may be some legal complications in naming minors, say your minor children, as beneficiaries of your life insurance. If a minor is named beneficiary and becomes entitled to the policy proceeds, the minor may not be able to give a legally valid release for receipt of the life insurance proceeds because a minor may not be legally competent to enter into contracts. Today, of course, many states have lowered the age at which a person attains majority to 18. Other states have adopted special enabling statutes applicable to insurance which authorize minors of a designated age, such as 15, to contract for insurance, give a valid receipt for benefits payable, and otherwise deal with policies as though the minor had attained majority. Other state statutes permit payment of a modest amount directly to a minor. But if such a statute does not apply, and proceeds are payable to a minor, it would be necessary to have a guardian appointed to receive payment of the proceeds on behalf of the minor. This normally involves legal formality, expense, and restrictions as to who may be guardian and what the guardian can do without specific court approval.

There are several possibilities for handling any problems that may arise out of naming minor beneficiaries.

1. You can *use an insurance trust* and name the trustee as beneficiary of your life insurance. The trust then would be administered for the benefit of your family, including any minor beneficiaries. (See Chapter 17 for the other advantages and the disadvantages of using a living insurance trust.)

2. You could name an adult (say, your wife or husband) as primary beneficiary and then use a *contingent life insurance trust* for the children (i.e., the minors), as described above.

3. In the case of some insurance companies, this problem can be simplified by allowing the proceeds to be retained at interest by the insurer with the full right reserved to withdraw the principal or to elect any other settlement option(s). The minor is named beneficiary, but it is provided that if he or she is still a minor when the proceeds are paid, a trustee named in the policy, rather than a guardian, will receive the payments on behalf of the minor and may exercise the privileges specified in the policy.

Providing for Simultaneous-death Situations

An insured and his or her spouse rarely die in a common accident or disaster. But it does happen, and so this contingency should be considered in planning your life insurance. For example, as mentioned previously, a beneficiary arrangement might provide, in substance: "Sue Smith, wife of the insured, if living at the death of the insured, otherwise equally to such of the children of the insured as may be living at the death of the insured." Under such a designation, assuming the proceeds are payable in a lump sum, if Sue survives her husband for only a few moments, her estate will be entitled to all the proceeds. In this event, the proceeds will be exposed to probate costs in her estate and to possible claims of her creditors and will pass in accordance with the terms of her will or according to the applicable intestate law if she left no will.

This result can be avoided by making all or a portion of the proceeds payable to Sue under the interest option subject to her full right of withdrawal, and naming the children (or a trust) as second beneficiaries to receive any remaining proceeds whether Sue dies before or after the insured. If Sue survives her husband, the proceeds are subject to her complete control. But if she dies before, simultaneously with, or shortly after the insured, the proceeds will be paid to the second beneficiaries rather than being tied up in the estate of the insured or his wife.

Another procedure for handling the common-disaster situation is to provide that the proceeds will be paid to the beneficiary only if he or she is living on, say, the thirtieth day after the insured's death. However, this procedure has some potential disadvantages that are avoided by using the interest option with the proceeds subject to withdrawal as described above.

An insurance trust also can be arranged to avoid the simultaneous-death situation.

HOW MUCH LIFE INSURANCE DO YOU NEED?

This question often perplexes consumers. They want to know how much life insurance they need to protect their families adequately, but they do not want to overinsure needlessly. Unfortunately, there probably is no one answer to this question; but as far as family protection is concerned, two approaches often are suggested for attempting to measure the amount of life insurance a person should have—the human life value approach, and the needs (or programming) approach.

Human Life Value Approach

The human life value approach attempts to measure the economic worth of an individual to his or her family or to others dependent upon his or her income. This approach seeks to measure the economic loss, defined as the loss of earnings devoted to an individual's dependents over his or her working lifetime, if the individual were to die today. This value is commonly computed by using the following five steps.

1. Estimate your average annual earnings from future personal efforts over the remaining years of your productive lifetime. This period normally is the difference between your contemplated retirement age and your present age.

2. Deduct from the average annual earnings your estimated federal, state, and other income taxes; personal life and health insurance premiums; social security (FICA) taxes; and your personal living expenses. The difference represents the amount of your earned income devoted to your family.

3. Determine the remaining years of your productive lifetime as explained above.

4. Select an appropriate interest rate at which your estimated future earnings devoted to your family can be discounted (for capitalization purposes).

5. Multiply the amount of your annual earned income devoted to your family by the present value of $1 per year for the period of the remaining years of your productive lifetime, assuming the interest rate selected in 4 above.

A simple example will help explain this procedure. Assume our old friend, George Able, age 33, earns $20,000 per year. Also assume (for the sake of simplicity) that this amount will remain level over his working lifetime and that $14,000 per year is devoted to his family. Thus, we can calculate George's present, estimated human life value by multiplying $14,000 by the present value of $1 per year for 32 years (65 − ¡33), discounted at an interest rate of, say, 5 percent, or a present value of $15.80. This product gives us an estimated human life value of $221,200 ($14,000 × 15.80). You can see that this human life value will diminish as George grows older, assuming no changes in income, retirement age, taxes, cost of self-maintenance, etc. Of course, if any of these factors change, this would affect George's economic worth to his family.

In practice, the human life value approach generally has not been used by agents in the sale of life insurance as much as the needs approach, which is described below.

Programming or Needs Approach

The other main method for figuring out how much life insurance you need to protect your dependents is the "needs" or "programming" approach. This approach attempts to analyze the various needs of a family in the event an income earner dies. Such needs vary, of course, from family to family, but the following categories of needs normally would apply to most families.

1. Final lump-sum expenses (e.g., last illness and burial expenses, probate costs, and the like)

2. Readjustment income (an income sufficient to allow the family to make any adjustment that may be necessary in living standards gradually)

3. Income for the family until the children are self-supporting (referred to as the "dependency period")

4. Life income for the widow after the children are self-supporting

5. Special needs (such as mortgage redemption, emergency fund, educational funds, and other specific needs)

6. Retirement needs

Once the family's needs are identified, the next step is to determine what income or benefits are available from other sources to meet those needs. The difference between the funds needed to meet the family's "needs" and those available from other sources represents the amount of life insurance you need.

The following is an illustration of the needs or programming approach. Assume the following facts:

Husband—George Able, age 33

Wife—Mary Able, age 30

Son—John Able, age 6

Daughter—Susan Able, age 4

Daughter—Cindy Able, age 1

Needs of the Able Family:

Lump-sum needs:

Funds for estate settlement at George Able's death: $15,000 (estimated funeral expenses, debts, estate taxes, and other estate settlement costs)

Emergency Fund: $2,000

Mortgage Cancellation Fund: $20,000 (already covered by decreasing term insurance)

Educational needs: $48,000 (assuming four years of college for each child at $4,000 per year for each child)

Income needs. George Able would like his family to have the following approximate monthly income if he were to die today:

$1,100 per month until his son (John) and daughter (Susan) reach age 18 (total of 14 years)

$1,000 per month from the time John and Susan reach 18 until Cindy reaches 18 (3 more years)

Thereafter, a life income of $600 per month to his widow (Mary)

A first step in the programming process often is to plot out in a simple graph what the family income needs are and to what extent those needs are met by social security and other benefits.[3] Social security benefits may be increased by automatic cost-of-living increases and, of course, by future changes in the law. The social security benefits used in the following programming illustration are the approximate benefits for the Ables as of 1975, assuming George Able has had maximum covered earnings. To find

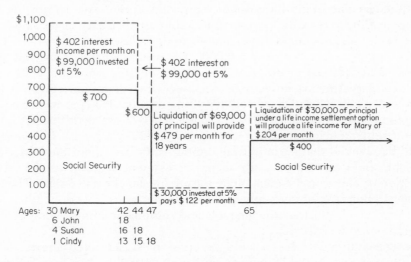

[3]This is an illustration of the so-called "regular" programming approach. Another approach, called the "capitalization and discount" method, also is commonly used. While these programming methods may differ in technique, they have the same objectives and the results normally are essentially the same.

your own current social security benefits, you can check with the Social Security Administration. Your insurance agent also may be able to help you on this.

Social security survivorship benefits would provide about $700 per month (maximum family benefit) until Susan reaches age 18 (and her benefits will continue to age 22 if she is a full-time student). For the next three years, until Cindy becomes 18 (or 22 if she is a full-time student), social security benefits would decrease to about $600 per month. When Cindy reaches 18 (or 22), social security benefits would cease until Mary reaches age 65 (or ages 60 through 64 at reduced benefits), at which time she would receive a life income of about $400 per month. The period during which no social security benefits would be paid is called the social security "gap" or "blackout period."

If it is assumed that life insurance is needed to make up the deficits in the amounts of monthly income desired, by a combination of the various settlement options described earlier in the chapter, and using the rates of a major life insurance company, approximately $99,000 of life insurance would be needed to meet the desired monthly income figures. The $99,000 of proceeds invested at 5 percent (the assumed current interest rate on settlement options) would yield $402 of interest each month. Added to social security of $700, a total monthly income of $1,102 could be provided until both John and Susan Able reach age 18. The proceeds still could be left at interest, yielding $402 per month, until Cindy Able reaches age 18. The $402 added to $600 from social security would give the family a total monthly income of $1,002 during this period. When Cindy reaches 18 three years later, the monthly income desired is reduced to $600. Thus, at this point it is necessary to plan to liquidate some of the life insurance proceeds (principal). To provide for the 18-year social security "gap" or "blackout period" (Mary's ages 47 to 65), $69,000 would provide $479 per month under a fixed-period option. The balance of the life insurance, $30,000, still would remain at interest and would yield $122 per month, making a total monthly payment of $601.

When Mary Able reaches age 65, social security will pay her a monthly life income of about $400. The remainder of the desired $600 per month could be obtained by liquidating the remaining $30,000 of proceeds through a life income settlement option which would provide $204 per month. Of course, it could be decided that a life income option would not afford the best yield available and that other, equally secure investment instruments should be considered. This would depend upon the circumstances at that time. The life income option is used here only for planning purposes. The dotted lines on the above graph illustrate the amounts and settlement arrangements for the life insurance described here.

Several additional ideas should be considered. As noted above, social security will pay a child's benefit until age 22 if the child is a full-time student. In this way, social security could be considered to provide about $22,000 of the total of $48,000 for educational needs in this case. This would leave a deficit of $26,000. This deficit could be provided for by life insurance or other means. The same applies to the need for an emergency fund of $2,000 and the $15,000 needed for estate settlement.

If all these needs are to be handled through life insurance, George Able would need the following:

1.	Emergency fund	$ 2,000
2.	Estate settlement	15,000
3.	Education (deficit)	26,000
4.	Family income	99,000
	Total	$142,000

Part of the needs or programming approach is to consider other resources available. Social security already has been considered. George Able's other present benefits and assets in the event of his death are as follows:

Group life insurance and profit-sharing death benefits from his employer	$ 52,000
Whole life policy with ABC Insurance Company	20,000
Whole life policy with family income rider with XYZ Insurance Company	40,000
Other investable assets	10,000
Total	$122,000

Therefore, George Able has a need for additional life insurance of about $20,000 under these assumptions.[4]

Of course, depending on the amount involved and your age, you must evaluate realistically your ability to pay the premiums for additional life insurance. It may be that you can purchase now only part of the life insurance you need, with the thought that the remainder will be purchased as soon as practicable. Or, you may want to use lower-premium forms of life insurance, such as term insurance, with the plan of converting some or all of it later to permanent forms of life insurance if this proves desirable. Naturally, it is important that any life insurance program be reviewed periodically in light of inevitable changes in your needs.

How can you make these calculations to determine how much life insurance you need? Normally, it is not necessary for you to do so because competent life insurance agents usually are more than willing to perform this service for you (on either the "needs" or the "human life value" approach). There is no cost or obligation to you in allowing them to do this for you. In fact, you can ask several agents from different companies to analyze your situation and present plans for you to compare.

[4]Other assumptions and techniques could properly be used in programming for these needs. However, while they might vary in detail, the basic ideas are the same. The above example is given only to illustrate the "needs" approach to determining how much life insurance a person should own.

5
HEALTH INSURANCE

There are two basic types of health losses against which you should protect yourself and your family—*disability income losses* and *medical care expenses*. Either type can result in financial catastrophe for your family and hence should be provided for in your overall financial planning.

HEALTH INSURANCE COVERAGES

Health insurance is insurance against loss by sickness or injury. It can provide coverage for disability income and medical expense losses caused by accident only or by accident and sickness.

The following are the major sources of health insurance coverage that may be available to you. Social insurance and group insurance are discussed first because they have become so important and because they usually are made available more or less automatically and so provide a basic level of protection which you can then supplement.

Social Insurance

The main social insurance programs that provide health benefits are:

1. The disability portion of the federal social security system (i.e., the "D" of OASDHI)
2. The "Medicare" portion (Hospital Insurance and Supplementary Medical Insurance) of the federal social security system (i.e., the "H" of OASDHI)
3. The state (and federal) workmen's compensation laws
4. The nonoccupational temporary disability benefits laws of California, Hawaii, New Jersey, New York, Puerto Rico, and Rhode Island

Group Insurance

Group insurance is the predominant way of providing private health insurance in the United States. Thus, group coverages represent the backbone of the health insurance planning for most people. As in the case of group life insurance, group health insurance is a contract made with an employer, or sometimes with another entity, that provides protection to a definitely identified group of persons.

Individual Insurance

Individual health insurance policies are contracts made with an individual to cover the individual and perhaps some specified members of his or her family (usually spouse and children). When the insured and specified family members are covered, the policy is often referred to as a "family health insurance policy." Family policies are used for medical expense benefits.

Franchise and Association Group Insurance

Franchise health insurance is a mixture of the individual and group approaches. It involves the issuance of individual policies to employees, or members of other groups, under an arrangement with the employer or other entity. Even though individual policies are issued, certain group underwriting standards may be used. Franchise insurance is the health insurance product comparable to wholesale life insurance.

Association group insurance is similar to franchise insurance except that it is typically issued to members of professional or trade association groups, covered persons usually pay their premiums directly to the insurer, and covered persons may receive certificates of insurance rather than individual policies. The premium rates for franchise and association group insurance typically are somewhat less than for individual insurance but more than for group insurance.

Other Insurance Coverages

Health insurance benefits also may be provided under a variety of other insurance coverages. Some of the more important are:

1. Disability benefits under group life insurance
2. Disability benefits under pension plans
3. Disability benefits under individual life insurance policies
4. Medical payments under liability insurance policies (and benefits under automobile "no-fault" plans)
5. Blanket health insurance and miscellaneous health coverages

DISABILITY INCOME (LOSS OF TIME) COVERAGES

In this section we shall describe the various kinds of disability income coverages you may use to protect yourself and your family against this important, and often neglected, risk. However, first let us review a few basic features you will encounter in buying or dealing with these coverages.

Features Affecting Your Disability Income Coverage

Maximum Benefit Period. This is the maximum period of time disability benefits will be paid to a disabled person. It represents a maximum limit of liability expressed in weeks or months or extending to a specified age. Sometimes disability benefits are payable for as long as the covered person remains disabled as defined in the plan, even for life. Lifetime benefits for disabilities caused by accident are common, and sometimes lifetime benefits are also provided for disabilities caused by sickness (perhaps for disabilities occurring before a certain age, like 50). Generally speaking, the longer the maximum benefit period, the greater the coverage for the insured.

Peril(s) Insured against. These perils normally are either *accident alone* or *accident and sickness.* Coverage of disability caused by accident only is limited in scope and normally should be avoided in buying health insurance. Try to get coverage for both accident and sickness.

Waiting (Elimination) Period. This is the period of time that must elapse after a covered disability starts before disability income benefits begin. Suppose, for example, a plan has a 30-day elimination period for accident and sickness. If an insured person becomes disabled as defined by the plan, he or she must wait 30 days after the start of disability before he or she can start collecting benefits. In health insurance, benefits normally are not paid retroactively to the start of a disability once such an elimination period has been satisfied.

Definition of Disability. This important provision basically describes when a person is considered to be disabled for purposes of collecting benefits. There are essentially three varieties of definitions of disability in common use today—the "any occupation" type, the "own occupation" type, and the so-called "split definition."

As it was originally conceived, and as it is still stated in some policies today, the *"any occupation" type* defines disability as the complete inability of the covered person to engage in any occupation whatsoever. This is a very strict approach. So the modern tendency among insurers is to phrase an "any occupation" definition in a way that will consider total disability as the "complete inability of the insured to engage in any gainful occupation for which he (or she) is or becomes reasonably fitted by education, training, or experience," or some similar wording. The "any occupation" approach is the least liberal as far as the consumer is concerned.

The *"own occupation" type* defines disability so that the covered person is considered disabled when he or she is "prevented by such disability from performing any and every duty pertaining to the employee's (or insured's, in the case of an individual policy) occupation." This approach normally is the most liberal from the consumer's viewpoint.

The so-called *"split definition"* really is a combination of these two approaches. An example is as follows:

> "Total disability" means complete inability of the insured to engage in *any* [emphasis added] gainful occupation for which he (or she) is reasonably fitted by education, training or experience; however, during the first 24 months of any period of disability, the Company (insurer) will deem the insured to be totally disabled if he (or she) is completely unable to engage in *his* (or *her*) [emphasis added] regular occupation and is not engaged in any form of gainful occupation.

This definition, in effect, applies an "own occupation" definition for a specified period—two years in this example—and then applies an "any occupation for which the insured is reasonably fitted" definition for the remainder of the benefit period. This is the modern approach to providing disability benefits for long-term disabilities. From the consumer's viewpoint, it is better to have as long an "own occupation" period under a split definition as possible. How long a period of "own occupation" coverage you can buy varies among insurers and with the circumstances, but it often is two to five years and may run to 10 years and even to age 65, depending on the circumstances.

Finally, a few insurers include in their definitions of total disability in individual policies the requirement that the disabled person must be confined "indoors" or "to the house." These are known as *"house confinement" provisions* or, as the consumer might view them, "prison clauses." House confinement provisions are almost invariably disadvantageous to the consumer and one should normally avoid them in buying disability income coverage whenever possible.

Social Security Disability Benefits

There are two basic kinds of social security disability benefits: cash disability income benefits and the "freezing" of a disabled worker's wage position for purposes of determining his or her future retirement or survivorship benefits. Most workers (and their dependents) in covered employment under the social security system would be eligible for social security disability benefits. Thus, they can consider these benefits as their base layer of protection against disability income losses.

An eligible worker is considered disabled for the purpose of receiving these benefits when he or she has a medically determinable physical or mental impairment which is so severe that the worker is unable to engage in *any substantially gainful work or employment*. This amounts to an "any occupation" definition of disability and is strict by health insurance standards. In addition, the *disability must last five months before benefits can begin*. After five months of disability, benefits are payable if the impairment can be expected to last for at least 12 months from when the disability began or to result in death or if it has actually lasted 12 months. This amounts to a five-month waiting (elimination) period. The combined effect of the strict definition of disability and long waiting period is largely to restrict social security disability benefits to total and severe (probably permanent) long-term disabilities.

The amount of the monthly social security cash disability benefits payable to a disabled worker and his or her dependents is based on the worker's wages subject to social security taxes.[1] Let us take an example to help clarify these benefits, and let us again take the case of George Able (age 33), who makes about $20,000 per year. You will recall that his wife, Mary, is age 30 and that they have three children, John, age 6, Susan, age 4, and Cindy, age 1. It is assumed the three children will go to college. One day George was involved in a serious automobile accident (not work-connected) and as a result became totally disabled and unable to earn a living. After five months of disability, George and his family would be entitled to the following social security cash disability benefits regardless of any private insurance benefits he also may have. For illustrative purposes, assume George's basic social security disability benefit is $400 per month.

George	$400 per month, until he recovers, dies, or reaches age 65
Mary	$200 per month, until Cindy (the youngest) reaches age 18 (or for 17 years)
John	$200 per month, until he reaches age 22 (or for 16 years)
Susan	$200 per month, until she reaches age 22 (or for 18 years)
Cindy	$200 per month, until she reaches age 22 (or for 21 years)

But this is reduced because of the *maximum family benefit* to about $700 per month.

Thus, as long as George remains disabled as defined in the law, his family will receive $700 per month for 18 years (by which time Mary, John, and Susan will no longer be eligible), $600 per month for three more years (by which time Cindy will no longer be eligible), and then $400 per month for the next 11 years, by which time George will be 65 (and his wife Mary will be 62). When George reaches 65, his regular social security retirement benefits will begin.

Social security disability income benefits, like other social security benefits, are not taxable income for federal income tax purposes.[2] Therefore, assuming George (filing a joint return with Mary) was in a 25 percent federal income tax bracket prior to his disability, the $700 per month of tax-free disability benefits would be equivalent to about $933 per month (or $11,200 per year) in taxable income. But it is clear that even this $11,200 of equivalent benefits is a far cry from the $20,000 per year George earned prior to his disability. Also, the social security disability benefits will decline as

[1] The same approach to calculating the average monthly wage applies to social security retirement, survivors, and disability benefits.

[2] They also are exempt from state income taxes, as well as the social security (FICA) tax itself.

George's children reach age 18 or age 22. Thus, George's disability protection needs to be supplemented by private insurance and/or other sources, or else his family would have to make drastic changes in their living standards and expectations for the future in the event of a serious disability such as that described above.

Workmen's Compensation Disability Benefits

For persons injured or suffering covered diseases arising out of and in the course of their employment, some coverage usually is provided under workmen's compensation laws. These laws are intended to provide benefits only for work injuries and diseases. Therefore, you really cannot rely on them in your health insurance planning because you may be injured off the job as well as on.

Group Health Insurance (Disability Income)

Group health insurance is a common method of providing disability income protection for the public. The two basic kinds of plans are (1) short-term group disability income insurance, and (2) long-term group disability income plans.

Short-term plans are widely written on a group basis and are characterized by: a schedule of weekly benefits based on earnings categories but with a relatively low maximum benefit, such as $100 per week; a short elimination period of from 3 to 14 days (or none for accident benefits); an "own occupation" definition of disability; and relatively short maximum benefit periods of, say, 13, 26, or 52 weeks. These plans generally are intended to provide relatively modest benefits for a short period of time. They do not attempt to meet the need for protection against more serious, prolonged disabilities that can be financially catastrophic for the family.

Long-term group disability income plans are designed to take care of the more serious, long-term disabilities, but these plans are not as common as the short-term variety. Group long-term plans are characterized by: benefits stated as a percentage of earnings (such as 50 or 60 percent of base salary) with a relatively high maximum monthly benefit of $1,000, $1,500, or more; a longer elimination period, such as 90 days or six months; a "split" definition of disability; and payment of disability benefits for longer maximum benefit periods, such as 5 years, 10 years, or to age 65. These plans usually try to avoid, at least in part, duplication with other disability benefits. To be eligible for coverage, it is common for employees to have to be employed by the employer for a substantial period, such as one or two years.

Thus, as an example, a group long-term plan might provide benefits equal to 60 percent of the covered employee's base salary but subject to a maximum monthly benefit of $1,500 and with a six-month elimination period for accident and sickness. The maximum benefit period is to age 65 for both accident and sickness. A full-time employee becomes eligible for the plan after being continuously employed for one year. The plan covers occupational as well as nonoccupational disabilities (so-called 24-hour coverage).

Most group long-term plans have *coordination of benefits* provisions that indicate how other disability income benefits available to the covered person will affect the benefits payable under the group policy. Such coordination-of-benefits provisions are important to the consumer in planning his disability protection. These provisions are not uniform, but a fairly typical coordination-of-benefits provision in a group long-term disability plan might provide, for example, that the maximum benefit will be reduced by any benefits paid or payable under:

1. Any workmen's compensation or similar law
2. The Federal Social Security Act (based on the "maximum family benefit")[3]
3. Any disability or early-retirement benefits actually received under the employer's pension plan
4. Any state disability benefits law or similar governmental legislation
5. Any other *employer-sponsored* [emphasis added] disability plan
6. Any full or partial wage or salary payments by the employer

You should review the coordination-of-benefits provision in any such group contract that may cover you. Many group plans, for example, do not reduce their benefits on account of individual disability income insurance that is not provided by the employer (as in the example above), but some do.

Let us see how the particular group long-term disability plan outlined above would affect our hypothetical case of George Able. George's base salary is $20,000 per year or $1,667 per month. Sixty percent of $1,667 is $1,000 per month, which is less than the plan's maximum monthly benefit. Therefore, after the six-month elimination period, George could recover up to $1,000 per month from the group plan. However, under the coordination-of-benefits provision cited above, the social security benefit of $700 per month would be deducted from the maximum benefit otherwise payable by the group plan. Thus, the group plan benefits would become $300 per month ($1,000 − $700) for the first 18 years of George's disability. Note that if George had a personally owned disability income policy, the benefits under that policy would not reduce his group benefit under the above-cited coordination-of-benefits provision. However, in some cases any personally owned disability income benefits would simply serve to reduce the group plan's benefits and would not result in any net benefit to the insured. Thus, the consumer should review each case on its own merits to see if additional personal coverage is warranted.

A covered employee's group disability income coverage typically terminates when (1) the employee leaves his or her employment; (2) the employee becomes 65; (3) the group policy is terminated by the employer; or (4) the

---

[3]Sometimes only the disabled employee's basic social security benefit is taken as a deduction.

employer fails to pay the premium for the employee, except through error. Thus, an employee's *group disability income insurance* normally terminates when the employee terminates his or her employment and, contrary to the case with group life insurance, the terminating employee usually does not have the right to convert the group disability coverage to an individual disability income policy. Therefore, when an employee leaves one job to take another, he or she will normally lose any group long-term disability coverage from the time of leaving his or her former employer until he or she meets the eligibility-period requirement of the group plan of the new employer. In the group long-term plan described above, for example, this eligibility period is one year.

The terminating employee might deal with the above problem in either of two ways: (1) some insurers are willing to waive the eligibility-period requirement for a new employee if the employer consents and the new employee provides at least some evidence of insurability, and/or (2) the employee could buy his or her own disability insurance for the period of time he or she is not covered by a group policy. There also is the possible problem that a terminating employee may find that his or her new employer does not provide as good a group disability plan as the former employer or, in fact, may not provide any such plan at all. Under these conditions, the terminating employee probably would need to carry (or increase) his or her own disability income coverage.

Individual Health Insurance (Disability Income)

Despite the importance and growth of group disability income insurance, individual policies remain an important way people can protect themselves against the critical disability risk. There are several reasons why you might need individual coverage in your financial planning despite the growth of group insurance.

1. Many people are not members of groups that provide such group insurance.

2. Others may be members of insured groups but for one reason or another are not eligible, or not yet eligible, to participate in the group plan.

3. Group disability income benefits may be inadequate, either in amount or in duration (as in the case of group short-term disability income benefits, for example).

4. Some people may feel it necessary to provide short-term individual disability income protection for themselves during the elimination (waiting) period of a group plan when this period is relatively long, such as six months or even a year.

5. Others may not want to rely entirely on employer's group insurance or other employee benefits for your financial security in this important area.

6. Individual policies are finding increasing use in situations where business health insurance is needed, such as buy and sell agreements or "key man" situations.

Benefits Provided. Like group coverage, individual policies provide weekly or monthly benefits for a specified period (maximum benefit period) during the continuance of the insured's total (and sometimes partial) disability. Individual disability income insurance should be analyzed mainly in terms of the *perils covered, maximum benefit period, definition of disability, elimination period,* and *amount of coverage.* Any individual health insurance policy should also be analyzed in terms of its *renewal or continuance provision.* Renewal provisions for all forms of health insurance are discussed later in this chapter. Naturally, *cost* also is an important consideration and is directly related to the above factors. Moreover, the premium cost for basically the same coverage can vary considerably among insurers, and, therefore, the consumer should "shop around" for coverage with several insurers before buying.

Individual disability income policies provide benefits for disability either (1) resulting from accidental bodily injury (accident only coverage), or (2) resulting from accidental bodily injury or from sickness (accident and sickness coverage). As we said before, *it is important for you to protect yourself against both accident and sickness, as opposed to accident only, if at all possible.* Of course, accident only coverage costs considerably less because you get much less protection.

The consumer today usually has a wide choice of maximum benefit periods in buying individual disability income policies, ranging from a period as short as six months to a period as long as the insured's lifetime for accident and to age 65 for sickness (and sometimes to lifetime for sickness as well).

The maximum benefit period you select should depend upon your needs. However, assuming you need permanent protection, *you should seriously consider buying coverage with longer maximum benefit periods, such as to age 65, for both accident and sickness.* To buy shorter benefit periods (usually to reduce the cost) of, say, two or five years may result in the disability benefits running out before the person reaches retirement age (when, presumably, his or her retirement benefits will start). This is false economy; there are better ways to save premium dollars.

Insurers commonly use a "split" definition of disability in individual contracts. In general, the longer the "own occupation" period, the better for the consumer.

You also normally have a fairly wide choice of elimination periods in buying individual disability income insurance. They may range, for example, from none for accident and seven days for sickness up to one year or more for accident and sickness. There are several *factors you may want to consider in choosing an appropriate elimination period.*

1. Coordination with other disability coverage. You may have other disability benefits available during the initial period of a disability. For example, your employer may have a noninsured salary continuation ("sick-pay") plan for the first month or so of any disability, or perhaps a group short-term disability income plan with a maximum benefit period of 13 or 26 weeks. Thus, you can

plan the elimination period of an individual policy so the benefits will start after such other benefits are exhausted.

2. Other resources. You may plan to maintain a conservatively invested emergency fund to take care of short periods of disability, among other purposes.

3. Cost saving. A relatively small increase in the elimination period will normally produce a considerable saving in premium. Such a saving may make it possible for you to have a more adequate program of protection than would otherwise be possible.

Within limits, you can choose the *amount of coverage* for which you want to apply in individual health insurance. This, of course, depends upon the amount of weekly or monthly benefits you need, want, and can afford to buy. It also may depend, however, on the amount of insurance that insurers are willing to write on a given individual. In underwriting individual disability income insurance, insurers have issue and participation limits that may affect the amount of insurance you can buy. An *issue limit* is the maximum amount of monthly benefit an insurer will write on any one individual, such as $1,500, $2,000, or more, depending on the particular insurer's underwriting rules. A *participation limit* is the maximum amount of monthly benefits from all sources in which an insurer will "participate" (i.e., write a portion of the coverage). Participation limits usually are higher than issue limits and might be $2,000, $3,000, or more per month. In addition, to try to avoid overinsurance, insurers limit the amount of disability income insurance they will issue to a person, so that the monthly benefits from all sources will not exceed a specified percentage of the person's earned income. The percentages used for this underwriting rule vary among insurers, but they might be 60 to 70 percent of earned income for persons with lower incomes and then graded downward to around 50 percent for earned income in excess of a certain amount. These underwriting rules may limit the amount of coverage available to the consumer, particularly for persons with higher incomes and/or with business health insurance needs. However, these underwriting limits do vary among insurers, and so you may be able to get the amount of coverage you want by "shopping around" a little.

A wide variety of *supplementary benefits* may be included in or added to a basic individual disability income policy. Some of the more important include the following:

1. Waiver of Premium. This provision is included automatically in most individual disability income policies and is comparable to the similar benefit in life insurance.

2. Partial Disability Benefit. This benefit may be an integral part of the disability contract but is often written as an optional rider at an extra premium. *Partial disability* is often defined as the inability of the insured to perform one or more, but not all, of the important duties of his or her occupation, and the benefit paid is frequently 50 percent of the amount payable for total disability for a limited maximum benefit period of from three to six months.

3. Guaranteed Insurability Provisions. These also are similar to the corresponding provisions in life insurance policies. They commonly provide that on stated

policy anniversary dates the insured may purchase specified additional amounts of disability income benefit as of his attained age and at the insurer's rates then in effect with no evidence of insurability being required.

4. Accidental Death or Accidental Death and Dismemberment (AD&D) coverage. This is similar to "double indemnity" in life insurance. And, as in life insurance, the logic of buying this kind of coverage is highly questionable.

5. Accident Medical Reimbursement, Hospital Income, or other medical expense benefits. These medical expense-type benefits usually can be added to disability income policies. But you should buy such benefits only if they fit into your overall health insurance planning, not just because they are available at a seemingly low premium outlay.

6. Benefits that increase the amount of the basic disability income coverage. One such benefit is a family income-type benefit that provides for a decreasing amount of disability income insurance. Another is a variable disability income benefit that allows the amount of monthly income to vary during an initial period of disability (such as during the first six months or year of disability) so as to coordinate with other disability benefits.

Coordination of Benefits. In general, individual disability income policies pay their benefits regardless of whether other disability benefits also are payable. However, health insurers *may* place certain policy provisions relating to other insurance in their disability income contracts. There are basically two such provisions: the "Insurance with Other Insurers" provision, and the "Relation of Earnings to Insurance" provision.

The *"Insurance with Other Insurers" provision* may be used by insurers in policies where the insurer retains the right to refuse policy renewal. It provides that if the insured has other disability insurance of which the insurer has no notice prior to a claim, the policy benefit will be paid in the proportion that the amount of insurance of which the insurer had notice bears to the total amount of insurance under all policies.

The *"Relation of Earnings to Insurance" provision* (sometimes called the "average earnings" clause) can be used only in guaranteed renewable or noncancellable policies (see later in this chapter for a discussion of these terms). It normally provides that if the total amount of "valid loss of time coverage" exceeds the insured's monthly earnings at the time of disability or his or her average monthly earnings over the two years immediately preceding the disability, whichever is greater, the policy benefit will be paid in the proportion that the monthly earnings (or average monthly earnings) bear to the total amount of monthly benefits under all such valid coverage. This provision ceases to apply when total benefits would be reduced to less than $200 per month.

Neither of these provisions must be used by insurers in their policies. Some insurers include them in their policies, while others do not. Strictly from the individual consumer's point of view, since these provisions might serve to limit benefits in the event of other insurance, a disability income policy is more liberal to the consumer if it does *not* contain these provisions relating to other insurance.

Most individual disability income policies are written on a "24-hour basis." This means they pay their benefits for both occupational and nonoccupational disabilities. In some cases, however, individual policies will exclude disability arising out of the insured's employment. Such "nonoccupational" coverage is, of course, less favorable to the consumer than "24-hour" coverage.

Termination of Coverage. Policies that are noncancellable or guaranteed renewable typically provide that coverage will continue, if the insured continues to pay the premiums, until a specified age, usually age 65. This is the age at which retirement benefits normally begin, and thus the insured can continue the coverage during his working years. Some policies, however, allow the insured to continue the coverage beyond age 65 on either a guaranteed renewable basis or at the option of the insurer, usually provided the insured continues to be gainfully employed. This kind of extension of coverage allows the insured to continue his protection (in fact, gives him the right to do so if the extension is on a guaranteed renewable basis) if the insured in fact continues working beyond normal retirement age. Many people today do continue working past 65. Thus, it is advantageous for the consumer to have such a provision in the policy. Policies may have a terminal age, such as 70, beyond which the coverage cannot be continued in any event.

Franchise and Association Group Disability Insurance

The benefits provided under franchise or association group disability insurance are much the same as under individual policies, except that the insured person has less flexibility in choice of plan, benefits, and optional coverages. There usually are limitations on the amount of disability income insurance you can apply for under these plans similar to those used in underwriting individual policies. Under these plans, the insurer usually waives its right to discontinue or modify any individual policy unless all policies in the group also are discontinued or modified.

Premiums for association group coverage usually apply to an insured as of his or her attained age at each annual renewal, frequently on the basis of 5- or 10-year age brackets. These are referred to as "step-rate premiums," and they increase as the insured grows older. This is different from "level-premium policies," where premiums vary with the insured's age at the time the policy is issued but then remain the same (level) for the duration of the coverage. Most individual policies are sold on a level-premium basis.

If you need disability coverage, you should check out any association group plan available to you. The rates may be lower than for individual policies and there often is less extensive underwriting. But be careful about how the rates are quoted, and remember that step-rate premiums can increase markedly as you grow older. You should also note the circumstances under which association group coverage can be terminated (as compared with an individual policy, for example). Association group coverage usually is terminated:

1. If the whole plan is discontinued for the group (either by the association or by the insurer)

2. If the covered person ceases to be a member of the association or franchise unit

3. If the insured person fails to pay his or her premium within the grace period

4. At the attainment of some age, such as 65

Other Insurance Benefits

There are various other kinds of coverages that can provide you with disability income benefits. Here are some of the more important.

Disability Benefits under Individual Life Insurance Policies. As we saw in Chapter 4, individual life insurance policies can contain disability coverage in the form of (1) waiver-of-premium benefits, and (2) disability income riders.

The *waiver-of-premium benefit* is modest in cost when a separate premium is charged for it, and consumers generally should include it in their life insurance programs. It also can provide substantial benefits. If a person is paying, say, $600 per year in premiums for individual life insurance, the waiver of these premiums is the equivalent of $50 per month of tax-free disability income benefits.

Disability income riders are less common. They are really a kind of individual disability income benefit that is tied to a life insurance policy. Both the waiver and the disability income rider typically use an "any occupation" definition of disability, although some insurers now use a more modern "split" definition.

Group Life Insurance Disability Benefits. There are three basic types of disability provisions used in group life insurance plans. The *maturity value type* provides for the payment of the face amount of a disabled employee's group term life insurance, usually in monthly installments over a fixed period of time such as 10, 20, 60, or 120 months.

The *waiver-of-premium type* provides for the continuation of a disabled employee's group term life insurance coverage after termination of employment if the employee becomes totally disabled.

The *extended death benefit (or one-year extension) type* is the least common and least liberal. It extends a disabled employee's group term coverage for only one year after termination of employment.

Disability Benefits under Pension Plans. While pension plans are intended primarily to provide retirement benefits, they may contain some disability benefits, such as the following:

1. A number of plans allow an employee who has become totally and permanently disabled to take early retirement under certain conditions.

2. Some pension plans provide a separate disability benefit for a totally and permanently disabled employee who has met specified requirements.

3. Many plans allow full vesting (see Chapter 12 for an explanation of vesting in general) of an employee's pension benefits in the event of total and permanent disability.

4. A few private pension plans provide a disability benefit akin to waiver of premium or the "disability freeze" in the social security system. This benefit allows a disabled employee's pension credits to continue to accumulate during his or her disability.

MEDICAL EXPENSE INSURANCE COVERAGES

The other broad category of health losses against which people seek to protect themselves and their dependents is medical expenses. People usually are well aware of the need for protection in this area and, in fact, sometimes tend to overemphasize the need for insuring against so-called "first dollar" medical expenses and to overlook less frequent, but larger, medical expenses.

Service versus Indemnity Benefits

Medical expense coverage is unusual among insurance coverages in that benefits can be provided in two different ways: on a *service basis* or on an *indemnity basis,* depending largely on the type of insuring organization involved. Which of these ways is used can be important to the consumer.

The main types of insuring organizations writing private medical expense benefits are the insurance companies and Blue Cross–Blue Shield associations. In addition, there are a number of so-called "independent" organizations (such as the new health maintenance organizations—"HMO's") that provide medical expense benefits.

A fundamental distinction between Blue Cross–Blue Shield plans and insurance company plans is the basis on which benefits are provided. Blue Cross plans normally provide service benefits to the subscriber (insured), such as, for example, 70 days of semi-private care in a member hospital with other specified hospital services included. With some exceptions, the subscriber is entitled to receive the specified service benefits in a member hospital without additional cost, regardless of what the hospital might have charged the patient if he or she had not been covered by Blue Cross. On the other hand, insured plans typically agree to indemnify (reimburse) an insured person for covered hospital (or medical) expenses up to specified maximum dollar amounts, such as, for example, up to $60 per day for a maximum of 120 days of hospital confinement and up to $1,000 for miscellaneous hospital costs incurred during the period of confinement. If the hospital's actual charges exceed the maximum dollar limits, the insured must pay the difference.

Even though most Blue Cross plans emphasize service benefits, they frequently provide cash (indemnity) benefits under certain circumstances. For example, cash allowances may be used: (1) for certain types of services, like maternity and hospital outpatient benefits; (2) for daily room-and-board charges in a private room; and (3) for a stay in a nonmember hospital.

Blue Shield plans which pay the expenses of surgery and other medical care costs also provide service benefits but to a lesser degree and on a generally different basis from Blue Cross. There are three general approaches to providing benefits under Blue Shield plans. A few plans provide *full-service benefits* to all subscribers. Under this approach, the participating physician agrees to render the covered surgical and medical services to subscribers without charging them any additional fee, regardless of the subscriber's income. Other plans provide *straight reimbursement (or indemnity) benefits.* Most plans, however, provide *partial service benefits.* Under this approach, certain income limits for subscribers are set by the plan. Those subscribers whose annual income is less than the limit receive service benefits, while those having an income in excess of the limit are provided cash (indemnity) benefits according to a schedule as a credit toward the physician's usual fee. Partial-service benefits really represent a middle ground between the full-service and indemnity approaches. For higher-income subscribers, however, the partial-service approach virtually eliminates the application of service benefits to them.

Kinds of Medical Expense Benefits

On either a service or an indemnity basis, there are a wide variety of medical expense benefits available to the public. Medical expense coverages, however, can be divided into two broad categories: the so-called "basic" coverages, and coverages under major medical-type policies.

By *"basic" coverages* we generally mean the traditional hospital, surgical, and regular medical expense coverages that provide benefits for specified kinds of care, usually starting with the first dollar of expense you incur, with relatively low maximum benefits.

The limitations of these "basic" coverages for the consumer led to the development of major medical expense insurance around 1950. Since then, major medical-type policies have shown very rapid growth. Briefly, *major medical-type policies* provide broad coverage for most types of medical expenses, make use of deductibles, require the covered person to bear at least a portion of his or her covered expenses through a so-called "coinsurance" provision, and pay covered expenses up to a relatively high maximum limit of liability.

Types of "Basic" Benefits. While there are a great many different kinds of basic medical expense benefits, written on either a group or individual basis, the following are the most common.

Hospital expense benefits. These benefits are designed to cover the expenses of hospital confinement and are available on a service basis (from

Blue Cross plans) or an indemnity basis (from insurance companies). The specific benefits provided by hospital expense coverage include:

1. The hospital daily-room-and-board benefit, which covers the per diem charges made by hospitals for room, board, and general nursing services. When provided on an indemnity basis, this coverage usually is written with a *daily benefit* of up to so much per day, such as $40, $50, $60, $80, or more, for a maximum period of hospitalization, which may range from as little as 30 days to as long as two years or more, depending on the plans available and how much premium the insured wants to pay. Blue Cross service benefits typically provide a certain number of days of semi-private hospital care, ranging from as few as 21 days to as many as 365 days or more.

2. The hospital services ("extras") benefit, which covers hospital services other than those included in the daily-room-and-board charge, including: use of operating or delivery rooms, diagnostic services (such as laboratory and x-ray), anesthetics, drugs, use of medical equipment and supplies during confinement, and the like.

3. Maternity benefits may be available and often are expressed as a multiple (such as 10 times) of the daily-room-and-board benefit or, in service plans, as a certain number of days of hospital care.

4. Other benefits may also be added, such as an emergency outpatient accident benefit, limited outpatient diagnostic benefits, and supplementary nursing benefits.

While deductibles traditionally were not used for hospital expense insurance, it has been increasingly common to use small deductibles (such as $25 or $50) for basic hospital expense insurance. Using such deductibles can reduce substantially the cost of hospital insurance for the consumer.

Hospital income benefits. This kind of hospital insurance differs from the coverages described above in that instead of reimbursing the insured for hospital expenses that the insured or his or her family have actually incurred, hospital income policies (or riders to other contracts) agree to pay stated amounts of weekly or monthly benefits while a covered person is confined in a hospital. These stated amounts, which may range from $50 to $1,000 per month or more, are paid regardless of any other health insurance benefits you may have. Thus, they often are purchased to supplement other coverage, such as Medicare, group insurance, or other individual policies. Remember, though, that hospital income contracts agree only to pay the fixed benefit during hospitalization, even though your actual hospital expenses may be greater than this amount. A fixed benefit of $1,000 per month, for example, represents only a daily benefit of approximately $33, which really is inadequate to meet fully the hospital expenses of today. But hospital income contracts may be helpful to you as supplementary coverage.

Surgical benefits. This type benefit customarily provides reimbursement for the charges of operating surgeons (and sometimes anesthesiologists) subject to a series of limits for various common surgical procedures set forth in a surgical schedule included in the policy. Surgical schedules are commonly described on the basis of the "schedule limit," which is the highest fee provided for in the schedule. Thus, a "$600 surgical schedule" means simply that the highest amount paid for any procedure(s) in the schedule is $600. Other amounts paid will be scaled down from this figure, depending on the nature of the procedure.

Regular medical (doctors' expense) benefits. These benefits cover physicians' charges for other than surgical procedures. Regular medical benefits generally pay so many dollars per day for doctors' visits for a specified number of days.

Other "basic" benefits. There are a great many other kinds of specific medical expense benefits available. Space does not permit their description here.

Limitations of Basic Coverages. The "basic" medical expense coverages have been, and continue to be, important ways of insuring against certain types of medical expenses. But when you are planning for your and your family's complete health insurance needs, you should keep in mind the following limitations of these basic coverages.

1. Many types of important medical expenses may not be covered.

2. In relation to how large medical care expenses can get today, the maximum benefits are quite low.

3. In a period of rapidly rising medical care costs, "basic" plans can easily become out of date.

4. There are many different "basic" coverages that the consumer must piece together to develop a complete insurance program.

Major Medical-type Benefits. Major medical and comprehensive medical expense coverages represent the backbone of protection for the insuring public against catastrophic medical expenses. Major medical was developed to meet the recognized limitations of basic hospital, surgical, and regular medical expense policies.

Types of plans. There are two broad types of major medical plans: major medical expense insurance and comprehensive medical expense insurance. *Major medical expense insurance* covers most types of medical expenses up to a high overall maximum limit of liability and uses a deductible and a so-called "coinsurance" provision. These policies contain relatively few exclusions and internal limits. They are often used to supplement basic hospital-medical-surgical coverages.

Comprehensive medical expense insurance is similar in concept to regular major medical coverage except that comprehensive plans usually provide, after a small deductible, a certain amount of basic hospital-medical-surgical coverage without applying any coinsurance provision, and then cover these expenses above this amount, as well as all other covered expenses, up to the policy's overall maximum limit of liability with a coinsurance percentage applying to these expenses. In essence, the comprehensive approach combines some basic hospital-medical-surgical coverage with major medical coverage in the same policy.

Covered expenses. Major medical plans cover most types of medical care expenses whether you are confined in a hospital or not. Covered expenses are specifically listed in the policy and most are covered subject only to the overall maximum limit of the policy. Some expenses, however, have special limits applying only to them. These are called "inside limits." Inside limits often apply to: daily-room-and-board charges, private-duty nursing, mental and nervous diseases (especially when the patient is not hospital-confined), nursing home or extended care facility coverage, and sometimes surgical charges. Generally speaking, *the fewer and higher such inside limits are, the more valuable is the major medical coverage for the consumer.*

Major medical policies almost always specify that only "reasonable and necessary" or "reasonable and customary" charges will be paid. This was intended to avoid payment of excessive charges made by some medical practitioners. However, some insurers may reduce covered charges that they feel do not fall within the prevailing pattern of charges in a community on this basis. But this is an administrative matter, and a covered person can contest what he or she may feel is an unjustified reduction in a claim made by the insurer on this basis.[4] You may be able to get an adjustment in these cases if you complain.

Maximum limit. Major medical policies usually contain an overall maximum limit of liability that may range from as low as $5,000 to as much as $500,000 or more, and a few plans have no maximum limit. Most plans, however, have limits of $25,000 or less.

Major medical maximum limits can be applied in several ways, including: on a *per cause* basis, on a *calendar-year* or *benefit-year* basis, on an *aggregate lifetime* basis, or using some *combination* of these, such as on a calendar-year basis but subject to an aggregate lifetime limit. Maximum limits can usually be reinstated after a specified amount of benefits, such as $1,000, have been paid and the covered person submits evidence of insurability or returns to work for a specified period of time. Some policies, however, provide for an automatic restoration of the maximum, such as a 10 percent restoration each year, for example. It is wise for a covered person to maintain his or her major medical coverage by reinstating the maximum limit if this is necessary.

Deductible. There are several types of major medical deductibles, such as an *initial deductible,* a *corridor deductible*, and an *integrated deductible.* As in the case of the maximum limit, major medical deductibles can be applied on a per cause or a calendar- or benefit-year basis. Use of a reasonably large major medical deductible can result in considerable premium savings for the consumer.

Coinsurance. After the deductible is satisfied, most major medical policies require the covered person to bear a certain portion, commonly 20 or 25

[4]Insurers often have review procedures for such contested claims.

percent, of covered expenses, with the insurer paying the remainder. This usually is referred to as a "coinsurance" provision. Coinsurance in major medical policies has the effect of forcing the covered person to bear a portion of covered losses above the deductible until the policy maximum limit is reached. Thus, it can result in your having to pay a significant portion of your medical expenses out of your own pocket. A few major medical plans do not use coinsurance provisions at all. Other modern plans, particularly group plans, apply the coinsurance percentage to only an initial amount of covered expenses. Clearly, the consumer is benefited by provisions which limit the rigor of a "pure" coinsurance provision, particularly for larger claims.

A simple illustration can help show the effects of the various provisions discussed above on a claim. Suppose you are covered by a major medical policy with a $100 deductible (on a per cause basis), a $25,000 maximum limit, an 80/20 coinsurance provision, and an inside limit on hospital daily-room-and-board charges of $60. Further suppose your wife (who also is covered) suffers a serious illness and is confined to a hospital for 100 days at a daily room charge of $80 and she incurs, say, $10,000 of other covered expenses. You would recover as follows:

Daily-room-and-board charges ($60 × 100) =	$ 6,000	(effect of inside limit)
Other fully covered charges	10,000	
Total covered expenses	$16,000	
Deductible	− 100	
	$15,900	(effect of deductible)
Coinsurance	× .80	
Recovery	$12,720	(effect of coinsurance)

Note that this still leaves $5,280 of uncovered expenses, and the total expenses have not yet reached the policy's maximum limit.[5] Thus, you can see that an emergency fund still may be necessary for medical expenses even if you have major medical expense insurance.

Excess Major Medical. Many personal excess (umbrella) liability insurance policies now include as a part of the contract an excess medical expense benefit. (See Chapter 6 for a discussion of personal excess liability insurance.) This benefit provides excess major medical coverage on an individual basis. The maximum limit under this coverage, normally on a per cause basis, typically ranges from $15,000 to $25,000. While this excess coverage has its limitations, it adds to the consumer's protection against very large medical expenses and should be considered carefully for any complete insurance program. A few insurance companies also write excess major medical coverage as an individual policy or on an association group basis.

[5]This would be an after-tax loss of $3,960, assuming the unreimbursed expenses are deductible in full and the insured is in a 25 percent income tax bracket.

Medicare

Persons age 65 and over usually rely primarily on Medicare for their medical expense protection, although many also use private plans to supplement Medicare. Private health insurance plans generally are coordinated with Medicare so that they do not provide overlapping benefits after age 65.[6] Medicare comprises two major programs, Hospital Insurance (HI) and Supplementary Medical Insurance (SMI).

Hospital Insurance. Nearly everyone age 65 or over is eligible for HI, which provides several types of benefits. Among the major ones are the following:

1. HI covers up to 90 days of inpatient care in any participating hospital for each "spell of illness." For the first 60 days, HI pays for all covered services except for a $92 deductible. For the sixty-first through the ninetieth day, it pays for all covered services except for a deductible of $23 a day.

2. There is an additional "lifetime reserve" of 60 hospital days. For each of these days used, HI pays for all covered services except for a $46-per-day deductible.

3. After hospital confinement, HI covers up to 100 days of care in a participating extended care facility (nursing home). It pays for all covered services for the first 20 days, and all but a $11.50-per-day deductible for up to 80 additional days.[7]

4. Also, after hospital confinement, HI covers up to 100 home health "visits" by nurses, physical therapists, speech therapists, and other health workers.

Supplementary Medical Insurance. The SMI portion of Medicare is voluntary, although persons eligible for HI are covered automatically unless they decline the SMI coverage. SMI is financed by individuals age 65 and over who participate and by a matching contribution from the federal government. It generally will pay 80 percent of the reasonable charges for covered medical services after a $60 deductible in each calendar year. The following are some of the major services covered by SMI:

1. Physicians' and surgeons' services, no matter where such services are rendered.

2. Home health services, even if a covered person has not been in a hospital, up to 100 visits during a calendar year.

3. Other medical and health services, such as diagnostic tests, surgical dressings, and rental or purchase of medical equipment.

4. Outpatient physical therapy services.

5. All outpatient services of participating hospitals, including diagnostic tests or treatment.

[6]An exception is hospital income plans, described earlier, which pay their fixed benefit regardless of other plans.

[7]All these deductibles are adjusted periodically to reflect changes in hospital costs.

Workmen's Compensation

In addition to the disability income benefits discussed previously, all workmen's compensation laws provide medical benefits to employees injured on the job. Most laws provide unlimited medical benefits. Health insurance policies providing medical expense benefits normally specifically exclude expenses of any injury or sickness for which a covered person is entitled to workmen's compensation benefits.

Group Health Insurance

The lion's share of medical expense benefits in the United States now is provided under group medical expense coverage. Therefore, you should determine what group insurance protection you and your family may have.

Who Is Covered? Group medical expense insurance normally covers the insured employee and the employee's "dependents." The definition of these "dependents" is important to you because it indicates, in effect, the scope of your group protection and perhaps will point up some dependents for whom you need to make other arrangements for medical expense coverage.

Definitions of "dependents" vary among group policies, but they often include any unmarried, dependent child of the employee who has not attained a certain age (such as 19 or 23) and the employee's wife or husband. In some contracts, this definition is extended to include certain other family members, such as dependent parents or handicapped children, but this is less usual.

Benefits Provided. Group plans can provide any of the types of benefits described above. The group technique generally makes possible the provision of broader benefits at lower cost than is given under individual policies.

Coordination of Benefits. Most group medical expense contracts include a "coordination of benefits" (COB) provision which has the effect of limiting the total amount recoverable from group contracts (and certain other coverages) in effect for a person to 100 percent of the expenses covered under any of the contracts. This serves to avoid duplication of benefits when a person is covered under more than one group contract, such as might occur, for example, when a husband and wife are both employed and each is covered as an insured employee under his or her own employer's group policy and his or her spouse also is covered as a dependent. Their children also might be covered as dependents under both group contracts.

In most cases, however, group medical expense policies do not coordinate their benefits with individual medical expense policies. Therefore, a group policy's benefits normally will not be reduced because you may have individual coverage on yourself or your dependents. But you should check your group plan's COB provision to see if it does coordinate with individual coverage. On the other hand, an individual policy's benefits may be reduced because of group coverage. (See the next section on individual health insurance.)

Termination of Coverage. Since group coverage often is the backbone of a family's medical expense protection, it is important to consider the alternatives in case your group coverage is terminated. An employee's group medical expense insurance normally terminates automatically when the employee terminates his or her employment with the group policyholder. Dependents' coverage terminates when the insured employee's coverage terminates and also when their dependency status changes, as, for example, when a child reaches age 19 or 23 or when a wife or husband gets a divorce. There is no grace period in group medical expense insurance as there is in group life insurance. Therefore, with a few exceptions, if your group coverage terminates, you should *immediately* take care that you have adequate alternative coverage.

There are several possibilities for a person whose group medical expense coverage has terminated.

1. He or she may be eligible immediately for other group insurance.

2. The person may be eligible for Medicare upon reaching age 65.

3. The person may elect to convert his or her terminating group insurance to an individual policy without showing individual evidence of insurability. This right of conversion, where it exists, can be important to an individual who is uninsurable or who is insurable only at higher rates or for restricted coverage under individual insurance. In addition to the conversion privilege provided the insured employee, his or her dependents may have a limited right to convert their terminating insurance. Such a privilege may be extended to a surviving spouse in the event of the insured employee's death. Further, conversion rights may be granted a dependent child whose group coverage terminates.

4. The person may purchase new individual insurance to replace the terminated group coverage or to supplement any new group coverage for which the person may be eligible that is not as liberal as his or her former coverage.

Individual Health Insurance

There are a great many different individual and family medical expense policies available to the public from many different insurance companies. These policies often offer the consumer broad coverage for his or her medical expense insurance needs, but some offer only limited coverage. Therefore, you should evaluate carefully what you are buying.

Blue Cross–Blue Shield associations and some "independent" plans also offer individual medical expense contracts. Subscription charges for nongroup subscribers normally are higher than for the plans' group subscribers. The Blues tend to solicit their nongroup subscribers at the time they leave a group covered by Blue Cross, in periodic open-enrollment campaigns, and to some extent through advertising and continuous enrollment. The Blues do not sell through agents and brokers as do most insurance companies in this field.

Who Is Covered? Individual medical expense insurance can be written to cover the insured person, the insured's spouse, and the dependent, unmarried children of the insured. The persons covered normally are listed in the policy, and each must be acceptable to the insurance company according to its underwriting standards. A separate premium often is charged for each covered person in insured plans.

Blue Cross–Blue Shield plans often have one rate for individuals, another rate for husband and wife (or a covered person with one dependent), and a third rate for families, or some similar rating system.

Benefits Provided. The same basic kinds of medical expense benefits can be provided under individual policies as under group coverages. Individual policies may offer somewhat less liberal benefits than could be purchased under comparable group coverages, but this is largely a matter of degree.

Of course, you can select the coverages you want and feel you need when buying individual coverage. Most health insurers offer a reasonably complete line of individual health insurance policies to the public.

Coordination of Benefits. Since people are free to buy individual medical expense policies from a number of different insurers, may have group coverage as well, and may also be covered by other medical expense benefits (such as automobile or homeowners medical payments coverage), you may find yourself with several sources of recovery for medical expenses. This is not necessarily bad, and in fact people often buy individual policies to supplement other coverage. But it is an area you can take a hard look at to see if you can save premium dollars by dropping any unnecessary coverage.

Individual hospital-medical-surgical policies usually do not contain provisions that would coordinate or prorate their benefits with other medical expense insurance. Insurers generally try to avoid overinsurance here by their underwriting requirements.

In the case of individual major medical coverages, the deductible is used to coordinate that coverage with other medical expense benefits. The effect of such a deductible is that the major medical policy picks up coverage only after other medical expense coverage has been exhausted. Thus, if you have only some form of relatively limited "basic" hospital-medical-surgical coverage—either group or individual—you can supplement this "basic" coverage with a more comprehensive individual major medical policy on top. However, insurers usually will not issue such a major medical policy if you are covered by another major medical plan or by a "basic" plan with benefit limits above certain levels.

Termination of Coverage. Most individual medical expense policies terminate the insured's or his spouse's coverage when he or she reaches age 65 or first becomes eligible for Medicare, whichever is earlier. Of course, policies specifically designed to supplement Medicare are not so terminated or reduced. As in group medical expense insurance, dependents' coverage is subject to termination under specified circumstances.

At one time it was customary for individual medical expense policies to terminate upon the insured's death. Now, however, it is common for policies to provide that a surviving spouse automatically becomes the insured upon the original insured's death. Some policies also provide that when no spouse survives the insured, coverage is continued for minor dependents up to the policy's limiting age for such dependents. These are provisions you should consider in buying such insurance. Another advantageous feature commonly provided in family medical expense policies is a conversion privilege for dependents whose coverage terminates.

Other Insurance Benefits

An injured person may be entitled to other medical expense insurance benefits. These may include: (1) medical payments benefits under various kinds of liability insurance, (2) automobile no-fault benefits, and (3) blanket accident medical reimbursement benefits under individual or group policies.

Benefits from such sources normally are payable only if a covered person is injured in an accident or a specified kind of accident. Therefore, this is not coverage you can rely upon for full protection.

INDIVIDUAL HEALTH INSURANCE POLICY PROVISIONS

There are several kinds of individual health insurance policy provisions that may be important to you in making policy purchase decisions. These include: (1) renewal or continuance provisions, (2) provisions concerning preexisting conditions, and (3) certain general provisions.

Renewal or Continuance Provisions

Renewal provisions relate to the insured's rights to continue his or her individual health insurance coverage in effect from one policy period to another. These provisions are significant to the consumer since they may determine his or her ability to retain the health insurance protection. They generally can be classified as policies that are (1) renewable at the option of the insurer (optionally renewable), (2) guaranteed renewable, and (3) noncancellable and guaranteed renewable (noncancellable).

Policies that are *renewable at the option of the insurer* specify that the insurer has the right to refuse renewal as of any premium due date or policy anniversary.[8] Under these policies, the insurer can raise premiums, reclassify the risk, and/or attach restrictive endorsements at time of renewal. This is the least liberal renewal provision from the consumer's viewpoint.

Another situation is where there are restrictions on the insurer's right of nonrenewal. An example of this is in franchise or association group cover-

[8]Some states have adopted regulatory restrictions on the rights of insurers to refuse renewal under optionally renewable contracts.

ages, where the insurer usually cannot refuse renewal unless the insured person ceases to be a member of the association, the insured person ceases to be actively engaged in the occupation, or the insurer refuses to renew all policies issued to members of the particular group.

The term "guaranteed renewable" (or guaranteed continuable) is reasonably descriptive of the nature of this type of renewal provision. The policy provides that the insured will have the right to renew the coverage for a specified period of time, such as to age 65, or in some cases for life. Also, during this period, the insurer cannot by itself make any change in the policy, *except that the insurer retains the right to make changes in premium rates for whole classes of policies.* This means the insurer cannot change the premium or classification for an individual policy by itself but may change the rates for whole rating classifications. Most individual medical expense policies that guarantee the right of renewal are written on a guaranteed renewable basis. Some insurers also write disability income coverages on this basis.

The final category of renewal provision is the *noncancellable and guaranteed renewable (noncancellable)* type. When the term "noncancellable" or "noncan" is used alone to describe a type of renewal provision, it means the noncancellable and guaranteed renewable type. This provision gives the insured the right to continue the policy in force by the timely payment of premiums *as specified in the policy,* usually for a specified period of time, such as to age 65. Also, the insurer retains no right by itself to make *any* change in *any* policy provision during this period. The distinction between this and a guaranteed renewable policy is that the insurer guarantees the premium rates for noncancellable and guaranteed renewable contracts, but reserves the right to change premiums for whole classes of insureds under guaranteed renewable contracts.

Not surprisingly, however, the greater the renewal guarantees contained in the policy, the higher the premium will tend to be, all other things being equal. Thus, assuming the consumer has a choice among renewal provisions, the question becomes, How much is he or she willing to pay for renewal protection?

Preexisting Conditions

Individual health insurance policies normally cover only losses that begin during the policy period. Thus, accidents sustained or sickness existing prior to the effective date of coverage are not covered. These are preexisting conditions. Group health insurance, on the other hand, normally covers preexisting conditions, except in certain cases, such as smaller groups.

However, a section of the "Time Limit on Certain Defenses" provision, which is a required provision in individual health insurance policies, in effect provides that after a policy has been in force for two (or three) years, coverage cannot be denied by the insurer on the ground that a loss was caused by a preexisting condition, unless the condition is specifically excluded in the policy. This provision can be a valuable protection to the insured, because after the two or three years, the insured does not need to worry about conditions that might have existed before he or she purchased the policy.

General Provisions

Here are some of the required policy provisions which are more important as far as the consumer is concerned.

Time Limit on Certain Defenses. In addition to the part of this provision dealing with preexisting conditions we noted above, this important provision specifies that after a policy has been in force for two (or three) years, no misstatements, except fraudulent misstatements, made by the applicant in securing the policy can be used to void the policy or to deny liability for a loss commencing after the two- (or three-) year period. It is similar in concept to the incontestable clause used in life insurance.

Grace Period. Like life insurance policies, individual health insurance contracts allow a grace period for the payment of premiums.

Notice and Proof Requirements. The policy indicates certain time limits for the insured to give the insurance company written notice of a claim and to furnish the insurer with completed proofs of loss. The insured should try to comply strictly with these notice and proof requirements to avoid any possible complications with claims.

6
PROPERTY AND
LIABILITY INSURANCE

Buying property and liability insurance is important to your personal financial security. You can be very successful in your job or profession; have a good life and health insurance program; be successful with your investments; have a nice home, cars, perhaps a boat, and other valuable personal property; and yet be almost destroyed financially by an accident or lawsuit for which you do not have adequate property and liability insurance. This is particularly true today for liability insurance, because people in general have become so claims-conscious.

PROPERTY INSURANCE

Most people face risks of loss or damage to their real and/or personal property. To most, the purchase of a home represents the largest single investment they make. Even those who rent face the chance of suffering a severe financial loss through damage to their personal property. The questions you should ask yourself in this area include the following:

What can possibly happen to cause loss or damage to my property?

What kind of insurance coverage best suits my needs?

What amount of insurance should I carry?

Which insurer or insurers should I select to provide the coverage?

There are two basic approaches to insuring your property: (1) specified perils coverage, and (2) "all risks" coverage. *Specified perils coverage* protects you against the specific perils (causes of loss) named in your policy. It does not cover against loss by other perils. Some common examples of specified perils coverages include: fire insurance, theft insurance, extended coverage, Homeowners policies 1, 2, and 4, and the Dwelling Buildings and Contents—Broad Form. Some of these coverages, like the extended coverage endorsement, Homeowners policies, and Dwelling Buildings and Contents—Broad Form, cover a number of specified perils in one contract and may offer you quite broad protection.

"All risks"-type coverage protects you against all the risks or perils that may cause loss to the covered property, *except* those specifically excluded in the policy. Thus, the exclusions stated in the policy or form are important in determining the real extent of "all risks"-type coverage. Remember that no insurance policy or form covers everything. There are always exclusions. However, "all risks" coverage frequently is broader than specified perils coverage, but it also usually costs more. So you have to decide whether "all risks" coverage is worth the extra cost. Some common examples of "all risks"-type coverages are: Homeowners coverages 3 and 5, Dwelling Buildings Special Form, Personal Articles Floater coverage (e.g., on furs, jewels, fine arts, stamp collections, cameras, and the like), and automobile comprehensive physical damage insurance.

Probably the most planned-for risk of loss to real or personal property is by fire and related perils. Unless an individual is quite wealthy, he or she really cannot assume the fire risk.

The fire insurance policy is perhaps the most standardized in the insurance industry. The perils covered by the basic policy are fire, lightning, and removal of covered property from the premises to escape damage. The policy can be tailored to cover various types of property, including, of course, a dwelling and its contents. The standard fire policy, incidentally, is included automatically in the Homeowners forms that are so commonly used today to cover residential risks. To the standard fire policy is attached at least one form or endorsement further describing covered property and/or perils. The fire policy frequently is broadened by endorsement to include the "extended coverage" perils, which are

Windstorm

Hail

Damage by aircraft and vehicles

Riot, riot attending a strike, and civil commotion

Explosion

Smoke

It is common practice to include these perils, since they are frequent causes of loss. Additionally, other endorsements can be added to the standard fire policy, such as:

Vandalism and malicious mischief

Additional extended coverage (e.g., weight of ice, sleet, and snow; collapse of buildings; limited water damage; falling objects; damage by burglars; glass breakage; and freezing of plumbing and heating systems)

"All risks" coverage

The insuring clause of an "all risks" contract typically states that the policy covers "all risks" (written in quotation marks to indicate the conditional nature of the term) of direct physical loss or damage, except as hereinafter provided. Some of the commonly used exclusions in "all risks" contracts are the following:

Wear and tear, deterioration, rust, mechanical breakdown, and the like—these are gradual, inevitable causes of loss which are uninsurable because the occurrence is certain.

Flood, surface water, water backing up through drains, water below the surface of the ground, etc. Most private insurance contracts do not provide flood coverage because of its catastrophic nature and because of the limited regions of exposure. However, many flood-prone areas have been designated as eligible for flood insurance through the National Flood Insurance Act, and you should check into this if you reside in a flood-prone area.

Earthquake, landslide, and other earth movement. In most states, this coverage can be "bought back" by the insured upon payment of an additional premium.

To many homeowners and apartment dwellers, the detailed conditions, exclusions, and extensions that seemingly characterize property insurance policies may appear like more trouble than they are worth. But in reality, they are not difficult and can be analyzed in a "building-up" pattern as follows:

1. Basic specified perils coverage—Fire, lightning, and extended coverage
2. Broader specified perils coverage—All the above plus vandalism and malicious mischief, theft, and additional extended coverage
3. "All risks"-type coverage—All the above plus anything not specifically excluded

Which Coverage and in What Amount?

The question then becomes, "Which policy should I buy?" A cost-benefit type of analysis can provide the answer. By comparing the additional coverage provided with the additional premium, you can decide on the coverage that best suits your needs. Yet, sometimes the cost differential for broader coverage may be so little as to make it a worthwhile purchase.

Once a decision has been made as to the type of coverage, the amount of insurance must be determined. Most Homeowners policies (to be discussed later in the chapter) are written with a *replacement cost provision* that applies to the dwelling and related structures. You should be sure you have enough insurance to meet the requirements of this provision, as explained later in the section on Homeowners insurance. Of course, you also want to *be sure that your property insurance policy limits are adequate to cover the maximum loss you are likely to suffer* as a result of damage or loss to the various kinds of property you own or otherwise have at risk. In most cases, these will be limits equal to the full value of the covered property. But different kinds of property can be insured in different ways, and we shall point out some kinds of property that may present special coverage considerations when we discuss Homeowners policies.

In the case of contents valuation, an additional problem confronts the insurance buyer. This problem is all too familiar to those who have suffered a loss of this nature; it centers around the difficulty of recalling the articles destroyed and their description, purchase price, and date of purchase. To alleviate this kind of situation, you might take and periodically update an inventory of your personal property. Many insurers encourage this by providing inventory checklists that include all pertinent information. When completed properly, this inventory should present a fairly accurate basis for setting the amount of insurance, and, of course, it should be stored *away from your premises*, preferably in a safe deposit box.

What May Suspend or Reduce Your Coverage?

There are a few things that may suspend or reduce your property insurance coverage. Therefore, you should watch out for them so that your insurance protection will not be impaired.

For example, coverage for certain perils may be suspended if a covered building had been vacant (or unoccupied) beyond a stated period of time immediately preceding a loss. In Homeowners policies, HO-2, for example, such a suspension of coverage applies to loss caused by vandalism or malicious mischief, breakage of glass, and accidental discharge or overflow of water or steam if the covered building had been vacant beyond a period of 30 consecutive days immediately preceding a loss. If you do plan to leave your property vacant beyond such a time limit, you should notify your insurance agent or broker so he or she can take the appropriate action to maintain your coverage.

Also, fire insurance policies provide that the insurance company will not be liable for a loss occurring while the hazard is increased by any means within the control or knowledge of the insured. The policy does not spell out exactly what constitutes an increase in hazard within the insured's control or knowledge. Suppose, though, that you store in your garage an amount of gasoline that is far in excess of your normal household needs. Not only is this unwise from the viewpoint of your and your family's physical safety, but it also *might* constitute an increase in hazard that would suspend your fire insurance coverage.

Finally, remember that you must pay (or have your agent pay for you) your property and liability insurance premiums by the due date or your coverage will expire. Property and liability insurance policies do not contain a provision similar to the grace period found in life and health insurance policies. Of course, many property and liability insurance agents extend credit for a short period to their customers for their premium payments.

PERSONAL LIABILITY

The risk of loss of financial assets is by no means limited to the physical destruction of the assets. A potentially greater risk is the loss of assets or earnings through the judicial process as a result of one's negligence. Large liability judgments and settlements are common, and awards as high as a million dollars or more are quite possible today. As in the case of property coverages, a careful review of exposures to loss, coverages, policy limits, and differences between insurers can assist you in developing a comprehensive insurance program at the lowest practical cost.

When an individual looks at his or her diverse personal liability exposures, the following general *categories of exposures* come to mind:

1. Ownership and/or use of automobiles
2. Ownership and/or rental of premises
3. Professional or business activities
4. Directorships or officerships in corporations, credit unions, school boards, and other organizations
5. Employment of others (workmen's compensation and/or employer's liability exposures)
6. Ownership and/or use of watercraft or aircraft
7. Personal activities

These exposures can be covered by a variety of liability insurance coverages. We shall consider first the so-called comprehensive personal liability coverage which can be purchased separately but usually is bought as a part of a Homeowners policy.

Comprehensive Personal Liability Coverage

Daily nonbusiness activities include a host of exposures to loss through legal liability. Your dog bites a neighbor, a visitor trips and falls on your front walk, or a tee shot on the eighth hole slices and hits another golfer—all these accidents could result in large liability losses, as well as put you to great expense and trouble in defending yourself from claims even if they are groundless. This widespread exposure to liability losses stresses the need for comprehensive personal liability (CPL) insurance protection.

CPL insurance agrees to pay on behalf of an insured[1] all sums (up to the policy limits) that the insured becomes legally obligated to pay as damages because of bodily injury and property damage, and the insurance company also agrees to defend the insured in any suit that would be covered by the

---

[1]The word "insured" includes the named insured and, if residents of his household, his spouse, the relatives of either, and any other person under the age of 21 in the care of any insured.

policy. The insuring agreement is quite broad but still is limited by certain *exclusions*. Coverage, for example, does not apply to:

1. Business or professional pursuits. (Separate liability insurance is available for such exposures.)

2. The ownership, maintenance or use of automobiles, larger watercraft, and aircraft. (Each of these exposures presents special needs, and policies exist to cover each of them.)

3. Injury or damage caused intentionally by the insured.

4. Benefits payable under any workmen's compensation law (to avoid duplication of coverage).

5. Injury or damage due to war, revolution, etc., or nuclear energy.

6. Liability assumed by the insured under any contract or agreement that is not in writing.

7. Property damage to property in the care, custody, or control of the insured. (Limited coverage is provided under a separate insuring agreement.)

In addition to the basic liability coverage, CPL insurance contains two additional insuring agreements: (1) medical payments and (2) physical damage to property of others. *Medical payments coverage* agrees to pay all reasonable expenses incurred within one year from the date of an accident for necessary medical, surgical, dental, etc., services for each person who sustains bodily injury caused by an accident: (1) while on the insured's premises with permission, and (2) elsewhere, if the accident is caused by an insured, a resident employee, or an animal owned by the insured. *Note that this provision is not based upon the insured's legal liability. That is, eligible medical expenses are paid under medical payments coverage (up to the policy limit) whether or not the insured was at fault.* For example, if a neighbor is injured on the insured's premises and incurs medical expenses as a result of the injury, there is medical payments coverage without the necessity of determining who was at fault.

Physical damage to property of others coverage promises to pay for loss of property belonging to others caused by an insured. "Loss" means damage or destruction, but not disappearance, obstruction, or loss of use.

Limits of Liability and Cost

Comprehensive personal liability insurance provides bodily injury liability and property damage liability coverage on a so-called "single limit" basis—which means one limit of liability, such as $25,000, $50,000, $100,000, or $300,000, that applies to each occurrence regardless of the number of persons injured or the amount of separate property damage. In other words, there are no separate per-person or property damage liability limits.

Medical payments coverage is written subject to a per-person limit and a limit per accident. The physical damage to property of others coverage is fixed at $250. Thus, an illustrative set of coverage limits under CPL insurance might look like this:

Personal Liability (Bodily Injury and Property Damage)	$50,000 each occurrence
Medical Payments to Others	$ 500 each person $25,000 each accident
Physical Damage to Property of Others (a supplementary coverage)	$ 250 each occurrence

Cost of protection is dependent chiefly upon the number and uses of properties owned or used by the insured. Many individuals, however, are surprised at the reasonableness of the premium for a person who owns or rents one home or apartment. The following are examples of CPL premiums for various limits of liability based on a single residence.

CPL Limit of Liability	Annual Premium
$ 25,000	$15
50,000	17
100,000	19
200,000	21
300,000	24

Perhaps as important as the absolute cost of the policy shown above is the relatively small cost of doubling or even quadrupling the coverage. For example, a doubling of coverage from $25,000 to $50,000 costs only $2 additional; for four times as much coverage, a $100,000 limit costs only $4 more than a $25,000 limit. This is an example of sound insurance buying—getting a great deal of additional protection against potentially catastrophic losses for a relatively small cost.

HOMEOWNERS INSURANCE

Earlier in this chapter, the basic fire policy with endorsements was discussed, as well as comprehensive personal liability insurance. When these basic coverages are added to personal theft insurance, the resulting package is called a "Homeowners" policy. Developed and refined through the years, the various Homeowners policies generally provide broader coverage than the separate policies discussed above, and at a lower cost. Hence the wide popularity of Homeowners policies.

Types of Policies

There are basically five variations of Homeowners policies, as follows:

Homeowners 1 (Standard)	Fire, lightning, extended coverage, vandalism and malicious mischief, theft, glass breakage, and comprehensive personal liability
Homeowners 2 (Broad Form)	All the above, and additional extended coverage which provides coverage for other specified causes of loss
Homeowners 3	"All Risks" on buildings and Broad Form on contents
Homeowners 4	Contents coverage only (Broad Form) for tenants
Homeowners 5	"All Risks" on buildings and contents

As is common with package policies, Homeowners policies contain a set of required coverages that may be altered by endorsements which increase the amount of insurance and/or broaden the coverage. An example of the coverages and limits under a Homeowners 2 is as follows[2]:

Section I *Property Coverages*

Coverage A	Dwelling	$40,000	(selected by the insured)
Coverage B	Appurtenant private structures	$ 4,000	(10% of dwelling amount, but may be increased)
Coverage C	Unscheduled[3] personal property:		
	On the premises	$20,000	(50% of dwelling amount, but may be increased, or reduced to 40%)
	Away from the premises	$ 2,000	(10% of the on-premises limit but not less than $1,000)
Coverage D	Additional Living Expenses	$ 8,000	(20% of dwelling amount)

Section II *Liability and Medical Payments Coverages*

Coverage E	Comprehensive personal liability	$25,000	each occurrence
Coverage F	Medical payments	$ 500	each person
	Physical damage to property of others	$ 250	each occurrence

[2]Homeowners policies follow this basic pattern, but slight variations exist in certain states and under the forms used by some insurers.

[3]"Unscheduled" means property that is not specifically named or listed in a schedule in the policy. As we shall see later, you sometimes need to list certain valuable property in a separate schedule for full coverage.

It is readily apparent that this "package" provides a combination of coverages that fits the needs of most homeowners. A tenant's Homeowners policy (HO-4) simply deletes Coverages A and B. A Homeowners 5, the broadest of the Homeowners forms, has a minimum unscheduled personal property limit of 50 percent of the dwelling amount for personal property both on and off the insured's premises.

To appreciate fully the extent and limitations of the Homeowners policy, let us look briefly at each division of coverage.

Coverage A   The dwelling amount includes all additions, extensions, and building and outdoor equipment concerning the service of the premises. Trees, plants, shrubs, and lawns are covered only for certain perils and with an aggregate limit of 5 percent of the dwelling amount and not more than $250 on any one tree, shrub, or plant. Particular care must be taken in selecting the amount of insurance because of the replacement cost provision described below.

Coverage B   Private structures (garages, sheds, etc.) wholly detached from the dwelling are covered in an amount as shown above *in addition to* the dwelling amount.

Coverage C   Personal property owned or used by the named insured and his or her family is covered against the policy perils (including theft). However, among the property items specifically excluded from coverage are: motorized vehicles, aircraft, business property while away from the premises, salesmen's samples, automobile sound recording equipment and "tape decks," and property which is specifically insured elsewhere (a painting insured under a Fine Arts Floater, for example).

Coverage D   Additional living expenses incurred by the family while the dwelling is untenantable because of damage due to an insured peril include hotel bills, meals, and the like, *but only to the extent they are in addition to normal living expenses.*

The remaining coverages apply to the liability portion of the policy. This is the comprehensive personal liability coverage which we have discussed previously. The amounts of insurance applying to Coverages E and F are minimum amounts that can be increased by the payment of an additional premium.

Replacement Cost Provision

There are several "additional conditions" in Homeowners policies that the consumer should watch for. One is the *replacement cost provision* that applies only to Coverages A and B (the dwelling and appurtenant private structures). This provision really is advantageous to the insured because if you maintain the proper amount of insurance on your dwelling, you can recover any loss to the dwelling and private structures (but not personal property) on the basis of the full cost to repair or replace the damaged or destroyed property *without any deduction for depreciation*. This can be important to you. Without such a replacement cost provision, the Homeowners policy (and the standard fire policy which is incorporated in it) would pay only the actual cash value at the time of a loss of lost or damaged property. Actual cash value (ACV) normally means the new replacement cost of the property at the time of a loss minus the amount the property has physically depreciated since it was built. *Note that property still physically depreciates (i.e., wears out) even though its market value*, which basically depends upon the supply and demand for real estate, *may be rising or falling*.

But you must carry enough insurance in relation to the value of your dwelling to get the benefit of the replacement cost provision. Specifically, the policy provides that *if the insured carries insurance on a building equal to at least 80 percent of its replacement cost new, any covered loss to the building will be paid to the extent of the full cost to repair or replace the damage without deducting depreciation*, up to the policy limit. What if you carry insurance of less than 80 percent of replacement cost? Then, in case of a loss to the building, the insurance company would pay only (1) the actual cash value of the loss, or (2) the amount produced by the following formula:

$$\frac{\text{Amount of insurance carried on the building}}{80\% \text{ of the building's replacement cost new}} \times \begin{array}{c} \text{Cost to repair or} \\ \text{replace the damage} \end{array}$$

whichever is greater. In either case, though, this would be less than what you would have to pay to repair or replace the damaged building.

Therefore, it is important for you to buy enough insurance to meet the 80 percent requirement and to keep your coverage up-to-date with rising construction costs. How can you do this? First of all, your property and liability insurance agent or broker probably can help you by recommending the proper amount of coverage based on up-to-date information on construction costs and dwelling values. Second, in most states you can buy a special endorsement on Homeowners policies, called an "Inflation Guard Endorsement," that automatically increases your coverage limits periodically by small percentage amounts. However, use of this endorsement does not necessarily mean you have enough coverage. Finally, for your general information we have indicated in the following table some replacement cost multipliers, based on national statistics, for the period 1950 to July 1974.

These multipliers can be used as follows: Suppose your home was built in 1964 at a cost of $20,000 (for the building only, not the land; land cannot burn). What was its replacement cost in 1974? To find out, multiply the $20,000 original cost for the dwelling by the multiplier as of 1964, or 1.867. This will give you an estimated 1974 replacement cost of about $37,500 ($20,000 × 1.867 = $37,340).

REPLACEMENT COST MULTIPLIERS

Year	Dwelling Building Construction (Wood Frame)	Year	Dwelling Building Construction (Wood Frame)
1974 (July)	1.000	1966	1.730
1973	1.047	1965	1.809
1972	1.154	1964	1.867
1971	1.234	1963	1.909
1970	1.364	1962	1.959
1969	1.453	1960	2.028
1968	1.552	1955	2.333
1967	1.673	1950	2.932

Source: Marshall & Swift Publication Co.

Internal Limits (Sublimits)

Another thing to watch for is the smaller internal limits (called "sublimits") that apply to certain kinds of property under Homeowners policies. The following are some of the more important of these sublimits.

1. $100 aggregate limit on money, numismatic property (coin collections), and bank notes

2. $500 aggregate limit on securities, accounts, deeds, and similar property, or stamps, including philatelic property (stamp collections)

3. $500 aggregate limit *for loss by theft* of jewelry, watches, necklaces, bracelets, gems, precious and semiprecious stones, gold, platinum, and furs, including articles containing fur which represents their principal value

4. $500 aggregate limit on watercraft, including their trailers, furnishings, equipment, and outboard motors

Remember, too, that there is the off-premises limit on unscheduled personal property of 10 percent of the on-premises amount (but not less than $1,000).

The effect of these internal limits may be to make it necessary for you to schedule specifically additional amounts of insurance on certain property items. Let us take a specific example. Suppose you have a Homeowners 2 policy with $30,000 of insurance on the dwelling. You also own a coin collection worth about $1,500 and you have recently given your wife a fur coat worth about $2,000. Here your basic Homeowners policy would provide only specified perils coverage of $100 on the coin collection. And on the fur coat it would provide only $1,500 of off-premises coverage ($30,000 × 50% × 10%) and, in any event, no more than $500 of theft protection. So in this situation you might want to insure specifically on an "all risks" basis the coin collection for $1,500 and the fur coat for $2,000 to get full coverage on these items. You could do this under a Scheduled Personal Property Endorsement added to your Homeowners policy or under a separate Personal Articles Floater. Kinds of property that often are separately scheduled and insured in this way include: jewelry, furs, cameras, musical instruments, silverware, golfer's equipment, fine arts, stamps, and coins. Finally, if you have a large amount of high-value personal property and want broad coverage, you may want to consider buying a Homeowners 5 policy.

Liability Exclusions

In the personal liability area, *remember the liability exclusions under Homeowners policies and be sure you do not have any uncovered liability exposures.* Specifically, the following are some of the potential liability exposure areas, excluded under Homeowners personal liability insurance, that you might consider:

1. Any watercraft owned by or rented to an insured if it has inboard or inboard-outboard motor power of more than 50 horsepower or is a sailing vessel of 26 feet or more in length; or if it is powered by outboard motor(s) of more than 25 horsepower (unless endorsed on the policy). (In other words, Homeowners policies provide liability coverage for smaller boats, but not larger ones. For excluded watercraft, you may need boat or yacht insurance.)

2. Any aircraft.

3. Any motor vehicle owned or operated by, or rented or loaned to, an insured.

4. Recreational motor vehicles owned by an insured used away from the residence premises (other than golf carts while used for golfing purposes).

5. Rendering professional services.

6. Most business pursuits of an insured.

7. Any premises, other than an insured premises, owned, rented, or controlled by any insured.

8. Cases where the insured is liable to provide workmen's compensation benefits or does provide such benefits.

9. For damage to property occupied by, used by, rented to, or in the care, custody, or control of the insured. (This is the so-called "care, custody, and control" exclusion in liability policies.)

Eligibility

For those eligible, Homeowners policies generally provide broad coverage at a reasonable price. To be eligible, a dwelling must be owner-occupied. Seasonal dwellings, not rented to others, are considered to be owner-occupied, but a common problem in this regard is the two- or three-family house bought for investment purposes which is rented to others. In many states, the liability coverage for such a rental property may be added to the liability portion of the Homeowners policy, but a separate fire policy must be purchased to protect the building and contents values. In determining the amount of insurance on an investment property, remember that the insurance may be written on an actual cash value basis. Market value may be different from replacement cost or actual cash value. Depending on the circumstances, an individual may want to have a building appraised to determine its present-day construction cost and value for insurance purposes.

Cost

Homeowners premiums reflect many factors, and, accordingly, rates can vary considerably. They can also vary among insurers, and so you may be able to save some money by shopping around a little for your Homeowners coverage.

Cost also depends on which Homeowners form you use. The following chart presents an example of the relative cost differentials among three Homeowners forms.

Homeowners 1	$97 annually
Homeowners 2	$141 annually
Homeowners 5	$272 annually

Homeowners policies usually have a $50 or $100 deductible. This may be a so-called "disappearing deductible" which diminishes as the size of a covered loss increases and eventually no longer applies when the loss equals a certain amount, such as $500. The acceptance of a deductible is made attractive by the reduction in premium.

AUTOMOBILE INSURANCE

Perhaps no product has been at once so creative and yet so destructive as the automobile. Modern society has been shaped by the influence of the automobile and along with it has evolved automobile insurance.

Coverage and Persons Insured

Automobile insurance policies typically provide coverage for your automobile liability, physical damage to the automobile, and related exposures, each of which can be further subdivided as follows.[4]

[4]Certain states have enacted so-called "no-fault" auto insurance statutes which remove at least some auto accidents from the realm of negligence liability. A discussion of these no-fault laws is beyond the scope of this chapter.

Part I   Liability

  Coverage A   Bodily Injury Liability

  Coverage B   Property Damage Liability

Part II   Expenses for Medical Services (Coverage C—Medical Payments)

Part III   Physical Damage

  Coverage D   Comprehensive

  Coverage E   Collision

  Coverage F   Towing and Labor Costs

Part IV   Protection Against Uninsured Motorists (Coverage G)

The insuring agreement of the automobile liability policy covers the insured's liability arising out of the ownership, maintenance, or use of *owned* and *nonowned* automobiles. Traditionally, this coverage has been written with "split limits"—that is, with separate limits applying to each person and each occurrence for bodily injury liability, regardless of the number of persons involved, and a further limit applying to each occurrence for property damage liability. Some sample limits for a Family Automobile Policy (FAP) are as follows:

$100,000 per person	Bodily Injury Liability
$300,000 per occurrence	Bodily Injury Liability
$50,000 per occurrence	Property Damage Liability
$5,000 per person	Medical Payments
$10,000 per person	Uninsured Motorists
$20,000 each accident	Uninsured Motorists

Actual Cash Value—Comprehensive
$100 deductible collision

Under the above limits, the policy would pay liability claims against the insured up to $100,000 for each person who suffers bodily injury, subject to an overall limit of $300,000 for all persons injured in any one occurrence. There is up to $50,000 of coverage for the insured's liability arising out of damage to the property of others in any one occurrence. The medical payments portion will pay up to $5,000 for medical expenses of each person, including the insured and any occupants of his or her auto, without regard to legal liability. Uninsured motorist coverage generally provides minimum limits (normally, state financial responsibility law limits) for bodily injury from uninsured and hit-and-run motorists. The remaining coverages refer to property insurance (technically called "physical damage" coverage) on the insured's own car. Comprehensive (sometimes referred to as "comprehensive, fire and theft") provides broad "all risks" coverage, except for collision, which is written as a separate coverage. Recovery is made on an actual cash value basis, and comprehensive may be written with a deductible. Collision is the last major coverage and also is written on an actual cash value basis with a deductible.

Under the Family Automobile Policy (FAP), the most common type of automobile policy, the following are considered to be persons insured:

1. With respect to the owned automobile,

   a. The named insured and any resident of the same household,

   b. Any other person using such automobile with the named insured's permission, and

   c. Any other person or organization, but only with respect to his, her, or its liability because of acts or omissions of an insured under (a) or (b) above.

2. With respect to a nonowned automobile,

   a. The named insured,

   b. Any relative, but only with respect to a private passenger auto or trailer, provided his or her operation or use of the nonowned auto is with the permission, or reasonably believed to be with the permission, of the owner, and

   c. Any other person or organization not owning or hiring the auto, but only with respect to his, her, or its liability because of acts or omissions of an insured under (a) or (b) above.

Accordingly, the named insured is covered by his or her FAP for anyone using his or her car, and further, if he or she, or any resident relative, borrows someone else's car. This can be summed up by saying that the insurance follows the named insured and the owned auto.

Here are some of the liability exclusions under the FAP. The policy does not apply:

1. To an auto while used as a public or livery conveyance (but this exclusion does not apply to car pools where the participants simply share expenses)

2. To any benefits payable under workmen's compensation laws

3. To property of the insured, or property rented to or in charge of the insured

Cost

The fact that automobile insurance often is costly is brought home to the consumer every time he or she gets a premium notice. Although it appears to be quite complex, the rating of automobile liability insurance generally is based upon four factors: (1) age of drivers, (2) use of the auto, (3) territory where the car is garaged, and (4) the operators' driving records.

Similarly, auto physical damage insurance rates generally are affected by two factors: (1) the cost (new) of the car, and (2) its age. Since comprehensive and collision coverages promise to pay for the repair costs of a damaged vehicle, it follows that a more expensive car will have a higher premium than a less expensive one. Additionally, as the years go by, the actual cash value of a car diminishes through depreciation, and so does the premium. However, at some point in the life of a car it normally is economical for the insured to consider dropping his or her collision (and perhaps comprehensive) coverage. The value left to insure simply is not worth even a reduced premium. This point is discussed further below.

The following table illustrates the additional cost associated with increasing the basic automobile liability limits of 10/20 and 5, assuming the basic bodily injury liability premium is $100 and the corresponding property damage liability premium is $20.

Bodily Injury Limits	Premium
$ 10/20	$100
25/50	119
50/100	130
100/300	141
Property Damage Limit	
5,000	20
10,000	21
25,000	22
50,000	23

It can be seen that the bulk of the premium is used to pay losses within the basic limits, and thus it costs very little to increase coverage to a more adequate level. In this regard, there is no simple formula to determine the "correct" limits of liability an insured should carry. The problem, however, often is solved by incurring the small cost differential for the higher limits.

The cost of automobile liability insurance can vary considerably among insurance companies for the same coverage in the same territory. In a recent study conducted by the New York State Insurance Department, it was shown that the basic rates for auto liability policies of different companies could vary by as much as 50 percent in certain territories of the state. *Thus, consumers can secure significant savings by shopping around for their automobile insurance.* Of course, premium cost is not the only factor that should be considered. Other important factors include: the service provided by the particular insurance agent or broker; insurer claims policies, underwriting and renewal policies, and financial strength; and any dividends that may be paid by some companies.

In the area of physical damage insurance, one major cost-cutting technique that often is not utilized fully is *the use of deductibles or higher deductibles.* For example, increasing a collision deductible from, say, $50 to

$100 may involve a premium saving of $25 to $30 per year, depending on the rating factors involved. Similar relative savings can be realized by writing comprehensive coverage subject to a deductible.

A question often asked is, "For how many years should I carry collision coverage?" The answer, of course, varies with the type of car, whether it is financed, the financial position of the consumer, his or her risk-taking philosophy, and the like. However, many consumers do not purchase collision coverage after an auto is, say, three to five years old.

Types of Policies

Up to this point, we have been talking about the Family Auto Policy (FAP). Most people have an FAP to cover their personal auto exposures. However, there are other automobile policies available, each serving its own purpose, that you should know about.

Special Package Automobile Policies (SPAP) are similar to the FAP but with a few restrictions on coverage. The insured also has less choice with respect to the coverages and policy limits, and the SPAP is written with a single (B.I. and P.D.) limit of liability per occurrence. To be eligible for these policies, the insured usually must be accident-free for a certain period, such as three years, prior to the inception of the policy. A reduced premium of 5 to 20 percent often is available for this policy. Thus, if you are eligible, you must decide whether the restrictions on coverage and reduction in flexibility are worth the savings in premium. Not all insurers offer the SPAP. A *Basic Automobile Form* is used to insure commercial vehicles as well as some private passenger automobiles. This form is limited in that it is basically designed to insure only automobiles described in the policy. A *Comprehensive Automobile Policy (CAP)* also may be used by businesses or individuals to cover their exposures arising out of the ownership, maintenance, or use of any automobile (owned or nonowned) that is not specifically excluded.

Most individuals and families, however, use the FAP, or perhaps an SPAP, to meet their automobile insurance needs.

OTHER PROPERTY AND LIABILITY INSURANCE POLICIES TO CONSIDER

We now have introduced the basic core of most people's property and liability insurance program—the Homeowners and automobile insurance policies. In keeping with our personal risk management approach, the next logical step is an analysis and evaluation of additional, but less frequent, risks of loss and the available methods for dealing with them.

Excess Liability

Less than a decade ago, the public began to read, with considerable interest, newspaper articles concerning jury awards of $1 million or more in some negligence liability cases. Professional men, businessmen, and other people of means (who would be "target risks" for liability claims) began to examine the extent of the liability protection afforded by their automobile and Home-owners policies. Also of importance were the claims which would not be covered under most standard policies. Thus, demands for higher liability limits and broader protection brought forth the personal "excess liability" (catastrophe liability) or "umbrella" contract, so called because, like an umbrella, it is designed to cover everything under it (but there are required underlying liability policies, such as automobile and Homeowners). Most policies are issued with a minimum limit of $1 million, but higher limits are available.

Personal excess policies now are issued by many insurers, but they are not standardized. Therefore, care must be taken when comparing the contracts of different companies. *Basically, the umbrella policy is designed to pay and defend liability claims after the limits of underlying liability policies are exhausted.* For example, John Doe is involved in an auto accident and as the result of his negligence Richard Roe is seriously injured. A jury finds John liable to Richard for damages of $500,000. John's automobile policy, written with bodily injury liability limits of $100,000/$300,000, pays its per-person limit of $100,000. Unfortunately for him, John remains personally liable for the remaining $400,000 of damages, unless he had the foresight to buy a personal umbrella policy that would pay this amount on his behalf. Similarly, an umbrella policy takes over and provides additional protection up to its limit after other forms of liability insurance are exhausted, such as the CPL or watercraft policies.

In response to the demand for broader coverage as well as higher limits, the personal excess liability contract is written on a basis similar to the "all risks" approach in property insurance. That is, all liability losses are included unless specifically excluded. Some of the important extensions of coverage are the following:

1. Liability loss to property of others in the insured's care, custody, or control (as mentioned above, this is excluded under the Homeowners liability coverage)

2. Worldwide coverage (no territorial restriction)

3. Coverage of "personal injury" claims, which might include libel, slander, false arrest, wrongful entry, invasion of privacy, and the like

These extensions, which normally are not covered by "underlying" liability policies, are subject to a deductible that ranges from $250 to $1,000.

Most people with any significant liability exposures, whether you think of yourself as "well off" or not, should consider buying personal excess liability insurance. While the likelihood of such a "jumbo" or catastrophe liability loss is quite small, if it did happen to you, it would destroy you financially. That is not a risk you can afford to take. Furthermore, the premium cost is relatively small. Also, the personal excess policy may require underlying liability insurance with lower limits of liability than you are now carrying. Thus, you may be able to reduce some of your present liability limits and save some premium dollars, which would reduce somewhat the cost of buying the personal excess policy.

Excess Major Medical[5]

Based upon the same "umbrella" concept, some insurers offer "excess major medical" coverage under their personal excess liability policies. Designed to take over when underlying major medical coverage is exhausted, this coverage usually has a $10,000 deductible and provides an additional $15,000 to $25,000 of medical expense protection for each person in the family.

Personal Combination Policies

A new development in property and liability coverages for the consumer is the introduction by a few insurance companies of personal combination policies. These policies basically involve the combination of personal automobile insurance, homeowners insurance, and various optional coverages (like personal catastrophe liability and medical expense) in one package policy. This packaging of these personal coverages can result in premium savings for the consumer. However, only a few insurers offer personal combination policies, and these package policies are not standardized.

Directors' and Officers' Liability

A trend by the courts to require additional responsibility of officers and directors of corporations (and other organizations) in conjunction with their duties therein has created a need for insurance to meet this risk. The Directors' and Officers' Liability (D & O) policy covers any "wrongful act," which generally is defined as a breach of duty, neglect, error, misstatement, misleading statement, or omission. This form of exposure to loss is quite new and few losses have been paid. However, as noted above for personal excess coverage, it is *the potential for catastrophic financial loss* that is important from the individual's viewpoint.

Workmen's Compensation

The states, the District of Columbia, and the federal government have workmen's compensation laws which set forth the benefits payable to employees who suffer on-the-job injuries. The relevance of this risk may seem somewhat remote from the realm of personal risk management, but certain states include domestic and/or casual employees under their Workmen's Compensation Act. Therefore, depending on your particular state law, you may need workmen's compensation insurance. Your insurance agent or broker can advise you on this.

---

[5]This major medical coverage really is a form of health insurance and is discussed in greater detail in Chapter 5.

Investment Properties

Investment properties you may own or manage present similar risks of loss, as does personally used property, and all the risk management steps taken in connection with the individual's own property can be applied successfully here. On the property side, insurance to value must be dealt with, and decisions must be made regarding type of policy, deductibles, and the like. Because Homeowners policies are limited to owner occupants, a commercial package policy or perhaps a fire policy with appropriate coverage extensions may be used to provide the necessary property protection. Similar considerations apply in the liability insurance area. A competent insurance agent or broker can be of great help to you in designing and placing the proper coverage for such commercial-type risks. In some cases, it may be valuable to retain an independent risk management consultant.

INSURANCE COMPANIES AND PREMIUMS

A common misconception is that most property and liability insurance companies are alike and that their rates for insurance are "about the same." This is not the case. Although rates are regulated, the *final cost to the consumer can vary considerably among insurers.* Therefore, you may save money on property and liability insurance by shopping for your coverage.

In this connection, you should understand two basic ideas—rate deviations and dividends. A "rate deviation" is a discount from the standard premium given in advance. For example, some insurers offer rate deviations on automobile insurance and/or Homeowners policies because of favorable loss experience, lower expenses, or both.

A "dividend," on the other hand, is a refund of premium usually paid by a mutual insurer at the end of the policy term. Some mutual insurers do not pay dividends but rather charge a lower initial premium, while others have traditionally paid a fairly constant percentage of the premium, ranging from 5 to 30 percent. These factors, of course, reflect only one element to be considered in selecting an insurer—cost.

Insurer Selection

Security, service, and cost are the three yardsticks against which insurers should be measured. These criteria for selecting an insurer were discussed in Chapter 3.

Types of Property and Liability Insurers

The debate concerning which type of insurer is best probably will continue as long as there are different types. No attempt is made here to evaluate the performance of each, but let us at least mention the different types. First, in terms of how they sell their products, property and liability insurers are (1) independent agency companies (distribution is made through independent insurance agents), (2) so-called exclusive agency companies (that distribute their products through agents representing only the one compnay), and (3) direct writers (distribution through company-employed salesmen or no salesmen). Additionally, insurers can be further subdivided on the basis of their organizational form (as described in Chapter 3) as stock insurers, mutual insurers, reciprocal exchanges, and so forth.

CONCLUSION

In this chapter, we have attempted to describe the basic elements of property and liability insurance as they apply to nonbusiness risks. In a somewhat oversimplified way, the technique that should be followed to formulate or evaluate a personal insurance program is as follows:

1. *Discover the risks.* Ask yourself the question, "What can possibly happen?" Look for loss-producing hazards. Analyze and evaluate each risk particularly from a potential loss severity standpoint.

2. *Determine which risk management method(s) should be used for each risk.* That is, determine which risks can be transferred and which should be retained. Plan and implement any possible loss prevention activities.

3. *Select the insurance policies and coverages you need.* Determine the coverages, amounts of insurance, and any endorsements needed to prevent gaps or overlaps in your insurance program.

   Also, consider ways to reduce your property and liability insurance premium costs by using or increasing deductibles, dropping marginal coverages, and the like.

4. *Obtain competitive quotations.* As we said before, too few consumers "shop" for their insurance. Having done so, select your insurer on the basis of coverage, service, and cost. Also keep in mind the quality of service you receive from your agent or broker in making your choice.

5. *Evaluate and update your program periodically.* Even a perfect program of insurance coverages can quickly become outdated, possibly causing disappointment at the time of a loss. At least a semiannual review of all your policies seems desirable.

With these basic steps, and a desire to control risk, you can be well on your way to protecting your personal financial security.

PART THREE
ACCUMULATING CAPITAL

7

BASIC INVESTMENT PRINCIPLES

A basic financial objective of many people is to accumulate capital. They want capital for emergencies, various family purposes, a general investment fund, or retirement needs.

You can acquire capital in a variety of ways. Probably the most common is through an excess of family income over family outgo. Other important sources of capital include inheritances; gifts; growth or liquidation of business interests; and receipt of distributions from pension, profit-sharing, and similar plans. Once you have acquired capital not needed for more or less immediate family expenditures, you need to consider how to invest your capital and make it grow.

YOUR BASIC INVESTMENT OBJECTIVE

Your basic investment objective is to *earn the maximum possible rate of return* on the funds you have to invest, *consistent with your objectives and the investment constraints under which you must operate.* This statement does not mean that rate of return (yield) is the only investment consideration. There are a number of factors, other than yield, to be considered in the choice of investments. However, it does mean that, after all these factors are taken into account, you want the highest rate of return you can get on the choices open to you. We saw in Chapter 2, for example, that even a 1- or 2-percentage-point difference in yield can result in a substantial difference in the amount of capital you can accumulate over a period of years.

FORMS OF INVESTMENT

The person with capital usually has a wide choice of investments open to him. In Chapter 2 we classified these forms of investment into fixed-dollar investments and variable-dollar investments, depending on whether the principal and/or income are guaranteed in advance.

Therefore, in this part of the book, Chapters 8, 9, and 10 deal largely with variable-dollar investments, including: common stock, mutual funds, real estate, other tax shelters, and other equity investments. Chapter 11 covers fixed-dollar investments, including: corporate bonds and preferred stock, United States government securities, municipal bonds, and other savings instruments.

INVESTMENT AND SPECULATION

At one time it was common to draw a rather sharp distinction between "investment" on the one hand and "speculation" on the other. For example, high-grade bonds were considered "investments" while common stocks were viewed as "speculative."

Now, however, such distinctions often are blurred. Good-grade common stocks generally are looked upon today as investment-grade securities. Also, many people today invest for capital gains as well as for dividends or interest income.

In general, however, the term "speculation" probably can be used to mean the purchase of securities or other assets where it is hoped that their fluctuations in value will produce relatively large profits over a comparatively short period of time. In other words, the "speculator" takes large risks in the hope of large gains.

Is speculation, as we just defined it, to be avoided by a prudent investor? The answer seems to be, It depends. It depends on such things as how much of your total investment portfolio you want to risk in speculation, what other kinds of assets you have to protect your family, how good you are at speculating, and whether you have the temperament to take speculative losses as well as speculative gains. Of course, you should expect a considerably higher rate of return on speculations than you can earn on more conservative investments to justify the greater risks inherent in speculation.

Thus, while speculation is not necessarily bad, and in fact some persons are successful speculators, it seems reasonable to say that most people are not really prepared to speculate successfully. They generally are much better off investing more conservatively for the long pull. However, this is a matter of individual choice, once you have considered the facts realistically.

FACTORS IN THE CHOICE OF YOUR INVESTMENTS

There are a number of factors or investment characteristics you may consider in choosing among different investments. Authorities differ somewhat on the exact number and what they are called, but the following commonly are included:

Security of principal and income

Rate of return (yield)

Marketability and liquidity

Diversification

Tax status

Size of investment units or denominations

Use as collateral for loans

Protection against creditor's claims

Callability

Freedom from care

Legality

Some of these clearly are more important than others, and their importance also varies among individual investors.

No single kind of investment is superior to all others in every one of these characteristics. In other words, there is no "perfect investment." Investments will be relatively strong in some of these characteristics but weak in others. For example, to earn a high rate of return, it is usually necessary to sacrifice security of principal and income (i.e., to take greater risk). Thus, when you consider any investment in relation to these factors, you should do it in terms of: (1) *your needs and objectives,* and (2) *the characteristics of alternative investments that are available to you.*

Security of Principal and Income

For many investors, security of principal and income is of paramount importance. They want to be able to "get their money back" or "not lose money" on their investments. This is perfectly natural.

But when you look at this factor more closely, a fundamental question arises: Do you mean "security" in terms of *dollars* or "security" in terms of *purchasing power?* In the best of all worlds, we all naturally would like both. In the real world, however, the decline in the purchasing power of the dollar, caused by inflation, has become a major consideration for investors in seeking security of principal and income.

Thus, when you analyze different investments in terms of security of principal and income, you really need to keep in mind four different types of risks to investment values. These are (1) financial risk, (2) market risk, (3) interest rate (money rate) risk, and (4) purchasing power risk.

Financial Risk. This risk arises because the issuers of investments may run into financial difficulties and not be able to live up to their promises or expectations. For example, a person who buys a corporate bond runs the financial risk that the issuing corporation will default on the periodic interest payments and/or the payment of the principal amount at maturity. The buyer of common stock runs the financial risk that the corporation will reduce or eliminate its regular dividend payments in the future. Consider, for example, the losses because of financial risk suffered by the stockholders and bondholders of the Penn Central Transportation Company when that giant corporation became insolvent.

Market Risk. This is the risk arising out of price fluctuations for a whole securities market, for an industrial group, or for an individual security, regardless of the financial ability of particular issuers to pay the promised or expected investment returns. Thus, an investor may buy the common stock of a company whose earnings and financial position are good (and perhaps even are improving), only to find that the market price of the stock is falling because the investor misjudged the timing of his or her purchases and the market in general is falling (i.e., it is a "bear" market). Of course, the price of a given stock may also fall because of financial risk or some combination of financial and market risks. But the point to remember is that even if an investor selects a high-quality stock that has prospects for good earnings growth (has low financial risk), the stock still may experience substantial price declines if the investor's market timing is bad.

Interest Rate Risk. This risk is a little complex and involves the price changes of *existing* investments because of changes in the general level of interest rates in the capital markets. In general, a *rise* in general market interest rates tends to cause a *decline* in market prices for existing securities, and, conversely, a *decline* in interest rates tends to cause an *increase* in market prices for existing securities. Thus, market prices for existing securities tend to move *inversely* with changes in the general level of interest rates.

It is not difficult to see why this is true. Assume, for example, that 10 years ago you purchased a newly issued, high-grade corporate bond with a 4 percent interest rate for $1,000 (at par). The bond was to come due (mature) in 30 years. Therefore, you receive interest of $40 per year from the bond. At the time you bought the bond (10 years ago), the prevailing level of interest rates in the capital markets for bonds of this type, grade, and duration was around 4 percent, otherwise this bond issue could not have been sold successfully to the public. But in the meantime the general level of interest rates in the capital markets for bonds of this type, grade, and remaining duration has risen, and now (10 years later) let us say the prevailing interest rate for comparable bonds with a 20-year duration is about 7 percent.

What effect does this have on your existing bond? First of all, the 4 percent interest rate on your bond does not change, because this is set by the terms of the bond you bought. So you still will get interest of $40 per year until the bond matures 20 years from now. Also, when the bond matures in 20 years, you will get the full $1,000 maturity value from the issuing corporation. Unfortunately, however, the current market price of your bond in the bond markets will have declined to somewhere in the vicinity of $680.[1] This is about what you would get if you sold it today. Why is this so if it's a $1,000 bond? Because at about this price the yield to maturity (in 20 years) of this bond would be 7 percent, and this is the prevailing market interest rate. Therefore, since we assume investors can buy newly issued bonds at around 7 percent, the prices of existing bonds carrying lower interest rates must decline in the market to the point where they will offer generally comparable yields to maturity for a buyer. When the market price of bonds declines in

[1]A bond table shows that a 20-year bond with a 4 percent coupon rate will yield 7 percent if it is priced at 67.97 ($679.70).

this manner below their maturity value, they are said to be selling "at a discount" and are called "discount bonds."

Now, what will happen if interest rates in the capital markets should decline? Assume, for example, that six months pass and during that time the prevailing interest rate in the capital markets for comparable bonds moves from 7 to 6.5 percent. This would mean that the current market price of your 4 percent bond would rise to somewhere around $725. Again, why? Because at about this price the yield to maturity (in 19$^{1}/_{2}$ years) of this bond would be 6.5 percent, and this is now the prevailing market interest rate.

The basic point here is that the market prices of existing bonds will fluctuate as the general level of interest rates changes so that their yields will be competitive with those of more recent issues.

We have illustrated the interest rate risk in terms of a 30-year corporate bond. Does the interest rate risk also apply to other types of securities? Yes; changes in the general level of interest rates in the economy have some influence on the prices of all securities. For example, when interest rates generally rise, bonds may become more attractive than common stocks for some investors, thus exerting a downward pressure on the stock market.

In general, prices of securities that are of high quality because of their low degree of financial risk tend to be the *most* affected by changes in interest rates. This is so because the financial risk factor has relatively little impact on their market prices. Thus, the interest rate risk for securities tends to vary *inversely* with their quality in terms of financial risk. High-grade securities (in financial risk), whose prices are affected mainly by changes in interest rates, often are called *money rate securities. High-grade bonds* normally fall in this category. However, the prices of other securities, such as *high-quality preferred stocks* and *certain types of common stocks (like high-grade utility and bank stocks)*, also are considerably influenced by changes in interest rates.

Purchasing Power Risk. This is uncertainty over the future purchasing power of the income and principal from an investment. The purchasing power of income and principal depends upon changes in the general price level in the economy. Generally, when prices rise, purchasing power declines, and when prices decline, purchasing power rises. Since around 1940, the United States has experienced a rather steady inflationary trend with a consequent consistent decline in the purchasing power of the dollar. This has made inflation, and hence purchasing power risk, a matter of great concern to investors.

The economic fact of persistent price inflation over the past 35 years has led many investors to seek investments that they believe will protect them against severe declines in purchasing power. Thus, investors seek investments whose principal and income they hope will increase during an inflationary period, so that the purchasing power of their investment dollars at least will not decline. Such investments are often called "hedges against inflation."

The purchasing power risk to investment values is a very real and important one, but the concept of some investments being good "hedges against inflation" must be considered with care. First, no investment is a perfect "hedge against inflation." That is, no investment currently available in the United States can be counted upon to fluctuate at all times so that its purchasing power will be maintained. Second, while some types of investments, such as common stocks, *may* increase in value (both market price and dividends) at the same time that the general price level is rising, there is no assurance that this will be true for an individual stock, or several stocks, or the stocks of a whole industry group. Third, no "sure" relationship has been proved between movements in consumer prices and movements in, say, common stock prices. The only thing that can be said is that economic studies have shown that over a long period of years, broad indexes of common stock prices have *tended* to move in the same general direction as consumer prices. There have been a number of times, however, during which common stock prices and consumer prices did *not* move together. Finally, *an investor's goal is not really to "hedge against inflation," but rather to obtain the best investment returns he can, consistent with his other objectives.* What is really important is whether an investment can be expected to produce an attractive rate of return relative to your other available investment opportunities.

It is true, however, that certain equity-type investments, like common stocks, real estate, business ventures, and commodities, *may* increase in value during an inflationary period and thus preserve the purchasing power of the returns from the investment. On the other hand, fixed-dollar-type investments, like bonds, savings accounts, savings bonds, and life insurance cash values, normally will not increase in value during an inflationary period. But in your investment decision making, you are probably better off to consider how you expect a given investment to perform in the future, what your other investment opportunities are, and what your investment needs are, rather than worrying about whether the investment is called a "hedge against inflation" or not.

Also, do not forget that while for the past 35 years consumer prices generally have been rising (inflation), it is also possible for them to decline (a deflation or depression). While fixed-dollar assets will *lose* purchasing power during an *inflationary period,* they will *gain* in purchasing power during a *deflationary period.* To some, this may seem academic in light of the inflationary trend we have had. However, *you should never ignore the possibility of a deflationary economic period in your personal financial planning.*

No one kind of investment can be considered "good" in terms of meeting all these investment risks. An investment may be "good" in avoiding one or more of these risks but will almost invariably be "poor" in meeting others. To illustrate this important idea, various types of investment media are graded on the following chart as "good," "average," and "poor" in terms of their ability to meet each of the four basic investment risks. Of course, any such classification is a matter of opinion to a certain degree, and all investment media obviously are not shown. However, what is important is the recognition that no single investment vehicle can be "good" in terms of avoiding all these investment risks. This clearly suggests *the need for diversification* in an investment portfolio.

CHART 7-1

CLASSIFICATION OF SELECTED INVESTMENT VEHICLES IN TERMS OF MEETING INVESTMENT RISKS

Investment Vehicle	Financial Risk	Market Risk	Interest Rate Risk	Purchasing Power Risk
Savings accounts (insured by FDIC or FSLIC)	Good	Good	Good	Poor
Life insurance policy cash values	Good	Good	Good	Poor
High-grade corporate bonds	Good	Good (or Average)	Poor	Poor
High-grade common stocks	Good	Poor (or Average)	Average	Good (or Average) (assuming a broadly diversified portfolio)
Speculative common stocks	Poor	Poor	Good	Average (or Good)

Rate of Return

The primary purpose of investing is to earn a return on your capital. This return can take a variety of forms, including: interest, dividends, rental income, and capital gains. Investors normally want to maximize *their total investment returns* (investment income and capital gains combined). But to increase your expected total investment return at any given time, you normally must take greater investment risks. Thus, yield and degree of investment risk are directly related—*the higher the yield, the greater the risk.* Unhappily, an investor cannot have his cake and eat it, too.

Since an investor wants to maximize total investment returns, it is important to know what those returns are. For this purpose, it is helpful to divide investment returns into investment income and capital gains. We should also distinguish between before-tax and after-tax returns.

Annual Rates of Return (Yield). There are several ways of measuring the annual rates of return represented by the periodic income from an investment. They include (1) the *nominal yield,* (2) the *current yield,* and (3) the *yield to maturity.*

Nominal yield. This is the annual amount of interest or dividends paid compared with a security's par or face value, shown as follows:

$$\text{Nominal yield} = \frac{\text{annual interest or dividends}}{\text{investment's par or face value}}$$

The nominal yield is often called the *coupon rate* when applied to bonds and the *dividend rate* when applied to preferred stocks with a par value. For example, a bond with a maturity value (face amount) of $1,000 that pays interest of $70 per year has a nominal yield (coupon rate) of 7 percent, and a $100 par value preferred stock that pays dividends of $6.50 per year has a nominal yield (dividend rate) of 6½ percent. Nominal yield really has no meaning in connection with common stocks and other forms of investment.

Current yield. This measure of investment return generally is more significant to an investor than the nominal yield, and the current yield normally is expressed as the annual amount of income received from an investment compared with its current market price or value. This is the measure of yield normally used for common and preferred stocks and frequently that used for bonds as well. It can be calculated as follows:

$$\text{Current yield} = \frac{\text{annual investment income}}{\text{investment's current price or value}}$$

An investment's current yield normally will change over time because its market price will fluctuate and its annual investment income may change.

As examples of current yield, a common stock selling at $50 per share with an annual dividend rate of $2.50 has a current yield of 5 percent, and a 6 percent bond that is selling for $800 (quoted as 80 in the bond markets) has a current yield of 7½ percent.[2]

Yield to maturity. Another measure of yield commonly applied to bonds is the yield to maturity, sometimes called the "net yield," "effective yield," or "true yield." Bonds have a definite maturity date when their par or face amount (usually $1,000 per bond) is to be paid off by the issuer. However, you can purchase bonds for less than their maturity value (at a discount) or for more than their maturity value (at a premium). Thus, in the calculation of the yield to maturity for a bond, the annual gain (discount) or loss (premium) of principal that will be realized if the bond is held to maturity is added to or deducted from the bond's annual interest income, and the result is divided by the average investment in the bond.

For bonds selling at a discount, the yield to maturity is greater than either the current yield or the coupon rate. For bonds selling at a premium, the opposite is true, and the yield to maturity is less than either the current yield or the coupon rate. Let us take some examples to illustrate this.

First, assume a 5 percent bond maturing in 10 years that currently is selling for $800. For this bond, the

---

[2]Annual bond interest of $60 ($1,000 maturity value × 6%) divided by $800 equals 0.075 (7½%).

Coupon rate   = 5%

Current yield   = 6.25%

Yield to maturity = 7.78%

On the other hand, assume a 9 percent bond maturing in 10 years that currently is selling for $1,100. For this bond, the

Coupon rate   = 9%

Current yield   = 8.18%

Yield to maturity = 7.62%

When a bond is selling at or near par, the coupon rate, current yield, and yield to maturity will be essentially the same. In most cases, when an investor plans to hold a bond until maturity, the yield to maturity is considered the most accurate measure of annual investment return.

The current yields for stocks and bonds often are shown in financial newspapers and similar sources. Also, bond yields to maturity for different coupon rates, bond prices, and remaining periods to maturity are available from "bond yield tables." In addition, investment houses supply information on the yields to maturity for bonds they may have for sale, and other financial publications may contain this information for the bonds whose prices they report.

Capital Gains Rates of Return. Many people invest for capital gains as well as regular annual income. Some people, in fact, are primarily interested in capital gains.

There may be good reasons for a policy of investing for capital gains. Capital gains are not taxed until actually realized. Even then, long-term capital gains receive favorable capital gains tax treatment (see Chapter 14). In addition, an individual may have adequate earnings or income from other sources and not need investment income currently.

But the rates of return from capital gains are difficult to measure. First, no one can know what, if any, capital gain there may be in the future on an investment. If the investment is successful, such a return can be very handsome. But if the investment turns sour, a loss may be suffered. Thus, you really can reason only from past experience with similar investments and from your or your investment advisor's analysis of future developments to estimate what your hoped-for capital gains might be.

Second, even measuring past capital gains rates of return can be difficult and confusing. You may hear a friend proudly remark, for example, "Boy, I really made a killing in the stock market. I bought XYZ Company at $20, and now it's worth $40 per share." But you do not know how long it took him to double his money, and this makes quite a difference. Also, you should compare such capital growth with, for example, what could have been earned, or can currently be earned, by simply putting your investment dollars in an insured savings account at compound interest, or by investing in corporate bonds or perhaps tax-free municipal bonds that involve less financial and market risk. Finally, remember that most investors suffer some capital losses as well as have capital gains. It sometimes is easy psychologically for an investor to remember successes but to forget losses when mentally calculating "how well he or she has done in the market."

One approach to measuring capital gains rates of return is to estimate an *average annual compound rate of gain* from capital gains for the period of time an investment has been held. Then, the *total annual investment return* may be determined by adding the yield from investment income to the rate of gain (or loss) from capital gains (or losses). You can estimate an approximate *average annual compound rate of gain* for a security that will be satisfactory for the purposes of most individual investors by referring to a compound interest table.[3] Thus, if you know *how much* an investment has grown over *how many years,* you can estimate roughly what the annual compound rate of gain (interest) has been over those years to produce the given capital growth. For example, let us say that your friend who bought XYZ Company common expands a little on his previous statement and tells you he bought the stock 10 years ago at $20 per share and now it is worth $40 per share. In other words, his capital growth has been 100 percent in 10 years, or his investment has doubled over this period. If we look at a compound interest table, we can see that your friend has had about a 7 percent average annual rate of capital gain from this particular stock over the 10 years. You may also be able to use the so-called "rule of 72" to estimate an average annual rate of gain. This is done by dividing the number of years it takes an investment to double in value into 72. The result (quotient) is approximately the annual rate of return over those years. In this situation, for example, 72 ÷ 10 = 7.2 percent per year.

If in addition, during this 10-year period, the current yield from the dividends paid on XYZ Company common has averaged, say, 2 percent, the *total annual investment return* on the stock for this time period would be about 9 percent. Of course, there is no assurance this return will be repeated in the future, but at least your friend should know how he has done in the past to help him make intelligent investment decisions for the future. He now would be in a much better position to compare this stock's total yield with that of alternative investments, such as bonds, savings accounts, and real estate.

After-tax Yields. Up to this point, we have not considered the effect of income taxes on investment returns. As a practical matter, however, investors want to know what their investment returns are after taxes. This is what they

---

[3]A compound interest table shows the amount $1 will accumulate to at various rates of interest over various time periods.

get to keep. Seeking this information complicates comparing investment yields because different kinds of investments are taxed in different ways and individual investors can be in widely varying income tax brackets. For purposes of estimating after-tax yields, we can view the returns from investments as: (1) income that is taxable as ordinary income, (2) income that is entirely tax-exempt, and (3) returns that are taxable as long-term capital gains.[4]

Investment income that is fully taxable as ordinary income, such as interest on savings accounts, interest on corporate bonds, and most of the dividends from common stocks, is easy to express on an after-tax basis. The *after-tax yield* can be determined by multiplying the current yield by 1 minus your highest income tax rate. Thus, if a married taxpayer's highest tax bracket is 25 percent (representing a taxable income from $12,000 to $16,-000), a savings account paying 5 percent interest would provide the following after-tax yield.

$$\begin{aligned} \text{After-tax yield} &= \text{current yield } (1 - \text{ tax rate}) \\ &= 0.05(1 - 0.25) \\ &= 0.05(0.75) \\ &= 0.0375 \text{ or } 3\tfrac{3}{4}\% \end{aligned}$$

The after-tax yield for a fully tax-exempt investment equals the current yield. Thus, the after-tax yield for a $4\frac{1}{2}$ percent municipal bond is $4\frac{1}{2}$ percent. It is common practice in investment literature also to express what a fully taxable security would have to earn to equal the yield from a tax-free security at various income tax rates. For example, a 5 percent tax-free yield received by a married investor in a 32 percent tax bracket (taxable income from $20,000 to $24,000) really is worth 7.36 percent to him or her on a fully taxable basis.[5] For a similar investor in a 50 percent bracket (taxable income from $44,000 to $52,000), the 5 percent tax-free yield would be worth 10 percent on a taxable basis.

It becomes more complicated to determine after-tax yields when investment returns are in the form of capital gains (or losses) or are partly ordinary income and partly capital gains (or losses). Some examples are when an investor purchases common stock that appreciates (or depreciates) in value, or a corporate or United States government bond at a discount and holds it until maturity. Basically, realized long-term capital gains generally are taxed at one-half the investor's ordinary income tax rate. However, the impact of capital gains taxation on investment decisions can be quite complex, depending on the circumstances, and this subject is covered in greater detail in Chapter 14.

---

[4]This is intentionally a somewhat simplified classification. See Chapter 14 for a discussion of the income taxation of different kinds of investments.

[5]You can calculate any similar equivalent yields by dividing the tax-free yield by 1 minus the investor's highest income tax rate. In this case, $5\% \div (1 - 0.32, \text{ or } 0.68) = 7.36\%$.

Marketability and Liquidity

These are important factors in choosing investments for many people. Life is uncertain and people want to know how readily they can dispose of their investments and how much they can get for them if they do.

Sometimes the terms "marketability" and "liquidity" are used to mean almost the same thing, but they do have an important difference in meaning. *Marketability* means the ability of an investor to find a ready market should he or she wish to sell or otherwise dispose of the investment. *Liquidity* means that an investment is not only marketable but also highly stable in price. In other words, an asset is liquid when an investor feels reasonably sure he or she can dispose of it quickly *and also* can receive for it approximately the amount put into it.

Some investments are neither marketable nor liquid, others are marketable but not very liquid, while still others are both marketable and liquid. In the following chart, various types of assets are graded for both marketability and liquidity. Of course, these classifications are again somewhat subjective, but they do give a general idea of the relative positions of these types of assets with respect to these investment characteristics. Naturally, the degree of marketability or liquidity of some of these assets depends on the particular circumstances.

CHART 7-2

CLASSIFICATION OF ASSETS IN TERMS OF
MARKETABILITY AND LIQUIDITY

Asset	Marketability	Liquidity
Savings accounts	Good	Good
Life insurance cash values	Good	Good
Corporate bonds (actively traded)	Good	Average
Municipal bonds (actively traded)	Good (or Average)	Average
U.S. government securities		
Short-term	Good	Good
Long-term	Good	Average
Savings bonds (e.g., Series E)	Good	Good
Common stock (actively traded)	Good	Poor
Real estate	Average (or Poor)	Poor
Business interests		
(proprietorships, partnerships, stock in close corporations, where there is no binding buy-sell agreement)	Poor	Poor

It is clearly preferable to hold highly marketable or liquid investments rather than less marketable or liquid ones. But you normally have to "trade" some yield for marketability and liquidity. That is, highly marketable or liquid assets usually yield less than less marketable or liquid ones. So you have to ask yourself, "Is marketability or liquidity important enough to give up some yield?" This, of course, depends basically upon your overall circumstances and objectives.

Diversification

Diversification is an important investment policy you should consider in constructing your investment portfolio. The basic purpose of diversification is to reduce or minimize an investor's risk of loss. It is primarily a defensive type of investment policy.

Diversification can take *several forms*. One is to *diversify an investment portfolio among the various types of investment media*—such as common stocks, bonds, savings accounts, and life insurance cash values. The prices or values of all types of investment media do not go up or down at the same time or in the same magnitude, and so you can protect yourself against economic fluctuations in this way.

A good example of this is the way the prices of common stocks and high-grade bonds typically have moved in opposite directions over the business cycle. During periods of economic prosperity the stock market generally rises because of increasing business and higher corporate profits and dividends. However, the prices of high-grade bonds often decline during prosperity because interest rates generally are rising (the interest rate risk) as the result of demands for capital at that time. During recession or depression, the opposite occurs: stock prices fall because of declining business, but high-grade bond prices tend to rise because of falling interest rates, because the demand for capital diminishes then. This is known as the *contracyclical price movement of high-grade bonds*.

You may also want to diversify among types of investment media to get balance in your portfolio between liquid and less liquid investments and between fixed-dollar and variable-dollar investments. It is normally considered sound practice to diversify your investments among several types of investment media.

Another form is *diversification within a particular class or type of investment*. For example, you may invest in the common stocks of several companies, may buy some "growth"-type stocks and some stocks to be held primarily for income, may purchase some "speculative" issues but generally invest in more stable stocks, and so on.

A third form is *diversification of investments according to maturity*. For securities with a fixed maturity date (like bonds or savings certificates), you can space the maturities so that you will have securities of various durations coming due periodically. This way you can have new principal to invest periodically, during periods of high and low interest rates, and thus reduce the interest rate risk. You may also want to buy other securities, like common stocks, from time to time rather than all at once, so that you can spread the market risk over both good and bad markets.

How can you get diversification in your investments? Here are several ways.

1. You can buy one or more securities periodically over a long period of time (for example, dollar cost averaging in buying common stocks, as discussed in Chapter 8).

2. You can invest through financial institutions that themselves diversify their investments. Such institutions include:

   a. Investment companies (including mutual funds)

   b. Life insurance companies, in connection with cash values, variable annuities, and the like

   c. Commercial banks, mutual savings banks, and savings and loan associations, in connection with savings accounts and savings certificates

   d. Real estate investment trusts (REITs)

3. You can set up a personal trust (or advisory account) with authority for the trustee to invest in a bank's common trust fund(s)

4. You can puchase participations in certain tax-sheltered investment ventures

Tax Status

As we saw above, an investment's tax status can have an important bearing on its attractiveness. But the investor's own tax bracket has an important bearing on this factor.

Size of Investment Units (or Denominations)

In some cases, you may be able to make an investment only in certain minimum amounts. For example, municipal bonds frequently are sold in lots of $5,000 or more, and participations in certain tax-sheltered investments often are limited to some minimum amount, like $5,000 or more. Also, direct investment in real estate requires a sizable down payment and payment of closing costs, as well as adequate mortgage financing. Normally, however, this is not a major factor in choosing an investment.

Use as Collateral for Loans

Many forms of property can be used as collateral for loans. Some kinds are more readily available than others, however. Life insurance policies, savings accounts, good-quality securities, and improved real estate may serve well in this regard. However, some types of property, like speculative common stocks, unimproved real estate, and closely held business interests, may be relatively poor for collateral purposes. Also, tax-free municipal bonds can involve tax pitfalls when used as collateral for loans, or even when they are owned and other property is used as collateral for loans, as is discussed in greater detail in Chapter 14.

Creditor Protection

Some assets can be arranged to provide their owners and/or their owners' heirs with protection against the claims of creditors in the event of bankruptcy or financial difficulties. So-called "spendthrift clauses" in life insurance settlement options and personal trust agreements are examples.

Callability

Callability (or redeemability) can be an important factor when investing in bonds and preferred stocks. Most issuers of corporate bonds reserve the right to call or redeem (i.e., pay off) the bonds before maturity, usually subject to certain conditions. Most issues of preferred stock also are callable. On the other hand, most United States government bonds and general-obligation municipal bonds are not callable prior to maturity.

Callable bonds and preferred stocks are usually redeemed by their issuers when market interest rates are below the coupon rates in the callable securities. The issuing corporation can then refinance the called securities in the capital market at the lower, prevailing interest rates and thus save money. But this is disadvantageous to the holder of the called securities. The holder has been deprived of a good investment, and now he or she can reinvest the principal from the redeemed securities in similar securities only at a lower yield. *Thus, other things being equal, securities that are not callable, or that have limited callability, are more attractive to investors than are callable securities.* But as is so often true, other things may not be equal because callable bonds and preferreds normally provide investors with higher yields than comparable noncallable securities.

What can you do to protect yourself against the threat of callability? Here are some ideas.

1. You can buy noncallable securities. However, as we saw above, most corporate bonds and preferreds are callable, and callable securities normally provide higher yields.

2. You can buy securities with strong "call protection."[6] However, you will probably have to pay a "price" in terms of lower yields for strong call protection.

3. You can buy bonds or preferreds selling at a "deep discount" from their maturity or par value. (See Chapter 11 for a discussion of "deep-discount" bonds.)

4. You may be able to diversify your purchases over time so that only a small portion of your portfolio will be called at any one time.

[6]The types of call protection used in bonds and preferred stocks are covered in Chapter 11.

Freedom from Care

This factor really has two dimensions: (1) freedom from the time and work involved in managing investments, and (2) freedom from worry and concern over investment results. These freedoms are quite important to some people but of little or no concern to others. Much depends upon your interests, financial position, experience, education, time available from business or professional pursuits, personal situation, and psychological makeup.

PERSONAL INVESTMENT MANAGEMENT

Having outlined some general factors you might consider in choosing investments, we now come to the overall question, How do you carry out your personal investment management? Your personal investment management can be broken down into the following fundamental areas: (1) considering your *investment constraints* or limitations, (2) defining your *investment objectives,* (3) establishing *investment policies* in light of your constraints and objectives, and (4) *implementing those policies.*

Investment Constraints

Every investor has certain personal factors that govern or limit how he or she should invest. As we said at the beginning of the chapter, the basic investment problem is to maximize your investment returns within the framework of these personal financial constraints. Here are some of the common investment constraints you might want to consider in the process of your personal investment management.

1. Your *ability to risk loss of investment income and principal.* This in turn is influenced by a number of personal factors, such as:

   a. Your earnings and the nature and stability of your employment

   b. Other sources of income

   c. Your age, health, family responsibilities, and other obligations

   d. Your overall assets, liabilities, and net worth position (your personal balance sheet)

   e. Whether you have closely held business interests or other relatively nonmarketable assets

   f. Any likely (or possible) inheritances

   g. Your plans to use investment principal for particular purposes, such as education expenses, retirement, future gifts, and estate settlement costs

   h. The extent to which you need your current investment income for your or your family's current living expenses

   i. The degree and duration of price inflation (or deflation) you feel are being risked, and how your other assets and sources of income will be affected by inflation (or deflation)

2. The *degree of liquidity and marketability* you need to maintain in your portfolio.

3. How well you are *able to weather the ups and particularly the downs in the securities markets.* In other words, can you afford to hold on to your securities during a bear market and wait for better times?

4. Your *overall tax and estate status,* including consideration of your income and estate tax positions.

5. The *quality of investment management services* available to you.

6. Your *attitudes and emotional tolerance for risk.*

Investment Objectives

Making investment decisions without defining your objectives is like trying to steer a ship without a rudder. You probably will not make consistent investment decisions without clearly understanding your investment objectives. While this seems obvious, many investors, in fact, make their investment decisions on such tenuous grounds as, "A golfing buddy told me confidentially that this stock is bound to 'go,'" or "A broker called me and told me I should get in on this one," or "This stock just looks good," without any consistent idea of their objectives in mind. Of course, your investment objectives are just one part of your overall financial objectives.

Investment objectives are shaped by a person's investment constraints and are influenced by many personal factors that vary among individuals and families. Further, a person's investment objectives normally change over his or her life cycle and as circumstances change. There are, however, certain common patterns of investment objectives into which people frequently fall. The following can be listed as typical of these.

Maximum Current Income. This objective emphasizes current yield over other factors. It is typical of people who must rely on investment income for part or all of their livelihood, such as retired persons.

Average Current Income with Moderate Capital Growth. This modifies the previous objective in that current investment income is not the predominate aim. While current income is important, capital gains also are sought.

Long-term Capital Growth. This objective aims primarily at capital gains over a relatively long period of time. It implies investment in securities that are expected to produce relatively consistent capital growth over the long pull. This kind of objective is typical of younger business and professional men and women who do not need current investment income to meet their living expenses, and who perhaps do not plan to spend a great deal of time and effort in investment analysis.

Aggressive Capital Growth. This objective seeks maximum capital growth and implies making riskier investments with considerable investment analysis and management. Current income is of minor importance.

Tax-Sheltered Investments. In some cases, a person's high income tax bracket makes tax-free or tax-sheltered investments very attractive. For the same reason, these persons may also seek their investment returns in the form of long-term capital gains rather than ordinary income.

These objectives are, of course, not mutually exclusive, and an investor often will have some combination of them. The investor might, for example, seek relatively conservative long-term capital growth for the bulk of his or her securities portfolio but hold another portion for more aggressive capital growth. Or, an investor in a high income tax bracket may place, say, one-half of his or her portfolio in municipal bonds or tax-sheltered investments and the other half in growth-type securities. There are many possible combinations depending upon individual circumstances. What is important, however, is for you to understand what your objectives are and to follow them.

Investment Policies

You should establish your investment policies to meet your objectives within the framework of your investment constraints. But in setting your investment policies, you might consider the following kinds of questions:

1. To what extent should I follow *aggressive* or follow *defensive* investment policies?

2. How much liquidity (and marketability) should I build into my program?

3. To what extent, and in what manner, should I *diversify* my investments?

4. What *kinds and grades* of securities should I include in my portfolio?

5. How should I react to changing market prices of securities? That is, what should my policy be with respect to *investment timing*?

Aggressive versus Defensive Investment Policies. There are investment risks (financial, interest rate, market, or purchasing power) inherent in any kind of investment policy, but some approaches or attitudes toward investment policy clearly imply more risk taking than others. Thus, we can broadly categorize investment policies as being aggressive or defensive in nature. *Aggressive policies* generally seek to maximize investment profits and, thus, accept above-average investment risks. On the other hand, *defensive policies* seek to minimize investment risks and, thus, accept correspondingly lower profits.

In general terms, you can distinguish between aggressive and defensive investment policies on the basis of the following characteristics.

Quality of securities purchased. To maximize returns, an aggressive portfolio includes securities of greater financial risk than would be true of a defensive portfolio. Thus, the aggressive investor is willing to take more financial risk.

Attitude toward investment timing. Again, to earn maximum returns, an aggressive investor tries to make profits by timing purchases and sales of securities according to his or her views on how the market will go. He or she tries to predict market movements and profit from them. A defensive investor, on the other hand, tends to use more or less automatic methods of timing purchases and sales, such as formula plans, and usually does not try to "outguess the market."

Frequency of investment transactions. An aggressive investor tends to buy and sell more frequently, while his defensive counterpart tends to follow a "buy and hold" policy. The aggressive investor wants to hold a security only during periods of rapid appreciation in its price.

Variety of investment vehicles used. In the search for greater profits from available investment capital, an aggressive investor may use many techniques and investment media, such as stock warrants, puts and calls, and short sales, that are not commonly used in more defensive portfolios.

Use of credit. An aggressive investment policy may involve borrowing, such as purchases of stock on margin, to increase the profit potential from available investment funds. A defensive policy generally does not contemplate the use of credit in this way. In other words, an aggressive policy tends to be highly leveraged.

Attitude toward diversification. An aggressive policy normally *concentrates* its purchases in a relatively small number of securities at any given time to maximize the investor's (or his advisor's) skill at selection and, hence, to maximize the profit from good selections. Risk is increased, however, because this approach loses the advantages of diversification.

Probably few people consistently follow only aggressive policies or only defensive policies in all respects. In fact, they employ some combination of the two; however, investors with medium-sized or smaller portfolios probably tend more toward defensive-type policies in general.

Liquidity and Marketability. The degree of liquidity you need in your portfolio is an important investment constraint. The following are some personal factors that can affect this decision:

1. The nature and immediacy of your financial obligations
2. The nature of your other assets
3. Your age and the potential liquidity needs of your estate
4. What credit facilities may be available to you
5. Availability of adequate health insurance and other insurance coverages to meet emergencies

Setting the proper degree of liquidity in a portfolio is largely a matter of judgment. It can be done by deciding to hold a certain number of dollars, say $4,000, in liquid assets; or to hold a certain percentage of assets, say 10 percent, in liquid form; or to hold some combination of the two, such as 10 percent of assets but no more than $10,000, in liquid form.

Diversification. Your policy here depends partly on whether you want to follow a more defensive or aggressive policy at a particular time. Diversification is basically a defensive policy.

The opposite of diversification is a policy of concentration. As we said above, *concentration* involves investing in only a few issues at any one time in hope of higher profit. People really are speaking of a policy of concentration (usually without using that term) when they say, "If I had put my money in Xerox 20 years ago, I'd be rich today." That probably is true. On the other hand, if they had put the bulk of their assets in Penn-Central stock, they would be far from rich today. The problem in applying a policy of concentration is to find the *next* Xerox *now*.

Composition of the Portfolio. This policy issue comes down to the question of what kinds and grades of investments you should include in your portfolio. It is the "$64,000 question."

The composition of an investment portfolio should, of course, be based on your investment objectives and constraints. It also depends on existing yield differentials among different kinds of securities in the market at a given time. Current economic conditions also are very important. You normally would not invest in common stocks at the start of a recession or depression, for example.

One common way to define the composition of a portfolio is in terms of the proportions or percentages that various assets or types of assets represent in the total portfolio. This is frequently done in terms of percentages of securities with different characteristics. For example, one such classification of securities might be:

1. Fixed-income securities
   a. Corporate bonds
   b. Municipal bonds
   c. United States government securities
   d. Other fixed-income securities
2. Convertible bonds and preferred stocks
3. Common stocks in mature companies
   a. Growth stocks
   b. Cyclical stocks
   c. Defensive stocks
4. Stocks in special situations and small growth companies

The idea behind any such classification is to help construct a portfolio of different types and grades of securities that can reflect your investment objectives. Naturally, a portfolio normally should change over time and with market conditions.

Two other ways in which you can subdivide your investment portfolio for purposes of analysis are according to:

1. The percentage of liquid assets to total assets
2. The percentage of fixed-dollar-type assets and variable-dollar-type assets

Investment Timing. As we saw before, an aggressive investment policy aims at making profits by successfully forecasting future price changes of securities and buying and selling accordingly. A defensive policy involves buying and selling from time to time without consciously trying to forecast how securities prices will change in the future.

There are a variety of *techniques or plans an investor can use in applying a defensive policy with respect to investment timing.* Among them are the following:

1. Dollar cost averaging. This is one of the best-known and most widely used defensive policies toward price changes. It is an application of time diversification and can be briefly defined as a policy of periodically investing equal dollar amounts in securities, usually common stocks.[7]

2. Formula plans. There are a variety of so-called "formula plans" for the timing of investment purchases and sales. Some of the more common are: (1) constant-ratio plans, (2) variable-ratio plans, and (3) norm-type plans. In general, they all attempt automatically, through a formula, to time purchases when stock prices are low and sales when stock prices are high.

3. Buying and holding a well-diversified group of common stocks for long-term investment. This can be characterized as a "buy and hold" or "sock 'em away" approach. It assumes that a policy of investing in a diversified list of common stocks of the more successful, leading companies in a number of major industries, purchased over a period of years, and held for the long pull, will provide a satisfactory rate of return when compared with other investments. This is a very defensive approach to common stock investment.

4. Buying and holding growth stocks. This has been a popular policy, but it assumes that an investor will be able to identify and purchase the "growth stocks" of the future. These, of course, may not be the same as the growth stocks of the past.

There are also a number of *techniques used by investors who want to follow an aggressive policy with regard to investment timing.* Many of these are aimed basically at forecasting cyclical swings in the stock market. There are many such techniques used, but they generally fall into three main classifications.

1. Forecasting overall stock prices by forecasting cyclical fluctuations in business activity (forecasting the business cycle). This is a common approach, but it obviously relies on predicting—or, at least, following others who predict—changes in the business cycle. This is no small feat, even for trained econo-

[7]Dollar cost averaging as applied to common stocks is discussed in Chapter 8.

mists. Also, while there clearly is a positive correlation between stock prices and business activity, they are not perfectly related. For example, overall cyclical changes in stock prices generally precede—or "lead," as economists would say—changes in the business cycle.

2. Forecasting overall stock prices by use of monetary statistics. This approach seeks to forecast stock prices by studying changes in the money supply (or "liquidity") in the economy. The theory is that when the money supply expands, stock prices (and business activity generally) will rise, and when the money supply contracts, so will stock prices.

3. Forecasting overall stock prices by use of the statistics of the stock market itself. The theory here is that basic patterns exist in the stock market which tend to repeat themselves. Therefore, if students of the market can determine what these patterns are, their fortunes will be made. Those who follow this general approach are called "chartists" or "technicians" in the securities industry.

There are a great many of these so-called "technical" methods for predicting stock price movements. However, some of the more widely known are:

1. The Dow Theory

2. Advance-decline series

3. Odd-lot studies

4. Volume studies

5. Breadth-of-market studies

6. Data on the market's short position[8]

Objective studies have not shown that any of the many technical methods for predicting stock market behavior can be completely relied upon. However, many market analysts believe such technical data are valuable as indicators of stock market behavior when used with each other and with other basic economic data.

Unhappily, none of the techniques or methods for investment timing is sure to yield the desired results. They can, of course, give clues to changes in the investment climate; however, that indescribable, undefinable factor called "judgment on the part of the investor" remains the key to successful investment timing.

Implementation of Policies

The final step in personal investment management is the implementation of your plan by selecting and purchasing the appropriate securities and making whatever changes are necessary in your portfolio from time to time. The selection and purchasing of specific securities will be discussed further in the following chapters.

[8]Detailed descriptions of the reasoning behind the techniques used in these methods are beyond the scope of this book. You can find such descriptions in most standard books on investments.

8
COMMON STOCK

Once you have adequate insurance protection and an appropriate emergency fund, you may be ready to think about establishing an investment program for any discretionary income and for capital you may have from other sources. As we said before, when such a point is reached, you are confronted with a number of possible investment outlets. This chapter concentrates on investments in common stocks; later chapters focus on other types of investment media.

INVESTMENT CHARACTERISTICS OF COMMON STOCKS

To develop a sound investment policy, it is necessary to understand the fundamental characteristics of common stocks. "Common stock" may be generally defined as the residual ownership of a corporation that is entitled to all assets and earnings after other claims have been paid and that has basic voting control. In short, common stock is the fundamental ownership equity. Common stockholders bear the main burden of the risks in a business enterprise and also receive the lion's share of any success.

The selection of common stock investments requires care and competence, but a careful investor should not fear investing in common stocks. In fact, many people may need stocks to have a balanced investment program. Therefore, you should either learn to select common stocks yourself or accept the alternative of placing that function in the hands of a professional investment advisor.

THE ARITHMETIC OF COMMON STOCKS

Once you decide to allocate part of your investment fund to common stock investments, you need to understand the "arithmetic of common stocks" in order to evaluate a particular stock or stocks. Four basic calculations may serve as convenient preliminary indicators of the worth of a common stock. These are (1) earnings per share, (2) net asset value per share, (3) price-earnings ratio, and (4) yield. These indicators, along with your general knowledge of the industry and company, should give you sufficient background information for you to know whether further investigation of the particular stock is warranted.

Earnings per Share

Since common stock is the residual claimant to the earnings of a corporation, it usually is possible to compute its earnings per share by taking net corporate profits after taxes, subtracting any preferred dividends, and dividing the remainder by the number of common shares outstanding. This may be illustrated by the following example: In its most recent fiscal year, the XYZ Company had a profit of $1,600,000 after deduction of expenses, interest, and taxes. Preferred dividend requirements for the year were $200,000. The remaining $1,400,000 amounted to $2 per share on the 700,000 shares outstanding ($1,400,000 ÷ 700,000 = $2). Earnings per share are computed in the same way for quarterly or semiannual periods when the data are available. Nonrecurring items contained in current income are generally excluded when computing earnings per share. Decisions based on trends or growth rates of earnings per share would otherwise be misleading.[1]

Investors generally place great emphasis upon earnings per share and the *trend* of earnings per share in evaluating common stocks. It can be argued that both present and future dividends are dependent upon earnings and that a stock's market price ultimately tends to keep pace with the growth (or decline) of its earnings per share.

Net Asset Value per Share

The net asset value per share, commonly referred to as the *book value* per share, attempts to measure the amount of assets a corporation has working for each share of common stock. It is arrived at by taking the net balance sheet value of the corporate assets, subtracting the face value of creditors' and preferred stockholders' claims, and dividing the remainder by the number of outstanding common shares. For example, the XYZ Company at the end of its last fiscal year had total net assets of $33 million and debts and preferred stock totaling $12 million. The remaining $21 million indicated a net asset value of $30 for each of its 700,000 common shares.

For businesses whose assets are a good measure of earning power, net asset value per share may be significant for investment purposes. However, it must be noted that corporate book values usually are based on cost, not earning power, and intangible assets not on the books may be more significant than book value in determining earning power.

In most cases, the net asset value per share of a common stock is of much less importance than the ability of those assets to generate a stream of

---

[1]Two earnings-per-share figures are sometimes reported. One is based on the number of common shares outstanding (as in the XYZ Company example above), and the other is adjusted to reflect potential dilution from warrants, convertible securities, stock options, and the like.

earnings. The market value of the common stock of so-called "growth companies" frequently will be many times the net asset value per share. On the other hand, for firms in a stagnant or declining industry, market value may be much less than net asset value. In some cases, the book value of a firm's assets might reasonably approximate their market or liquidating value. In such cases, the net asset value may keep the price of the firm's stock at a higher level than might be justified by the firm's earning potential. On the whole, however, net asset value per share for a publicly held corporation is not a very useful measure for evaluating the investment merits of its common stock.

Price-Earnings Ratio

The price-earnings (P/E) ratio of a common stock is simply the market price of the stock divided by the current per-share earnings of the corporation. Thus, if XYZ Company common stock sold for $40 per share at a time when its annual earnings amounted to $2 per share, its P/E ratio would be 20 ($40 ÷ $2).

The price-earnings ratio is a conventional and highly regarded measure of stock value because it gives an indication of stock prices measured against the earning power of the stock. A high P/E ratio normally can be justified only if the company's earnings are expected to grow. Thus, a high multiple for a stock normally indicates that the stock market expects the stock's future earnings to be higher than its current earnings.

An investor may find a review of the past price-earnings ratios of a stock a helpful means for estimating its current value relative to the past. Assume, for example, that over a 10-year period, XYZ Company common stock has shown consistent growth in earnings per share and market price, and that its P/E ratios have ranged from the low 20's on the low side to the 30's and even low 40's on the high side. Therefore, since this stock currently is selling for $40, and the annual earnings per share for the latest year are $2, a potential investor would know that the stock now is selling for a price-earnings ratio (20) that is historically low and thus *might* be a "good buy" at this time. On the other hand, if XYZ common currently were selling for $76, its P/E ratio (38) would be on the high side historically.[2] Of course, you must consider other factors about the stock in making your final decision. You also must evaluate the stock's current P/E ratio in light of present economic and stock market conditions and what you expect those conditions to be in the future.

However, the P/E ratios for stocks of small or speculative companies, or of companies with erratic earnings records, often do not provide dependable data upon which to base valuation estimates.

[2]Historical data on price-earnings ratios for common stocks are readily available to investors. For example, the Standard and Poor's Corporation *Standard Stock Reports* give this information for many stocks.

The financial sections of newspapers and financial periodicals often indicate the P/E ratios of the stocks whose prices they report.

Yield

As we saw in Chapter 7, the *yield for common stocks* typically refers to the percentage that the annual cash dividend bears to the current market price of the stock (i.e., the current yield). Thus, if XYZ Company common stock pays dividends at the rate of $1 per annum and sells for $40, the dividend yield is 2.5 percent.

The yield can be an indicator of the reasonableness of a stock's market price. This can be particularly true if the dividend used is a normal prospective annual rate and the company is expected to have stable, rather than rapidly increasing, decreasing, or erratic earnings. The stocks of many utilities may be good examples of stocks that might be appropriate for this kind of evaluation. As in the case of price-earnings ratios, the principal purpose in studying dividend yield history is to obtain a basis for stock valuation. If the dividend to be paid by a stock is reasonably certain, and if a "normal" yield that investors generally expect to receive on stocks of its type can be determined, an evaluation can be made on this basis. If, for example, a stable utility pays a $1.80-per-share annual dividend, and if a stock of this quality normally might yield about 7 percent, dividing $1.80 by 0.07 results in a valuation estimate of around $26 per share. If, however, this utility is selling for $30 per share, the current yield would be 6 percent, and an investor may feel this is too low in terms of the yield expectations for a stable utility. Naturally, the yields investors expect from different kinds of securities change as economic conditions change.

INFORMATION ABOUT COMMON STOCKS

Once a decision to invest in common stocks has been made, an investor is ready to acquire information about industries and companies that may be of investment interest. There are many potential sources of information about common stocks. Only the more common are discussed here.

One of the first sources is the financial pages of a good newspaper. In a newspaper can be found the stock tables, where daily price changes are reported. For example, on a particular day, here is how the record for the common stock of a hypothetical firm called "Typical Manufacturing Company" might appear in the New York Stock Exchange tables:

197-		Stock and Div.		Sales					
High	Low	in Dollars	P/E	in 100s	Open	High	Low	Close	Net Chg.
32¼	20¾	Typ Mfg. 1.20	13	29	25¼	26	25	25½	+½

Reading from left to right, this shows that the price range for Typical Manufacturing common on the New York Stock Exchange during the current year has been from a low of $20\frac{3}{4}$ ($20.75) to a high of $32\frac{1}{4}$ ($32.25). The stock currently is paying an annual dividend rate of $1.20 per share, has a price-earnings ratio (P/E) of 13, and 2,900 shares were bought and sold during the day in question. The first sale of the day was at $25\frac{1}{4}$ ($25.25) a share; the highest price for the day was 26; the lowest was 25; and the last sale for the day was at $25\frac{1}{2}$, half a point (50 cents a share) above the previous closing price (which must have been 25).

There are several stock market barometers (market averages) you might find useful. The best-known probably are the Dow Jones Stock Averages, Standard & Poor's 500-Stock Index, and the New York Times Index. The Dow Jones consists of four averages: (1) 30 industrials, (2) 20 transportation, (3) 15 utilities, and (4) a composite of the 65 stocks. The Dow Jones Industrial Average (DJIA) probably is the most widely followed of the four and is the one usually referred to in summaries of daily stock market activity.

There are a number of financial newspapers and periodicals carrying news of interest to investors and prospective investors. Some of these are: *The Wall Street Journal, Barron's, Financial Daily, Commercial and Financial Chronicle, Standard & Poor's Outlook, Forbes,* and *The Magazine of Wall Street,* plus such business news magazines as *Fortune, Business Week,* and *Nation's Business.* In addition, daily newspapers usually have a financial section for reporting such news. Investors also may subscribe to many different investment advisory newsletters and technical charting services of varying quality and price.

These sources are useful for obtaining current information on developments in the economy and the stock market and for individual industries and companies. If you want to know more than can be gained from reading these sources, you can simply write to any company that interests you and ask for a copy of its latest annual report, from which you can learn much about that company's financial situation.

Another way of getting information on a specific company is to look it up in one of the two major reference works of financial information, *Standard & Poor's* or *Moody's.* One of these services is almost certain to be available in any large library or through banks or stockbrokers.

Another important source of information on common stocks is from stockbrokers. Brokers are not infallible, of course, but most of them make a point of being well informed and of making their information available for the benefit of investors and prospective investors. Depending upon their investment research facilities, brokerage houses frequently have reports containing brief summaries of pertinent investment information on a great many companies. Some brokerage houses issue periodic reports that analyze the effect of current and anticipated developments on individual securities, companies, and industries. Brokers may also maintain lists of "recommended" stocks for various investment objectives. These lists are constantly revised on the basis of current developments. Again, depending upon the extent and quality of a broker's research facilities, such lists can be helpful to you in selecting industries and stocks to consider for investment.

THE INVESTMENT PROCESS

So far, we have touched on some basic essentials of common stock investment. But there still remains the important problem of selecting appropriate stocks for investment.

Investing is an art, not a science. Many helpful tools and techniques are available to help analyze a particular stock, but no one can say that, given a certain set of conditions, such-and-such will happen in the stock market. What will happen depends at least partially on human nature, and nothing is less predictable. Stock prices are subject to constant change, and a stock is worth only what somebody is willing to pay for it at a given time. "Buy low and sell high" certainly is good advice, but so far no one has been able to devise a way of determining exactly where the high and low will be. Money is not made through hindsight. Successful investing in common stocks cannot intelligently be based on hunch, hope, or hearsay; it must be founded on a study of the particular company and industry involved.

The first step in choosing a stock is evaluating the industry. The following are some of the important questions you should consider in evaluating different industries:

1. Does the industry provide products or services widely used and needed and for which the demand is substantial or the growth steady?

2. Is the industry cyclical, i.e., subject to major ups and downs, or is it relatively stable?

3. Is the industry likely to be adversely affected by new developments or technological changes? For example, is its source of raw materials in an area where crises are frequent or is it strongly subject to government orders?

4. What is the industry's labor situation?

5. Is the use of the industry's products growing rapidly (i.e., is it a "growth" industry), growing at a more stable rate, or perhaps declining relative to other industries?

6. Is the industry dependent largely on one or a few products, or is it diversified?

After answers to such questions have been secured, the competitive positions of the various companies within the industry can be analyzed. In doing this, the investment analyst must consider such questions as:

1. What is the company's relative position in its industry?

2. Is this position improving, stable, or declining?

3. How good does the company's management appear to be?

4. Does the company seem to work hard to expand its market and grow?

The answers to these and other pertinent questions about the company's fundamental position will help the analyst to *estimate the company's future earning power, and that is the key to its quality as an investment.* The size of a company, in itself, is not necessarily a major consideration, but many investors tend to buy securities of large, well-known companies.

As a practical matter, it is difficult, if not impossible, for most individual investors personally to research and analyze such factors as industry characteristics, competitive positions of companies, and the fundamental position of any given company. However, various professional investment concerns, stockbrokers, and investment advisors are in a position to do such research, and this type of investigation frequently is readily available to individual investors. An investor normally should make it a practice not to buy a stock unless he has determined its fundamental business position from such sources or perhaps from his own personal research.

One of the advantages of owning securities in companies listed on one of the major stock exchanges is that information about them is readily available. Another is that such listed stocks generally can be sold without difficulty whenever you wish (they are marketable). On the other hand, there are likely to be some attractive investment opportunities—particularly if you are searching for growth stocks—in companies whose stocks are traded over the counter. Also, some other types of stocks, like those of banks and insurance companies, frequently are traded over the counter.

As we saw before, most experienced investors like to know the price-earnings ratio for a stock before they invest. Price-earnings (P/E) ratios vary from industry to industry and from company to company within an industry. The P/E ratio for a particular stock also will vary as the economic outlook for the company, industry, or the whole economy is favorable or unfavorable. And, of course, the ratio is higher for a "growth stock" than for others. By and large, however, if a stock is selling at a ratio very much higher or very much lower than the average for the stocks of other companies in the same industry, it is wise for the investor to find out why before making an investment.

SHOULD YOU DIVERSIFY, AND HOW MUCH?

Most people who have contemplated investment have heard about common stock diversification, and some people have interpreted it to mean "buy a little of everything." But diversification can be misunderstood and sometimes can be more harmful than helpful.

As we saw in Chapter 7, diversification is a sound investment principle designed to minimize the risks of investing by dividing your holdings among various industries and companies, as well as among different kinds of securities or other investments. However, investment diversification in common stocks does not mean that if you are investing, say, $10,000, you should try to split it too many ways and arbitrarily buy stock in, say, 40 different companies. Regardless of the size of your investment portfolio, you should not own stock in more companies than you or your investment advisor can keep track of. In fact, some studies of diversification have shown that after a certain point, more diversification provides very little spreading of risk. It probably would be more sensible to put the $10,000 investment fund into, say, five to ten stocks.

As we noted in the previous chapter, concentration is the opposite of diversification. Concentration is typical of a more aggressive type of investment policy, while diversification represents a more defensive approach to investments. For most investors, however, a reasonable program of investment diversification probably is superior to alternative investment strategies.

PERIODIC REVIEW

You should reexamine your investment situation periodically and adjust your commitments accordingly. Also, any major change in your personal or family status or in the general economic situation may call for a review of your whole financial plan, including your common stock investments.

WHEN TO SELL?

Although most of the emphasis usually expressed over the last 20 or so years concerning common stock investment has been on buying, the question of when to sell can be equally important. If the 1970s are becoming known as a decade of change, the investor should be aware of what these changes, whatever they are, can do to his stocks.

There are many *reasons for selling stocks*. Obviously, one is the *need for money* for a variety of reasons. If an investor has to sell when the price of a stock is down, he may be forced to take a loss. That is why people are urged to invest in common stocks only if they have surplus cash beyond the needs of their daily life. You should not run the risk of having to sell at a bad time to meet other obligations.

Another reason for selling is to *take a profit* (or reduce a loss) when an individual thinks a stock has reached its upper limit. Or, one may sell when he believes his *money can earn a higher rate of return if invested elsewhere.* Remember, though, that it may be to your advantage to hold a profitable stock for more than six months so that the gain may be taxable as a long-term capital gain—unless there are compelling reasons for selling earlier. (See Chapter 14 for more on the effect of capital gains taxation on your investment decisions.)

Still another reason for selling a stock is to get rid of it if its *performance has not been up to expectations* and if it gives no sign of improving in the future. In general, it is unwise to stay with an unprofitable stock for too long. It normally is better to take a small loss now and make a change to something better.

You should not "have a love affair" with a stock. Do not consider any investment decision permanent or irrevocable. Keep track of the current performance of your stocks and change your investment program as conditions and prices dictate. And, as a rule of thumb, whenever the price of any security you own is so high that you would not consider it a good buy now, consider selling the security.

On the other hand, do not panic into selling without good reason. If you have invested with care and for the long term, do not let every change in the price of your stocks be a signal for gaiety or gloom. Remember that the nature of the stock market is fluctuation.

DOLLAR COST AVERAGING

One widely used timing technique for long-term investing is dollar cost averaging. "Dollar cost averaging" is the investment of a certain sum of money in the same common stock or stocks at regular intervals. It is basically an application of time diversification and may enable investors to capitalize on price fluctuations instead of just worrying about them. The method normally results in a lower average cost per share than the average market price per share during the period in question because the investor buys more shares of the stock with the fixed amount of money—say, $500 a year or quarter—when the stock is low in price than when it is comparatively high. Then, when the stock rises again (if it does), the investor shows a profit on the greater number of shares purchased at the lower prices.

The following table shows how the principle of dollar cost averaging could work.

TABLE 8-1
ILLUSTRATION OF DOLLAR COST AVERAGING

Date	Amount Invested	Market Price Paid	Number of Shares Purchased
1st Period	$500	$20	25
2nd Period	500	12½	40
3rd Period	500	10	50
4th Period	500	12½	40
5th Period	500	25	20
	$2,500		175

Total amount invested over 5 periods	$2,500
Number of shares purchased	175
Average market price	$16 per share
Average cost ($2,500 ÷ 175 shares)	$14.29 per share

Dollar cost averaging frequently works, unless the stock goes into a persistent decline. It works better if the stock has had an early decline and a later rise than if the reverse is the case. It takes a certain amount of strength of conviction. The investor must be convinced that, whatever happens from time to time, his stock is a good investment. He must be prepared to invest at regular intervals regardless of the price of the stock. He also must have the ready cash to stick to a regular program of buying even in periods when stock prices are down. Additionally, you must remember that dollar cost averaging does not protect you against loss of stock values in declining markets, and that you will show a loss if you must sell when the market price of the stock is below the average cost of the shares you purchased.

Thus, dollar cost averaging may be particularly well suited for investors with more or less uniform amounts of money periodically available for investment, who tend to follow a general investment policy of "buying and holding" securities, and who generally do not want to try to forecast stock prices. As noted in the previous chapter, dollar cost averaging is a defensive investment policy with respect to price changes of securities, particularly common stocks. Individual common stocks, mutual fund shares, and stock purchased under the Monthly Investment Plan (discussed below) are common vehicles for dollar cost averaging.

THE MONTHLY INVESTMENT PLAN (MIP)

Many people cannot manage to accumulate a large lump sum for investing all at once. For them, periodic investing may be the answer. To help meet this kind of situation, the Monthly Investment Plan (MIP) was developed by the New York Stock Exchange to serve as a method for people to invest as little as $40 in any of the common stocks listed on the New York Stock Exchange. As we saw above, it can be used for dollar cost averaging and to enable individuals to invest on a pay-as-you-go basis.

MIP is noncontractual. That is, you can start and stop whenever you wish, and there is no penalty if a payment is skipped. Stock is purchased for the MIP investor whenever his periodic payment is received, and his account is credited with the number of full shares he has purchased, plus any fractional interest in a share. Dividends are usually applied automatically to the purchase of additional shares. Although MIP may hinder an investor's flexibility, it is a convenient arrangement for people who want to have a regular program of common stock investment.

THE MECHANICS OF BUYING AND SELLING COMMON STOCKS

Buying and Selling Orders

There are various kinds of buy and sell orders you may use in your common stock transactions. Some of the more common are described below.

Market Orders. The most common type of order is the "market order," an order to buy or sell securities at the best price obtainable in the market at the moment. It is expressed to the broker as an order to buy or sell "at the market," that is, at whatever the market price happens to be.

Limit Orders. For many stock transactions, a market order is a reasonable one to use. However, when market prices are uncertain or are fluctuating rapidly, it may be better for an investor to enter a "limit order" that specifies the maximum price the investor is willing to pay, or, if selling, the minimum price he is willing to accept. For example, you might instruct your broker to buy 100 shares of a certain stock at 50 but no more.

The opposite is true when selling. For example, you might give your broker a limit order to sell 100 shares of the stock at 53. Here the broker may sell the shares at 53, or at a greater price if he can, but not at less than 53.

A price limit order must have a time limit so that it expires if not executed within a specified period of time.

Orders Based on Time. Most types of orders to buy and sell common stocks have a time reference contained in them. Such orders can take several forms. *Open orders* are good until canceled and are designated as GTC orders ("Good Till Canceled"). Another type is the *day order*, which is good only for the day on which it is ordered.

Stop Loss Orders. Another common type of order you may use is a "stop loss order." It is generally used as a basis for selling a stock once its price reaches a certain point, usually below the current market price. The reason you might use a stop loss order can best be explained by an example. Suppose you own a stock whose current market price is 100. You feel the condition of the stock market is so uncertain that the price of the stock could fluctuate markedly in either direction. To minimize any potential loss from the 100 level, you might enter a stop order at, say, 90. If the market price declines, you will be sold out when the market price reaches 90. A stop loss order becomes a market order once the specified price is reached, and the stock will be sold immediately at whatever price the broker can secure. Of course, if the market price goes up and never declines to the stop loss price, you would have lost nothing by placing this order.

If an investor wishes to use a stop order for a stock only at a specific price, he would enter a *stop limit order*. In the above illustration, for example, this order could instruct the broker to sell out at, for example, 90 and 90 only. If the transaction cannot be executed at 90, it will not be executed at all.

Margin Accounts

Most individual investors open *cash accounts* with their brokerage firms. As the name implies, all transactions in this type of account are for the full amount of the trade in cash. That is, a $1,000 trade requires a $1,000 cash settlement five full business days after the trade was made.

Many investors, however, are interested in buying securities "on margin." A *margin account* is used to allow an investor to assume a larger position in a security than he could if he used only his own funds. The investor puts up some of his own money and borrows the remainder. Margin accounts frequently are used by investors following more aggressive policies who want to lever their investment position and thereby magnify their return. They typically hold a security for relatively short periods of time, and they do not intend to pay off their margin account. In a few cases, margin accounts are used to finance long-term holdings of a security that currently is considered by the investor to be underpriced. In this situation, margin is used to purchase as many shares (or bonds) as possible, and the investor eventually intends to pay for his securities in full.

Margin accounts for listed securities can be opened through either a brokerage house or a commercial bank. The minimum "down payment," or margin requirement, is set by the Board of Governors of the Federal Reserve System. Let us take a specific example. Suppose the margin requirement is 70 percent, and Mr. A buys 100 shares of XYZ Corporation common stock at $50 per share. If this is a margin trade, Mr. A is required only to come up with $3,500 in cash (or its equivalent in other securities). He then borrows the rest ($1,500) from a bank or broker at the going interest rate for this type of loan. The entire $5,000 worth of securities is then put up as collateral for the $1,500 loan. Federal Reserve margin requirements specify only the minimum amounts of margin required at the time a loan is made. Minimum margin required after loans are made is discussed below.

But if the price of XYZ common declines, so that Mr. A's equity in the account decreases, he may get a "maintenance margin" call. *Maintenance margin* is the minimum equity position an investor can have in his account before he is asked to put up additional funds. In the above illustration, for example, assuming maintenance margin at 40 percent, XYZ common could fall to a price as low as 25 without a margin call.[3]

However, by borrowing to buy securities, an investor stands a chance of magnifying his losses, just as he does of magnifying his gains. Also, aside from the risks involved, other factors may discourage an investor from buying on margin. First of all, member firms of the New York Stock Exchange are required to establish a minimum margin account requirement. Also, a number of brokerage houses have a house policy concerning the minimum size of margin accounts. The idea behind these requirements, aside from trying to discourage speculative excesses, is to dissuade smaller investors from becoming overly committed in the stock market to their potential detriment.

Brokerage firms do not make securities loans on unlisted or over-the-counter (OTC) shares. However, an investor wishing to margin them can do so through a commercial bank.

Selling Short

"Selling short" means selling securities that the investor either (1) does not possess, and therefore must borrow to settle the account for them; or (2) does

---

[3]Since Mr. A must maintain an equity position of 40 percent in his margin account, he can borrow up to 60 percent of the value of the securities. His present loan is $1,500. Therefore, $1,500 divided by 0.60 (60%) equals the minimum value of securities Mr. A can have in his margin account without having to add more margin (cash or securities). In this case, this amount is $2,500 ($1,500 ÷ 0.60), or $25 per share.

possess but does not wish to deliver.[4] The former is the typical short sale arrangement used when the investor expects the stock to decline in price. The latter is called "selling short against the box" and is not as frequently used. "Selling short against the box" can be used to lock in a paper profit on a stock and postpone paying taxes on the capital gain. (See Chapter 14.)

To understand the technique of the short sale, let us first consider how an account is settled once an ordinary trade is made. Most settlements take place by regular-way delivery. This requires settlement on the fifth full business day after a trade has taken place. In other words, when an investor buys shares, he must pay for them by the fifth business day after the day the trade was made (the trade date). Similarly, when an investor is selling shares, the brokerage house must come up with the cash payable to its customer on the fifth full business day after the trade date, and the investor must make actual delivery of the shares sold.

Since investors must make regular-way delivery five full business days after a trade is made, a short seller must borrow the necessary securities within that time to make delivery. Usually, the securities can be borrowed directly from the short seller's broker, or the broker can arrange for such borrowing. The short seller is responsible for making up any dividends, rights, etc., that are declared on stock he has borrowed.

The most obvious reason for selling short is that the investor anticipates a declining market price for the security.[5] A typical example would be selling today at 100 with the hope of "covering," say a month from now, at 80 or less. Covering involves buying securities to replace the borrowed ones and, thus, delivering the securities originally sold short. However, regardless of the time elapsing from sale to the "covering" purchase, all gains resulting from short sales are treated as short-term capital gains for income tax purposes.

Of course, the reverse of the above situation may occur, and therein lies the danger of the short sale. That is, the price of the stock may not decline—it may even rise, thereby making it necessary to buy the stock later at a higher price than that at which it was sold. Thus, selling short involves considerable investment risk. It is normally considered an aggressive investment policy.

Securities Investor Protection Corporation

Following several sizable brokerage house failures, the federal government passed the Securities Investor Protection Act of 1970, which created the Securities Investor Protection Corporation (SIPC). SIPC is intended to pro-

---

[4]In the common sequence of transactions, where an investor buys a security which he hopes eventually to sell at a higher price, he has assumed what is called a *long position*. When the order of these transactions is reversed—sell first, and hopefully cover the sale later by buying at a lower price—the investor has taken a *short position*. In either case, the overall objective is to buy low/sell high.

[5]To prevent accumulating selling pressures in a downward market, short sales are permitted only if the last price change between successive round-lot transactions for a stock was *up* $\frac{1}{8}$ of a point or more.

vide funds, if necessary, to protect customers of an SIPC member firm in the event the firm is liquidated under the provisions of the Act. If a member firm is to be liquidated, a trustee is appointed to supervise the liquidation. The trustee attempts to return to customers out of the liquidated firm's available assets the securities that can be "specifically identified" as theirs (generally, these are fully paid securities in cash accounts and excess margin securities in margin accounts that have been set aside as the property of customers). SIPC pays any remaining claims of each customer up to $50,000, except that claims for cash are limited to $20,000. In general, customers' securities and cash held by SIPC member firms are covered by the Act. Other kinds of property, such as commodities accounts, are not covered.

Thus, the SIPC provides protection to investors who wish to leave securities or cash with member firms against the risk of the insolvency of such firms, up to the $50,000/$20,000 limits.[6] The SIPC, of course, is not intended to provide any protection to investors against losses resulting from everyday fluctuations in securities prices.

INVESTMENT CATEGORIES OF COMMON STOCKS

In determining what type or types of common stocks you might want to buy, it is important for you to understand the investment "grade" or "quality" of various stocks. Many different classification systems are used by brokerage houses and investment analysts. The basic system we shall follow is to classify stocks as: (1) blue chip, (2) growth, (3) income, (4) defensive, (5) cyclical, and (6) speculative. Of course, these categories are not necessarily mutually exclusive.

Blue Chip Stocks

"Blue chip" stocks generally are considered to be high-grade, investment-quality issues of major, well-established companies that have long records of earnings growth and dividend payments in good times as well as bad. Stocks like American Telephone & Telegraph, General Motors, Du Pont, and Procter and Gamble are generally considered "blue chip."

The ability to pay steady dividends over bad years as well as good for a long period is, of course, a strong indication of financial stability. Some "blue chips" of previous eras, such as the railroads, have ceased to be considered such now. On the other hand, some stocks, such as Xerox, that were not previously considered "blue chip," probably are today.

Growth Stocks

Many blue chips also are considered growth stocks. A growth stock is hard to define, but it is usually considered to be the stock of a company whose sales and earnings are expanding faster than the general economy and faster than those of most stocks. The company usually is aggressive, is research-minded,

[6]Some firms also provide private insurance protection for their customers up to higher limits.

and plows back most or all of its earnings into the company for future expansion. For this reason, growth companies, intent on financing their expansion from retained earnings, pay relatively small dividends and their current yield generally is low. Over time, however, investors hope substantial capital gains will accrue from the appreciation of the value of their stock as a result of this plow-back and expansion.

The market price of growth stocks can be quite volatile, particularly over the short run. They often go up in price faster than other stocks, but at the first hint that the *rate of increase* in their earnings is not being sustained, their prices can come tumbling down. And when the earnings of a "growth" stock actually falter, the result on its market price can be disastrous. Smaller and newer "growth companies" are especially vulnerable when their earnings fail to live up to investors' expectations.

In an effort to define a "growth" stock with more precision, several investment services have developed statistical tests to identify and select growth stocks. Standard & Poor's, for example, has developed a list of "200 Rapid Growth Stocks" by screening over 6,000 issues by computer.

However, growth stocks can mean different things to different people, and it makes a big difference whether an analyst takes a conservative or an adventurous view of the market.

Income Stocks

Sometimes people buy or own common stocks for current income. While in recent years common stocks, on the average, have had lower current yields than bonds or savings certificates, there are stocks that may be classified as income stocks because they pay a higher-than-average return. Income stocks are those that yield generous current returns.

Some care is needed in selecting income stocks. A stock may be paying a high current return because its price has fallen as the result of uncertainty about whether the company can continue to maintain its present dividend rate in light of declining earnings. Or, the stock may be of a lackluster company in an unpopular industry with little future. Or, the company may be located or mainly located in a foreign country where there is great risk due to political instability.

On the other hand, there are many sound stocks that are paying higher-than-average current yields because of the nature of their products or industries. When general economic conditions become more uncertain, investors often become more interested in the current income from stocks. Possible future capital growth seems less attractive then.

Defensive Stocks

Some stocks are characterized as "defensive." Such stocks are regarded as stable and comparatively safe, especially in periods of declining business activity. During such periods, these stocks tend to decline less than others, and some may actually rise.

Defensive issues are often found among companies whose products suffer relatively little in recessionary periods. Also, companies that provide the essentials of life tend to hold up well. The shares of utilities, banks, and food companies are examples of defensive issues.

In many cases, defensive stocks can also be classified as income stocks. For example, utilities generally are an example of both.

Cyclical Stocks

Considerably different from defensive stocks are cyclical shares. A cyclical company is one whose earnings tend to fluctuate sharply with the business cycle. When business conditions are good, the company's profitability is high and the price of its common stock rises. But when business conditions deteriorate, the cyclical company's sales fall off sharply and its profits are greatly diminished. Automobile manufacturers and machine tool companies are good examples of cyclical companies.

Speculative Stocks

In one sense, all common stock investment is "speculative" in that common stocks provide a variable- rather than a fixed-dollar outcome. Yet, this view of common stock investment is no longer commonly held (although it may return), and what are "speculative common stocks" has a more limited meaning. Some high-flying glamor stocks are speculative. Likewise, hot new issues and penny mining stocks are speculative. Other types could be identified from time to time as they come and go. Some are easy to identify; some are more difficult. Speculative high-flying glamor stocks can usually be identified by their *very* high price-earnings ratios. For example, at one time when the Dow Jones Industrials were selling at an average of about 18.5 times earnings, many leading "runaway" stocks were selling at multiples of 50 to 100 times earnings.

Also, there usually comes a point in a bull market when small, hitherto unknown companies go public or new small companies are formed. The offering of their low-priced shares finds a fierce speculative demand at this stage of the economic cycle and their prices often rise precipitously. Unfortunately for the uninitiated buyers of such issues, a day of reckoning often follows. (See Chapter 10 for more on speculation in "new issues.")

SOME THEORIES OF COMMON STOCK INVESTMENT

People have many theories of how to invest in common stocks. Yet, there probably is no one or even several theories on which everyone would agree. This probably is so because no one theory has consistently proven to be "the" answer to investment success. If one were, those who knew the theory (including the authors) would be rich. Very much depends upon the investor's particular needs and objectives, his overall financial and tax positions, the investment policy or policies he has elected to follow (see Chapter 7), the yields on alternative investments, the general economic outlook, and so forth.

Despite these cautions, however, some examples of commonly held theories of common stock investment are given here. You may find one or more that are of interest to you. Of course, there are other theories of common stock investment not described here because a full description of such theories would be beyond the scope of this book. You can refer to standard textbooks on investments for others. Also remember that the popularity of such theories (as well as the popularity of investing in common stocks) varies with the times. There is a certain amount of "faddism" in investment theories.

Growth Theory

The growth theory has been a popular one and is followed by those who hope to secure greater capital appreciation than is evidenced by the Dow Jones averages or some other indicator of trends in common stock prices. The theory now advocates careful analysis of corporate and industry records to select those "quality" issues that show continuing growth from one business cycle to another and a growth rate equal to some multiple, such as perhaps twice or more, of the growth rate for the overall economy.

There can be no doubt that some investors who have made long-term commitments to industries which have had a strong, continuous, and exceptional growth trend of earnings have had considerable investment success. They may have bought common stock in companies in such industries—sometimes in only one company—and then simply held these securities over the years.

If an investor can identify and purchase the stock of such a company in an industry in its earliest growth stages and the company goes on to become a leader in an important field, the investor probably will accumulate substantial capital. However, the odds against selecting the right company that will survive this initial stage are very great.

Thus, in many cases the most likely course for the growth-theory investor to follow is to wait until an industry has passed through its initial competitive crises, and then attempt to select one or more of the strongest companies that have emerged from the struggle. If the investor makes the correct selection or selections when the industry still has a significant period of growth ahead of it, and the investing public has not already pushed the stock price up to discount future growth for too many years in advance, the investor can do well at this stage.

What happens in many cases, however, is that investors substantially overprice stocks in such favored "growth" industries. They may either buy in too late, or they may stay with the securities too long, or both. Many investors buy into such growth stocks after a long rise. The higher the stock prices go, the more popular and fashionable the industry appears. Yet, the higher the market price goes, the greater the market risk becomes, and at some point the former growth stock no longer "grows."

There are no "pat" answers with respect to growth stocks. Properly selected and bought at the right time, they can produce substantial profits for investors over the long pull. But they are no investment panacea, and the investor who purchases "growth stocks" when they are most popular and high-priced often is not psychologically conditioned for any substantial decline in the market prices of such stocks. And as fashions change, these popular stocks may go out of fashion, at least temporarily. While this situation may be temporary, many investors do not have the required patience to hold securities under such circumstances.

Also, of course, the decline (or lack of growth) may not be temporary. This may be a difficult situation for the investor to judge accurately.

Depressed-industry Approach

Almost the opposite of the popular growth-stock approach is the depressed-industry approach, where the investor is endeavoring to select "comeback" industries and companies. As we noted above, certain stocks labeled as growth stocks may be very popular and selling at high prices that overdiscount their future growth, even if it materializes. Similarly, stocks in depressed industries may be selling at prices that substantially overdiscount their troubles.

Note, however, that this theory does *not* mean that investors should purchase a stock just because it is low in price. Stocks should be purchased only on the basis of careful analysis of expected future earnings. To follow the depressed-industry approach, an investor should have the time and experience to analyze securities carefully to make sure he is not purchasing stocks of companies that are at all likely to go bankrupt (e.g., Penn Central) or in an industry that is going out of existence. In fact, for the most part, investors probably are best advised to select the highest-grade, or at least one of the highest-grade, securities in a depressed industry.

Moderately Growing Industries

Many investors prefer a policy of purchasing common stocks of good-quality companies in moderately growing industries. This is particularly true if they are seeking income and stability along with moderate capital appreciation. Such stocks may not appear so attractive to the great bulk of investors and, as a result, they tend to be moderately priced. They sell at reasonable price-earnings ratios and provide good yields most of the time. While the investor in such stocks may not stand to make spectacular capital gains, neither is he likely to be exposed to substantial capital losses. Certain utility stocks may be cited as an example of this category.

COMMON STOCKS AND MARKET CYCLES

When you invest in common stocks, always be aware of stock market cycles. When carried very far in either direction, stock market price movements are exaggerated and irrational in retrospect, no matter how logical they may have appeared at the time they were taking place. Investor psychology toward common stocks can change swiftly, and attitudes toward different companies and industries can follow a similar pattern. Thus, you should try not to be in a financial position where you would *have to liquidate* your common stocks to secure cash. As we said in Chapter 7, you should have emergency reserve funds in bonds, savings accounts, life insurance cash values, and the like. Also, as we said in Chapter 7, you should consider what your investment policy should be with respect to stock market cycles (i.e., with respect to investment timing).

COMMON STOCK WARRANTS

Common stock purchase warrants are certificates that give the holder the option to purchase the common stock of a corporation at a stated price, which normally is higher than the market price at the time the warrant is issued. Some warrants are perpetual, but most expire five to ten years after being issued.

Warrants represent a call on the future earnings of a corporation. Their value is speculative and depends upon the terms of the contract, the current and estimated future price range of the common stock, and the relationship between the number of warrants outstanding and the number of common shares outstanding. The price of warrants fluctuates widely. Thus, they provide a risk vehicle for speculation. Like other options, warrants give the buyer greater leverage to magnify his return, and thus they tend to be used by investors following more aggressive policies.

HOW GOOD ARE COMMON STOCK INVESTMENTS?

To many people, "investment" means buying common stock. There are or have been several reasons for this. First is the decrease in the purchasing power of the dollar (i.e., the purchasing power risk). Secondly, a generally rising stock market during much of the 1950s and 1960s provided substantial capital gains for many people who then were "in the market." This fostered the idea that the purchase of common stock is a good way to keep abreast of declining purchasing power. In fact, during the 1950s and 1960s, common stocks in general did far better than just keeping pace with inflation.

This is all well and good for this period, but have there been any extensive research studies on how well common stocks have done over long periods of time? The answer is, Yes! The Center for Research in Security Prices of the University of Chicago has conducted several such studies. The first study contained rates of return on all common stocks listed on the New York Stock Exchange for 22 periods between January 1926 and December 1960.[7] If, for example, a married man who had an income of $10,000 in 1960, and its equivalent in earlier years, had bought an equal dollar amount of every common stock listed on the New York Stock Exchange starting in 1926, and if he had reinvested his dividends in all the stocks listed there year after year through 1960, his total return would have equaled 8.2 percent compounded annually (after paying commissions and applicable income and capital gains taxes). Of course, if he had bought at the high of 1929 and sold at the low of 1932, he would have shown a loss—a whopping loss, at that. But in almost all the 22 selected time periods covering boom and bust and war and peace from 1926 through 1960, he would have earned a good return—often a better return than he could have earned on most other investment media.

While the first study from the Center for Research in Security Prices showed what average rates of return an investor would have earned from common stocks in the various time periods under the assumptions used, it did not answer the question of what risk (i.e., variability of rates of return) he might have encountered.

Another study from the Center bears on this point. It covers all possible combinations of month-end purchase and sale dates for all common stocks listed on the New York Stock Exchange from January 1926 through December 1969—56,557,538 transactions. Among the conclusions are:

An investor in all common stocks would have made a profit 78.3 percent of the time.

Over two-thirds of the time the rate of return would have exceeded 5 percent per year compounded annually.

Almost one-fifth of the time the rate of return would have exceeded 20 percent per year compounded annually.

Losses of 20 percent per year occurred only about once in 13 times, and losses exceeding 50 percent per year only once in 50 times.

The median rate of return was 9.8 percent.

Remember, however, that the overall purpose of investing is to earn the best possible return on your capital. In some recent years, inflation has continued strongly while most stock prices have declined. Also, yields on other kinds of investment media, like corporate bonds and bank certificates, have climbed drastically. These phenomena just stress the idea presented in Chapter 7 that, before investing, you should decide upon specific investment objectives and policies and then invest accordingly. This may or may not involve investing in common stocks. The fact that common stocks generally have been good investments over extended periods of time in the past does not necessarily mean they are good investments now or that they will be in the immediate future.

[7]Lawrence Fisher and James H. Lorie, "Rates of Return on Investments in Common Stocks," *Journal of Business,* University of Chicago, January 1964.

9
MUTUAL FUNDS

Mutual funds are, in effect, large portfolios that are formed by many individual investors collectively pooling their resources. Many different types of funds exist, with varied investment objectives. Individual mutual funds also differ in the degree of success they achieve in meeting their stated objectives. Investing in mutual funds and how it may affect personal financial planning are discussed in this chapter.

In popular usage, the term "mutual fund" often is used to mean any kind of investment company. Actually, however, there are three basic kinds of investment companies: (1) those selling face-amount certificates, (2) unit investment trusts, and (3) so-called "management companies." Management companies, in turn, can be classified as (1) closed-end funds, and (2) open-end or *mutual funds*. However, the open-end or mutual fund is by far the most important variety of investment company and, hence, we devote most of our attention to it in this chapter.

WHY INVEST IN MUTUAL FUNDS?

Three *major advantages* are frequently given for investing in mutual funds. First, by pooling their investable capital, smaller investors are able to enjoy a degree of *diversification* they could never achieve on their own. Second, a mutual fund offers *experienced professional management* to select the securities to which the fund's resources will be allocated. And, third, a mutual fund offers *convenience* and *ready marketability* through the fund's obligation to redeem its shares. Thus, an individual investor in a mutual fund does not have to keep on top of his or her current holdings; an investor does not have to be constantly on the alert for new investment opportunities; tax statements concerning fund distributions are prepared by the fund and sent to the investor; if the investor wishes, fund distributions can normally be systematically reinvested; the investor's holdings in the fund usually can be systematically liquidated if he or she wants to supplement current income; and the like.

Given these advantages, it is not surprising that mutual funds can play a major role in one's financial planning. Today, hundreds of mutual funds actively compete for the public's investment dollars, so you have a wide choice among funds. An intelligent investor, however, should consider whether mutual funds or other investment outlets would be best for accomplishing his or her objectives, and whether the services provided by a mutual fund are worth the expense. If the investor decides a mutual fund is best for him or her, the investor still must be able to find those funds whose investment objectives are consistent with his or her own and then choose from among them. To provide meaningful answers, the investor should be familiar with the different types and structures of mutual funds, know where to obtain relevant information on mutual funds, and know how to evaluate such information.

TYPES OF FUNDS

As noted above, investment companies can be classified in several ways. However, one of the major distinctions is between open-end and closed-end funds.

Open-end Funds

A mutual fund is, by definition, an open-end investment company. Open-end companies represent the dominant and most rapidly expanding type of investment company. They are called "open-end" because the number of outstanding shares—or capitalization—is not fixed. Instead, the number of shares is continually changing as investors purchase new shares or redeem old ones. Thus, when you want to buy shares in an open-end fund, you, in effect, buy them from the fund itself. And when you want to redeem such shares, the fund must stand ready to buy them back from you.

The price for purchase or sales of open-end fund shares is based on the most recently computed net asset value (NAV) of the fund. Net asset value per share is the total value of all securities and other assets held by the fund divided by the number of outstanding shares and is calculated twice daily.

Closed-end Funds

A closed-end investment company is similar in many respects to a typical corporation. It issues a fixed number of shares which normally does not fluctuate, except as new stock may be issued. It can issue bonds and preferred stock so as to leverage the position of the common shareholders. The closed-end fund uses its capital and other resources primarily to invest in the securities of other corporations. Abacus Fund, Madison Fund, Niagara Share, and Tri-Continental Corporation are examples of closed-end funds.

The shares of closed-end funds are bought and sold in the market just like the stock of other corporations. The stock of closed-end funds can be listed on stock exchanges or traded over-the-counter. The price quotations for the stock are given daily in the same manner as for other traded common stocks (see Chapter 8). The seller or buyer contacts his or her stockbroker, who handles the transaction and charges the usual commission for the broker's services. The total number of outstanding shares is not affected by transactions in a stock, because both buyers and sellers are outside investors and not the fund itself.

Unlike open-end shares, the price for purchases and sales of closed-end fund shares is determined by the supply and demand for the shares in the market—just as with any other common stock—and is not directly tied to a fund's net asset value (NAV) per share. When the stock market price of a fund's shares exceeds its NAV, the fund is said to sell *at a premium* (over its NAV). On the other hand, when the stock market price is less than a fund's NAV, it is said to sell *at a discount* (from its NAV). Thus, at any given time, some closed-end funds may sell at a *premium* while others sell at a *discount*.

Open-end versus Closed-end Funds

If you want to buy a fund, should you consider an open-end or a closed end fund? This is a debatable question, and no pat answers exist. But here are some things you may want to consider. First of all, both types provide professional investment management, diversification, and periodic distributions of investment income and capital gains to investors. They both also are readily marketable, but in different ways—an open-end fund through redemption of its shares by the fund itself and a closed-end fund by sale of its shares on the open market. There are more open-end funds to choose from, and they often are sold by sales representatives who handle mutual funds. Therefore, when you are solicited to buy a fund, it will almost certainly be an open-end fund. Thus, people tend to be more aware of, and know about, open-end funds than closed-end funds. When you buy or sell a closed-end fund, you pay regular stock market commissions and other costs. What sales charge you must pay for a mutual fund depends on whether it is a "load" or "no-load" fund, as described below.

What your fund shares are worth at any given time is not guaranteed for either type, but their value is determined differently. In the case of a mutual fund, it is the NAV of the fund shares at that time; for a closed-end fund, it is the price of the fund shares on the stock market at that time. But in both cases you can make money, break even, or lose money on the fund shares, depending largely on how the particular fund's investments do. You cannot buy a mutual fund for less than its NAV per share, but you can normally buy a closed-end fund at a discount (or a premium). Sometimes closed-end funds sell at substantial discounts, particularly during downturns in the stock market ("bear" markets).

In the final analysis, of course, your investment success with a fund will depend upon the investment performance of the particular fund you buy rather than upon what type it is. However, there are good funds of both types, and so you must make a choice here.

Load and No-load Mutual Funds

As we said above, the price of an open-end fund is based on the net asset value (NAV) per share. However, two significantly different pricing arrangements are used for open-end funds, and you should understand the difference. Open-end funds are sold on either a load or a no-load basis. A "load" refers to the commission charged an investor by a fund for executing a transaction for the investor. The most common arrangement is where the investor pays the full commission when he or she purchases shares in the fund but pays no commission when redeeming them. Some examples of load funds are Aetna Fund, Delaware Funds, Dreyfus Funds, Investors Group Funds, New England Life Funds, Oppenheimer Funds, and Wellington Funds. Naturally, these are cited only as illustrations of the large number of load-type mutual funds.

The typical load is $8\frac{1}{2}$ or $8\frac{3}{4}$ percent of the public offering price.[1] Thus, when you purchase a load fund, you pay net asset value plus the load. If you redeem your shares, you normally receive the net asset value. For example, suppose the L Fund, which charges a load of $8\frac{1}{2}$ percent, has an NAV per share of $10. The load for an investor wanting to purchase shares of the L Fund would be 93 cents per share or $8\frac{1}{2}$ percent of $10.93. So the investor would pay the sum of the NAV and the load, or a total of $10.93 per share. However, if he or she wants to redeem the shares in the future, and the NAV at that time is, say, $10.50, he or she would receive the NAV, or $10.50 per share.

No-load funds do not charge a sales commission (load) when the shares are purchased or redeemed. Thus, both transactions would occur at the fund's NAV per share. Some examples of no-load funds are Financial Program Funds, Loomis Sayles Funds, Penn Square Fund, Price (T. Rowe) Funds, and Scudder Funds.

Open-end fund values and prices are given daily in the financial pages of most newspapers in a special section on mutual funds. Prices are quoted on a net asset value (NAV) basis and an offering price (offer) basis. These prices for the L Fund (a load fund), mentioned above, would be NAV—$10 and offering price—$10.93. The spread between the NAV and the offering price is the load. For a no-load fund, the quoted NAV and the offering price would be the same.

To illustrate the differences in these funds, and to help you identify closed-end funds, load-type mutual funds, and no-load-type mutual funds, the following examples may be helpful.

First is a daily quotation for a *closed-end investment company*—the Tri-Continental Corporation—that is listed on the New York Stock Exchange (the Big Board):

---

[1]Note that this results in a slightly higher percentage load based on the net amount you actually invest (i.e., the offering price less the sales load, or the NAV per share). An $8\frac{1}{2}$ percent load, for example, is equal to 9.3 percent of the amount actually invested.

1974		Stocks	Div.	P/E Ratio	Sales in 100s	High	Low	Close	Net Chg.
High	Low								
27½	20⅞	Tri Con	2.76e	—	96	21⅞	21¼	21¼	−¼

This basically is the same quotation as for any stock listed on the Exchange, except that no price earnings (P/E) ratio is given and the dividends of $2.76 are those declared or paid in the preceding 12 months. Note that the net asset value is not given in this quotation. However, an interested investor can find out the NAV of closed-end funds from various sources. For example, each Monday *The Wall Street Journal* publishes a weekly listing of net asset values of closed-end investment company shares as of the previous Friday's close. By referring to this listing or a similar one in other sources, we can find that Tri-Continental Corporation shares had an NAV of $25.43 as of the date of the above quotation. Thus, Tri-Continental stock was selling at a 16.4 percent discount on that date. Also, the current yield, based on the last 12 months' dividends, was 12.8 percent.

Now, let us take two mutual funds—one a load fund and another a no-load fund. The daily quotation for the *load fund*—the Delaware Fund—that is listed in the mutual funds section of daily newspapers would be as follows:

NAV	Offer Price	NAV Change
8.65	9.45	+.02

From other sources, you could find out what the payments (from income and/or capital gains) by the fund have been for the latest 12-month period.[2] The difference between the quoted NAV and the offer price is, of course, the sales load (80 cents per share in this example).

A similar quotation for a *no-load fund*—Price (T. Rowe) Growth Stock Fund—that also is listed in the mutual funds section of daily newspapers would be as follows:

NAV	Offer Price	NAV Change
10.84	10.84	+.03

Here the no-load fund can be distinguished from the load fund in that its NAV and Offer Price are the same. Again, you can find the recent investment income and/or capital gains payments made by no-load funds from other sources.

[2]Such payments are listed weekly in the Mutual Funds section of *Barron's,* for example.

Reducing the Sales Load

For load funds, the percentage load is normally reduced as an investor makes larger dollar purchases. The minimum initial investment is usually specified in dollar amounts, such as $200, rather than in numbers of shares. A typical schedule of reducing load charges is given below.

Amount of Investment	Sales Charge as Percent of Offering Price
Less than $10,000	8.5%
$ 10,000 but less than $ 25,000	7.5%
$ 25,000 but less than $ 50,000	6%
$ 50,000 but less than $ 100,000	5%
$ 100,000 but less than $ 250,000	4%
$ 250,000 but less than $ 500,000	3%
$ 500,000 but less than $1,000,000	2%
$1,000,000 or more	1%

The amounts at which the percentage sales charge declines (e.g., $10,000, $25,000, etc., as shown above) are called "discounts" or *breakpoints*. Obviously, it is to the investor's advantage to be in the highest breakpoint bracket he or she can because the reduced sales charge applies to the entire investment the investor makes.

There are some *ways you can save money by taking maximum advantage of the reduced sales load applicable to larger investments in a load fund*. First of all, you, your spouse, and all your children under age 21 are considered as one "person" in determining how much is being or has been invested in a fund's shares. The trustee or other fiduciary of a single trust or other fiduciary account also is considered a single "person" for this purpose, even though the trust or account may have a number of beneficiaries. If you are entitled to a sales charge discount on the basis of this "family (or trust) aggregate rule," you should be sure to so indicate at the time you buy the fund shares.

Second, you may be entitled to an "accumulation discount" or "right of accumulation" on the basis of previous fund purchases. In calculating your total investment in a fund's shares, the aggregate value (usually at the current offering price) of *all* the fund's shares you hold at the time you make an additional purchase is taken into account in determining the sales load to be applied to the additional purchase. Suppose, for example, you (or your spouse or children under 21) own shares in our hypothetical L Fund that currently are worth $5,000. If you now buy another $9,000 worth of L Fund shares, you would have crossed the $10,000 breakpoint, and the sales load applicable to the $9,000 purchase (but not retroactive to the first $5,000 worth of fund shares) would be 7.5 percent, according to the above schedule.

This would save $90 in sales charges in this example (8.5% − 7.5% = 1% times $9,000). There is no time limit on when additional shares must be purchased to take advantage of this right of accumulation. Again, if you are entitled to a reduced percentage load because of such a right of accumulation, you should be sure to say so when you buy fund shares.

Third, you can use a "letter of intent" to save on mutual fund sales charges. Suppose you are planning to buy enough of a mutual fund to reach a certain breakpoint, but you do not have the cash to do it all at once. You can sign a so-called "letter of intent" indicating that you (or your spouse or children under 21) intend to invest a stated amount in the fund within a specified period—usually 13 months. Then, the sales load on all purchases you make during the 13-month period is at the rate applicable to the total stated amount you indicated you would invest in the letter of intent. For example, you might sign a letter of intent indicating your intention to invest $25,000 in a fund over 13 months. If you actually do this by buying, say, $5,000 worth of the fund's shares on each of five occasions during the 13-month period, only a 6 percent, rather than a higher, sales charge will be made on each purchase. A letter of intent costs you nothing, and it does not obligate you actually to buy the fund shares (a sales charge adjustment is made if you do not). You can also decide at any time up to 90 days after having made an initial purchase of fund shares whether you want to sign a letter of intent for the future and have those shares included in it. Furthermore, many management companies that have several funds under their management will allow letters of intent and rights of accumulation to apply to purchases of one or a combination of their mutual funds.

In addition to the sales load charged by load funds, both load and no-load funds charge management fees. A common management fee starts at ½ of 1 percent per year of the fund's assets.

Load versus No-load Funds

Assuming you have decided to invest in a mutual fund (as opposed to a closed-end investment company), you should *consider whether to buy a load fund or a no-load fund*. Prospective investors often are uncertain whether load or no-load funds are best for them. This is a controversial question, and again there are no pat answers. However, here are some things you may want to think about in making your decision. Load funds are more numerous and generally better known to the public. Also, investors historically have put considerably more money into load funds than into no-load funds. On the other hand, in recent years the proportion of total mutual fund assets held by no-load funds has been increasing.

The greater part of the load paid by an investor when he or she purchases load fund shares is received as a commission by the mutual fund salesman. No-load funds ordinarily are not sold through salesmen. Their shares normally are purchased and redeemed directly by mail through the fund itself.[3]

[3]Brokerage houses through which no-load funds channel their business are generally willing to handle transactions for affiliated no-load funds.

Thus, no-load funds avoid the salesman's commission. On the other hand, the mutual fund purchaser loses the advice and sales efforts of the salesman. Many people would never invest in any fund if it were not for the sales efforts of mutual fund salesmen.

As a group, load funds probably have historically performed no better and no worse than no-load funds. Of course, some load funds can justifiably claim to have outperformed particular no-load funds, or even the average performance of all no-load funds, over an extended period of time. On the other hand, some no-load funds also can show better results than most other no-load funds as well as the average results of all load funds. It is difficult to draw the conclusion that either type fund is inherently superior to the other in terms of investment performance—so much depends on the individual fund.

An investor should be relatively sure when buying a load fund that he or she will not have to liquidate his or her position in the near future. If there is a possibility that some shares will have to be redeemed to meet other needs, this would be a factor in favor of a no-load fund. If, on the other hand, your investment can be committed for a long period of time, the initial sales load itself becomes relatively less important.

HOW CAN YOU INVEST IN MUTUAL FUNDS?

There are a number of ways you can invest in mutual funds, including outright purchase, voluntary accumulation plans, contractual periodic payment plans (so-called "contractual" plans), single-payment plans, and the reinvestment of dividends and realized capital gains payable from the fund.

The *outright purchase* of mutual fund shares is similar to such a purchase of any other kind of security. The investor receives a stock certificate for the number of shares purchased.

Acquisition plans are available for the investor who wants to make mutual fund purchases on a regular, periodic basis. These plans are similar in concept to the Monthly Investment Plan for common stocks (which, incidentally, can be used to make regular investments in closed-end funds) that was discussed in Chapter 8. Thus, an investor may seek to accumulate fund shares by making periodic, say monthly, payments to the fund, although a minimum monthly payment, such as $25 or so, may be required. A larger minimum initial investment also may be required.

A popular kind of periodic mutual fund investment plan is the so-called *voluntary accumulation plan.* Under this plan, the investor indicates, without any binding commitment on his or her part, that he or she will periodically invest additional amounts of money in the fund. However, the investor does not agree to make these periodic investments for a specified time period or to invest a certain total dollar amount. An investor, for example, might start such a plan with an initial investment of $200, with subsequent investments of $50 per month.

The sales charge (load) under a voluntary accumulation plan is level for each purchase made. The investor fills out an application to start this kind of plan, and the shares and fractional shares the investor acquires under the plan are often held for him or her by the fund's custodian. Fund distributions are often automatically reinvested in fund shares. The investor can terminate the plan any time he or she chooses without penalty. Some plans also make available decreasing term life insurance as an optional feature.

Another kind of periodic investment approach is the so-called *contractual plan*, whereby the investor agrees to invest a certain amount in periodic payments over a specific period of time, perhaps 10 or 15 years. Such a plan provides for the reinvestment of capital gains and dividend distributions at no charge (i.e., at the fund's NAV). Loans secured by the accumulated shares can be conveniently arranged. Decreasing term life insurance coverage can be added to ensure completion of the plan in the event of the purchaser's death. Finally, despite the term "contractual" used to identify these plans, the investor is under no legal obligation to make the regular payment each month, or even to complete the plan. The investor may request at any time that the shares for which he or she has paid be redeemed.

Contractual plans have been subject to criticism, and they are not permitted to be sold by the securities laws of some states. The bulk of this criticism has been directed at the practice of deducting the total sales (load) charges that would be made if the plan were completed from the periodic payments made by the investor in the first few years of the plan. For this reason, these plans generally are called "front-end-load" plans. Up to 50 percent of the payments made during the first year of a contractual plan may be deducted as sales charges.[4] Thus, the amount of the actual investment made by an investor during the first few years of a contractual plan is substantially reduced. This practice exacts a particularly heavy burden on those investors who, for whatever reason, are unable to complete the plan.

A *single-payment plan* for buying mutual fund shares is essentially an outright purchase under a contractual-type arrangement. The shares are held by a bank as custodian, and the owner can name a beneficiary to receive them directly in the event of his or her death. Thus, the shares do not have to pass through the owner's probate estate. (See Chapter 15 for the advantages of bypassing your probate estate.) Dividends are reinvested at net asset value under this plan.

Mutual funds (and some closed-end investment companies) have *automatic reinvestment plans* whereby you can reinvest your dividends and capital gains distributions from the fund in additional fund shares. Depending on the method of investing in the fund, and on the fund's prospectus, the automatic reinvestment may be at the fund's offering price or the net asset value at the time of reinvestment. Of course, reinvestment at net asset value is more advantageous to the investor.

Mutual funds may also offer a *systematic withdrawal plan* to investors whose shares are worth a certain minimum amount, like $5,000 or $10,000. The investor may establish a withdrawal plan to pay a specified, periodic

---

[4]The portion of the first 12 monthly payments that can be deducted as a sales load is legally limited to a maximum of 50 percent.

amount to him or her, such as $500 per month. The investor may want to do this during his or her retirement years, for example. Remember, however, that such a systematic withdrawal plan is not the same as a life annuity sold by an insurance company. To the extent that the periodic payments under a withdrawal plan involve the use of your fund capital, your share balance in the fund may become depleted over time, particularly in a declining stock market. Thus, the periodic payments are not guaranteed for your and/or your spouse's lifetime(s). If you want such a life annuity guarantee, coupled with a common stock or balanced investment program, you might consider redeeming your fund shares and buying an individual variable annuity. (See Chapter 13 for a discussion of variable annuities.) Of course, if you cash in fund shares (either for periodic payments to be made to you under a withdrawal plan or otherwise), you may have a capital gain or loss for income tax purposes, depending on whether your fund shares have appreciated or depreciated in value while you held them.

Remember, too, that withdrawals under a systematic withdrawal plan made at the same time as you are buying mutual fund shares in the same or another load fund normally are disadvantageous because you are, in effect, paying duplicate sales charges. However, management companies that handle several mutual funds often permit investors to *exchange* all or part of their shares in one fund for those in another fund or funds they manage at net asset value. Thus, an investor who may have purchased shares in a growth fund during his or her working years might exchange them for shares in an income fund at retirement. Such an exchange, however, might result in the investor's realizing a capital gain or loss at that time.

MUTUAL FUNDS AND THEIR INVESTMENT OBJECTIVES

There are mutual funds available to meet just about any investment goal you may have. The most common classifications based on investment objectives are growth stock funds, income funds, balanced funds, and diversified common stock funds, although in reality investment companies often provide a broad range of investment objectives rather than aims that fall neatly into one of these categories.

As the name suggests, the primary objective of *growth stock funds* is capital appreciation. Current income is of minor importance. The so-called "performance" (or "go-go") funds are simply more aggressive in their investment policies in seeking to attain capital growth.

The primary objective of *income funds* is to provide a sizable and stable flow of investment income to their shareholders. They generally invest in common stocks, preferred stocks, and bonds, with higher current yields being their investment goal.

Balanced funds usually are the more conservative of these common types of mutual funds. Balanced funds also invest in common stocks, preferred stocks, and bonds, but their investment objectives can be characterized as security of principal, reasonable current income, and reasonable capital appreciation over the long term. During declining stock markets, they are generally expected to suffer less than growth funds, but, of course, they also are generally expected to lag behind growth funds during rising markets.

Diversified common stock funds also tend to be more conservative, but they invest mainly in good-quality common stocks. Their objective is long-term capital growth with reasonable, but varying, current income.

Just as these funds differ in their basic objectives, they also differ in the degree of aggressiveness with which they approach these objectives. Thus, while a young person on the way up the executive ladder might want a "growth" fund, he or she still has decisions to make. Some "growth-oriented" funds invest mainly in large, well-established companies that they hope will provide steady, if unspectacular, growth. Other funds are constantly searching for small, newer companies that could provide very large returns—although perhaps at considerable risk. So the investor needs to specify his or her own risk-return preferences more precisely than just expressing a desire for "growth" in order to identify only a few funds that may best meet his or her needs.

Several other types of funds in addition to those described above may be helpful to you in meeting certain investment objectives. Thus, we have *preferred stock funds, bond funds*, and *tax-exempt bond funds*. In addition, some *specialty funds* concentrate on the common stock of firms in particular industries or in a given geographic area. For example, funds have specialized in the airline, chemical, and atomic energy industries. Some funds make heavy use of options, while others are interested primarily in new issues. There are even so-called "super funds"—mutual funds that invest in other mutual funds. So the investor, in approaching the mutual fund market, has many alternatives from which to choose.

Another rather specialized type of fund is the *dual fund*. A dual fund actually is organized as a closed-end investment company and is really two funds in one. Dual funds are based on the fact that some investors are interested exclusively in capital gains while others are interested only in income. Thus, half of a dual fund's shares are sold as capital shares and the other half as income shares. The capital shares benefit from any capital appreciation of the entire fund, while the income shares receive all the income. Capital gains are not distributed annually. Rather, the fund is organized for a specific period of time, typically 10 to 15 years, after which the income shares are retired at a fixed price. All capital growth of the fund then would go to the growth shareholders at that time.

Leverage and hedge funds utilize the same concepts and strategies but give them different labels. While both terms are encountered in practice, we can think of them for practical purposes as the same. Their investment objective is maximum capital appreciation, but at the expense of substantially increased risk. Thus, they can be considered as inherently speculative. In their quest for maximum capital appreciation, hedge funds may use such aggressive investment techniques as financial leverage, short sales, and options, in addition to the more conventional investment methods. Hedge funds generally appeal to investors who want to follow aggressive investment policies.

There are also some *tax-free exchange funds* which were formed to allow investors to exchange stock they owned for fund shares without any capital gains tax liability at that time. But because of an adverse tax ruling, no new offerings of these funds have been made since 1967.

HOW CAN YOU FIND OUT ABOUT MUTUAL FUNDS?

Several sources of information on mutual funds are readily available. From these sources you can determine a fund's investment objectives and philosophy, study the current composition and changes in its portfolio, and see how the fund has performed historically as compared with other funds with similar objectives. The intelligent use of available information can help you avoid selecting a fund that is not appropriate for your particular circumstances. The well-informed investor should also be better able to ask appropriate questions of a mutual fund representative.

Probably the most commonly used source of information is the *prospectus* prepared by mutual funds. While a fund naturally will attempt to present itself as attractively as possible, its prospectus must be accredited by an outside auditor and approved by the Securities and Exchange Commission (SEC). It must also be prepared in accordance with SEC guidelines regarding form and content. The prospectus, for example, gives information on the fund's investment objectives and program; how to purchase, redeem, and transfer shares; minimum initial and periodic investments; periodic purchase and systematic withdrawal plans; the officers and directors of the fund; recent purchases and sales of securities; the current composition of the fund's portfolio; the fund's financial statements; and so on. In addition to the prospectus, funds prepare less comprehensive quarterly reports for shareholders.

Closed-end funds prepare annual reports similar to those of most other publicly held corporations. *Moody's* and *Standard and Poor's* financial manuals also provide comprehensive information on closed-end funds.

Forbes magazine publishes an annual review of the performance of most of the widely held funds. It also compares the funds' performance with several of the better-known stock market indexes.

Arthur Wiesenberger Services Corporation publishes a very comprehensive summary of essential information and performance records. This annual volume, entitled *Investment Companies*, covers all leading open- and closed-end funds. It is available in most brokerage houses and public libraries. Other recognized sources of information include: *Johnson's Charts*, published by Hugh Johnson and Company; *Mutual Fund Guide*, published by Kalb, Voorhis and Company; and *Fundscope* magazine.

MUTUAL FUND PERFORMANCE

Anyone interested in investing in a particular mutual fund would certainly want to know how that fund has performed historically relative to other, comparable funds and perhaps to the market as a whole. It is difficult to devise a widely acceptable, reliable, and understandable measure of performance, however. Actually, several areas of performance might be of interest. One might be to measure administrative efficiency; this is generally evaluated by expressing total operating expenses as a percentage of a fund's assets (the expense ratio) or sometimes as a percentage of fund income (the income ratio).

However, an assessment of the investment performance of a fund probably would be of far greater interest to a prospective investor. One commonly used measure of performance is simply to analyze the annual income dividends paid, realized capital gain distributions, and price fluctuations of the fund's shares over a period of time. But such "performance" data should be used by an investor with care. First, you should make comparisons based on a number of years' performance, like 10 to 15 years'. The results of any one year could be misleading or distorted. You should also be sure to use similar time periods. Be careful, too, about evaluating mutual fund performance only during "good times" (years of business prosperity). Second, it is important in analyzing performance to consider the investment objectives of a fund. For example, a balanced fund should do better than a growth fund in a declining market, while the opposite should be true in a sharply advancing market. Also, you should consider the risks involved. For example, since investors in a growth fund normally would be exposed to greater investment risks than would investors in, say, a balanced fund— given the nature of the investments of the two types of fund—the growth fund shareholders should expect to be rewarded with a higher average rate of return over a period of years.

SELECTING A FUND

Suppose, after considering all the preceding factors, you have decided you would like to invest in mutual funds. But which one? And when is the right time? These are not easy questions, and there is no "sure" answer; but here are some ideas that may help you in this important choice.

1. See if *the fund's objectives and investment policies* meet with your own objectives. As we saw above, funds can have a wide variety of investment objectives and you can normally find a fund or funds to meet most objectives. So it is largely a matter of finding the right fund(s) to meet your objectives. A mutual fund's investment objectives and how it seeks to attain those objectives (its investment policy) are described in its prospectus.

2. Consider *the fund's past performance* (see above) in light of its objectives. Some information in this regard also is contained in a mutual fund's prospectus (see the prospectus section, "Per-share Income and Capital Changes").

3. Determine, as best you can, *the qualifications and experience of the people in management* who are managing the fund's portfolio. Information on the officers and directors of a mutual fund is contained in the prospectus.

4. Briefly look over *the securities in the fund's portfolio* (e.g., in the "Statement of Investments" section of the prospectus) to see how they

appear to you. Do they generally seem to be the kind of securities you would like to own?

5. If it is a load fund, *consider its sales charges* to see how they compare with those of similar funds.

6. Consider the *various shareholder services* the fund will make available to you, including: the right of accumulation, available investment plans, a systematic withdrawal plan, and any exchange privilege.

7. Remember that *funds normally are considered long-term investments.* Therefore, do not be too concerned with strictly short-term changes in fund values.

8. However, *investment timing* can be as important in buying fund shares as in investing in individual stocks or bonds. Therefore, you should consider the investment climate and your own strategy with respect to investment timing (see Chapter 7) before buying fund shares.

10
TAX SHELTERS AND OTHER EQUITY INVESTMENTS

This chapter winds up our discussion of equity-type investments as ways of accumulating capital. It also deals with a subject of increasing attention in recent years—tax-sheltered investments.

Probably the most important of these investments is real estate. The subject of real estate as an investment really transcends its use as a tax shelter but is included here because real estate is often discussed in terms of its tax advantages. Real estate was a favored investment for many people long before it was viewed as a tax shelter.

The equity-type investments of most people revolve largely around listed common stocks, mutual funds investing in common stocks, and recently perhaps variable annuity contracts sold by life insurance companies (see Chapter 13). However, for some investors, particularly those in high income tax brackets, carefully studied and selected tax-sheltered investments may be very logical as a portion of their investment portfolio. Moreover, other investors may find one or more kinds of investments described here, which they had not considered before, interesting to them for one reason or another.

TAX-SHELTERED INVESTMENTS

This is a broad term that can apply to many kinds of investments from the tax-free (deferred) buildup of life insurance cash values and Series E savings bonds to the interest on municipal bonds. However, as the term has been applied in recent years, it means certain specialized kinds of tax-favored investments, like real estate, oil and gas businesses, and certain farming operations such as cattle feeding. These tax-sheltered investments generally involve one or more of the following tax benefits.

1. Accelerated depreciation and amortization
2. Deferral of taxable income through current income tax deductions
3. Use of current income tax deductions to shelter (offset) other taxable income
4. Special statutory deductions, such as percentage depletion
5. Taking returns as long-term capital gains

In addition, such investments usually rely on the investor's borrowing heavily to finance the investment (high leverage) and taking an income tax deduction for the debt interest.

Reasons for Tax Shelters

Tax-sheltered investments are basically attractive to those in high income tax brackets who can afford to take considerable investment risks. Such individuals want to invest their money so as to "shelter" their returns as much as possible from what are in some cases almost confiscatory combined federal, state, and local income tax rates. They also may want the higher returns possible on high-risk investments.

Also, some of these investments, particularly real estate, may be of interest to other people primarily for their merits as investments, aside from possible tax advantages. In general, however, the income tax aspects of these investments have tended to become dominant, and they often are not suitable for persons in lower brackets.

Pitfalls in Tax-sheltered Investments

Tax-sheltered investments should be made with great care and normally only after seeking competent professional advice. This is particularly necessary with respect to these investments for several reasons.

First, they are of a *specialized nature* in areas where the investor frequently is not knowledgeable (oil and gas drilling, cattle ranching, particular real estate deals, and so forth). Thus, the investor really cannot judge the quality of such an investment without outside technical advice, which, of course, costs money. The investor also should have proper tax and legal advice on those important aspects of such an investment. One should also bear in mind that presently favorable tax rules can change in the future.

Second, the *ability, reputation, and character of the promoter and his or her possible financial stake in the deal* are of critical importance. Also, *consider the "load" or profit to the promoter* that you may be paying. This is shown in the prospectus of a public offering. If this "load" is too high, so little of the amount you pay actually will be available for investment that your chances for profit will be substantially diminished.

Many tax-sheltered investment deals are sold as limited-partnership interests. While this usually means that the investor (as a limited partner) is not liable for the debts, obligations, or any losses of the partnership beyond the limited partner's original contribution to the partnership capital, it also usually means that the general partners (the promoters and/or their associates) have the exclusive right to manage and operate the partnership. The limited partners have no control. This again speaks to the need for evaluating the promoter.

Third, it is easy to be blinded by promised tax benefits in making these investments. You should *be sure a tax shelter offers economic potential as an investment* before committing any funds to it. Sometimes such investments are touted or viewed entirely as "good tax deals." This is not to say that their potential tax benefits are not important to such deals, but they are not by any means the only consideration. It stands to reason that, when all is said and done, you cannot make money by losing it. The economic merit of an investment also is important to securing expected tax benefits. The tax authorities may attack a transaction as a "sham" that only trades on its tax results with no other economic merit (see Chapter 14).

Fourth, *high interest rates may make many tax shelters questionable investments.* As we said above, many of these deals are heavily financed with borrowed funds, and even if the interest is deductible, the high cost of money can make them impractical economically. Also, one of the investment alternatives of the high-bracket taxpayer is income-tax-free municipal bonds. Higher yields, in general, may make municipals relatively more attractive.

Finally, tax shelters generally are *high-risk, long-term investments with very limited liquidity and marketability.* In a limited-partnership situation, for example, a limited partner usually cannot assign or sell his or her interest in the partnership without the consent of the general partner(s). Also, there are no established markets or price quotations for such limited-partnership interests, and a minimum investment usually is required.

However, with all these warnings, we recognize that various tax-sheltered investments that are properly selected and evaluated for their investment merits, highly leveraged, and entered into by high-bracket taxpayers (say, at least a 40 percent federal income tax bracket) may result in attractive after-tax yields (say, annual yields of 10 to 35 percent or more), depending on the particular investment. Such investors may want to consider tax shelters *as a part of* their total investment portfolio. However, they should make sure they have adequate liquid assets and life insurance protection before doing so. Also, they would be well advised to have impartial, outside experts evaluate a tax shelter before investing in it. Some banks, accounting firms, tax specialists, and other advisors specialize in evaluating tax-sheltered investments on a fee basis.

TYPES OF TAX-SHELTERED INVESTMENTS

Many kinds of tax-sheltered investments exist, but only some of the more important will be mentioned here. Also, we cannot attempt to go into all the tax and yield ramifications of each in the limited space available here.

Real Estate

Historically, real estate has been a widely used investment medium for income and capital gains. It also offers tax advantages which permit it to be classified as a tax shelter.

A great many people have, in a sense, an investment in real estate in that they own their home, condominium, or cooperative apartment. Many people also own a second or vacation home. Some others may own smaller, income-producing properties that they hold as an investment, while a few have larger real estate interests of various kinds.

Should You Consider Real Estate as an Investment? This is a hard question, for the answer depends upon such factors as your own circumstances; what kind of real estate you are talking about; the state of the local real estate market; and general economic conditions, including interest rates.

To help you answer this question for yourself, let us first consider *the advantages cited for real estate investments.*

1. The possibility exists of earning a higher-than-average total yield on your investment. This may result from the inherent advantages of owning well-selected real estate (the idea that real estate basically is a good investment), the use of financial leverage, and tax advantages. But one difficulty in comparing the yields on real estate investments with those of other investments is that there are several concepts and techniques used for measuring real estate rates of return, and some of them are quite complex for most people to apply. However, to help give you a point of reference, here is a simple formula that often is used by real estate brokers and individual investors as a rough rule of thumb for comparing the yields on different investment properties:

$$\text{Rate of return} = \frac{\text{net income from property before interest and depreciation}}{\text{purchase price for property}}$$

Thus, if a small apartment house produced a net annual income, after allowances for property taxes and expenses, but before interest on a mortgage, depreciation, and income taxes, of $12,000, and its purchase price is $120,000, the rate of return under this formula is:

$$\text{Rate of return} = \frac{\$12,000}{\$120,000} = 10\%$$

Now, how does *financial leverage* enter the picture? "Leverage" is simply the use of borrowed funds (normally under a long-term mortgage in real estate) by an investor to try to increase the rate of return the investor can earn on his or her own funds invested in the project.[1] In general, when the cost of borrowing is less than what can be earned on the investment, it is considered *favorable leverage,* but when the reverse is true, it is called *unfavorable leverage.* Of course, when real estate is used as a tax shelter, it is expected that the project will produce a tax loss during a period of years that will result in a return to the high-bracket taxpayer of tax savings plus a favorable cash flow.

The main tax advantage of investment in improved real estate is depreciation, which will be discussed a little later.

[1]Sometimes leverage is also viewed as the use of borrowed funds with the *hope* that the *value* of the real estate will increase at a faster rate than the cost of borrowing the funds.

2. Some consider real estate, like other equity investments, as a hedge against inflation.

3. Good-quality income property normally will produce a favorable cash flow. This results despite the fact that the property technically may produce a tax loss on paper, because depreciation is a noncash expense, and because depreciation, particularly accelerated depreciation, is a big expense factor in real estate.

4. There are tax advantages. As we said above, the main tax advantage of investing in improved real estate is the opportunity of taking depreciation (writing off the cost of buildings and other physical property, but not land, over their useful life) as an income tax deduction against the income from the real estate. Also, depending on the nature of the real estate, various accelerated depreciation methods can be used. It is this tax-deductible depreciation that, in effect, shelters the real estate income (and perhaps other taxable income as well) from income taxation. Further, costs to operate and maintain property, such as property taxes, insurance, and repairs, are deductible. Also, real estate can be traded or exchanged for similar property on a tax-free basis. Finally, on the sale of improved investment real estate, any gain normally is a long-term capital gain, except that the excess of accelerated depreciation over straight-line depreciation (called "additional depreciation") may be subject to depreciation recapture as ordinary income (to the extent of any gain).

Now let us look at some of the *possible disadvantages of real estate investment.*

1. There is relatively poor marketability in real estate, as compared with other investment media, and the expenses of buying and selling are relatively high.

2. Similarly, there is a lack of liquidity in real estate.

3. A relatively large initial investment often is required to buy real estate.

4. It may be difficult to determine the proper value for real estate, particularly for the uninitiated. Real estate is not uniform, and there are definite cycles in the real estate market. All real estate does not go up, even in times of economic prosperity.

5. Real estate is considered by many to be an inherently risky form of investment. It is basically fixed in location and character. Also, it is an equity-type investment, and real estate values will collapse during a period of economic depression as rapidly as, or perhaps even more rapidly than, other kinds of equity investments.

6. High interest rates may adversely affect real estate investments.

How Can You Invest in Real Estate? If you want to do so, there are several ways you can invest in real estate. First of all, you can simply buy property in your own name or as joint tenants or tenants in common with someone else. This is the traditional way of holding real estate, but it limits the size of the investment that can be made to the amount of capital you and perhaps a few others can raise. Real estate, of course, can also be owned by corporations and general partnerships.

You can also invest in real estate by buying units of a *limited-partnership interest* in a real estate venture. The limited partnership is a commonly used vehicle for real estate investment where the investors are the limited partners and the promoter, builder, or developers are the general partners. In this way, the limited partners can invest their capital with only limited liability for partnership debts, and the earnings (and tax losses) from the real estate can be "passed through" the partnership form of organization to the individual limited partners without being taxed to the partnership. The earnings (or losses) are taxable to (or deductible by) the individual partners. The general partners can manage the real estate investment, which usually is their business. But, again, note the importance of the character, ability, and experience of the general partners in any such deal, because the general partners are in control. There have been many offerings to the public in recent years of real estate limited-partnership interests. Some of them may be attractive to you as tax-sheltered investments, but before investing read any prospectus carefully, evaluate the deal or have someone evaluate the deal for you, and remember the pitfalls of tax-sheltered investments we discussed earlier. However, some such deals may be good investments for you, depending on your needs and circumstances.

Another method of real estate investment for the public is through a *real estate investment trust (REIT)*. A REIT is generally similar in concept to a closed-end investment company (see Chapter 9, "Mutual Funds"), but it is organized to invest in real estate. A REIT can give the real estate investor many of the investment advantages of corporate ownership, including centralized management, limited liability, continuity of interests, and transferability of ownership. Thus, the investor can have, through a REIT, the advantage of investment marketability, which is not generally present in a limited-partnership real estate syndicate.

The main advantage of a REIT over a public real estate corporation is the REIT's unique tax status. Corporations are subject to the corporate income tax (i.e., they are taxable entities), while a REIT (like a mutual fund) can avoid, or largely avoid, the corporate tax by distributing its earnings to its shareholders. The distribution is then taxed to the shareholder as ordinary income or capital gains. However, a REIT cannot pass on an operating loss to its shareholders, as can a limited-partnership syndicate. Thus, REIT shareholders cannot use such operating losses to shelter other taxable income—a procedure which, as we saw above, often is one of the tax advantages sought in tax-sheltered real estate investments.

REITs vary considerably in size, origin, and types of real estate investments made. Some are speculative and others are quite conservative in their investments. Therefore, be sure to find out the investment objective of any REIT you are considering. Also remember that *management is critical. The public generally is not able to judge the investments a REIT makes, so your main concern should be the quality of its management.*

You can buy shares in REITs through your broker on organized stock exchanges or over the counter. Some examples of REITs traded on the New York Stock Exchange are Chase Manhattan Mortgage and Equity Trust, Cousins Mortgage and Equity Investments, The Equitable Life Mortgage and Realty Investors, IDS Realty Trust, and North American Mortgage Investors.

Kinds of Real Estate in Which You Can Invest. Not all real estate investments are the same. Some are very speculative while others are quite conservative. As far as tax and investment considerations are concerned, real estate probably can be classified as:

1. Unimproved land investments ("bare land")
2. Improved real estate

   New and used residential property (apartment houses and the like)

   Low-income housing (where investors are allowed special tax incentives)

   Other income-producing real estate (such as office buildings, shopping centers, and various industrial and commercial properties)
3. Mortgages (such as through government-guaranteed Ginnie Mae passthroughs, for example—see Chapter 11)

Oil and Gas Ventures

These are probably the most risky of the tax-sheltered investments, but by the same token they can yield very handsome returns if successful. It has been estimated, for example, that about 1 in 15 wildcat wells results in a small oil field, 1 in 200 results in a medium-sized field, and only 1 in 1,000 results in a large field.

Two basic tax incentives have existed for oil- and gas-drilling investments. The tax law permits:

1. The deduction from taxable income (i.e., the sheltering of other income) of intangible drilling costs, which could be about 60 to 70 percent of the cost of a productive well. If the well is dry, the entire cost can be deducted from taxable income. For high-bracket taxpayers, this substantially reduces the after-tax cost of failure (dry holes).
2. A percentage depletion allowance, whereby the taxpayer can deduct this allowance from his or her gross income from oil and gas investments.

People can, of course, invest directly in oil and gas operations. However, in recent years many oil and gas limited partnerships, registered with the SEC, have been offered to the public as a way of investing in oil and gas tax shelters. All the comments and suggestions made earlier concerning such limited partnerships also apply here.

Other Tax Shelters

There is a variety of other kinds of tax-sheltered investments that could be mentioned. They include: *cattle breeding and other farming enterprises, timber, minerals and mining operations, equipment leasing,* and *purchase of deep-discount bonds with a large percentage of the purchase price borrowed,* among others. They each have their particular tax features and advantages and limitations for the high-bracket taxpayer. Space does not permit full discussion of each of them in this book, but interested persons can get information on them from other sources and from professional advisors in this field.

OTHER EQUITY INVESTMENTS

There is a variety of equity-type investments or techniques for making such investments. Some may be inappropriate for your circumstances or interests, and others may be too speculative, but you at least may want to know about them. Not all "other equity investments" are discussed here because space does not permit it; however, your investment advisors can discuss them with you if you are interested.

How to Use Put and Call Options

"Puts" and "calls" are *options* to sell and buy securities within a specified, usually fairly short, time period. A *call* is an option allowing the buyer of the call *to purchase* from someone a certain stock at a set price (called the exercise or "striking" price) at any time within a specified period. On the other hand, a *put* is an option allowing the buyer of the put *to sell* to someone a certain stock at a set price at any time within a specified period. These options normally are for round lots (100 shares) of common stock. In the over-the-counter (OTC) option market, options can be written for periods (maturities) of one month, two months, three months (or 95 days), six months and 10 days, or a year. In the case of option trading on the Chicago Board Options Exchange (CBOE), options on a stock are available for only a few standardized expiration dates, which are the last business days of January, April, July, and October.

Buying Options. You normally buy options (either calls or puts or both) when you want *to speculate* on whether a stock is going up or down or is going to fluctuate beyond certain limits. The price you pay for the option is called the *premium.*

Let us see how buying options might work. Suppose you think XYZ Common is too low and the price soon will go up substantially. In this case, you might buy a *call option* for XYZ Common. Suppose, for example, you could acquire a six-month-and-10-day call option (for 100 shares) on XYZ at an exercise price of $50 per share for a premium of $625. Now, if your judgment is correct and XYZ climbs to $70 per share during the six-month period, your profit (exclusive of commissions and other charges) would be as follows:

Gross return	$2,000 ($70 − $50 = $20 × 100 shares)
Cost of call	625
Profit	$1,375

You can see that this profit would be more than a 100 percent increase over your $625 "investment." This *speculative leverage generally is the attraction of options*. But if you are wrong, and XYZ stays at $50 or declines during the six months and 10 days, you will lose all your $625 premium. However, your loss will be limited to the cost of the call ($625 in this example). Thus, your *chance* of profit can be high but your loss will be limited.

You could, of course, have simply bought XYZ Common outright or on margin if you thought the price was going up (see Chapter 8). But because of the speculative leverage involved, you get a much bigger "swing" out of a dollar "invested" with options even than with buying on margin.

While leveraged speculation is the main reason for buying calls, there are some other possible reasons: to sell some of your existing investments to release cash while still maintaining your short-term market position; as a protection against short-term market uncertainty; and as a hedge against short sales you may have made.

On the other hand, if you think XYZ Common is overpriced and soon will fall substantially, you might buy a *put option*. It would basically work the same way as a call, except in the opposite direction. You want the stock to fall substantially to make your speculative profit. Another reason for buying puts may be to protect yourself for the short term in a declining market.

The *amount of the premium* you must pay for an option naturally varies with market and other factors; but as a generalization, premiums may range from 5 to 15 percent of the market value of the underlying stock. For you to make a profit on options (puts or calls), the price of the underlying stock must fluctuate rapidly and substantially (and, of course, in the right direction). In many cases, options prove to be unprofitable for the speculator because the underlying stock prices do not fluctuate enough over the relatively short option period to offset the premium paid for the option.

The exercise (or "striking") price of options in the over-the-counter market generally is tied to the last trade in the underlying stock at the time the option contract originates. On the options exchange (CBOE), on the other hand, options have standardized exercise prices so that organized options trading is possible.

More sophisticated traders can engage in a variety of option techniques. One is the *straddle*, in which you buy a put *and* a call in the same stock with the same terms and dates. Here the speculator will profit if the underlying stock's price moves *far enough in either direction* to more than offset the premiums on both options. *Strips, straps,* and *spreads* can also be used as techniques.

Remember that buying options is an *aggressive, speculative* investment strategy. Therefore, even persons who want to follow this kind of strategy should normally commit only a relatively small percentage of their assets to buying options, as is true for risky, speculative investments in general.

Selling (Writing) Options. Now we are on the other side of the fence. We are selling options (calls or puts) to others.

The motivation for selling options normally is entirely different from the motivation for buying them. The option writer (individuals or institutions with portfolios of stock or cash) normally wants to secure an attractive yield on his or her existing investment. This increased yield comes from the premiums received by the option writer on the options he or she grants to buyers. For example, a 10 to 15 percent premium for writing six-month call options would amount to a 20 to 30 percent annual return.

The option writer, however, gives up the opportunity for capital appreciation on stock he or she owns that is called away. But if the price of the stock declines, the option writer bears this risk (except, of course, that the writer has the premium on any call he or she wrote on the stock).

But there are some warnings commonly given to careful option writers. Do not write "naked" call options. These are options where you do not own the underlying security. Generally, you should sell calls only on securities in your portfolio or on securities purchased for this purpose. Also, sell puts only against cash and only on stock you would otherwise want in your portfolio. However, some pure speculators do write options with the objective of profiting from price changes. Only speculators who can afford to take the considerable risks involved should do this.

Buying New Issues

Stocks and bonds offered by corporations for the first time are called *new issues.* Some new issues are offered by corporate giants, like Campbell Soup, Exxon, and American Telephone and Telegraph, either to raise money or to "go public." Such corporations often are of the "blue-chip" variety, and the investment merits of their new issues can be judged by an investor accordingly. In many cases, the market price of these new issues rose substantially immediately after they were sold and there was considerable interest in them at the time.

However, most new issues are made by smaller, relatively unknown, or newly formed corporations. Many of them do not have an established "track record" of operations and earnings. Hence, they are often highly speculative. Some investors, however, like to buy such new issues as speculations. Those, like the Kentucky Fried Chicken Corporation, that prove successful offer phenomenal gains for their original buyers. But a great many such new issues do not prove successful in the long run, and so the chance of loss in such speculative investments is high.

Another aspect of investing in new issues, however, is that some studies have shown that the prices of new issues *during the first year of their life* have outperformed already existing stocks. This may be because of the speculative interest at that time in such new issues.

Commodity Futures Trading

Persons usually engage in commodity futures trading in hopes of profiting from price changes in one or more of a number of basic commodities. These commodities include wheat, corn, oats, soybeans, potatoes, platinum, copper, silver, orange juice (frozen concentrated), cocoa, eggs, frozen pork bellies, lumber, iced broilers, and many more. You can speculate on price changes in these commodities by buying and selling futures contracts in the particular commodity.

A *futures contract* is an agreement to buy or sell a commodity at a price stated in the agreement on a specified future date. While futures contracts call for the delivery of the commodity (unless the contract is liquidated before it matures), this is rarely done, and the speculator in commodity futures almost always "closes out" his or her position in a futures contract before the contract matures. This way the commodity itself never actually changes hands among speculators. On the other hand, contracts to buy or sell the physical commodities are made in the cash (or "spot") market. The listing of the prices of commodity futures and cash (spot) commodity prices is shown in the financial pages of many daily newspapers and in various financial newspapers.

Let us see how you might trade in commodity futures. Suppose you think the price of, say, corn is going up. You might back up your opinion by entering into a futures contract *to buy* 5,000 bushels of corn (a full contract in corn) for delivery in December at a price of $3 per bushel, which would be the market price for December corn at the time the buy order was executed (assuming it was a market order). This is referred to as being "long" in the commodity.

Now suppose that you were correct and in a month the price of December corn futures rises 20 cents per bushel to $3.20. You now might decide to close out your transaction by selling 5,000 bushels of December corn and take your 20 cents per bushel profit, or a total of $1,000 (5,000 × 0.20 = $1,000), exclusive of commissions and other costs. However, you could have effectively magnified this profit through the leverage of trading on margin. Margin requirements in commodities are relatively low—usually being 10 to 20 percent of the value of the commodity traded. If the margin requirement in this example had been 10 percent (for purposes of illustration), you would have had to put up only $1,500 for your original futures contract and would have borrowed the rest on margin. You can see how this leverage can magnify a speculator's potential profits (and losses) in terms of the amount the speculator actually puts up. Of course, if the price of December corn futures had declined and you had closed out your transaction, you would have suffered similar speculative, leveraged losses. As in other areas, *leverage works both ways.*

Suppose, instead, that you think the price of corn is too high and is going down. In this case you would *sell short.* You might, for example, enter into a futures contract *to sell* 5,000 bushels of corn for delivery in December at a price of $3 per bushel. But here you would hope to close out your transaction (cover your short position) when the price of December corn had fallen below $3 per bushel, and your profit (exclusive of commissions and other costs) would be the difference between your original selling price ($3 in this example) and your eventual (hopefully lower) purchase price. Of course, if the price of December corn futures rises, and you cover your short position, you will lose on the transaction.

There are, of course, many other techniques for dealing in commodity futures that are not discussed here. Your broker or dealer can advise you about them if you are interested.

A word of caution is in order. While the opportunities for speculative profits in commodity futures trading can be enormous and quick, the risks are equally so. Trading in commodity futures is inherently speculative and risky. Authorities in the field estimate, for example, that speculators lose 75 to 80 percent of the time. Therefore, you generally should not get involved unless you have substantial risk capital in liquid form, adequate other resources, and the ability to control your emotions—mainly fear and greed. Also, as we said above with respect to puts and calls, you normally should not commit more than a relatively small percentage of your total resources to speculation. In other words, if you cannot afford to lose, you should not get involved. But if you follow these cautions, you will have a much better chance to be a successful speculator, if you should decide that commodities are for you.

Art, Antiques, Coins, Stamps, Gold, Silver, etc.

Some people are interested in investing in these more unusual items. In recent years, properly selected items in some of these areas have shown substantial increases in price. This has led some to regard buying such items as a "hedge against inflation." As we have said before, however, this is true only if their prices keep rising, and there is no necessary connection between the prices of such items and inflation. This is not to say that these items may not be good investments for some people under the right circumstances. It is just that inflation does not have much to do with it.

These items are unique and specialized, and so buying them successfully requires a knowledge of what you are doing. Also, they produce no investment income—only possible price appreciation. Of course, many people have a collector's interest in such property anyway, and so it is quite logical for them to acquire these items. However, viewed purely as an investment, they would not seem to be suitable for most people.

11

INVESTING IN FIXED-INCOME SECURITIES

Two earlier chapters—Chapter 2, "Setting Your Objectives," and Chapter 7, "Basic Investment Principles"—covered many of the essentials needed for making investment decisions as a key part of your personal financial planning. These earlier chapters stressed the need to look objectively at your attitude toward taking risks—your basic investment objectives—and presented the necessary criteria and arithmetic for you to understand the strengths and weaknesses of many different kinds of investments. The previous three chapters have dealt with various equity-type investments— the most important for most people probably being common stocks and mutual funds. Yet, for most individuals, they form only part of their overall investment program. Many types of what might be called "fixed-income" investment outlets also are available to you. In fact, the variety of these fixed-income investment outlets has increased in recent years. This chapter examines many of these fixed-income securities and investments to see how they might fit into your financial planning.

WHAT ARE FIXED-INCOME INVESTMENTS?

Simply stated, fixed-income investments promise the investor a stated amount of income periodically. For example, a savings account may pay 5 percent interest a year, a certificate of deposit (CD) 7½ percent, and a corporate bond 7 to 9 percent. Naturally, such rates may vary over time.

The buying and selling of fixed-income securities after their initial offering create a public market in many of these securities. Dealings in short-term securities—those sold to satisfy short-term money needs—create the money market. Dealings in long-term securities—those sold to finance long-term capital needs—create the capital market. Both markets are large, broad, and active.

About fifteen different kinds of securities are traded in the money and capital markets. The kinds of securities available can satisfy a variety of investment goals. For example, investors can obtain current income with maximum safety by buying treasury bills, or maximum income over a period of time by buying long-term corporate bonds, or a tax-free return by buying municipal bonds. Also, attractive opportunities for capital growth may be provided by convertible bonds, preferred stocks, and so-called "deep-discount" bonds. Thus, the markets for fixed-income securities offer investors a variety of possibilities for meeting at least some of their investment objectives.

In the following sections of this chapter, we discuss the various kinds of fixed-income investments and the influences that affect the market prices of fixed-income securities. We also offer some guidelines to successful investment in the fixed-income markets and how such investments can be used and coordinated in achieving your personal financial goals and security.

TYPES OF FIXED-INCOME INVESTMENTS

Many varieties of fixed-income securities and investments are available to the individual investor. They include the following:

Preferred stocks

Convertible preferred stocks

Corporate bonds

Convertible bonds

"Deep-discount" bonds

Municipal bonds

Tax-free notes

Bond funds

United States Treasury bills

United States Treasury notes

United States Treasury bonds

United States savings bonds

United States government agency securities

Flower bonds

Ginnie Mae pass-throughs

Certificates of deposit

Savings accounts

Preferred Stocks

Preferred stocks represent equity capital of a corporation, and the claim that preferred stockholders have against the assets of the corporation follows the claim of bondholders but precedes that of common stockholders. In almost all cases a company must pay dividends on its preferred stock before paying anything on its common. But a corporation can pass (omit) its preferred dividends without becoming insolvent. The dividend rate on preferred stock usually is fixed, and when dividends are cumulative, any arrears of preferred dividends must be paid before dividends can be paid on the common stock.

Although preferred stocks ("preferreds") do not have fixed maturities like bonds, they may be subject to call. Preferreds also may have sinking fund provisions that require the company to allocate funds to retire a certain number of shares each year. Preferred stockholders normally do not have voting rights unless dividends have been in arrears for a specified period or certain sinking fund provisions have not been met.

Except for public utilities and companies with similar needs for maintaining a certain relationship between equity and debt, corporations have almost ceased to offer preferred stocks as a means of raising new capital. The tax laws allow corporations to deduct interest payments on debt in computing their taxable income, but dividends on preferred stock must be paid from after-tax income. Also, a steady decline in the gross-yield advantage provided by preferred stocks in relation to high-quality bonds has occurred in recent years. Since preferreds rank below bonds in the corporate capital structure, investors actually should expect to receive higher yields on preferreds than on bonds. Thus, preferred stocks generally have become less attractive to individual investors.

Corporate Bonds

All bonds, whether corporate or otherwise, are promises to pay interest at stated rates (coupon rates) and to repay principal at a specified maturity date, with certain minor exceptions. They differ mainly in their terms concerning security pledged, their provisions for repayment of principal, and various other technical features.

In recent years, corporate bonds have commanded an increasing share of the funds invested for fixed income. There have been sharp rises in long-term interest rates and in the volume of corporate bond financing.

Kinds of Corporate Bonds. Year in and year out, public utilities offer the largest percentage of corporate bond issues. Most utility bonds are *mortgage bonds,* secured by a lien on all or a portion of the fixed property of the company.

The demand of manufacturing corporations for funds has a pronounced influence on the corporate bond market. Most bonds of manufacturing and other industrial corporations are *debentures*—bonds that are backed by the full credit of the issuing corporation but that have no special lien on the corporation's property. Debentures generally have first claim on all assets not specifically pledged under mortgage bond indentures. Debentures also may be protected by a guarantee that specified assets will not be pledged for issues of new mortgage bonds, or otherwise encumbered, unless the debentures are secured by assets of equal value. *Subordinated debentures* have a claim on assets only after the claims of senior debt are satisfied. *Income debentures* are a kind of subordinated debenture on which interest is payable only if it is earned. If the company's income is insufficient to pay the interest, however, the interest usually is accumulated and must be paid before any dividends can be paid on preferred or common stocks.

In recent years, increasing numbers of finance companies, banks, and real estate companies have made use of public bond offerings. Also, various kinds of *equipment trust certificates* (like railroad equipment trust certificates) rank among top-quality corporate securities because of their direct claim on specific property that can be used by other corporations (e.g., railroads) if the issuer should default on its obligation. A trust certificate can be issued against various kinds of equipment that a trustee, usually a bank, buys from an equipment manufacturer and then leases to the user. The holder of the trust certificate becomes the beneficial owner of the property, and the user makes rental payments at fixed intervals to retire the certificates.

Call Provisions. Most corporate bonds can be retired or "called" before maturity, and periods of declining interest rates historically have provided opportunities for corporations to refund their bond issues at a lower interest cost. However, many corporations now issue securities that offer investors protection for a specified period of time against call or refunding (the redemption of an entire issue by the sale of a new issue) at lower interest rates. This period of call protection varies but may be 5 years on utility issues and 10 years on industrial issues. Investors often are willing to accept a moderately lower yield in exchange for some call protection. This assures them that their interest income will be maintained at a certain level for at least a given time, even if interest rates decline in the future. In recent years, virtually all new issues have provided some type of protection against early call or refunding.

Sinking Fund Provisions. Many bond issues also have sinking fund provisions designed to retire a substantial portion of the bonds before maturity. Bonds in a designated amount are selected by lot for retirement at fixed intervals; in that way, the issuer repays the debt gradually. Some companies may also satisfy sinking fund provisions by buying their own bonds that are to be retired in the open market. Sinking funds strengthen the fundamental position of a bond issue; however, in recent years such provisions have become less popular with investors who are seeking to preserve liberal returns for as long as possible. For that reason, sinking fund provisions often are deferred.

Deep-discount Bonds

These bonds sell in the market for much less than their face amount (par value) because they were issued at a time when interest rates were lower. For example, take a bond with a 4⅜ percent coupon rate that is to mature in 15 years. Assume the current market price of this bond is 68. This means a $1,000-face-amount bond is selling in the market for $680, or at a 32 percent discount from par. This is a deep-discount bond. Investors may like such bonds for several reasons.

1. They provide *automatic call protection* because their coupon rates are relatively low compared with current market interest rates—4⅜ percent in the example cited.

2. They provide, in effect, *a built-in capital gain upon maturity*—32 percent in 15 years in the above example—coupled with a reasonably good current yield in the meantime.

3. A *tax advantage* exists because the difference between the face amount at maturity and the purchase price ($1,000–$680 = $320, in the above example) is taxed as a long-term capital gain (if held more than 6 months, see Chapter 14) rather than as ordinary income.

But because of these advantages, investors tend to bid up the prices of these bonds, and deep-discount bonds normally sell in the market at somewhat lower yields than comparable bonds with higher coupon rates. Nevertheless, deep-discount bonds are still attractive to many investors.

Any kind of bond—corporate, municipal, or United States government—may sell at a discount. The above tax advantage becomes reversed for "municipals," however, because their coupon rate is tax-free anyway, and so a capital gains tax actually becomes a disadvantage for them.

Municipal Bonds

Tax-exempt interest is the most important feature of municipal bonds (see Chapter 14). Municipals are particularly attractive to persons whose income tax brackets enable them to realize a greater after-tax net return from tax-free interest than from interest that is fully taxable. Table 11-1 illustrates the relationship between the effective return on municipal bonds and that of other fixed-income investments.

TABLE 11-1

1.	2.	3.	4.	5.	6.	7.
				Your Take-home	Your Take-home	
		Your Take-home From a Tax-free 6% Bond Is	Your Take-home From a Bank Paying 5% Taxable Is	From a US Govt Bond Paying 6% Taxable Is	From a Corporate Bond Paying 7½% Taxable Is	To Keep 6% From a Taxable Bond It Would Have to Pay You
If Your Net Joint Taxable Income Is	Your Federal Tax Bracket Is					
$ 16,000	28%	6%	3.60%	4.32%	5.40%	8.33%
$ 25,000	36%	6%	3.20%	3.85%	4.80%	9.37%
$ 35,000	42%	6%	2.90%	3.48%	4.35%	10.34%
$ 50,000	50%	6%	2.50%	3.00%	3.75%	12.00%
$ 75,000*	55%	6%	2.25%	2.70%	3.38%	13.33%
$100,000*	62%	6%	1.90%	2.28%	2.85%	15.79%

*Taxable income from all sources, "earned" and otherwise.

You can use this table by finding your own income bracket in column 1 and then reading across the columns. For example, a husband and wife who file a joint return on $25,000 of income (after deductions and adjustments) are in a 36 percent federal income tax bracket (column 2). The income from a municipal bond paying 6 percent would be all theirs to keep. But in a 36 percent tax bracket, they could keep only 3.20 percent from a savings account paying 5 percent (taxable), 3.85 percent from a United States government obligation paying 6 percent (taxable), and 4.80 percent from a $7\frac{1}{2}$ percent corporate bond (taxable). Based on these figures, this couple probably should consider municipals. Note that while the above-quoted yields will change over time, it is the *relationship* between municipal bond yields and other yields that is the basic point for the investor.

Municipal bonds are issued by cities, towns, and villages; by states, territories, and possessions of the United States; and by housing authorities, port authorities, and other political subdivisions. The tremendous increase in the volume of new municipal issues has resulted from the continuing demand for public facilities of all kinds.

Kinds of Municipal Bonds. There are several kinds of municipals of which the investor should be aware. The kind of bond has an impact on the security behind it.

General obligation bonds. This is the largest category of municipal bonds; they are secured by the full faith, credit, and taxing power of the issuing municipality. The principal and interest on state obligations, for example, are payable from the state's many and varied sources of revenue. The principal and interest on general obligation bonds of local governments usually are payable from unlimited ad valorem taxes on all taxable property within the area. General obligation bonds are normally considered to offer a high level of security for the investor, consistent, of course, with their credit rating (see below).

Sometimes an issuer borrows funds and pledges only a limited portion of its taxing power for the payment of principal and interest. Under these conditions, the bonds still are considered general obligation bonds, but they are referred to as *limited tax bonds.*

Special tax bonds. These bonds are payable only from the proceeds of a single tax, a series of taxes, or some other specific source of revenue. Such bonds are not secured by the full faith and credit of the state or municipality.

Revenue bonds. Revenue bonds are issued to finance many different kinds of projects, such as water, sewerage, gas, and electrical facilities; hospitals; dormitories; student-union halls and stadiums; hydroelectric power projects; and bridges, tunnels, turnpikes, and expressways. The principal and interest on such bonds are payable solely from the revenues produced by the project. Perhaps the largest and best-known kind of agency issuing revenue bonds is the toll-road or turnpike authority, which raises funds by means of bond issues and pays interest and principal out of the net earnings from the particular toll road.

Housing authority bonds. These bonds are issued by local authorities to finance the construction of low-rent housing projects and are secured by the pledge of unconditional, annual contributions by the Housing Assistance Administration, a federal agency. Housing authority bonds are considered top-quality investments because they are backed by the full faith and credit of the United States.

Industrial revenue bonds. These bonds are issued by a municipality or authority but are secured by lease payments made by industrial corporations that occupy or use the facilities financed by the bond issue.

Other Basic Facts. Most municipal bonds are bearer bonds. They also *mature serially;* that is, a certain number of bonds in each issue reach maturity in each year over a period that may range from one month to 50 years or longer. Such a range of maturities offers investors a great deal of flexibility in selecting maturities according to their needs. However, most general obligation bonds are redeemable only at maturity.

Quality ratings on municipal bonds are provided by Moody's and Standard & Poor's, the financial services that also rate corporate bonds (see later section in this chapter, "What You Should Know about a Bond"). The ratings are objective because these rating services conduct no security transactions. In general, municipal bonds rank second in quality only to securities issued by the United States government and government agencies. During the depression of the 1930s, for example, payments on more than 98 percent of all municipals were met without fail.

Short-term Tax-free Notes

These are project notes of local issuing agencies, states, municipalities, or other political subdivisions in denominations of $5,000 or more. They are issued to mature in one month to one year. These notes normally are secured by the full faith and credit of the issuer. Interest is paid at maturity. Some investors in high tax brackets use these tax-free notes as a way to keep their money working between major commitments.

Bond Funds

Many types of bond funds are available. These are similar in concept to mutual funds, except that instead of frequently being common stock-oriented, these funds are composed of bonds. There are general-purpose bond funds made up of bonds of all types, including corporate, government, and municipal. Other funds specialize in certain types of bonds, such as corporate bond funds, municipal bond funds, and government bond funds. Professional managers choose the bonds, arrange for their safekeeping, and collect the interest.

Many bond funds now are unit investment trusts where a portfolio of securities is selected at the time the trust is organized and is not subsequently changed. The sponsor of the trust (say, a broker or investment banker) then sells units in the trust to investors. There may be no management or redemption fees in connection with these trusts, and the units may be redeemable by the trust for an amount depending on the value of the bonds in the trust at the time of redemption.

There are also closed-end bond funds you can buy on organized stock exchanges. (See Chapter 9 for a discussion of closed-end investment companies.)

United States Government Obligations

Because the federal government generally is accepted as having the highest possible credit rating, yields on government obligations are basic for all maturity ranges throughout the capital markets. Rates on other securities tend to follow the rate structure set by government obligations but are generally higher.

Treasury Bills. Treasury bills are bearer obligations issued on a discount basis and redeemed at face value at maturity. Treasury bills dated March 5, 1970, and thereafter are issued in minimum denominations of $10,000. At present, the Treasury offers two new issues of bills each week for competitive bids; one issue matures in three months, the other in six months. Noncompetitive tenders from $10,000 to $200,000 of each issue can be submitted without a stated price. Such bids are allotted in full at the average price of accepted competitive bids.

Each month the Treasury offers, under the same general rules that apply to three- and six-month bills, a series of bills with maturities of nine months and one year. From time to time the Treasury also offers *tax-anticipation bills* for bids on a competitive basis. These bills may be used at face value to pay the buyers' income taxes, even though the maturity date usually is seven days after the tax payment date. Therefore, the yield is greater if buyers use the bills for tax payments instead of redeeming them for cash at maturity.

Treasury Notes. Treasury notes have maturities of from one to seven years. The notes are issued in bearer or registered form, and interest is paid semiannually.

Treasury Bonds. Treasury bonds, which mature in more than seven years, constitute the largest segment of the government's public debt. All bonds are available in registered or in bearer form. Interest is paid semiannually. Many of the bonds are callable at par five years before maturity on interest payment dates.

Savings Bonds. United States savings bonds are registered, noncallable, and nontransferable securities. They also are not acceptable as collateral for loans. Two kinds of savings bonds are now being issued—Series E and Series H.

Series E bonds are sold in face-value denominations of $25 to $10,000; denominations of $100,000 are available for employees' savings plans. Except for employees' savings plans, the maximum purchase in any one calendar year is $5,000. Series E bonds pay no current interest; instead, they are issued at a discount and are redeemable at face value on the maturity date. The effective interest rate depends on the length of time between the issue date and the maturity date. To raise the interest rate on these savings bonds, the government can shorten the time span between issue and maturity dates. Series E bonds are redeemable at any time starting two months after the issue date, but redemption before maturity usually reduces the effective yield.

Unlike Series E bonds, *Series H bonds* are sold at par, and the interest is paid every six months. Denominations of H bonds range from $500 to $10,000, but a single purchaser is limited to $5,000 in any one year. Series H bonds may be redeemed six months after the issue date.

Other United States Government and Agency Securities

United States Government Agency Securities. These securities are not issued directly by the federal government, but some have government guarantees. They typically carry yields somewhat higher than for comparable United States government securities. Some of the governmental agencies that issue these types of securities are: the *Federal Intermediate Credit Banks*, the *District Banks for Cooperatives*, the *Federal Land Banks*, the *Federal Home Loan Banks*, the *Federal National Mortgage Association* (Fanny Mae), the *Government National Mortgage Association*, the *International Bank for Reconstruction and Development* (World Bank), and the *Inter-American Development Bank*.

Flower Bonds. These are United States government bonds with a special feature. The federal government will accept them at full par value in payment of federal estate taxes. However, you may be able to buy them at a discount in the market. Therefore, your estate can realize a gain if they are used to pay your estate taxes.

Ginnie Mae Pass-Throughs. This is a new type of security that permits an individual to earn high mortgage yields with both principal and interest payments guaranteed by the federal government. These securities feature an average life of 10 to 12 years with a minimum investment of $25,000.

A special feature of these securities is that part of the principal is returned with the interest each month. Thus, they may be useful for such purposes as providing a retirement income with guaranteed, higher-yielding securities.

Commercial Paper

"Commercial paper" is the name applied to the promissory notes of well-known corporate borrowers. The minimum amount for commercial paper usually is $10,000. Commercial paper may be issued with maturities of as much as 270 days; in practice, however, the maturities available usually are somewhat shorter. Commercial paper is sold on a discount basis.

Certificates of Deposit

Certificates of deposit (CDs) are interest-bearing, negotiable, marketable evidences of time deposits. They are sold by banks in varying amounts and maturities. The maximum interest rates at which certificates of deposit may be issued are regulated by the Federal Reserve System.

Savings Accounts

Savings accounts represent one of the most popular forms of fixed-income investment. They are a highly safe and liquid investment outlet and offer almost complete flexibility to the depositor.

These conveniences must be weighed against other factors, the principal one being rate of return. Savings accounts traditionally return lower yields than many other forms of fixed-income investments.

CONVERSION PRIVILEGES IN FIXED-INCOME SECURITIES

Much confusion often is evident among investors concerning whether to consider buying *convertible bonds* or *convertible preferred stocks*. The conversion privilege is a provision available in some preferred stock and bond issues. The purpose, operation, and significance of this provision to investors is the same whether the provision appears in a preferred stock or a bond. This section looks at the factors you should evaluate in considering securities with the conversion feature.

The purpose of a conversion privilege is to make a bond issue (we shall use bonds for our illustrations) more attractive to investors by giving them both the financial security of a bond and the opportunity for gain from the possible appreciation of common stock. But you should not be misled into thinking that this option is free. The conversion privilege is an option to buy stock at a predetermined price, and as an option, it has a price. The price is the difference between the yield on a convertible bond and the yield on a nonconvertible bond with the same investment merits. This difference varies with economic and market conditions, but it might be, say, as much as a full percentage point. That is, a bond selling at an 8 percent yield as a straight bond might sell at a 7 percent yield on a convertible basis. The price of the conversion privilege depends upon the terms of conversion and estimates of the possibility that the common stock obtainable by conversion will significantly exceed its conversion price in the future.

Convertible bonds generally are callable. Although the callability feature of securities was discussed earlier, it deserves special mention with respect to convertible securities. The callability feature allows the issuer to call convertible bonds whenever the market value of the stock obtainable by conversion is greater than the call price of the bonds, and thus, in effect, to force conversion. To illustrate, a bond callable by the issuer at 105 may be convertible into 50 shares of common stock at $20 per share. Whenever the market price of the common stock exceeds $21 per share, the issuer can force conversion by calling the bonds for redemption. The bondholders then have a choice of receiving $1,050 per bond in cash or converting the bond to 50 shares of stock (worth 50 × $21, or $1,050). The importance of the callability feature combined with the conversion privilege is that it may be used to shorten the maturity of convertible bonds.

You should weigh the types of considerations discussed above when contemplating the purchase of convertible securities and determine how they mesh with your short- and long-term investment objectives.

WHAT YOU SHOULD KNOW ABOUT A BOND

One of the first things the individual investor should realize is that all bonds are not created equal. The ability of the issuer of a bond to meet its obligations may vary. Bonds issued or guaranteed by the United States government generally are considered to be the safest of investments. As for other bonds, the probabilities that all bond provisions will be met range from virtually certain to questionable.

Bond investment ratings are available to the public and are published by independent rating agencies. These ratings range from "triple A" to C or D, and they basically follow two systems. In one system, *Standard & Poor's*, the ratings descend from highest quality down, as AAA, AA, and A to BBB, BB, B, etc. The other system, *Moody's*, starts as Aaa, Aa, and A, proceeds to Baa, Ba, B, etc. Therefore, BBB under *Standard & Poor's* system is generally the equivalent of Baa under *Moody's* rating system.

Obligations meriting one of the top four ratings are considered of "investment grade" by the rating agencies and investment analysts. To merit the very top rating (AAA or Aaa), the speculative element must be considered to be almost nonexistent. By the fifth rating level, the speculative element has become quite significant; and by the seventh rating, the speculative element predominates.

STRATEGY FOR INVESTING IN FIXED-INCOME SECURITIES

Shot-term Investments

Each short-term fixed-income security is at least a partial substitute for another, and to the extent that substitutions can be made, investors may be able to improve their overall yield by shifting their funds among fixed-income instruments. The *yield spread*, or differences between and among yields on different securities, is the key to flexible portfolio management. Although one security can be compared with another only to a limited extent, such comparisons do help the investor to ascertain situations that are out of line.

As a general rule, *maturities should be lengthened when interest rates are expected to decline and should be shortened when interest rates are expected to rise.* In this way, an investor will have committed his or her funds at the present high rates when future rates are expected to be lower, and will have his or her funds available to commit later at the expected higher rates when it is anticipated that interest rates will be higher in the future. Of course, judging future moves in interest rates is not easy and is far from certain. It is like trying to judge which way the stock market will go. But, as in buying stocks, the investor really has to make some kind of judgment. Even doing nothing is taking a position to keep things as they are.

Long-term Investments

A study of yield averages is a valid starting point for a comparison of price movements in the bond markets over time because those averages are compiled from actual market prices and reveal the relationships between yields on various kinds of bonds at certain periods of time. Such a study also reveals information on trends in yields over time. For example, there has been a rather consistent upward movement in bond yields since the end of World War II.

In addition, yield spreads—the relationships between yields on various kinds of fixed-income securities—are helpful in long-term investing as well as for short-term portfolios. Among the spreads that are regarded as significant are those between yields of new corporate bonds and seasoned corporate bonds, between discount and current-coupon corporate bonds, and between callable and deferred-call corporate bonds. The difference between the return realized from municipals and that from fully taxable securities also is important. Yield spreads are not the same over time, and changes in these differentials can provide investors with opportunities for capitalizing on those changes. Consequently, paying attention to yield spreads can be profitable. For example, because United States treasury securities are of the highest quality, they sell at lower yields than do other fixed-income securities. On the other hand, investors should not pay too high a premium for this absence of credit risk.

The record shows that despite the generally rising trend in interest rates noted above, the long-term fixed-income securities markets have presented numerous capital gains opportunities to the active, flexible investor who is willing and able to take advantage of turns in the market.

On the other hand, although capital gains opportunities do exist in fixed-income securities for the aggressive, alert investor, long-term investments in nonconvertible bonds and preferred stocks normally are made primarily for income. Thus, long-term bond investments can provide secure, liberal income for the investor.

PART FOUR

PLANNING FOR YOUR RETIREMENT

12
PENSION AND PROFIT-SHARING PLANS

Earlier chapters have discussed the personal risks and potential solutions to the financial losses caused by premature death, disability, property and liability losses, and unemployment. The final personal risk, and one of growing importance, is that of "living too long" or outliving your income. How to provide for your retirement is a significant question.

ECONOMIC PROBLEMS OF RETIREMENT YEARS

The assumption is often made that people's financial needs decrease after retirement. To some extent, this assumption may be valid. The retired individual's children probably are no longer dependent, and his or her home and its furnishings have perhaps been paid for. There also are some income tax breaks available to persons when they retire.

However, the actual total reduction in the financial needs of a person upon retirement probably has been overstated. Social pressures may discourage any drastic change in your standard of living at retirement. There is an increasing tendency for retired persons to remain active, particularly in civic, social, travel, and other recreational activities.

Some people also want to be able to make gifts to their grown children and grandchildren after they retire. Finally, you cannot forget what economic forces, like *inflation* or *deflation* (recession or depression), may do to your carefully planned retirement income. The trend in social thinking seems to be in the direction of not expecting retired individuals to have to take a drastic reduction in their standard of living after retirement.

The proportion of persons age 65 and over with some earnings from active employment is about 20 percent, and this percentage has been declining. Obviously, many reasons account for the withdrawal of older persons from the labor force. A large number of older workers voluntarily retire, particularly if they can afford to do so. Others find it necessary to retire for reasons of health. Further, the OASDHI program and private pension plans, although created to alleviate the financial risk associated with retirement, in a sense also have aggravated the problem in that these programs have tended to "institutionalize" age 65 as the normal retirement age. Of course, self-employed persons and business owners may have greater control than employees as to the timing of their retirements from active employment. For example, professional persons, like physicians and lawyers, frequently continue in practice, at least on a part-time basis, until advanced ages. The fact remains, however, that most workers really cannot count on employment opportunities during their retirement years (e.g., after age 65).

Also, the high levels of federal and state income tax rates reduce an individual's capacity to save. Thus, tax-favored retirement plans are very attractive to many people today. In addition, in recent decades inflation has been an additional deterrent to increased levels of saving. Inflation is, of course, a particularly serious threat to the savings and retirement programs of persons who are already retired.

Another dimension to the problem is the increasing average life expectancy of people. Within the last 60 years, for example, the life expectancy at birth has increased from 47 years to approximately 70 years.

HOW CAN YOU PROVIDE FOR YOUR RETIREMENT?

The task of providing retirement income today seems to fall on (1) an individual's ability to accumulate his or her own retirement fund during his or her working years, (2) government retirement programs, and (3) employer-provided retirement plans. People frequently receive retirement benefits from all these sources. In fact, it seems prudent not to rely entirely on only one or even two of these sources. A balance (or diversification) of retirement income sources seems best in most cases.

For a considerable period throughout our social and economic development, it was generally thought that the problem of providing for an old-age income should be solved by the individual. However, in today's economy, with high taxes and inflation, the problem of amassing an adequate capital sum out of one's earnings is indeed a difficult one. Still, many people accumulate an investment fund during their working years to help provide for their retirement. In fact, as we said before, this seems only prudent so that you are not completely dependent on social security or your employer.

A second approach to the problem of financing old-age security is for the government to sponsor retirement programs. Because of the difficulties many people face in accumulating funds by direct savings, the government has found it both economically desirable and politically expedient to enter the pension-financing business. This has basically been accomplished through the Social Security Act of 1935 and its many subsequent amendments and expansions. It is generally felt that the essential purpose of social security is to provide a *guaranteed income floor* upon which a more comfortable retirement income can be built by the individual.

The third main method of handling the problem of retirement financing is for the employer to assume some of the burden. And, in response to this need, by inducements offered under federal tax laws and due to other factors, employers have established tax-favored retirement plans in increasing numbers. Thus, for many people private pension and profit-sharing plans are expected to provide a major part of their economic security during retirement. The remainder of this chapter will be devoted to private pension and profit-sharing plans, while the next chapter will cover other types of private retirement plans that may be available to you.

KINDS OF PENSION PLANS

Private pension plans often are considered as complex arrangements that only the most sophisticated financial experts can understand. People know they are covered under a pension plan, but they may not be exactly sure what it provides or what their rights are under it. However, with an understanding of some basic concepts, pension plans can be understood by most people, and their importance in your financial planning can be evaluated better.

Briefly, private pension plans may be *informal or formal.* If formal, they may be *funded or unfunded.* If they are funded, they may be classified as to whether they are *uninsured or insured* and whether they are *qualified under the Internal Revenue Code or are nonqualified plans.* Further, they may be classified by whether the funds paid in by the employer and/or employees are *allocated* to the individual participants at the time these funds are paid in or whether these funds are held in an *unallocated* account and used to purchase annuities for employees when they retire.

Formal versus Informal Plans

The informal pension plan is hardly any plan at all. The employer simply decides to whom it will give a pension and for how much at the time the pension payment commences. On the other hand, a formal pension plan defines the rights and benefits of the employees in advance, setting forth eligibility standards for participation in the plan and for the receipt of benefits. It also establishes a formula for determining the amount of pension and other benefits under the plan. Most pension plans today are formal plans.

Funded versus Unfunded Plans

Informal plans usually are not funded. A formal plan, however, may be unfunded or funded. When an employer pays retirement benefits out of current earnings directly to the employees as their benefits come due, the plan is considered unfunded. This type of unfunded plan is called a "pay-as-you-go" (or "current disbursement") pension plan. But when the employer puts aside money in excess of that required to pay current pension benefits to retired employees and transfers this money to a trustee (usually a bank) or an insurance company, the plan is funded in advance. When the employer puts away enough each year to fund the accruing pension liability for the current service of covered employees and in addition accumulates sufficient assets to offset the initial past-service liability (pension credits earned before the plan was installed), the plan is said to be *fully funded*. Most pension plans today are funded, but not all of these are fully funded. Certain minimum funding standards are required by the Employee Retirement Income Security Act of 1974 (Pension Reform Act or ERISA) for "qualified" pension plans.

Insured versus Uninsured Plans

Two agencies typically are available to fund a pension plan: trust companies and insurance companies. When a trust is used as the funding agency, the plan is called a "trusteed" (or uninsured or self-insured) plan. When an insurance company is used, the plan is called an "insured" plan. And when both funding agencies are used in connection with the same plan, it is said to be a "combination" or "split-funded" plan.

Allocated versus Unallocated Funding

Pension-funding instruments may be classified as to whether the funds are allocated to each participant under the plan (allocated), or whether the allocation is deferred until the employee reaches retirement age (unallocated). Trust fund plans usually are unallocated, while insured plans may be allocated or unallocated, depending on the plan used.

"Qualified" versus Nonqualified Plans

A nonqualified plan is one that does not meet the requirements for "qualification" set by the tax law. An employer using a nonqualified plan is willing to sacrifice the considerable federal income tax advantages, discussed later in this chapter, accorded to "qualified" pension plans so that the employer can retain greater freedom to establish whatever coverage requirements, benefit structure, financing methods, and the like for the plan. To be qualified for tax purposes, a pension plan must meet certain requirements in these areas. The tax advantages of being a qualified plan usually are so great, however, that most pension plans today are designed to meet the tax law requirements for qualification.

IMPACT OF THE FEDERAL TAX LAW ON PRIVATE PENSION PLANS

As we said above, meeting the tax law requirements for a qualified plan usually is very important in pension planning. It also significantly affects the covered employees' rights and tax status under a plan.

Tax Advantages

The tax advantages arising from "qualified" pension and profit-sharing plans are most significant, and an understanding of them is important to your personal financial planning. The principal tax advantages of such plans are summarized as follows:

1. A covered employee is not considered to be in receipt of taxable income from the plan until benefits are actually distributed or made available to the employee.

2. Death benefits paid on behalf of an employee are not considered part of the employee's gross estate for federal estate tax purposes to the extent the death benefits are attributable to his or her employer's contributions to the plan and to the extent the death benefits are paid to a named personal beneficiary of the employee.

3. A lump-sum distribution to a covered employee on account of his or her severance of employment may be taxed on a favorable basis.

4. Contributions made by the employer, within certain limitations, are deductible by the employer for income tax purposes as a business expense.

5. Investment income on these contributions normally is not subject to federal income tax until paid out in the form of benefits.

Qualification Requirements

Some of the important requirements of a qualified plan may be summarized as follows: (1) there must be a *legally binding arrangement* that is in writing and communicated to the employees; (2) the plan must be for the *exclusive benefit* of the employees or their beneficiaries; (3) it must be impossible for the principal or income of the plan to be *diverted* from these benefits for any other purpose; and (4) the plan must benefit a broad class of employees and *not discriminate* in favor of officers, stockholders, or highly paid employees.

WHEN ARE RETIREMENT BENEFITS PAYABLE?

Because the primary purpose of a pension plan is to provide a retirement income for covered employees, the usual requirement you must meet to qualify for benefits is attainment of a certain age. The plan usually will specify a normal retirement age. It may also provide for early or late retirement as well.

Normal Retirement Age

The normal retirement age, commonly 65, is the earliest age at which a covered employee is entitled to retire with full benefits under the plan's benefit formula. A minimum-service requirement also may be superimposed on the age requirement.

Early Retirement

Under many pension plans, employees who meet certain conditions, such as reaching at least age 55 and completing at least 10 years of service, may, at their option, retire early and receive a reduced benefit. The benefit is scaled down from the normal retirement amount to reflect the difference in the actuarial cost of early retirement. For example, assume normal retirement age is 65 and a pension formula produces a retirement income of $300 a month at that age. The pension plan allows participation in retirement benefits at age 55 at the option of the employee. At age 55, however, the pension formula produces a retirement income of only $150 a month (fewer years of service, lower average earnings, etc.). If early retirement were elected at age 60, the formula in our example would produce $200 a month of retirement income. However, early retirement may be conditioned not only upon an employee's age and service, but also upon the employer's consent or the physical condition of the employee. Some plans require the employee to be totally and permanently disabled before qualifying for early retirement.

Obviously, the value to an employee of an early-retirement privilege depends on the amount of income that must be sacrificed to take advantage of it. As noted above, the reduction may be substantial. It is, of course, one of the factors you should consider in deciding whether to retire early.

Late Retirement

A number of pension plans make a *distinction between normal and mandatory retirement ages.* For example, a plan may permit early retirement at reduced benefits, as discussed above, at age 55 at the employee's election; normal retirement with full benefits at age 65; and late retirement with normal benefits at age 68 at the employee's election. Note that even though the benefits of employees who elect early retirement are reduced, the benefits of employees who elect late retirement may not be increased because of the incentive it would give employees to delay their retirement. Many plans also contain provisions under which a willing employee at his employer's request can be retained beyond the mandatory retirement age. Usually each such case is considered individually.

WHAT KINDS OF PENSION PLAN BENEFITS MAY YOU HAVE?

Many people think all they can receive under their employer's pension plan is a retirement pension when they reach age 65. While this is the primary purpose of pension plans, several types of benefits may be available to participating employees, as follows: (1) retirement income benefits for the employee and his or her spouse (or for the employee); (2) benefits in the event his or her employment is terminated prior to reaching the minimum retirement age (vested benefits); (3) death benefits; (4) a widow's pension; and (5) disability and medical benefits.

Retirement Income Benefits

The Pension Reform Act of 1974 requires that, effective for plan years beginning after December 31, 1974, if an employee has been married for at least one year prior to retirement, the normal form of retirement benefit must be a joint and at least one-half survivor annuity payable to the employee and his or her spouse. This joint and survivor annuity form normally will produce an actuarially reduced retirement benefit from what would have been paid as a life income to the employee alone (a so-called pure life annuity). This is so because the joint and survivor form gives the employee's spouse greater security through the survivorship benefit, but naturally this added benefit has a cost. (See the discussion of joint and survivorship annuity forms below under "Death Benefits.") However, the law permits an employee to elect any other form of retirement benefit (annuity form) provided by the plan. But the plan may require the employee to make such an election in writing a reasonable time before his or her retirement date.

Some plans give employees the option to have their pension benefits converted (commuted) into a lump-sum payment at retirement. Lump-sum distributions may offer employees an income tax advantage, as will be explained later.

Benefits upon Termination of Employment

Under a contributory pension plan, where the employees pay part of the cost, an employee is always entitled to a refund (or the right to a deferred benefit) in the amount of his or her contributions to the plan upon termination of employment. The usual practice is to return these contributions supplemented by a modest rate of interest.

With respect to benefits upon termination of employment, the principal concern of most people lies in the disposition of the benefit rights *attributable to employer contributions*. The disposition of these rights depends upon the vesting provisions of the plan.*Vesting* is defined as the employee's rights to benefits, *attributable to his or her employer's contributions*, that are not contingent upon the employee's continuing in the specified employment. In other words, your vested pension rights are those rights in the pension benefits paid for by your employer that you can keep even if you should leave your employer. Vesting is very important to the certainty of your retirement income and hence to your personal financial security.

Vesting can take several forms. Immediate and full vesting of pension benefits as they are earned is far and away the most liberal form of vesting from your standpoint. Only a very few private pension plans have such a vesting provision. The use of one of three minimum vesting options was required by the Pension Reform Act of 1974.

Under one option, you receive no vesting until you have been with an employer for 10 years. After that you become fully vested. For example, assume your pension plan promises $10 a month at retirement for each year worked. If you leave your company before 10 years, you would get no vesting credits. If you stay 10 years, your pension upon retirement would be 10 years times $10, or $100 a month.

Vesting is gradual under the remaining options. The second option provides 25 percent vesting after five years of service. This is followed by annual 5 percent vesting increases in the subsequent five years, and 10 percent annual vesting increases for five years after that. Under this plan the employee reaches full vesting of pension rights after 15 years.

The third vesting option is called the "rule of 45." The employee is given 50 percent of his or her pension rights when the employee's age and number of service years total 45. For example, an employee would have a right to 50 percent vesting of retirement benefits if he or she has worked 8 years for the company by the time he or she is 37. Also, under this same option, the employee will be 50 percent vested after 10 years and fully vested after 15 years with the company.

Of course, these *minimum* vesting standards under the Pension Reform Act do not prevent an employer from establishing more liberal vesting for its employees.

Death Benefits

In keeping with the idea that an employee's contributions to a pension plan must be recovered by the employee or the employee's beneficiary, contributory plans provide for a refund of the employee's contributions in the event of his or her death prior to retirement. If death follows retirement, contributory plans customarily refund to the participant's beneficiary at least the difference, if any, between the contributions paid by the individual to the plan and the total amount of retirement benefits paid by the plan to the individual prior to his or her death.

In addition, when an employee receives his or her retirement income in the form of a joint and last survivor annuity (or a refund annuity), benefits may become payable to a surviving annuitant or beneficiary upon the employee's death. As noted above, such benefits result from a "tradeoff" of lower lifetime income payments to the retired employee in exchange for the survivorship or refund benefit.

Note that by providing a joint and last survivor form of annuity, rather than a pure life annuity, a pension plan in effect is providing death protection for an employee's spouse in the event the employee predeceases his or her spouse. The "cost" to the employee of this death protection is the after-tax difference between the employee's pension benefit as a pure annuity and the reduced pension benefit payable on a joint and last survivorship basis. Assume, for example, a man who is retiring at age 65 has a wife aged 63. Further assume he can elect to receive his pension benefit at age 65 on a pure annuity basis of $800 per month, rather than on a joint and last survivorship basis with his wife under which their monthly pension benefit will be $680. Now, if the entire pension benefit is taxable as ordinary income in this case, and if our couple is going to be in a 22 percent income tax bracket after he retires, the "cost" of the guarantee of continuing the $680 monthly pension to the wife if the employee dies first would be $94 a month ($800 − $680 = $120 × 0.78 = $94). Remember, too, that if the retiring employee's wife in our example is not provided for in this way, he will have to do so in some other manner, such as continuing (or even purchasing) life insurance coverage on his life for her benefit. Of course, her social security benefits will increase upon his death (she will be a surviving spouse rather than the wife of a retired worker), but this will not nearly make up for the loss of his pension benefit if he should elect to take it on other than a joint and last survivor basis (e.g., as a single life (pure) annuity).

Just as an example, the following illustration shows the changes in pension income that would result from the use of a joint and two-thirds survivorship benefit and a joint and full survivorship benefit, rather than a single life annuity, under various age and sex assumptions. These are the annuity rates used by one life insurance company.[1] Other companies or plans will employ different rates, and so you should check your own plan for this information as it applies to you. By referring to this illustration, you can see how we got the reduced benefit in our previous example. We assumed a male retiring at age 65, his spouse is 63, and a joint-and-full-benefit-to-the-survivor annuity form is used. The illustration shows that these assumptions produce a monthly benefit equal to 85 percent of his single life (pure) annuity ($800 × 0.85 = $680 per month). As we noted above, under the Pension Reform Act the

---

[1]These rates are all based on the further assumption of a 10-year guaranteed period of annuity payments (called "10 years certain and continuous") in any event.

JOINT-LIFE OPTIONS

Two-Thirds Benefit to Survivor with 10-Year Guaranteed Period (At death of either spouse, payments reduce to a ⅔ benefit for the survivor for life.)

If You Are MALE Retirement Age Shown Below				If Spouse's Age Is Then	If You Are FEMALE Retirement Age Shown Below			
62	65	68	70		62	65	68	70
94%	92%	89%	88%	60	101%	99%	97%	96%
96%	94%	92%	90%	63	103%	102%	100%	98%
97%	95%	93%	92%	65	105%	103%	102%	100%
100%	98%	96%	95%	68	108%	106%	105%	103%
102%	100%	98%	97%	70	110%	108%	107%	106%

Full Benefit to Survivor with 10-Year Guaranteed Period (The full benefit continues as long as either spouse lives.)

If You Are MALE Retirement Age Shown Below				If Spouse's Age Is Then	If You Are FEMALE Retirement Age Shown Below			
62	65	68	70		62	65	68	70
86%	83%	80%	78%	60	94%	92%	89%	87%
88%	85%	82%	80%	63	95%	93%	91%	89%
89%	87%	84%	82%	65	96%	94%	92%	91%
91%	89%	87%	85%	68	97%	96%	94%	93%
93%	91%	88%	87%	70	97%	96%	95%	94%

normal annuity form is at least a joint and one-half survivor annuity, unless the covered employee elects otherwise. So if a retiring married employee wants a single life annuity form, for example, he or she must take the initiative to elect it under the rules of the pension plan.

Some pension plans also include a pre-retirement death benefit. This is true, for example, of plans funded through individual life insurance policies and group permanent life insurance contracts. But group annuity plans or trust fund plans usually do not provide for a pre-retirement death benefit.

In most cases, group life insurance plans rather than pension plans are considered to be the better vehicle for providing lump-sum death benefits. Lump-sum death benefits in excess of $5,000 paid under a pension plan are subject to federal income taxes, while death benefits paid under a life insurance plan are not taxable as income. For federal estate tax purposes, however, the law tends to favor death benefits under pension plans because these benefits, if paid to a named beneficiary, are not includable in a deceased employee's estate to the extent they are attributable to employer contributions. Proceeds paid under a life insurance plan are includable in an employee's estate if the employee had incidents of ownership in the life insurance at his death. However, where a potential estate tax liability poses a significant problem, it may be possible for the employee to arrange his or her group life insurance coverage so as to eliminate the insurance proceeds from his or her estate for tax purposes. (See Chapter 17 for the details on this.)

Widow's Pension

A *widow's pension* commonly refers to the right of a surviving spouse to receive a pension benefit in the event the pension plan participant dies prior to his or her retirement age. It thus provides preretirement survivorship benefits to a surviving spouse under the pension plan. The joint and last survivor annuity forms discussed under "Death Benefits" above related to survivorship benefits after the pension plan participant reached retirement age.

In addition to the surviving-spouse benefits described above, the Pension Reform Act of 1974 also provides for certain preretirement survivorship benefits if a pension plan provides for early retirement and a participant was married at least 12 months before his or her death. In this case, the pension plan must include an option that provides for the payment to a participant's surviving spouse of a benefit that is not less than one-half the participant's actuarially reduced pension benefit, provided the participant dies after becoming eligible for early retirement. This optional preretirement survivorship benefit does not need to be made available to participants until they are eligible for early retirement or are within 10 years of normal retirement, whichever is later. Of course, the "cost" of this option can be an actuarially reduced pension benefit for the participant or his or her survivor (as also is true of the joint and last survivor option discussed above). The effect of this optional benefit is to provide a limited widow's pension in these cases.

The law allows a two-year prior-election period for this option. Thus, a pension plan may provide that the election is not effective if the participant dies within a specified period, but not more than two years, after making or revoking the election.

While widow's benefits have not been common in pension plans in the United States, they are now receiving a great deal more attention and probably will be included in many pension plans in the future.

Disability Income Benefits

Workers on occasion are required to retire from a job because of permanent disability. Such a disability retirement can create a severe financial strain on the employee and his or her family. Thus, a number of pension plans recognize the problem of permanent and total disability and make some provision for this risk.

In some pension plans, a form of permanent disability protection is afforded by allowing the disabled worker to retire early at an actuarially reduced benefit level. Also, under some plans, pension credits continue to accumulate for a disabled participant, who then receives full retirement benefits at normal retirement age.

Other pension plans provide for a disability income benefit unrelated to retirement benefits and express this benefit as a percentage of earnings at the time of disability or as so much a month for each year of service. Eligibility requirements usually restrict such disability benefits to employees who have accumulated some service period, such as 10 years, and have reached some age, such as 50. Therefore, younger employees generally are given no permanent disability income protection through pension plans. An exception may be found in pension plans that are funded through individual life insurance policies that may provide a monthly disability income benefit, such as $10 per $1,000 of face amount of life insurance.

Medical Expense Benefits

Assets accumulated in pension funds may be used to provide specified medical expense benefits for *retired employees, their spouses, and their dependents.* Thus, some pension plans have incorporated provisions for accumulating funds for medical benefits and using the funds to pay medical expenses up to the amounts specified in the plan or to pay premiums on behalf of retired employees for group health insurance or for the voluntary Supplementary Medical Insurance available under Medicare.

HOW MUCH PENSION BENEFIT WILL YOU RECEIVE?

The size of the benefits to be paid upon retirement is an extremely important consideration in your overall financial planning. Pension benefits usually are expressed in terms of a fixed number of dollars. However, some plans are expressing benefits in terms of an investment unit with a variable dollar value (so-called "variable annuities"). Some plans combine the fixed-dollar and variable-dollar features.

Benefit Formulas

Pension plan benefit formulas establish either a definite benefit or a definite contribution to the plan. Definite-benefit formulas may be a flat amount, a flat percentage of earnings, a flat-amount-unit benefit, or a percentage-unit benefit. Definite-contribution formulas also are known as "money-purchase" formulas.

Definite-benefit Formulas. Under a *flat-amount* formula, all participants upon retirement are given the same benefit, regardless of their earnings, their age, and, to some extent, their years of service. For example, all employees meeting some minimum credited service requirement, such as 15 years, might be given a monthly retirement benefit of, say, $200 a month. Employees who reach retirement age with less than 15 years of credited service may be given progressively reduced benefits.

A formula that relates pension benefits to earnings but not to years of service is the *flat-percentage formula.* Under this formula, a pension equal to a given percentage of the employee's average annual compensation may be paid at retirement to all employees completing a minimum number of years of credited service. Employees who fail to meet the minimum service requirement may be given a proportionately reduced pension. The percentage used varies among plans, with a common range being 20 to 50 percent. The average compensation to which the percentage applies may be the employee's average earnings over the full period of his participation in the plan or, more commonly, the average of his earnings over the final few years of his participation.

A formula that relates benefits to years of service but not to earnings is the *flat-amount-unit-benefit formula.* Under this kind of formula an employee is given a flat amount of benefit per month for each year of credited service. Thus, for example, an employee may be given $20 per month for each year of credited service. Under this formula, an employee with 15 years of service would receive a monthly pension of $300.

A widely used variation of the unit benefit formula is the *percentage-unit-benefit formula.* Under the percentage formula, an employee may be given, say, 1½ percent of earnings for each year of credited service. Using this formula, an employee with 30 years of service would receive a monthly pension of 45 percent of earnings. The earnings to which the percentage is applied may be the earnings during the year in which the unit benefit is accumulated (career average) or the earnings during the last 5 or 10 years before retirement (final average). Many variations of the final-average compensation plan are in use, such as compensation for the five consecutive years of highest pay.

Defined Contribution (Money-purchase) Formulas. Some business firms and other organizations use a money-purchase type of pension benefit formula. Under this plan, a percentage of an employee's pay (normally from 5 to 10 percent) is set aside in a pension fund by the employer and sometimes is matched by the employee. The amount of an employee's retirement benefit will be determined by how much the contributions in the pension fund made on his or her behalf can buy. The amount of retirement benefit that can be purchased with each dollar of contribution will decrease as the employee grows older.

Integration with Social Security

Pension benefit formulas frequently take into consideration the old-age benefits payable under social security. This is referred to as "integrating" the private pension plan with social security. These integrated pension plans usually either reduce the benefits otherwise provided under the formula by a percentage of the employee's social security benefit, provide a lower pension benefit on wages subject to social security (covered compensation) than on wages above this amount, or exclude employees who earn less than a given level of compensation.

Level of Retirement Income

In the past, pension experts generally have agreed that the *minimum* pension, when combined with social security, should equal at least 50 percent of an employee's preretirement income to be considered adequate. But if a pension benefit is fixed at this level throughout retirement, the retired person is exposed to a purchasing-power risk due to inflation and is denied the opportunity to share in any increasing standard of living arising out of a growing economy.

The issue of inflation (or deflation) and retirement-plan income is so important that a later section of this chapter, "Inflation and Retirement Planning," will be devoted to it.

Maximum Benefit Limits

The Pension Reform Act of 1974 has set new overall limits on benefits or contributions that can be allowed under "qualified plans," annuities, and retirement accounts which receive favorable tax treatment. In general, annual employer-provided pensions under a definite benefit plan cannot exceed (1) $75,000 or (2) 100 percent of the employee's average annual compensation for his or her three highest consecutive years under the plan, whichever is less. These limits are to be adjusted annually for future cost-of-living increases in a manner similar to that used for social security purposes. However, there is a $10,000 benefit exception which generally permits an annual pension of $10,000 or less even though it exceeds 100 percent of compensation. The above limits are to be reduced proportionately if an employee has less than 10 years of service prior to retirement. They will be cut in half, for example, if an employee has only five years of service. These overall limits apply to employer-provided benefits, not employee-provided benefits (as in a contributory plan, for example).

There are certain transitional rules that are basically intended to avoid or limit benefit cuts for persons covered under defined benefit plans in existence on October 2, 1973.

There are also limits on employer contributions to defined contribution-type plans. In general, annual employer contributions to a defined-contribution-type plan cannot exceed (1) $25,000 (adjusted for future cost-of-living increases) or (2) 25 percent of the employee's annual compensation, whichever is less. There is a provision dealing with the situation where an employer has both defined-benefit and defined-contribution-type plans, such as a defined-benefit pension plan and a deferred profit-sharing plan, for example. In this case, the combination of annual employer-provided benefits and contributions for an employee may not exceed 140 percent of the limits for the plans considered separately.

Most employees probably will not be directly affected by these maximum limitations on benefits and contributions set by the Pension Reform Act. In individual cases, however, they may significantly affect pension and other retirement benefits.

YOUR TAX STATUS UNDER QUALIFIED PENSION AND PROFIT-SHARING PLANS

Employee participants in qualified pension and profit-sharing plans can be affected by three types of federal taxation: the income tax, the estate tax, and the gift tax.

The Federal Income Tax

As we saw above, a favorable federal income tax consideration of qualified pension and profit-sharing plans is that a participating employee does not have to report as current income contributions made on his behalf by his employer, except where life insurance is a part of the plan. Even in this case, the employee must report only the term insurance cost for the actual amount of life insurance at risk. This taxable term cost normally is small, where it exists at all.

Income Taxation upon Distribution. When pension or deferred profit-sharing funds are distributed (made available) to a participating employee (or to the employee's beneficiary), an income tax liability may arise. The nature of this liability depends on whether the plan is contributory or noncontributory, the reason for the distribution, and the time period over which the distribution is made.

Under contributory plans, an employee's payments into the plan are made with after-tax dollars and, therefore, the employee incurs no additional income tax liability when these funds are returned to him or her. The employee's total contribution to the plan is called the *consideration paid.*

Distributions from pension and profit-sharing plans may be made to participating employees at normal retirement, at early retirement, because of total and permanent disability, upon termination of employment, or upon termination of the pension or profit-sharing plan itself. Distributions also may be made to pay medical expenses of retired employees. In addition, distributions can be made from deferred profit-sharing plans to participating employees during periods of illness, on the occasion of layoffs, and for medical expenses prior to retirement. Distributions from pension and profit-sharing funds also may be made to the beneficiary of a participating employee following his or her death.

When the full amount credited to an employee participant's account is paid to the recipient within one taxable year, the distribution is called a "lump-sum" distribution; when the distribution is made as periodic payments over several years, the distribution is called an "annuity" distribution. Whether the distribution is made as a lump sum or as an annuity is important in determining the participant's income tax liability.

Lump-sum Distributions. The tax law has accorded and still accords special income tax treatment to certain lump-sum distributions from qualified plans to participating employees or their beneficiaries. The Pension Reform Act of 1974 has changed the tax rules governing such distributions for lump-sum distributions made in taxable years beginning after December 31, 1973. In general, the Act allows that part of the taxable portion of a lump-sum distribution attributable to the employee's service prior to 1974 to be taxed as a long-term capital gain, while the part of the lump-sum distribution attributable to the employee's service after 1973 is taxed separately at ordinary income rates. The taxable portion of a lump-sum distribution is the difference between the payment received and any consideration paid by the employee. In essence, then, the pre-1974 part of a distribution gets long-term capital gains tax treatment while the post-1973 part is considered ordinary income. The Act also provides for a special 10-year forward-averaging technique that lessens the impact of the ordinary-income treatment.

To qualify for this special income tax treatment, a lump-sum distribution must be a full payment within one taxable year of the recipient of the value standing to the credit of an account under a "qualified" plan to or on behalf of an employee who has been a plan participant for at least five years. The distribution must be made under one of the following conditions: (1) upon the employee's death or disability, (2) upon the employee's separation from the employer's service, or (3) after an employee attains age 59½.

Thus, favorable long-term capital gains tax treatment still may be available for a portion of lump-sum distributions from qualified plans. Also, the effect of the new tax rules is mitigated by the special 10-year forward-averaging rule. Further, the Pension Reform Act established a so-called "tax-free rollover" provision that permits the tax-free transfer of assets from a "qualified" plan to an individual retirement account or annuity (see Chapter 13 for a discussion of individual retirement accounts) subject to certain conditions. This "tax-free rollover" provision may permit a lump-sum distribution to be so transferred without any income tax currently being payable.

As we saw above, the lump-sum distribution rules apply to a distribution made because of an employee's death to a sole beneficiary. In this case the beneficiary is accorded the special employee death benefit exclusion under which the first $5,000 of otherwise taxable benefits is exempt.

In general, death benefits payable under life insurance policies are excludable from taxable income. However, where life insurance policies are used to fund qualified pension and profit-sharing plans, only the amount by which the value of the policy is increased by the employee's death is excludable. Thus, the beneficiary must report as income an amount equal to the policy's cash value immediately before the insured's death.

Annuity distributions. Benefits payable to an employee participant or his beneficiary as periodic payments are subject to rules governing the taxation of annuities, with some special modifications applicable to employee benefit plans. In determining the income tax liability for annuity payments received from a qualified pension or profit-sharing plan, one of two rules will be applied.

Under one rule, the annuitant determines the ratio of his or her investment in the plan to the expected return from the plan and excludes a similar proportion of each annuity payment from his or her gross income. Suppose, for example, that a male employee receives a retirement income of $6,000 a year for life, starting at age 65. Using the expected-return multiple of 15 prescribed in the tax regulations for a male aged 65, he would have an expected return of $90,000 ($6,000 × 15). If the employee had contributed $20,000 to the pension fund, the ratio of his investment in the plan to his expected return would be $20,000 to $90,000, or two-ninths (22.2 percent). Therefore, the employee would exclude two-ninths of each annuity payment from his gross income and report as ordinary income only seven-ninths of the $6,000, or $4,667, a year. The exclusion ratio will continue even though the employee may live beyond his expected 15 years. If an employee's retirement income is guaranteed for a fixed number of years, the actuarial value of this guarantee would be deducted from the employee's investment in the plan, and this would increase the taxable portion of his pension payment.

In noncontributory plans, an employee usually does not have any investment in the plan. The exclusion ratio, therefore, will be zero. Thus, the employee will have to report all the annuity payments as gross taxable income.

An alternate rule applies if, during the three-year period beginning on the date the annuity payments commence, an employee receives an aggregate amount equal to or greater than his or her investment in the plan. In this case, the employee simply excludes from gross income all annuity payments received until he or she has excluded an amount equal to his or her investment in the plan.

These rules also apply to annuity benefits payable to the beneficiary of an employee participant following the employee's death. When a retirement income is paid to a retired employee under a joint and survivorship annuity, the survivor continues to use the same exclusion ratio.

The Estate Tax

A lump-sum payment (or the value of an annuity distribution) paid to a beneficiary of a deceased employee under a noncontributory, qualified pension or profit-sharing plan is exempt from federal estate taxes. But this exemption does not apply to amounts payable to the estate of a deceased employee. In a contributory plan, the portion of the death benefit attributable to an employee's contributions is taxable. See Chapter 16 for the estate-planning aspects of these estate tax rules.

In some states, death benefits under employee benefit plans are subject to state inheritance and/or estate taxes, while in other states these benefits are exempt. Wide variations exist among the states.

The Gift Tax

If an employee designates a beneficiary irrevocably under a qualified pension or profit-sharing plan, the employee makes a taxable gift equal to the value attributable to his or her contributions. Under a noncontributory plan, therefore, no gift tax liability is incurred.

INFLATION AND RETIREMENT PLANNING

Over the years, concern has been growing over the adverse effects of inflation in our economy and particularly over its impact on retired persons. The purpose of this section is to mention some of the approaches that are being used in pension planning to minimize the adverse effects of inflation on pension income. In the final analysis, however, perhaps the best defense of the individual to this problem is not to be completely dependent on your employer's pension plan. Try to have other sources of retirement income as well. This may be good advice in the face of *inflation or deflation*.

Inflation and Pension Income

For many decades, the traditional concept of retirement security reflected the desire for an adequate income at retirement relative to the salary you earned during your working lifetime. A "secure" pension plan meant the employer was willing and able to provide a fixed level of benefits to its employees at retirement and that the plan was adequately funded. But with the emergence of inflation as a major problem in the last several decades, pension planners recognized that planning only in terms of fixed dollar levels might not be enough.

Approaches to Dealing with Inflation in Pension Planning

Pension adjustment techniques are designed to give employees greater assurance that pensions that were deemed adequate when credited will continue to prove adequate at or even after an employee's retirement.

Final-pay Plans. An employee's retirement benefit may be based either on his *career earnings* or his *final salary,* depending on the plan's benefit formula. In those plans utilizing a career-average formula, an approach to purchasing-power security consists of updating accrued benefits to reflect changing salary levels and to provide more reasonable benefit levels for longer-term employees.

Benefit formulas can also be solely a function of the final active work earnings, such as final earnings averaged over the last 5 to 10 years. This approach emphasizes levels of compensation just prior to retirement that may reflect increased productivity, greater employee value, and more recent inflationary trends.

Cost-of-living Plans. An obvious vehicle for providing pension benefits with more secure purchasing power is a plan that would stipulate that payments be adjusted according to variations in some sort of price index. For example, such a plan might provide for an upward adjustment in a year when the index exceeds a certain percentage, say, 105 percent, of a chosen base-period level, and a downward adjustment when it drops below, say, 90 percent of that level.

Variable Annuities. The variable annuity is an emerging idea for dealing with the purchasing-power risk to pension security. Basically, variable annuities provide for the investment of pension contributions in a segregated portfolio of equity securities. The contributions are used to establish a fund or account which, with additional deposits and investment growth, is used to purchase a lifetime income (usually expressed in investment units rather than dollars) at retirement date. Thus, the account values under these contracts and the retirement income purchased with the proceeds reflect the performance of the invested funds, rising or falling as the market value of their underlying securities portfolio increases or decreases. The theoretical basis for the variable-annuity concept is the long-range historical relationship between the cost of living and the investment performance of diversified portfolios of common stocks.

The claimed advantages of the variable-annuity concept are: (1) protection against long-term inflationary erosion of pension purchasing power, and (2) possible performance surpassing that of fixed-dollar annuities. The attendant disadvantage is the risk of loss of capital.

PENSION BENEFIT GUARANTY CORPORATION

Another development of the Pension Reform Act of 1974 was the establishment of a Pension Benefit Guaranty Corporation, to be administered by the U.S. Department of Labor. This corporation, in effect, sets up an insurance program for employees and pensioners of companies that have gone out of business. The act insures pensions up to $750 a month. Moreover, should a company go out of business, up to 30 percent of its assets can be taken away by the government and applied toward the pension program. This program will provide a major additional element of safety, so important in a person's retirement planning.

PROFIT-SHARING PLANS

The Concept of Profit Sharing

Some employers prefer to relate the amount of their contributions for employee retirement to profits rather than to payroll, especially if their profits fluctuate widely from year to year. Also, employers may use a profit-sharing plan to supplement a pension plan.

Much of what was previously discussed in this chapter concerning pension plans applies equally well to profit-sharing plans. Therefore, this section will concentrate only on basic differences between these two approaches to retirement planning as they may affect your personal financial planning.

Benefits under Profit-sharing Plans

The primary objective of deferred profit-sharing plans is to help build financial security for employees and their families in the event of the employees' retirement, permanent disability, or death. However, severance benefits are an important by-product of these plans. While the principal functions of a qualified profit-sharing plan are basically similar to those of a qualified pension plan, deferred profit-sharing plans usually have had more liberal vesting arrangements. But under the Pension Reform Act, qualified profit-sharing plans must meet the same vesting standards as qualified defined-benefit pension plans.

Additional benefits may be available under some deferred profit-sharing plans to make the plans more flexible and also to make them more appealing to younger employees. However, when such benefits are made available, certain restrictions on the participants' access to the benefits are necessary so that all funds to the credit of the participants will not be treated as current income for tax purposes when employer contributions are made and as interest is earned.

Withdrawal and *loan privileges* are the principal additional benefits provided under deferred profit-sharing plans, although most noncontributory plans do not offer either type of benefit. Most contributory plans offer either loan or withdrawal privileges, or some combination of the two. These provisions can be very useful in your financial planning or in case of emergencies.

Distributions are legally permitted under profit-sharing plans after two years. Thus, if a plan permits withdrawals, the maximum that can be allowed is the total amount in the fund less the contributions made and the interest earned during the previous two years. The plan itself, however, may not permit withdrawals up to the legal maximum. A number of contributory plans restrict withdrawals to employee contributions. Others restrict them to a given percentage of the amount vested. Furthermore, withdrawals usually are allowed only for hardship cases. However, where employee contributions are voluntary, employees usually are allowed to withdraw their own contributions without restriction. Any amount withdrawn, less the participant's own contributions, is taxable as income in the year received.

You may also have access to profit-sharing funds through a loan provision. A loan has an advantage over withdrawal in that the borrowed funds are not treated currently as taxable income to the participant. The participant can also deduct the interest he pays on the loan for federal income tax purposes. Equally important is the fact that the loan must be repaid, thereby preserving the long-term objective of the plan.

A qualified profit-sharing plan must include the terms under which loans will be made. Generally, the amount that can be borrowed is limited to 75 percent of the participant's equity in the employer's contributions and 100 percent of the equity in his or her own contributions. Loans may be restricted to specific purposes, such as home construction or repair, home mortgage payments, expenses of illness or death in the family, education of children, or any sound purpose in keeping with the long-term objectives of the plan. A loan waiting period may be required.

13
OTHER RETIREMENT AND EMPLOYEE BENEFITS

There is a wide range of employee benefits (fringe benefits) beyond the group life insurance, group health insurance, and pension and profit-sharing plans we have discussed before. Some of these additional employee benefits can include any or a combination of the following:

Company purchase programs

Nonqualified deferred compensation arrangements

Dental insurance plans

Group property and liability insurance plans

Thrift (or employee savings) plans

Stock option and stock purchase plans

Unemployment and severance pay arrangements

Vacation plans

Vision care plans

Employee financial counseling

The above programs constitute only a sample of the employee benefit plans that could be arranged. It is beyond the scope of this book to cover all the many types of employee benefits.

In addition to employee benefits, this chapter also covers some individual retirement plans other than employer-provided pension and profit-sharing plans. We shall start with some of these individual plans.

INDIVIDUAL ANNUITIES

The annuity can be an important instrument in planning for your retirement. In its simplest form, an annuity can be described as follows. An individual pays an insurance company a specified capital sum in exchange for a promise that the insurer will make a series of periodic payments to the individual (called an "annuitant") for as long as he or she lives. The periodic income collected under an annuity contract is composed of three parts: principal;

interest; and a survivorship benefit, which arises from the fact that those who die release their investment to be spread among the survivors.

Objective of an Annuity

The basic purpose of an annuity is to assure a person an income he or she cannot outlive, as well as one that is relatively large when compared with the amount paid for the annuity. The periodic income under the annuity should be relatively large because the annuity principle involves the gradual consumption of the purchase price of the annuity. The individual in deciding what route to take should evaluate payments under an annuity as compared with the return from relatively safe certificates of deposit or high-grade municipal, corporate, or government bonds.

Types of Individual Annuities

Annuities may be of several varieties. The key distinction in terms of an individual's personal financial planning is whether one or more lives are, or should be, covered.

Retirement Annuity Contract. A common form of individual annuity is the retirement annuity, which is offered by many life insurance companies. This annuity contract has a wide range of options that make the contract very flexible.

A retirement annuity can be purchased with a single premium or by premiums paid over a period of years prior to retirement. In the event of the annuitant's death prior to age 65 (or other selected maturity date of the contract), the contract provides for the payment of the accumulated gross premiums (without interest) or the cash value, whichever is larger, as a death benefit to a beneficiary designated in the contract. During the deferred period, the annuitant may withdraw the cash value at any time and terminate the contract.

Premiums for this contract are usually quoted on the basis that the accumulated sum at maturity will be applied under a life annuity with 120 or 240 monthly installments guaranteed. At maturity, however, the annuitant may elect any form of life annuity, with the actual monthly income being appropriately adjusted. In addition, the annuitant usually has the option of taking the accumulated contract value in cash instead of in the form of an annuity. This can be a valuable option, which the annuitant might want to exercise, for example, if, at the time the contract matures, there are more attractive investments available or the annuitant is in poor health.

The usual form of retirement annuity also permits the annuitant to have the annuity income begin at an earlier or later date than the one originally specified in the contract, with an appropriate adjustment in the amount of income. The option to postpone the income payments may be particularly attractive if increasing longevity produces a greater working expectancy.

Joint and Last Survivor Annuities. This kind of annuity provides a specified amount of income over the lifetimes of two or more persons named in the contract, with the income (or a reduced amount) continuing to the survivor after the first death among the covered lives. The joint and last survivor annuity is finding increasing acceptance, primarily as an alternative income settlement option under individual life insurance and endowment contracts and in private pension plans. It is appealing since the income payments continue as long as either of two or more annuitants lives. It is frequently useful for a husband and wife or in other family relationships.

Since the annuity provides for payment until the last death among the covered lives, it will pay to a later date on the average and, therefore, is more expensive than other annuity forms. Saying it another way, a given principal sum will provide less income under a joint and last survivor annuity form than under a single-life annuity at either of the two ages.

The joint and last survivorship form may be offered on either a pure annuity basis or with a certain number of installments guaranteed. In its normal form the joint and last survivor annuity continues the same income until the death of the last survivor. Most insurance companies, however, offer various modified forms which provide (assuming two covered lives) that the income will be reduced following the first death to two-thirds or one-half, depending upon the contract, of the original income. This is known as a "joint and two-thirds" or "joint and one-half" annuity.

The Variable Annuity. We introduced the variable-annuity idea in Chapter 12 ("Pension and Profit-Sharing Plans") because employer-provided pension plans can provide variable annuities to employees. But people frequently buy variable annuities on either a group or individual basis for various tax-sheltered retirement plans (such as HR-10 and tax-sheltered annuity plans, to be described later in this chapter) or as individual annuities for themselves. Hence, variable annuities will be discussed in greater detail here.

In times of *deflation*, the value (in terms of purchasing power) of fixed-dollar, guaranteed-income annuities increases because of a falling price structure. That is, the purchasing power of a fixed-dollar income tends to go up in periods of falling prices. On the other hand, when *inflation* produces a rising price level, the purchasing power of a fixed-dollar income tends to fall off. Consequently, in times of deflation fixed-dollar annuities find increasing popularity, whereas in periods of inflation such annuities tend to be widely criticized. The impact of inflation since World War II has led to a search for a way of providing a life annuity with a reasonably stable purchasing power. The variable life annuity based on equity-type investments (usually common stock) has been advanced as a possible answer to this problem.

Nature of the variable annuity. As in the case of the conventional deferred retirement annuity, during the accumulation period a level premium is paid to the insurance company. But in the case of a variable annuity, the annuity premiums are placed in a special "Separate Account" for variable annuities. The funds in this separate account are invested separately from the life insurance company's other assets, mostly in common stocks. Each year, the variable annuity owner's level premiums are applied to purchase units to his or her credit in the special separate account. The number of these units purchased each year depends upon the current valuation of a unit in dollars. Thus if each unit, based on the current value of the investments in the separate account, has a value of $10, a level premium of $100 (after expenses) will purchase 10 units. However, when the value of a unit changes, depending upon investment results, the next $100 level premium will purchase more or less than 10 units.[1] This procedure would continue until the maturity of the contract. At that time, the accumulated total number of units credited (called "accumulation units") would be applied, according to actuarial principles and based on the current valuation of a unit, to convert the credited units to a retirement income of so many units (called "annuity units"), to be valued according to the account's investment experience for the lifetime of the annuitant.

Thus, instead of providing for the payment each month of a fixed number of dollars, the variable annuity pays the current value of a fixed number of annuity units. The dollar amount of each payment is the current value of the fixed number of annuity units and, of course, will *vary* over the annuitant's lifetime, depending upon the investment experience of the separate account. If, for example, an annuitant is entitled to a lifetime annuity of 10 annuity units each month, and the dollar values of an annuity unit for three consecutive months were $10, $9, and $11, the annuitant would receive a dollar income for these months of $100, $90, and $110.

Under almost all variable-annuity plans, the current value of the accumulation units is payable to his or her beneficiary upon the death of the participant during the accumulation period. Also, depending on the purpose of the plan, a participant may be able to terminate his or her contributions and receive the present value of his or her accumulation units in cash or as a deferred annuity.

Investment risk assumed by the participant. Under a conventional fixed-dollar annuity, the insurance company assumes the mortality, expense, and investment risks. The company invests the assets behind conventional annuities mostly in stable, fixed-dollar-type investments. Under variable annuities, the insurance company assumes only mortality and expense risks. The assets behind variable annuities are invested in a separate fund in equity-type investments, and the annuitant's dollar income is permitted to fluctuate according to the investment performance of the separate fund. Neither the value of the accumulation units nor that of the annuity units is guaranteed by the insurance company. Thus, you are assuming the investment risk when you buy a variable annuity, but it is important to remember that the insurance company still is guaranteeing that you will not outlive your income in terms of annuity units.

---

[1] This aspect of a variable annuity operates something like an open-end mutual fund, with the calculation of the value of an annuity unit being similar to the determination of the net asset value of a fund's shares.

Equity-type investments, it is asserted by proponents of the plan, yield more under normal business conditions, and thus the annuitant has a more than reasonable chance of receiving a higher income under a variable annuity than he or she would under a fixed-dollar annuity. On the other hand, in times of depressed business conditions, the variable annuitant will receive less in dollars of income than he or she would under a conventional, fixed-dollar annuity.

Sales and administrative fees. Insurance companies that sell variable annuities may charge participants two kinds of fees. One is a *sales fee* deducted once from each annuity contribution as it is received. This sales fee might range, for example, from 4 to 8 percent of each contribution, depending on whether it is a group or individual variable annuity and on the insurance company involved. Some insurers charge higher sales fees than others. Thus, if the sales fee is 6 percent, for example, and a participant makes monthly contributions to a variable annuity of $100, $94 of the $100 will go to buy annuity units (i.e., to be invested) and $6 will go to the insurer as the sales fee. This fee is collected only once from each contribution, however. It is similar in concept to the sales load charged by load-type mutual funds.

Another charge is a *periodic fee for investment management* and perhaps other services or guarantees. This also can vary among insurers, but typically it is at an annual rate of $\frac{1}{2}$ of 1 percent of the net asset value of the fund.

SETTLEMENT OPTIONS

Life insurance contracts contain a series of options concerning the disposition of life insurance proceeds and, usually, cash surrender values. These settlement options were discussed in Chapter 4; however, they are mentioned again here because of their relationship to annuities and retirement income. Most life insurance companies make available by contract, or as a matter of practice, settlement options providing a pure or straight life income, a life income with installments guaranteed, or a joint and last survivor life income. Note that these life income settlement options are, in effect, simply immediate annuities purchased by applying the cash value or the proceeds of a life insurance policy as a single premium.

TAX-SHELTERED RETIREMENT PLANS

We saw in Chapter 12 the tax advantages that can go to employees who are covered under "qualified" pension and profit-sharing plans. These advantages are one of the reasons why these plans are so popular, and in effect they result in a tax-sheltered retirement plan for covered employees. But important tax-sheltered retirement advantages can also be secured by certain other groups through special tax-favored retirement plans available only to them. These groups are self-employed persons under so-called HR-10 plans, individuals not covered by qualified or governmental retirement plans under individual retirement accounts and annuities, and employees of certain nonprofit and educational organizations under tax-sheltered annuity (TSA) plans. These plans are discussed below. In a way, nonqualified deferred compensation plans, usually used by high-salaried executives, also are "tax sheltered," and they are considered later in the chapter.

Tax-sheltered Retirement Plans for the Self-employed (HR-10 Plans)

Before 1963, sole proprietors and partnerships could have qualified pension and profit-sharing plans covering their employees, but the owners of these businesses could not get the tax benefits of these plans. This was true even though the sole proprietor or partner was actively engaged in the operation of the business. However, the Self-Employed Individuals Tax Retirement Act of 1962 (also called the "Keogh Act" or "HR-10"), and its subsequent amendments, made it possible for owner-employees of unincorporated businesses and other self-employed persons to be covered under qualified retirement plans. An HR-10 plan, therefore, is a formal arrangement whereby an owner of an unincorporated business (sole proprietor or partner) establishes a program to provide tax-favored retirement benefits for himself and his eligible employees, if any.

Who Can Participate? The plan must cover all full-time employees with at least three years of continuous service. The employer can exclude part-time employees who work less than 1,000 hours during a calendar year. A self-employed person may establish a plan even if he or she has no employees who are eligible. However, an employee must be brought into the plan when he or she satisfies the eligibility requirements.

How Much Can You Put into Such a Plan? A self-employed person can put up to 15 percent of his or her earned income, but no more than $7,500 per year, into an HR-10 plan. But a self-employed person can contribute $750 per year or less to a plan regardless of the 15-percent-of-earned-income limitation.

What Are the Tax Advantages? Contributions to the plan *are not currently taxable* to the plan participants, and they *accumulate income tax—free.* Also, contributions to the plan are *fully deductible* by the self-employed individual for federal income tax purposes.

Payment of Benefits. Except in the case of permanent disability or death, benefit payments may begin no earlier than age $59\frac{1}{2}$ nor later than $70\frac{1}{2}$. If a premature distribution is made (i.e., a distribution prior to age $59\frac{1}{2}$, and not as a result of a participant's death or disability), the owner-employee will be disqualified from plan participation for five years, and a penalty tax will be levied in addition to the tax resulting from including the taxable portion of the distribution in his or her gross income for that year. Thus, premature distributions from HR-10 plans are disadvantageous and you should not start such a plan unless you can leave your money in it until at least age $59\frac{1}{2}$.

Taxation of Benefits. Benefits from the plan are taxable as ordinary income when received. In effect, you are deferring taxation by such a plan rather than avoiding it. However, your ultimate tax liability may be lessened considerably because the benefit payments are deferred until retirement, and most people expect to be in a lower tax bracket during their retirement years than in their current earning years. If a self-employed person chooses to take a lump-sum distribution, the special tax rules applying to lump-sum distributions (discussed in Chapter 12) basically apply.

Employment Termination Benefits (Vesting). Covered employees are always entitled to their accumulated benefits under the plan if they leave their employer before retirement. This amounts to full vesting of these benefits.

Advantages of Using Before-tax Dollars to Save for Retirement. The advantages of using an HR-10 plan can be illustrated by the following example. Assume a self-employed individual (female, age 45) is in a 30 percent income tax bracket and that she wants to save $1,000 of her gross income for retirement. Also suppose she has no employees and uses a retirement annuity contract (explained above) to fund an HR-10 plan.

Without Plan		With HR-10 Plan (Retirement Annuity)
$ 1,000	Savings out of gross income	$ 1,000
300	Federal income tax	—
700	Net after-tax contribution	1,000
28,200*	Cash accumulation at age 65	44,173**
206	Monthly income (life income 10 years certain)	336**

This is income derived from funds accumulated with *after-tax* dollars. When applied to buy a single-premium annuity, only a portion of the income is taxable.	This is income derived from funds accumulated with *before-tax* dollars. Generally, most of the income is taxable.

*5% gross interest (3.5% net after taxes—interest on accumulations taxable each year).

**Figures involving accumulated dividends and life incomes are illustrations based upon the experience of a major life insurance company.

HR-10 Funding Methods. There are three basic approaches to funding an HR-10 plan. They are: (1) a *fully insured plan;* (2) a *noninsured plan;* and (3) a *split-funded plan,* which uses a combination of insurance and noninsurance funding. All these funding methods have one basic objective—to build a retirement fund for plan participants. In addition to the accumulation of a retirement fund, some funding methods also provide certain supplemental benefits, such as life insurance protection, disability waiver of premium benefits, and the like.

A self-employed individual establishing an HR-10 plan must select the funding method through which the plan benefits will be provided. There are many factors that may influence the choice of funding method in a specific situation. Among them are the self-employed individual's investment philosophy, present investments, present insurance program, and the number of years remaining until his or her expected retirement.

Fully insured plan. Under this approach, all contributions are invested in individual retirement income and/or retirement annuity policies. Thus, it follows that all benefits are derived from these contracts. This approach offers a maximum of guarantees and administrative simplicity. The values established by the HR-10 contributions grow at a guaranteed interest rate and provide a guaranteed monthly life income and preretirement death benefit. A fully insured plan is simple to put into operation. An employer may use a prototype instrument that most insurers have and purchase insurance policies on the lives of the participants.

Noninsured plan. Under this plan, the HR-10 contributions are deposited with a corporate or other trustee who is responsible for administration and investment. One type of investment medium commonly used in noninsured plans is mutual funds. For those willing to assume the risk, mutual funds offer the *possibility* of equity appreciation. It is thus argued that they may offer a potentially greater retirement fund than an equivalent investment in insurance or guaranteed annuities. Of course, there is a corresponding lack of guarantees associated with such plans. A participant's retirement fund will grow or shrink with the fortunes of the securities held in the mutual fund's portfolio.

Split-funded (or blended) plan. Under this arrangement, a self-employed person utilizes a combination of individual life insurance or annuity policies and a separate noninsured investment fund. The main appeal of such a plan is combining the death benefits and guarantees of life insurance with the equity potential and flexibility of noninsured plans. Contributions to the plan are divided in two ways: part of the contribution for each participant is used to pay the premiums on his or her own life insurance policy, and the remainder is invested in a separate investment fund (such as mutual funds, for example). The split-funded plan requires the use of a trustee to supervise this fund.

Defined-benefit HR-10 Plans. Prior to the Employee Retirement Income Security Act of 1974 (Pension Reform Act), the limitations on the contributions that self-employed persons could make to HR-10 plans in effect meant that defined-benefit plans were not available to fund such plans. However, the Pension Reform Act allows self-employed persons to set up defined-benefit pension plans to fund their HR-10 plans for tax years beginning after 1975. Under such defined-benefit plans, the maximum annual fixed benefit that may be accrued is computed by applying an appropriate percentage (which varies by age) to the individual's compensation (up to $50,000 per year) that is covered by the plan. There is a table in the law giving the percentages. These maximum limits on benefits are used for defined-benefit plans instead of the 15 percent or $7,500 limit on contributions.

Individual Retirement Accounts and Annuities (IRAs)

A new tax-favored retirement plan for individuals not covered by private qualified retirement plans (e.g., union or company) or government retirement plans was instituted by the Pension Reform Act of 1974. Under the Act, these individuals may initiate their own tax-favored retirement plan through an *individual retirement account* with a bank or other responsible organization as trustee or custodian, an *individual retirement annuity* with an insurance company, or certain *retirement bonds* issued by the U.S. government. Into such an account, annuity, or bonds, the individual may put each year up to $1,500 or 15 percent of his or her annual compensation, whichever is less. The annual contributions made by the individual (or on his or her behalf) are income tax–deductible up to the $1,500 or 15 percent limits. For example, if an individual puts $1,000 into the special account, he or she pays no income tax on the funds until he or she withdraws the money at retirement. Additionally, investment earnings on the special retirement account are not taxed until the funds are withdrawn at retirement.

There is a so-called "tax-free rollover" provision in the Act that affords a certain amount of flexibility with respect to funds placed in individual retirement accounts and annuities. This provision permits tax-free transfers of funds between an individual retirement annuity or bonds and an individual retirement account. It also permits such transfers from a qualified plan to an individual retirement account or annuity, and amounts received from one qualified plan may be transferred to another qualified plan on a tax-free basis through an intermediary transfer via an individual retirement account. This may allow a plan participant or employee to transfer retirement funds between plans without incurring a current income tax liability, provided he or she complies with the requirements of the Act for such tax-free transfers.

Tax-sheltered Annuity (TSA) Plans

A tax-sheltered annuity (TSA) plan is an arrangement permitted under federal law whereby an employee of a "qualified organization" can enter into an agreement with his or her employer to have part of the employee's earnings set aside for retirement. No federal income tax is payable on the amount set aside each year to purchase retirement benefits provided: (1) the amounts are used to buy an annuity contract, a retirement income insurance policy, or mutual funds; and (2) the contribution amounts do not exceed the employee's "exclusion allowance." Thus, a TSA plan enables employees of "qualified organizations" to save for retirement with *before-tax* dollars. Such plans are considered by many to be one of the most advantageous and flexible tax-deferral devices available, provided you are eligible.

Who Is Eligible? Any employee who works for a public school system or a tax-exempt organization established and operated exclusively for charitable, religious, scientific, or educational purposes is eligible. Some examples are organizations such as the Red Cross; Community Chest; Visiting Nurses

Associations; Salvation Army; nonprofit hospitals; and educational organizations, including private primary or secondary schools, colleges, and professional or trade schools. Public schools include county and city school systems, state universities, colleges, technical schools, and state teachers colleges.

How Much Can an Eligible Employee Contribute Each Year? Assuming no current participation in a formal, qualified retirement program, as much as 20 percent of an employee's salary can be put into a TSA plan, with additional amounts possible if the employee has had past service with the organization. There are two ways of approaching contributions to a TSA plan by eligible employees:

1. A salary increase to the employee, or
2. If the employer cannot afford to make contributions in addition to an employee's regular compensation, the employee can still do so by arranging for a salary reduction—in effect, a salary savings plan using before-tax dollars.

Example of contribution via a salary increase. Assume an eligible employee earns $10,000 per year and that the employer will contribute to a TSA plan on the employee's behalf under the salary increase arrangement. In this case, up to 20 percent per year of the employee's salary ($2,000) could be invested this way. The 20 percent maximum is called the *exclusion allowance.* In this example, if the employer agrees to a $400 annual increase for this purpose, this amount would be within the employee's exclusion allowance and there will be no federal income tax on the salary increase. The employee's total earnings are now $10,400, but only $10,000 is taxable.

Example of contribution via salary reduction. Under a salary reduction arrangement, the exclusion allowance is 20 percent of salary *after* it has been reduced by the amount of the contribution to the TSA plan. The maximum annual contribution can be determined by taking $\frac{1}{6}$ of the employee's unreduced salary, or $\frac{1}{6}$ of $10,000 = $1,666, using the above facts. The resulting figure will be 20 percent of the employee's reduced salary (20% of $8,334 = $1,666). Assume in this example that a female employee wishes to reduce her salary and authorizes her employer to contribute $400 annually to a tax-sheltered plan. This amount is within the maximum exclusion allowance and the employee's taxable income will be $9,600, with $400 of before-tax dollars going into the TSA plan.

The advantages of using *before-tax dollars* to save for retirement that were illustrated above for HR-10 plans would also apply to TSA plans, and so they will not be repeated here.

Contributions to Existing Qualified Plans. If a participant under a TSA program also participates in a qualified pension plan or state retirement plan (in the case of public school teachers), any *employer* contributions to the pension plan are taken into consideration in terms of reducing the employee's TSA exclusion allowance. In addition, the new maximum limitations on annual contributions to a qualified defined-contribution plan ($25,000 or 25 percent of pay), described in Chapter 12, also apply to TSA plans, subject to certain special "catch-up" rules.

Past Service. An employee's annual exclusion allowance can be increased if he or she has past service with the organization. This would have the effect of increasing the employee's maximum allowable contribution by giving him or her credit for past service with the employer.

Taxes on Benefits. Benefits from a TSA plan are taxed as ordinary income when received by the participant. Since this usually will occur at or after retirement, the effective income tax liability probably will be lessened because the retirement years of most people will be lower income tax years. Should a TSA participant borrow on a life insurance or annuity policy (used to fund the plan), surrender the policy for cash, or withdraw any accumulated dividends, this would be considered a distribution from the plan and would be reportable for federal income tax purposes.

PROFESSIONAL CORPORATIONS

Many considerations are involved in determining whether physicians, dentists, attorneys, and other professional people should incorporate their practice. State law, financial considerations, size of the practice, and the number of practitioners are among the factors that play a role in this decision. Should they incorporate, they will generally receive the same tax advantages and disadvantages and operating conveniences as other corporations.

A very important reason for incorporating arises from the fact that the professional is now a *stockholder-employee* of the corporation. As such, he or she is eligible to participate in employee benefit plans along with the regular employees. These programs are available on a tax-favored basis only to employees; the owners of unincorporated businesses are not considered to be employees. Thus, the following fringe or employee benefit programs become available to the stockholder-employee of a professional corporation on a tax-deductible basis.

1. *Qualified retirement plans.* This area provides possibly the greatest single incentive for professionals to incorporate. Corporate retirement plans can provide greater benefits for the owners of a professional corporation than are available to them under HR-10 discussed earlier in this chapter.

2. *Group term life insurance.* Premiums paid for group term coverage are deductible as a business expense and are not considered taxable income to covered employees (up to $50,000 or the applicable state limit, if any), including stockholder-employees.

3. *Medical expense insurance.* Premiums for this coverage also are deductible by the corporation and not taxable income to covered employees.

4. *Disability income insurance.* Here again, premiums paid for this coverage are deductible by the corporation and not taxable to covered employees. Also,

benefit payments received after 30 days of continuous disability are income-tax-free to the employee up to $100 per week.

5. *$5,000 employee death benefit.* In addition to any group insurance coverage, the corporation may pay a $5,000 death benefit to a deceased employee's beneficiary, which is deductible by the corporation and income-tax-free to the beneficiary.

NONQUALIFIED DEFERRED COMPENSATION

A deferred compensation arrangement is an agreement whereby an employer promises to pay an employee in the future for services rendered today. The plan usually is set up to provide for salary continuation over a period of years following retirement or other termination of employment. Such payments are referred to as "deferred compensation" because they represent compensation currently earned with payment postponed to the future. They are called "nonqualified" because they do not meet the requirements for a tax-favored "qualified" retirement plan. They are usually given to highly paid executives.

Why Deferred Compensation?

Some businesses do not have "qualified" retirement plans to offer their employees. But many others, who have such plans covering the bulk of their employees, may still want to provide additional benefits for certain key people that would not be permissible under "qualified" plans. Also, because of today's high federal income tax rates, many highly paid executives would like to defer income from their peak earning years to some future date when they expect to be in a lower tax bracket—usually at retirement.

The Key Executive's Problem

Because of increased living costs and high income taxes, a key employee with a better-than-average income often is looking for a tax-saving plan. High federal income tax rates make it difficult for him or her to create a substantial retirement, death, or disability fund. A salary increase may not solve this problem because a substantial portion would be depleted by income taxes. For example, the following illustration shows what a 15 percent salary increase for a married taxpayer means at various income levels.

Present Taxable Income	15% Increase	Federal Income Tax on Increase*	Additional Net Spendable Dollars
$30,000	$4,500	$1,830	$2,670
40,000	6,000	2,920	3,080
50,000	7,500	3,750	3,750
60,000	9,000	4,500	4,500

*The maximum tax rate on earned income is 50 percent.

On the other hand, if the executive could defer the receipt of this increased income until retirement, death, or disability when his or her taxable income presumably will be less, he or she will net more spendable dollars.

The Deferred Compensation Solution

A solution to this problem can be a nonqualified deferred compensation plan. Thus, instead of a current salary increase, the key executive and the employer agree on a plan that will defer the compensation until a later date. This is done by having the key executive enter into an employment contract with the employer stipulating that specific payments will be made to the executive or his or her beneficiaries in the event of the executive's death, disability, or retirement. Therefore, the employer has entered into an enforceable obligation to provide the agreed-upon benefits. The deferred compensation agreement may further provide that the key executive will continue in the employment of the company and may also obligate the executive, within limits, to refrain from engaging in a competitive business and/or to be available for consultation after retirement.

Note, however, that from the executive's viewpoint the benefits of such a plan are deferred into the future and the executive cannot get them in advance even if his or her circumstances should change. Also, the employer's obligation to provide the deferred benefits *cannot be secured for the employee's protection* by any outside financial device (like a life insurance policy) without adverse tax consequences. Of course, the employer itself can fund its obligation by carrying life insurance on the employee's life, but here the policy becomes part of the general assets of the employer and cannot be earmarked specifically for the purpose of carrying out the employer's obligations under the deferred compensation agreement. Thus, in the final analysis, the employee must rely on the employer's future financial strength to carry out its obligations under the deferred compensation agreement.

SURVIVOR'S INCOME BENEFITS

In recent years, interest has been growing in "survivor" death benefit plans. These plans are distinguishable from traditional employer-sponsored group life insurance plans in that a benefit is payable only to certain specified dependents of the employee and only if these dependents survive the employee. Moreover, the benefit is payable only in installments and, as a rule, only for the period that a dependency status continues to exist.

Forms of Survivor Benefits

Survivor benefits, as presently provided in the United States, usually take one of the following forms.

1. Spouse or dependent spouse benefits payable under the employer's retirement plan.

2. "Bridge" group life insurance benefits, which typically provide a benefit of $100 a month or more to a wife age 50 or older (at the time of the employee's death) until the wife reaches age 60 or 62, with benefits not payable after remarriage or if the wife is receiving social security benefits.

3. Survivor income life insurance for employees with dependents. This coverage is similar to group life insurance, except that the stipulated payments are provided only if a qualified dependent survives the employee, and such benefits usually are paid in monthly installments. Under some plans, the benefit may be forfeited if the spouse remarries.

Duration of Income

A survivor income plan may be designed to provide transition income to enable survivors to adjust to the loss of the employee's income or to replace, at least in part, the income the employee would otherwise have earned had he or she remained alive. Transition income may be paid for comparatively short periods, such as 2, 3, or 4 years, or for as long as 15 or 20 years. On the other hand, lifetime benefits may be provided, or income may be paid until age 65 or the survivor's eligibility for social security benefits. Payments are often discontinued if a surviving spouse remarries.

Benefits for a dependent child typically are paid until the child reaches age 18 or 21 (sometimes until age 23 in the case of full-time students). A child's benefits may also be discontinued upon marriage.

EMPLOYEE THRIFT OR SAVINGS PLANS

An increasingly popular form of employee benefit plan is the thrift or savings plan. Technically speaking, a tax-favored thrift or investment savings plan must be formulated as a pension, profit-sharing, or stock bonus plan.

The true thrift savings plan which has emerged in recent years has the following general characteristics:

1. The plan has been established either separately or in conjunction with a regular pension or profit-sharing plan for the purpose of encouraging thrift or investment savings on the part of employees.

2. Participation in the plan normally is voluntary on the part of eligible employees.

3. Contributions to the plan by participating employees are made through payroll withholding and are accumulated in separate, nonforfeitable trust accounts for their benefit, and, in most plans, the employees have at least some choice with respect to how their contributions will be invested by the trustee.

4. If employer contributions also are made under the plan, their allocation is normally related, at least in part, to the amount contributed by employees.

Standard Thrift Savings Plans

Standard thrift savings plans are normally established as separate plans and involve at least a minimum employer contribution, which may be related to the amounts contributed by employees or determined, partially or wholly, in relation to profits. Under standard plans, prescribed rates are established for required employee contributions. "Required contributions" are any contributions which result in an employee's receiving a greater share of employer contributions. The prescribed rate may be a set amount, such as 5 percent of pay, but more often it is based on an optional scale, with a prescribed minimum amount, such as 2 percent of pay, and then a set maximum amount, which usually does not exceed 6 percent of pay. In addition to "required contributions," standard thrift plans may permit additional, voluntary contributions by participating employees.

In many plans, the employer contribution and/or allocation formula escalates in accordance with service or participation (for example, 25 cents on the dollar the first year, 50 cents the next two years, and $1 for $1 after four or more years).

Eligibility provisions are generally very liberal; and vesting, if not immediate, usually is rapid. Normally, employees are given the right to suspend participation at any time, and most plans allow participants to make partial or full withdrawals from their accounts after a set period of participation or in the event of financial hardship.

Advantages of Thrift Savings Plans

There is no tax advantage, as such, with respect to an employee's own contributions to a thrift savings plan (since they must come out of after-tax dollars). However, such plans afford the other tax advantages of qualified plans in that they provide the opportunity to compound any investment increments on a before-tax basis and that employer contributions are not currently taxed to the participants.

The main appeal of thrift savings plans from an employee's standpoint, however, is the opportunity they afford for systematic investment of small amounts through weekly or monthly payroll deductions on a comparatively low-cost basis. An employee attempting to set up a systematic investment program on his or her own may pay out 10 percent or even more of the periodic investment in brokerage charges or mutual fund commissions. But under most thrift savings plans, these costs can be substantially reduced through pooled investment purchases, or even eliminated where the employer pays the costs of investment administration.

STOCK OPTIONS AND STOCK PURCHASE PLANS

Although perhaps not as well known as other types of benefit programs, stock options and stock purchase plans are important for many people in their personal financial planning. Since this can be a most complex subject, it is only briefly introduced here.

In general, there are three basic types of such plans that receive favorable tax treatment from the federal government. They are: *qualified stock options, employee stock purchase plans,* and *restricted stock options.* The Internal Revenue Code contains a long list of requirements necessary to obtain favorable tax consequences under the various types of statutory stock options. Under these rules, in certain situations, it is possible to convert a portion of what would otherwise be considered ordinary income into capital gains. The Revenue Act of 1964 has served to limit, but not eliminate, the use of statutory stock options under new and complex rules. Changes made by the Tax Reform Act of 1969 place further limitations on the benefits accruing under certain statutory stock options as tax-saving devices.

PART FIVE
TAX AND ESTATE PLANNING

14
INCOME TAX PLANNING

Most people are very much concerned with saving on their income taxes. Income taxes must be paid each year, the rates are high, and the total tax burden takes a large portion of the income of most families. Also, many states (and cities) have enacted income taxes on top of the federal levy.

THE FEDERAL INCOME TAX

Basic Structure

The federal income tax law is very detailed and complex. Obviously, all its rules, provisions, and exceptions cannot be discussed here. But the basic formula for determining an individual's tax can be shown briefly as follows.[1]

GROSS INCOME

LESS—DEDUCTIONS TO ARRIVE AT ADJUSTED GROSS INCOME

Including:

Employee business and trade expenses

Sick-pay exclusion (if sick-pay is included in income)

Moving expenses

Deductions attributable to a business or trade carried on by the taxpayer other than as an employee

Deductions attributable to property held for the production of rents and royalties

Other allowable deductions for depreciation and depletion

Contributions to a self-employed retirement (HR-10) plan

Net operating loss deduction (carryback and carryover of net business losses)

Net capital losses

[1]The basic income tax structure presented here is not meant to be exhaustive. There are a number of excellent income tax publications the taxpayer can consult to get more detailed information on the deductions, exemptions, etc., due him or her.

EQUALS—ADJUSTED GROSS INCOME

LESS—ITEMIZED DEDUCTIONS (or the Standard Deduction)

Including:

Medical and dental expenses (including medical expense insurance premiums)

Taxes

Charitable contributions

Interest expense

Casualty losses

Child and disabled-dependent care expenses

Miscellaneous deductions

LESS—EXEMPTIONS

EQUALS—TAXABLE INCOME

TAX (determined by applying income tax rates to taxable income, but subject to a maximum 50 percent tax bracket on earned income)

LESS—CREDITS (i.e., amounts deducted from the tax itself)

PLUS—OTHER TAXES PAYABLE

Including:

Self-employment tax (social security tax paid by the self-employed on their earnings subject to social security taxes)

Minimum tax on "tax preferences" (described below)

Federal Income Tax Rates

The federal tax rates on taxable income can reach fearsome heights. Table 14-1 shows the federal income tax rates as of the beginning of 1975 applying to married individuals filing joint returns (these rates also apply to a qualified, surviving spouse during the first two years after the year in which his or her spouse died), unmarried (single) individuals, and trusts and estates (these rates also apply to married individuals who elect to file separate returns). There is a separate set of tax rates (not shown here) applying to "heads of households," which are less than those for single persons but more than the rates applying to married persons filing joint returns.

You can see that individual income tax rates can go as high as 70 percent and can reach high rates even for those who certainly are not wealthy. For example, a single person with a taxable income between $22,000 and $26,000 is in a 40 percent tax bracket, and married persons filing a joint return with taxable income (combined) between $24,000 and $28,000 are in a 36 percent bracket. If the married couple can reduce their taxable income by $1,000, they will save $360 in federal income taxes.

A person may find that several federal income tax rates apply to him. First, there are the regular rates on ordinary income (and net short-term capital gains) noted above. But there is a ceiling of 50 percent on the maximum marginal tax rate on earned income. In addition, net long-term capital gains are taxed at *one-half* the person's regular tax rates on ordinary income, but with a maximum rate of 25 percent on capital gains of less than $50,000 in any one year. Since the rules governing capital gains taxation are so important to income tax planning, they will be explained in greater detail later in this chapter. Finally, there is a minimum tax of 10 percent on "tax preference" items that exceed an annual exemption of $30,000 plus the taxpayer's regular income tax liability. "Tax preference" items include net long-term capital gains deductions, the amount by which the value of stock purchased under restricted or qualified stock option plans (see Chapter 13) exceeds its option price, and the amount by which accelerated depreciation exceeds straight-line depreciation for real estate, among others. Actually, this minimum tax will not affect many people because of the annual exemption of $30,000 plus the regular tax.

Capital Gains Taxation

Capital gains and losses may be short-term or long-term. A *short-term capital gain (or loss)* results from the sale or exchange of a capital asset held for six months or less. Similarly, a *long-term capital gain (or loss)* results from the sale or exchange of a capital asset held for more than six months.

In calculating capital gains or losses, the taxpayer first combines his short-term transactions (gains and losses), if any, and arrives at either a net short-term gain or a net short-term loss. Next, he combines his long-term transactions (gains and losses), if any, resulting in either a net long-term gain or a net long-term loss. The taxpayer then combines his short-term and long-term transactions as follows.

1. If the taxpayer has a net short-term loss, a net long-term loss, or both, he can use the loss to reduce his other ordinary income up to a maximum of $1,000 in any one year. However, a net long-term loss is reduced by 50 percent when used to reduce ordinary income. In other words, it takes $2 of net long-term capital loss to reduce ordinary income by $1. On the other hand, it takes only $1 of net short-term capital loss to offset $1 of ordinary income. *Hence the attractiveness of net short-term capital losses to the taxpayer.* Any unused net capital losses (long- or short-term) may be carried forward by the taxpayer indefinitely and used in future years, first to offset any capital gains he may have and then to offset ordinary income up to $1,000 per year.

Suppose, for example, that Mr. Able has the following capital gains and losses on his stock and bond transactions for the year.

Short-term capital gains	$ 750
Short-term capital losses	1,500
Long-term capital gains	1,000
Long-term capital losses	3,000

In addition, Mr. Able has ordinary taxable income of $15,000.

TABLE 14-1

FEDERAL INCOME TAX RATES FOR MARRIED INDIVIDUALS FILING
JOINTLY, UNMARRIED INDIVIDUALS, AND TRUSTS AND ESTATES

(1) Taxable Income after Deductions & Exemptions	(2) MARRIED INDIVIDUALS FILING JOINTLY*		(2) UNMARRIED INDIVIDUALS		(3) TRUSTS & ESTATES**	
	Rate on Excess over Amount in Column 1	Tax on Amount in Column 1	Rate on Excess over Amount in Column 1	Tax on Amount in Column 1	Rate on Excess over Amount in Column 1	Tax on Amount in Column 1
$	14%	$	14%	$	14%	$ ......
1,000	15	140	15	70	15	70
2,000	16	290	16	145	16	145
3,000	17	450	17	225	17	225
4,000	19	620	19	310	19	310
8,000	22	1,380	21	690	22	690
12,000	25	2,260	24	1,110	25	1,130
16,000	28	3,260	25	1,590	28	1,630
20,000	32	4,380	27	2,090	32	2,190
24,000	36	5,660	29	2,630	36	2,830
28,000	39	7,100	31	3,210	39	3,550
32,000	42	8,660	34	3,830	42	4,330

36,000	45	10,340	18,000	36	4,510	45	5,170
40,000	48	12,140	20,000	38	5,230	48	6,070
44,000	50	14,060	22,000	40	5,990	50	7,030
52,000	53	18,060	26,000	45	7,590	53	9,030
64,000	55	24,420	32,000	50	10,290	55	12,210
76,000	58	31,020	38,000	55	13,290	58	15,510
88,000	60	37,980	44,000	60	16,590	60	18,990
100,000	62	45,180	50,000	62	20,190	62	22,590
120,000	64	57,580	60,000	64	26,390	64	28,790
140,000	66	70,380	70,000	66	32,790	66	35,190
160,000	68	83,580	80,000	68	39,390	68	41,790
180,000	69	97,180	90,000	69	46,190	69	48,590
200,000	70	110,980	100,000	70	53,090	70	55,490

*Also applies to certain surviving spouses.

**Also applies to married individuals who file separate returns.

Mr. Able first has a net short-term capital loss of $750 and a net long-term capital loss of $2,000. He can use his $750 short-term loss and $500 (because of the limit to the total deduction per year) of his long-term loss ($500 × 50% = $250) to reduce his other ordinary taxable income by $1,000, or to $14,000. (Assuming Mr. Able is married and files a joint return, this would be worth $250 in income tax saving this year.) Mr. Able can carry his remaining $1,500 of net long-term capital loss forward to the next and subsequent tax years. Thus, a taxpayer with capital losses can use these losses to save income taxes.

2. If the taxpayer has a net short-term gain, the gain is taxable at the same rates as ordinary income. This normally makes it *desirable to reduce or eliminate short-term capital gains when possible.*

3. If the taxpayer has a net long-term capital gain, either 50 percent of the gain is included in his ordinary income (effectively taxing the entire gain at one-half the taxpayer's ordinary income tax rates) or, instead, the full gain can be taxed at the alternative capital gains rate of 25 percent. Under the alternative method, however, if there are more than $50,000 of long-term gains in any year, one-half of the excess over $50,000 is taxed as ordinary income, as noted above. It is a common misconception that net long-term capital gains are taxed at 25 percent. The 25 percent alternative rate becomes advantageous only when a taxpayer's tax bracket on ordinary income exceeds 50 percent. Thus, for most taxpayers, long-term capital gains are taxed at lower rates than 25 percent. This, of course, is why *taking returns as long-term capital gains, rather than as short-term gains or ordinary income, is attractive tax-wise.*

Suppose, for example, that Mr. Baker has the following capital gains and losses for the year:

Short-term capital losses	$1,000
Long-term capital gains	6,000
Long-term capital losses	2,000

Mr. Baker also has ordinary taxable income of $22,000.

Mr. Baker's net short-term capital losses are $1,000 and his net long-term capital gains are $4,000. Thus, his net long-term gain is $3,000 and he would elect to add one-half of this amount, or $1,500, to his $22,000 of ordinary income. If Mr. Baker is married and files a joint return, his ordinary top tax rate is 32 percent and the effective rate on the entire long-term capital gain (i.e., the $3,000) would be 16 percent. Note that in this example it would have been better tax-wise for Mr. Baker to have delayed taking the long-term capital gains (if possible) to a later tax year, because then his short-term losses could have been used on a dollar-for-dollar basis to offset his ordinary income, on which the tax rate is higher.

4. If the taxpayer has both net short-term capital gains and net long-term capital gains, the long-term gains are taxed as described above and the short-term gains are taxed at the full ordinary income rates.

BASIC TAX-SAVING TECHNIQUES

We now turn to some specific ways in which taxpayers may be able to reduce, shift, or postpone their income taxes. These basic tax-saving techniques can be broken down into those that essentially involve: (1) tax elimination, (2) shifting the tax burden to others, (3) taking returns as long-term capital gains, and (4) postponing taxation. Some plans involve a combination of these ideas. This kind of classification helps evaluate properly what might be accomplished by a given tax-saving plan.

Tax Elimination or Reduction

Tax-saving techniques aimed at producing income tax deductions, exemptions, and credits that reduce otherwise taxable income (or the tax itself), and techniques that result in nontaxable income or in economic benefits that are not taxable, are perhaps the most desirable because they avoid tax altogether. Here are some such techniques.

Use of Checklists of Income Tax Deductions, Exemptions, and Credits. There are a great many specific income tax deductions, exemptions, and credits available to taxpayers. Space does not permit all of them to be discussed here, but some are mentioned in this and other chapters and in the "Personal Financial Planning Checklist for Decision Making" following Chapter 18. Also, there are checklists of the following: items included in gross income; income (and other items) that are not taxable; deductions to arrive at adjusted gross income and itemized deductions; nondeductible items; other taxes (federal, state, and local); and various taxable or deductible items applying particularly to certain occupations or businesses, all available from the government and from commercial publishers. In addition, banks, insurance companies, stockbrokers, and other businesses may make available pamphlets and other information to the public on how to save income taxes with regard to their special areas of activity. A taxpayer can often save taxes by finding deductions, exemptions, and the like, that he had not considered previously, by going through one or more of these checklists when he prepares his return. Use of such checklists is a part of the personal financial planning process.

A related matter is your taxpayer status. Be sure to claim the *head of household status* or the *special widow or widower status* if you qualify. Also, remember that while married persons usually file joint returns, they can elect to *file separate returns.* Thus, if both husband and wife have an income (e.g., both are working), they generally should calculate their income tax first on the assumption of a joint return and then on the assumption of separate returns, to see which method produces the lower tax. Married persons living in community property states also may find this procedure useful.

Also, if a taxpayer has a considerable increase in taxable income in one or more years, he should see if his income tax can be reduced by *using income averaging*.

Receipt of Nontaxable Income. There are various forms of nontaxable income. However, from the viewpoint of taxpayer decision making, perhaps the most important is interest paid on state and local government bonds—so-called "municipal" bonds. Investment in municipals is becoming an increasingly popular way to avoid federal, and often state and local,[2] income taxes.

But it is only the interest paid on the municipal (i.e., the coupon rate times the par value) that is income tax–free. When a municipal is issued, or bought in the open market, at a price less than par, the difference between the purchase price and the par value of the bond (the "discount") is taxable as a long-term capital gain (assuming the bond is held more than six months) at the time the bond comes due. If the bond is sold before maturity, the difference between the purchase price and the net sales price also is taxable as a long-term capital gain.

Unhappily for taxpayers, when bonds are purchased at a "premium" (purchase price in excess of par), the difference between the purchase price and par value at maturity is *not* considered a capital loss.

But in order to safeguard his tax break on municipal bonds, an investor must watch his borrowing policies. If a taxpayer borrows money "to buy *or carry* tax exempts" (emphasis added), he cannot deduct the interest on the loan. But when is a taxpayer borrowing to buy or carry municipals? In general, if a taxpayer has debt outstanding which is not (1) incurred for purposes of a personal nature (such as consumer credit or a mortgage on real estate held for personal use) or (2) incurred in connection with the active conduct of a trade or business, *and* if the taxpayer also owns tax-exempt bonds, the IRS will *presume* the purpose of the indebtedness was to carry the tax-exempt bonds, and will thus deny an income tax deduction for the interest on the indebtedness (the interest on the tax-exempts, however, remains tax-free). Of course, this presumption may be rebutted by the taxpayer, but the taxpayer may not win. Suppose, for example, a taxpayer owns debt-free municipal bonds but borrows money from a bank to buy taxable common stock. Under these circumstances, the IRS may deny an interest deduction for the bank loan, even though the common stock dividends are mostly taxable income.

Remember also that the first $100 per year of dividend income from common stocks is excluded from gross income for tax purposes. If the stock is jointly held by a husband and wife filing a joint return, $200 per year is excluded. For investors owning smaller amounts of common stock, this can mean that all or a sizable portion of their dividend income is tax-free. If, for example, a common stock has a current yield of 5 percent, a husband and wife owning the stock jointly and filing a joint return could hold $4,000 worth before any of the dividends would be taxable.

[2]States generally give preferential tax treatment to their own municipal bonds but they tax bonds issued by other states. However, the states cannot tax the interest on United States government obligations, even though such interest is subject to federal income taxation.

Nontaxable Employee Benefits. One of the great advantages of many kinds of employee benefits is that they provide real economic benefits for the covered persons, but in many cases there is no income tax to the employee on the value of these benefits. In other cases the income tax is deferred, and these plans are considered later in this chapter under "Postponing Taxation."

Among the more popular employee benefits that provide protection for the employee and his family but may involve no taxable income for the employee are

1. Group term life insurance (except for a maximum limitation)
2. Group medical expense insurance (except that benefits may reduce otherwise deductible medical and dental expenses if deductions are itemized)
3. Noninsured medical expense reimbursement plans (except that benefits may reduce otherwise deductible medical and dental expenses if deductions are itemized)
4. Group disability income insurance (except that benefits in excess of the "sick-pay exclusion" are taxable)
5. Noninsured sick-pay plans (again except that benefits in excess of the "sick-pay exclusion" are taxable)
6. Group accidental death and dismemberment, travel accident, and related plans

If such benefits were not provided for employees, in most cases employees would have to purchase similar benefits for themselves and their families with after-tax dollars.

The employer gets an income tax deduction for the premiums or contributions he pays toward such benefits for his employees. Thus, the cost of the benefits is deductible by the employer but generally not taxable to the employees—an advantageous tax situation.

Planning Sales of Securities for Tax Losses. Investors can often save taxes by selling (or holding) securities at the right time. Basically, this involves using the capital gain and loss rules we discussed before to the taxpayer's best advantage. We should state at the outset, however, that tax considerations should not be permitted to outweigh sound investment decisions in buying or selling securities. The tax "tail" should not wag the investment "dog." But in many cases the astute investor can plan his securities transactions so as to realize tax savings and yet not significantly affect his basic investment decision making.

Such tax savings also can take some of the sting out of unrealized investment losses (so-called "paper losses") that an investor really has even though he has not actually sold the security. Psychologically, this is hard for some investors to accept. If you buy a stock at $90 per share and over time it rises to, say, $180 per share, the stock has doubled in value, and at the time it is quoted on the stock exchange at 180, each share actually is worth $180 in cash (less selling expenses), not $90. Investors, of course, readily accept this concept. Similarly, if you buy a stock at $90 per share and over time it falls to, say, $45 per share, the stock has declined 50 percent in value, and at the time it is quoted on the stock exchange at 45, each share actually is worth only $45 in cash (less selling expenses), not $90. It may never again rise to 90. Understandably, some investors find it harder to accept this concept. They somehow feel they have not really had a loss unless they sell the stock. But this is not true; they really do have the loss—the only question is whether or not they realize the loss by selling the stock. From an investment standpoint, an investor must consider the investment merits of his securities *at their current prices*, not at what he paid for them.

Thus, if an investor already has an unrealized loss on a security and is lukewarm on the future investment performance of the security anyway, or can make a satisfactory tax exchange (explained below), he should seriously consider selling the security, realizing the loss, and taking an income tax deduction for it now. Assume an investor in a 32 percent income tax bracket owns a stock he purchased five months ago for $4,000 and which now is worth $3,000 in the market. If he has no capital gains for the year, and sells this stock now, he will realize a $1,000 short-term capital loss, which he can deduct from his ordinary income and save $320 in taxes (less selling expenses). His actual after-tax loss then is $680. Viewed in another way, if our investor holds the original stock, he has an investment worth $3,000; but if he sells the stock and gets his tax deduction, he has $3,320 (less selling and any buying expenses) to reinvest ($3,000 from the sale of the original investment plus $320 in income tax saving).

The above example illustrates the general concept of *tax-loss selling* of securities (it works with bonds as well as stocks). The following are some specific ideas on how to maximize your tax savings in this area.

1. Taxwise, it is better to take your *losses* as *short-term capital losses* (rather than long-term capital losses), and your *gains* as *long-term capital gains* (rather than short-term capital gains).

Assume that in the previous example our investor owns two stocks—one with the $1,000 short-term capital loss and another with a $1,000 short-term capital gain. For investment purposes, he is willing to sell them both. Should he sell both now and offset his loss with a gain? No. Taxwise, he would be better off to take his $1,000 short-term loss this year and save $320 in taxes. Then, for best tax results, he should do two things. First, he should let his gain run until it becomes long-term. And second, he should wait until next year or some future year to sell the stock so that his gain will not offset his tax-saving loss this year. When he does sell the stock for a long-term gain, his capital gains tax will be only $160, and so he will save $160 in taxes plus having the use of the tax savings from his previous short-term loss.

2. If you already have taken capital gains, either short- or long-term, on securities or other property, you can *offset* these *gains by taking losses on other securities* you may own.

But if you have a net long-term capital gain, it may not be desirable to offset this gain with a short-term capital loss. If the short-term loss can be carried over to the next tax year (and remain short-term), it may be better, taxwise, to take it then when it may offset ordinary income dollar for dollar.

3. You can use *tax exchanges* to enable you to sell a security for a tax loss and yet still keep an investment position in the same field or industry.

Suppose an investor owns a stock in which he has a capital loss that he would like to take now for tax purposes, but he also feels the stock has investment merit for the future and would like to retain it or one like it. So our investor asks himself, "Why not sell the stock, take my tax loss, and then immediately buy it back again?" The reason is that this would be a "wash sale," and the loss would be disallowed for tax purposes. The tax law does not recognize losses taken on the sale of securities if the taxpayer acquires, or has entered into an option or contract to acquire, substantially identical securities within 30 days before or after the sale. Therefore, our investor would have to wait at least 30 days after the sale or else run afoul of the "wash sale" rule.

Undaunted, our investor then says, "Why not sell the stock to my wife (or other family member), take my tax loss, but still keep the stock within the family?" Unhappily for our taxpayer, this will not work either. The tax law disallows all losses in sales within the family (that is, those made directly or indirectly between husband and wife, brothers and sisters, and ancestors and lineal descendants).

Our investor, however, can maintain approximately the same investment position in the field or industry, even for the 30-day period before or after the tax sale, by selling the stock in which he has the loss and then immediately purchasing a stock of about the same (or perhaps even greater) investment attractiveness. This often is referred to as a "tax exchange." Many stock brokerage houses each year maintain lists of suggested tax exchanges to aid investors in this regard.

4. If an investor has substantial net long-term capital losses he wants to take now, but no gains with which to offset the losses,[3] he might consider selling the securities, taking his tax loss, and replacing them with good-quality bonds selling at a discount. As the bonds mature—and some or all of them could be purchased with only a relatively short time to maturity—the difference between the bonds' purchase price and maturity value would be a capital gain which can be reduced or eliminated by the capital loss carried over. This, in effect, makes the capital gains on your bonds entirely or mostly tax-free.

5. If an investor wants to "lock in" a capital gain he already has in a stock, but for any of several reasons does not want to take it yet for tax purposes, he can use the technique of *"selling short against the box."* Here the investor borrows an equal amount of stock from his broker and sells the stock short. This locks in the gain on the stock he owns. Then, when the investor is ready to take his gain, he uses the stock he owns to close out his short position.

Losses on Sales of Residences. For tax purposes, a personal residence is considered a capital asset, but one held for personal use. Therefore, while a short-

---

[3] The investor could, of course, offset the losses against his ordinary income to the extent of $1,000 per year, but perhaps he wants to get tax benefits more rapidly from these losses.

or long-term gain on the sale of a personal residence is taxable (unless postponed, as explained below), a loss on the sale of such a residence is not deductible because the loss was not incurred in a trade or business or in connection with a transaction entered into for profit. The same is also true, incidentally, for other assets held strictly for personal use, such as cars, boats, airplanes, or furniture. In effect, the gain is taxable, but the loss is the taxpayer's.

The tax law does allow some relief from the rigor of these rules in connection with gains on the sale or exchange of a residence (including sale of ownership in a cooperative apartment or a condominium) which is the taxpayer's principal place of abode. In this case, if the taxpayer buys and occupies another existing residence within one year before or after the sale of his former home, or begins construction of a new residence either before the sale of his former home or within one year after that sale and occupies the new residence as his principal home within 18 months after the sale of his former residence, any gain on the sale of his former residence is not taxed at that time, except to the extent that the sales price exceeds the cost of his new residence. But technically the capital gains tax is only postponed, not forgiven, because any gain not taxed at the time of a sale reduces the tax basis of the new residence.

Let us briefly illustrate this. Assume a taxpayer sells his principal residence for $60,000; has broker's commissions, legal fees, and other expenses of the sale of $4,000; and incurred "fix-up" expenses[4] prior to the sale of $2,000. The residence originally cost him $30,000 (his adjusted tax basis). A month after the sale, the taxpayer buys another home as his principal residence for $65,000. The taxpayer's tax status with respect to this sale is as follows:

Gross sales price for former residence		$60,000
Less:		
Expenses of sale	$4,000	
"Fix-up" expenses	2,000	−6,000
Adjusted sales price for former residence		$54,000
Less:		
Adjusted tax basis of former residence		−30,000
Gain on sale		$24,000

But since the purchase price of the new principal residence = $65,000, which exceeds the adjusted sales price ($54,000) of the former residence, no *current* gain is recognized on the sale.

---

[4]These are expenses such as painting, repairs, and replacement of shrubs incurred to make the residence more attractive for sale. Such work must be performed within the period of 90 days prior to the date of the contract of sale.

However, the tax basis of the newly acquired residence now is:

Cost of new residence	$65,000
Less:	
Gain on sale of former residence not taxed currently	−24,000
Adjusted tax basis of new residence	$41,000

There is a further limited exclusion of gain on the sale of a residence by a taxpayer or spouse over age 65 under certain conditions.

If, however, property held for personal use is converted to property used for the production of income, as when a residence is rented to others, depreciation is allowed as a tax deduction from rental income and a capital loss on a subsequent sale of the property is deductible. Thus, if the owner of a residence actually rents it, he can treat a loss on its sale as a deductible capital loss.

The tax status of an inherited residence depends upon the use made of it by the person inheriting it. If the new owner does not use it as a residence, but immediately attempts to sell or rent it, the property then is considered held for profit, and a loss on its sale is a deductible capital loss. The same also is true even though two persons own the residence jointly, use it as a personal asset, and one of them dies. The tax status of the residence in the hands of the survivor depends upon how the survivor then uses it.

Making Charitable Contributions. Another way to reduce taxable income and save taxes is by making charitable contributions which are itemized deductions. Such contributions often are expected of the taxpayer anyway, and so he might as well make them in the most advantageous way he can.

One possibility is gifts of appreciated long-term capital-gain property, such as common stock with a sizable "paper gain." Here the gift of stock generally would be deductible at its fair market value on the date of the gift and no capital gain on the stock would be realized by the donor.[5]

Suppose, for example, an investor has owned common stock in a growth company for a long time and has a sizable "paper gain" in it. He would like to dispose of some of this stock but has no offsetting losses. He also customarily gives about $1,000 per year to his church. If our investor were to give $1,000 worth of this stock (rather than his customary cash donation) to his church, he would be better off taxwise and the church would get the same dollar donation (less any selling expenses on the stock).

Let us see why. Assume our investor's cost basis in the $1,000 of stock is $100 and he and his wife are in a 36 percent income tax bracket. We shall compare the tax results of a gift to charity of the stock itself with the sale of the stock, retaining the after-tax proceeds of the sale, and making the investor's customary $1,000 cash contribution to charity.

[5]The limit on such contributions to most charitable organizations generally is 30 percent of the taxpayer's adjusted gross income.

	Sale of Stock and Gift of Cash	Gift of Stock
Market value of stock	$1,000	$1,000
Sale of stock:		—
Cost basis	100	—
Capital gain	$ 900	—
Capital gains tax	$ 117*	—
Charitable contribution	$1,000 (cash)	$1,000 (stock)
Tax deduction	−360	−360
	$ 640	$ 640
Capital gains tax (from above)	117	—
After-tax cost of transaction to taxpayer	$ 757	$ 640

*Equal to 13% of the $900 long-term capital gain.

The net effect of this illustration, under the assumptions given, is a tax saving equal to the capital gains tax on the sale of the appreciated securities. But this works only if the taxpayer is going to make a charitable contribution anyway.

However, if you are holding securities on which you have a loss, the reverse is true. You are better off taxwise first to sell the securities, take your tax loss, and then give the proceeds to charity in cash. That way you get both the capital loss on the sale and the charitable deduction.

Another technique that may be useful in some cases is the charitable remainder trust. Under this approach, a taxpayer can transfer property in approved ways (i.e., to a charitable-remainder annuity trust, a charitable-remainder unitrust, or a pooled income fund, commonly maintained by charitable organizations); receive an income for life, for a term of years, or for the joint lives of himself and his wife; and then provide for the remainder interest in the property to go to charity. This gives the taxpayer a *current* income tax deduction for the value of the remainder interest but allows him to continue to receive an income from the property for life or a term of years.

One final thought on charitable remainders. The tax law permits gifts to charity of a remainder interest in a personal residence or farm without meeting the strict requirements for charitable-remainder trusts. This can result in a sizable *current* tax deduction for some persons who are willing to give away their residence or farm effective after their death.

Shifting the Tax Burden to Others

Because of the highly progressive federal income tax structure, it is often attractive taxwise to use plans that basically are intended to shift income from persons in higher tax brackets to those in lower brackets. This is normally done within the family so that the economic benefits remain "at home." Let us look at some of the tax-saving plans for doing this.

Outright Gifts of Income-producing Property. One of the simplest and most obvious ways of shifting income to others is the outright gift to them of income-producing property. Father gives stock to his adult children; Grandmother gives bonds to her grandchildren; Mother puts money in savings accounts in her children's name; and so on. When a donor gives the donee property, future income from the property is taxable to the donee, not the donor.[6] However, to escape income tax liability, the donor must give away the property as well as the future income from it. Gifts of only the income from property will not shift the income tax to the donee.

For capital gain purposes, the donee of a capital asset takes the donor's tax basis in the property, plus generally the amount of any gift tax paid on the transfer by the donor. Thus, if a donor paid $1,000 five years ago for common stock which is now worth $2,000 and gives the stock to his son, the son's tax basis is $1,000. If the son later sells the stock for $2,200, he will have a long-term capital gain of $1,200. Thus, the donor (father) can transfer a potential capital gain to his presumably lower-tax-bracket son.

On the other hand, if the owner (the father) simply holds the stock until his death, it will get a new income tax basis (a stepped-up basis) generally equal to its market value at the time of his death. Thus, if the stock's market value at the owner's (father's) death is $2,000, that becomes its income tax basis rather than the previous $1,000. This means the potential capital gain in the stock prior to the owner's death will be wiped out and never be taxed to anyone.

For capital loss purposes, however, different rules apply. In this case, the donee's tax basis is either the donor's basis or the fair market value of the property at the date of the gift, whichever is lower. This means capital losses cannot be transferred to the donee. Therefore, *property in which the owner has a sizable "paper" loss is not desirable gift property from an income tax-saving standpoint.* Here it would be better for the owner to sell the property, take the capital loss for himself, and then give away other assets.

Property on which the donor's cost basis is about the same as its current market value does not present a built-in capital gains tax for either the donor or the donee. Therefore, some argue that it generally is the most desirable gift property.

Gifts of Income-producing Property in Trust. Rather than give property outright, it can be given in trust—an irrevocable lifetime trust. An irrevocable lifetime trust is one established by the creator during his lifetime and in which he did not retain the power to alter or terminate the trust. The nature,

---

[6]Lifetime gifts can have other advantages as well, such as saving federal estate taxes, saving state inheritance taxes, and reducing probate costs. However, lifetime gifts can result in gift taxes. These concepts are discussed further in Chapters 16 and 17.

uses, and advantages of trusts in estate planning are described in Chapters 15, 16, and 17. In this chapter, we are concerned with how trusts can be used to save income taxes.

First, let us briefly describe how the income from property in irrevocable trusts is taxed. The basic concept of the taxation of trust income is that the trust serves as a conduit for such income—somewhat similar to the concept applied to mutual funds. Thus, the tax initially falls on either the trust or the beneficiary, depending on the trust's terms, and ultimately it falls on the beneficiaries to whom the income is distributed. Tax-exempt trust income (such as interest on municipal bonds) is received by the beneficiary tax-free.

Gifts to Minors. People frequently want to make gifts of income-producing property to minors—children or grandchildren, for example. One of the hoped-for advantages in doing this is for the income from the property to be taxed to the minor.

Some kinds of property often can conveniently be given directly to minors—such as savings accounts, United States savings bonds, and life insurance on the minor's life. Income from such property also may be shifted to the minor. Interest from a savings account opened for a child is taxable to the child, provided that under state law the *account belongs to the child* and the child's parents may not use any of the funds in the account to support the child. Also, interest on United States savings bonds bought *in a child's name* is taxable to the child, even though the child's parent(s) may be named as beneficiary(ies) in the event of the child's death. But interest on United States savings bonds bought by a parent who names his child only as co-owner is taxable to the parent.

However, outright gifts to minors of other kinds of property, such as securities or real estate, may cause problems because outsiders may not be willing to deal with the minor in managing the property because he generally is not considered legally competent to contract. Of course, a legal guardian could be appointed for a minor to manage property he owns, but guardianship tends to be inflexible, it ends when the person becomes of age, and donors generally prefer other ways of giving property to minors.

Other than outright gifts, there are several possibilities for making gifts to minors. They include: (1) use of regular trusts, (2) gifts to minors in trust under the special Internal Revenue Code section (Section 2503(c)) enacted for this purpose, and (3) gifts under a Uniform Gifts to Minors Act or comparable state law.

Gifts may be made to minors through *regular irrevocable trusts* the same as they can to anyone else. The only practical problem with this is that a formal trust must be established and, depending upon the size of the gift and the terms of the trust, the donor may not be able to take advantage, or full advantage, of the $3,000 federal gift tax annual exclusion (described in Chapter 16) when he sets up the trust. Thus, such trusts can result in the shifting of income for income tax purposes, removing the trust property from the donor's gross estate for estate tax purposes, but perhaps resulting in the loss or reduction of the gift tax annual exclusion.

Under Section 2503(c) of the Internal Revenue Code, a donor can have full use of the gift tax annual exclusion for a gift in trust if it meets the requirements of the law. The law provides that the trust income and principal may be expended by the trustee for, or on behalf of, the minor beneficiary. Any amounts remaining in the trust when the beneficiary becomes 21 must be distributed to the beneficiary then. This may be a disadvantage, because many donors prefer to postpone the distribution of trust property to a beneficiary until after age 21, or perhaps in installments, such as one-third at 21, one-third at 25, and the final third at 30. If the beneficiary dies prior to age 21, the trust property must go to his estate or as he designated. If the donor is not the trustee or one of the trustees under this kind of trust, the trust property will be removed from the donor's gross estate for estate tax purposes.

The *Uniform Gifts to Minors Act* (or Model Gifts of Securities to Minors Act or comparable state legislation) is a popular way to make smaller gifts of securities and sometimes other property to minors. Laws of this type have been enacted in all states. Briefly, they provide for the registration of securities, and sometimes other kinds of property, by a donor in the donor's own name, or in the name of any adult member of the minor's family, to act as "custodian" of the securities for the minor. Thus, Grandfather might give stock to his grandson with the boy's father named as custodian.

The stock would be held by the custodian, who would manage, invest, and reinvest it for the minor's benefit. The custodian can apply the property or the income from it for the benefit of the minor in the custodian's sole discretion. But to the extent the property and income are not expended for the minor's benefit, they must be delivered or paid over to the minor when he reaches age 21. If the minor dies before attaining 21, the property and income must go to his estate. These provisions are similar to those required of a Section 2503(c) trust, noted above, and have the same possible disadvantage of a required distribution at age 21.

The Uniform Gifts to Minors Act, or comparable legislation, simplifies making smaller gifts to minors. No formal trust agreement is required. Income from property transferred in this way is taxable to the minor, unless the income is used to satisfy a legal obligation to support the minor. Also, the donor gets full use of the gift tax annual exclusion.

There are two income tax "wrinkles" that can be involved in gifts of income-producing property to minors or in the use of short-term reversionary trusts for minors (described below) which should be mentioned here. First, trust income or income from property held for a minor under a Uniform Gifts to Minors Act that is used to discharge a parent's or guardian's *legal* obligation to support the minor will be taxed to the parent or guardian. Thus, parents cannot use these arrangements to discharge their own legal obligations to support their children at favorable tax rates. However, just what a parent's legal support obligation is in a given case may not be entirely clear. The obligation is limited by the duties imposed on parents by the law where they live.

The other "wrinkle" is that any individual who is eligible to be claimed as a dependent by any other taxpayer for the year (e.g., a dependent child) can only use his standard deduction (i.e., his percentage standard deduction or low-income allowance, whichever is larger) to reduce his *earned income*. The standard deduction cannot be used to reduce his unearned income, as from a trust, for example. But the dependent's $750 personal exemption still applies to all his income—earned and unearned. The effect of these rules is to make the shifting of unearned income to persons who are claimed by another as dependents less attractive taxwise than it once was. Of course, minors frequently fall into this category. However, there can still be significant net tax savings for a family in using plans to shift property income to low-bracket dependent children. For example, even if a dependent child has no earned income, $750 per year (the amount of his personal exemption) can be shifted to him income tax–free.

Short-term Reversionary Trusts ("Clifford Trusts"). A commonly used device for shifting income to others—a minor child, a son or daughter just getting started, an aged relative, and the like—is to establish an irrevocable short-term reversionary trust (commonly called "Clifford"-type trusts or just "short-term trusts"). With this type of trust, the owner of income-yielding property in effect can give the property away for a period of years and then get it back again. This is what is meant by a "reversionary" trust. In the meantime, the income from the property will be taxed to someone else, who presumably will be in a lower tax bracket than the owner.

The tax law provides that the income from a trust with a duration of more than 10 years will be taxed to the trust beneficiary if it is currently distributable to the beneficiary, or initially to the trustee if the income is accumulated in the trust and then later to the beneficiary when it is distributed to him. Thus, the trust income during its term is taxed either to the beneficiary or the trustee, but not to the person establishing the trust (the creator). The duration of a short-term trust can also be measured by the lifetime of the income beneficiary. Thus, such a trust can be created for the benefit of an aged relative and provide that it will terminate either at the end of 10 years and a day or upon the beneficiary's death, whichever occurs first.

At the end of the trust term, the trust terminates and the property placed in it reverts back to the creator of the trust. Thus, the creator gets his income-producing property back, but the income from the property for the term of the trust goes to the beneficiary.

Let us take a specific example. Suppose an executive and his wife are in a 42 percent income tax bracket. They have an 11-year-old dependent daughter who currently has no earnings. The executive transfers $50,000 of his common stock holdings to a 10-year-and-a-day short-term reversionary trust with the net trust income of about $2,500 per year distributable currently to his daughter as the income beneficiary of the trust. At the end of the 10-year-and-a-day trust term, the stock will revert back to the executive. During the 10-year term, the $2,500 per year will be taxable to the daughter at her tax bracket and not to her father (assuming the income is not used to discharge his support obligation). Thus, her annual tax would be:

Gross income from the trust	$2,500
Dividend exclusion	−100
	$2,400
Daughter's personal exemption	−750
Taxable income	$1,650
Income tax (daughter is in a 17% top tax bracket)	$250

Note that the daughter can take no standard deduction in this case because her father takes her as a dependent and all her income is unearned.

If our executive had not set up this trust, the approximately $2,500 per year from the stock (ignoring trustee's fees in this example for the sake of simplicity) would have been taxable to him and his wife at their 42 percent tax bracket. This would mean an annual tax to them of about $1,050 on this income as compared with their daughter's tax of $250.

Instead of distributing the income from a short-term trust to the beneficiary currently, as in the above example, the trustee can be given the power to accumulate the income and to distribute it to the beneficiary when the trust is terminated or otherwise. Another possibility is for the trustee to be empowered to use trust income to buy life insurance (say, a 10-pay life policy) on the beneficiary's life. This policy (and any accumulated income) would be distributed to the beneficiary at the end of the trust term. Many people like this way of giving life insurance to their children at favorable tax rates.

There can be a possible gift tax liability, however, on the creation of a short-term reversionary trust. The value of the gift for gift tax purposes is the discounted value of the assumed income stream from the trust for its term. For a 10-year term, this equals 44.16 percent of the value of the property originally put into the trust. For example, in the illustration above of a $50,000 10-year trust, the value of the gift made to the executive's daughter would be $22,080 ($50,000 × 0.4416). But this gift tax value would be considerably less than the executive's and his wife's combined $60,000 gift tax lifetime exemptions (and their annual exclusions, if applicable), and so in all probability no gift tax would be payable in this case.

Taking Returns as Long-term Capital Gains

We saw above that the income tax rates on long-term capital gains are no greater than one-half the rates on ordinary income. Further, since capital assets receive a "stepped-up" income tax basis upon the owner's death (equal to their then market value), an unrealized gain at the owner's death may never be taxed. People can plan for capital gains in a variety of ways. Some of the more common are mentioned below.

Ownership of Investments (or Property) That May Appreciate in Value. This is one of the cornerstones in the investment policy of many people. Purchase of so-called "growth stocks," for example, is aimed at reaping long-term capital gains, rather than dividend income.

But investors should not feel that common stocks are the only vehicle for securing capital gains. Other equity-type investments—such as real estate— also *may* grow with the economy in the future. Also, marketable bonds, such as corporate or United States government bonds, *may* result in capital gains (see the discussion below of bonds purchased at a discount).

Return-of-capital Dividends. Some corporations pay common stock dividends that are entirely or partially income tax–free. Technically, this is because the nontaxable portion of the dividend is a return of capital, rather than true corporate profits being paid to the stockholders as dividends. But the investor is not taxed currently on this portion of the dividend, and so the stock's current after-tax yield is increased. However, such nontaxable dividends or portions of dividends reduce the tax basis (cost) of the stock. Therefore, if the stock is sold at a price equal to or in excess of its original cost, such dividends, in effect, will be taxed as a long-term capital gain.

Bonds Purchased at a "Discount." As we pointed out before, when bonds are purchased in the open market (or issued) at a price less than their par (maturity) value, the difference between a bond's purchase price and its par value at maturity is a capital gain, not ordinary income. Such bonds are often referred to as "deep-discount" bonds (see Chapter 11). This really is a built-in capital gain, since the bond will eventually mature at its par value. Of course, the bond may also be sold prior to maturity at a capital gain (or loss, for that matter).

The taxation of a bond's "discount" as a long-term capital gain will serve to increase the effective after-tax yields of bonds whose current interest return is taxable—such as corporate and intermediate- and long-term United States government bonds. However, for municipals, whose current interest return is not taxable, any such "discount" still is taxable as a capital gain. Therefore, this is not a desirable tax feature for municipals.

Note, however, that the "discount" of treasury bills, which customarily are purchased by investors at a discount from their maturity value to provide a given yield, is ordinary income, not capital gains, for federal income tax purposes.

Lump-sum Distributions from "Qualified" Plans. A lump-sum distribution in one year from a "qualified" pension, profit-sharing, or thrift plan on termination of employment may receive partial long-term capital gains treatment. See Chapters 12 and 13 for an explanation of the taxation of employee benefits.

Postponing Taxation

A number of important tax-saving techniques basically involve postponing taxation until the future rather than the reduction or elimination of taxes now.

Postponing taxes can be advantageous to the taxpayer for several reasons. He may be in a lower tax bracket in the future; his financial circumstances may be better known then; he gets the investment return on the postponed tax while it is postponed; he may not be in a financial position to pay the tax now; and, under some circumstances, the tax may never have to be paid. However, when reviewing a proposal involving tax saving, you should recognize whether taxes are being permanently reduced or merely postponed.

Various kinds of employee benefit plans, executive compensation plans, and tax-sheltered (or deferred) annuity plans represent important ways by which many people postpone taxation until a presumably more favorable time for them. As noted above, some of these plans can also permit at least partial long-term capital gains tax treatment of their benefits.

The nature and taxation of these plans were discussed in Chapters 12 and 13. Among the more important are:

Qualified pension, profit-sharing, and employee thrift plans

Stock options and employee stock purchase plans

Nonqualified deferred compensation plans

Tax-sheltered (deferred) retirement (HR-10) plans for the self-employed

Individual retirement accounts and annuities (IRA plans)

Tax-sheltered (deferred) annuity (TSA) plans for employees of nonprofit organizations and public school systems

Other approaches to postponing taxation have already been mentioned in this chapter, including:

Postponing the sale of appreciated securities or other investments

Selling stock "short against the box" to lock in a capital gain

Postponing capital gains taxation on the sale of a taxpayer's principal residence

In addition, the following are other commonly used ways of postponing the impact of income taxation.

Postponing Income Taxation on Series E Savings Bonds. Series E United States savings bonds are issued on a discount basis and the interest they earn is represented by the periodic increase in their redemption value over time. Other United States savings bonds, such as Series H bonds, pay their interest periodically to the owner in cash.

Owners of Series E bonds have a choice as to when they want to be taxed on the increase in value of their bonds. They may elect: (1) to report and pay tax on the increase in redemption value as interest each year, or (2) to postpone paying tax on the increase in value until the bonds mature or are redeemed. Interest on Series E bonds held beyond their maturity date, where the owner previously had elected to postpone taxation, does not need to be reported until the bonds are actually redeemed or the period of extension ends.

Under Series H bonds, however, there is no choice of deferring taxation, and the owner is taxed on the interest each year as it is paid.

Series E bonds, on which the owner postponed taxation, can be exchanged for Series H bonds without the owner's being taxed in the year of the exchange, except to the extent that he may have received cash upon the exchange. Thus, a person can buy Series E bonds during his working years, elect to postpone taxation, and then exchange the E bonds for H bonds when he retires to receive a periodic retirement income. The increase in value of this taxpayer's E bonds (which he exchanged tax-free for the H bonds) will not be taxed until the H bonds mature or are disposed of by the taxpayer. Thus, the tax on the return from the E bonds (which, when held to maturity, was 6 percent as of 1975) can be postponed for a long time.

Selecting the Particular Stock Certificates to be Sold. The tax law permits an investor to select the particular stock certificates he wants to sell, assuming he is going to sell only part of his holdings of a stock.

Suppose you own 60 shares of a common stock with a present market value of $50 per share. You acquired the stock over the years as indicated below, and now wish to sell 20 shares.

Purchased 20 shares 10 years ago at $20 per share

Purchased 20 shares 5 years ago at $50 per share

Purchased 20 shares 2 years ago at $60 per share

Thus, depending on which certificates you decide to sell, you could have a capital gain, no gain or loss, or a capital loss. In the absence of identification as to which certificates are sold, the tax law assumes the first purchased are the first sold (a first-in, first-out concept).

Tax-free Buildup of Life Insurance Policy Values. Life insurance cash values increase over time, on the assumption of a guaranteed interest rate stated in the policy. In addition, policy dividends based in part on an "excess interest" factor are paid on participating policies. These amounts are not subject to income taxation as they increase year by year, but only when the policy matures (as an endowment) or is surrendered. This commonly is referred to as the "income tax–free buildup" in life insurance.

In a sense, however, this is only a postponement of income taxation, because if a policy matures or is surrendered for more than the net premiums paid, the gain is taxable as ordinary income. But if the insured dies, the "gain" permanently escapes taxation. These matters are discussed in greater detail with regard to the taxation of life insurance in Chapter 17.

Installment Sales. For certain kinds of property, when the selling price is paid to the seller in installments by the buyer, the seller may elect to pay tax on any gain arising from the sale as the installments are collected rather than in the year the sale is made. Thus, if a transaction meets the requirements for the installment method of reporting income, the seller can spread out the payment of his tax liability over the installment payment period.

TAXATION AND THE CAPITAL GAINS TAX "LOCK-IN" PROBLEM

The capital gains tax can produce a situation in which an investor feels "locked in" to a stock because of his own investment success. For example, a person may have made the "right" investment decision on a "growth stock" many years ago; he may have been buying a stock, or several stocks, right along under a dollar-cost-averaging scheme; or he may have acquired stock many years ago, or periodically, under employee stock options, a stock purchase plan, or a profit-sharing plan. Other possibilities could be named. They basically involve a situation in which the investor finds himself (happily, of course) with a "paper gain" in a stock and is afraid to sell the stock because he will have to pay taxes on the capital gain.

This kind of lock-in problem can have several bad effects for the investor and his family. The investor's portfolio may become heavily "lopsided" in favor of the locked-in stock, and diversification may be badly needed. What goes up can also come down, and in a declining market the investor may suffer losses in the locked-in stock. In addition, there may be better investments around now than the locked-in stock—another stock in the same industry or a different industry, mutual funds for diversification, high-yielding corporate bonds, municipal bonds for those in higher tax brackets, and so forth. Furthermore, while an investor's personal situation may have changed and he could use the money, he may be afraid to sell the stock and pay the tax for fear of depriving his children and other heirs of part of their inheritances.

Assuming a lock-in problem, let us briefly review what an investor's choices are:

1. He can simply hold the appreciated stock—never sell it during his lifetime—and since it will get a stepped-up income tax basis equal to its then market value upon the owner's death, he can pass it on to his heirs capital-gains-tax-free.

2. He can give away the appreciated stock to someone in his family during his lifetime. The donee will take the donor's income tax basis in the stock; but if the donee is in a lower tax bracket than the donor, the capital gains tax on a subsequent sale by the donee will not hurt so much.

3. The investor can give some or all of the appreciated stock to charity. As we saw before, he can then get a current income tax deduction for the full current market value of the stock and not realize any of the appreciation in the stock's value as a capital gain. If the investor is going to make charitable contributions in cash anyway, gifts of appreciated securities are an attractive alternative taxwise.

4. The investor can sell some or all of his appreciated stock, pay the tax (or offset the gain with long-term capital losses), and reinvest the net (after-capital-gains-tax) proceeds elsewhere. In this choice, the investor basically must decide whether an alternative investment is sufficiently better than the appreciated stock to justify paying a capital gains tax.

Of course, our investor does not have to follow just one of these alternatives. He can mix them. He might, for example, sell some of his appreciated stock and reinvest the proceeds, use some to make his customary charitable donations, give some away within his family, and keep the rest. Further, if he happens to have acquired the stock at different times with different tax bases, he can sell the stock with the highest bases and give away to charity and/or keep the stock with the lowest bases.

TAX-PLANNING CAVEATS

While tax planning is important and can produce significant savings, it should not be overemphasized. Overemphasis on tax savings can result in unwise or uneconomical transactions in other respects. Therefore, in pursuing the legitimate objective of reducing his or her tax burden, the taxpayer should also keep in mind some tax-planning caveats or warnings so that the decisions made in this area will be sensible from all points of view.

Avoid "Sham" Transactions

Taxpayers sometimes undertake transactions that have no real economic significance other than the desire to save taxes. Such "sham" transactions will not work. A fundamental principle of tax law is that a transaction will not be recognized for tax purposes unless it makes sense aside from its tax consequences.

Also, a transaction must be in fact what it appears to be in form. Thus, if a father ostensibly gives property to his children, but in fact continues to deal with the property as if he were the owner in accordance with an "understanding" with his children, the father will run a real risk that the "gift" will be regarded as a "sham" with no tax consequences.

In general, if a tax-saving plan makes no sense, other than for tax purposes, it should not be adopted.

Do Not Let Tax Factors Outweigh Other Important Objectives

Most financial decisions involve a number of considerations of which taxes are only one. The possibility of having to pay taxes, or of saving taxes, should be considered carefully but not to the exclusion of other nontax objectives. The capital gains tax "lock-in" problem, discussed above, is an example of this.

Consider What You Must Give Up for the Tax Saving

A proposal that involves tax savings almost always also requires the taxpayer to give up some flexibility, control, or other advantage that he would otherwise have. In other words, it is unlikely that you can "have your cake and eat it, too."

As an example of this, many people invest in municipal bonds because the interest is tax-exempt. But the "price" of this tax-free income is that the yields on municipals are lower than those on generally comparable corporate bonds.

A taxpayer should ask himself, when confronted with a tax-saving proposition, "What will I have to give up to secure the expected tax saving?"

Be Sure the Tax Saving Is Enough to Justify the Transaction

In some cases there may be a real tax saving, but it may not be large enough to justify the transaction. Also, look at how long it takes to get the anticipated tax savings. Sometimes tax-saving proposals show promised savings at the end of 10 years, 15 years, 20 years, age 65, or some other lengthy period of time. But the promised tax savings really may not be very substantial when calculated on a per-year basis.

Keep Your Planning Flexible

The popular saying, "The times, they are a-changin'" is as true for financial plans as any other. Tax rates, laws, family circumstances, and the taxpayer's financial condition all may change over time. Therefore, a taxpayer should consider carefully any loss of flexibility that will result from a tax-saving proposal.

Be Sure the Analysis is Complete

Before a taxpayer undertakes a financial plan that is based to any significant degree on expected tax savings, he should be sure he understands all the tax implications or dangers of the plan—not just the expected tax benefits. As part of such an analysis, he should consider how other types of taxes, such as estate and gift taxes, will affect the plan.

15
ESTATE PLANNING PRINCIPLES

Estate planning can be defined as arranging for the transfer of your property from one generation to the next so as to achieve, as far as possible, your objectives for your family and perhaps others. In our tax-oriented economy, tax minimization often is an important motivator for estate planning. And, in fact, proper planning can reduce taxes substantially. Tax saving, however, is not the only goal of estate planning and should not be overemphasized.

Before we go on to talk about specific estate planning techniques, let us review briefly the basic objectives of estate planning for most people.

OBJECTIVES OF ESTATE PLANNING

The estate owner should ask himself, "What am I really trying to accomplish through estate planning, given my own circumstances?" This general question, in turn, can be broken down into a number of specific estate planning objectives, some or all of which apply to most people.

1. Determining who will be the estate owner's heirs or beneficiaries and how much each will receive. This depends mainly on the estate owner's family and personal situation.

2. Planning adequate financial support for the estate owner's dependents. This means providing adequate income (after taxes) for his dependents to live on, as well as capital they can draw on in emergencies. In practice, an adequate life insurance program often is the answer to this objective.

3. Reducing estate transfer costs (i.e., death taxes, expenses of administration, and the like) to a minimum, consistent with the estate owner's other objectives.

4. Providing sufficient liquid assets for the estate to meet its obligations (i.e., adequate estate liquidity). This often becomes critical when an estate consists primarily of closely held business interests or similar unmarketable property.

5. Planning for the disposition of closely held business interests.

6. Deciding who is to settle the estate and how the property is to be administered. This involves selecting the executor or co-executors and deciding on investment and property management.

7. Planning how the estate owner's property is to be distributed. A person's property can be passed on to his heirs through arrangements taking effect

during his lifetime (called "living" or "inter vivos" transfers) or by transfers taking effect only at death. Most estate plans use several methods of transferring wealth—including both lifetime transfers and transfers at death.

These methods of estate transfer will be described later, but for now they can be outlined briefly as follows:

1. Lifetime methods of estate transfer

   a. Joint ownership of property with right of survivorship

   b. Lifetime gifts

   c. Life insurance proceeds paid to others

   d. Other beneficiary arrangements (e.g., death benefits payable under pension plans, profit-sharing plans, tax-sheltered annuities, and deferred compensation agreements)

   e. Irrevocable living trusts

   f. Revocable living trusts

   g. Business buy-sell agreements

   h. Exercise of powers of appointment

2. Estate transfer at death

   a. Intestate distribution

   b. Outright by will

   c. Testamentary trusts (i.e., trusts established under your will)

PROPERTY AND PROPERTY INTERESTS

Your estate can consist of a variety of different kinds of property and property interests. Therefore, let us briefly review what some of the more important of these are.

In general, property is anything you can own. Basically, there are two kinds of property—real property and personal property. *Real property* (or real estate) is land and everything attached to the land with the intention that it be part of the land. *Personal property* is all other kinds of property. Personal property can be *tangible*—property that has physical substance, like a car, boat, or furniture—or it can be *intangible*—property that does not have physical substance, like a stock certificate, bond, bank deposit, or life insurance policy.

Forms of Property Ownership

Property can be owned in various ways, and this can greatly affect your estate planning. Here are some of the common ways.

Outright Ownership. This is the highest form of ownership and is what people generally mean when they say someone "owns" property. The outright owner of property holds it in his own name and can deal with it during his lifetime. He can sell it, use it as collateral, or give it away. He can also pass it on to his heirs as he wishes (within some broad limits that will be mentioned shortly). Examples of outright ownership are almost limitless— sole ownership of cars, furniture, boats, furs, jewelry, etc.; ownership in one's own name of stock, bonds, bank accounts, and other accounts; and being the owner of a life insurance policy.

Joint Ownership. This exists when two or more persons have ownership rights in property. The more important kinds of joint ownership are as follows.

Joint tenancy (with right of survivorship). The outstanding characteristic of joint tenancy with right of survivorship (WROS) is that if one of the joint owners dies, his interest in the property passes automatically (by operation of law) to the other joint owner(s). This is the meaning of "with right of survivorship." Thus, if John and Mary own their residence as joint tenants and John dies, Mary automatically owns the residence (now in her own name) by right of survivorship. The same would be true if John and his brother Frank owned some investment real estate as joint tenants. Joint tenancy can exist between anyone—not just husband and wife.

During the lifetime of the joint tenants, the survivorship aspect of a joint tenancy can be destroyed by one of the joint tenants. Thus, if John and Frank own property as joint tenants, and John sells his interest to Harry, Frank and Harry then own the property as tenants in common (described below). Similarly, if John's creditors were to attach his interest in the property and have it sold to meet their claims, the purchaser and Frank would own the property as tenants in common.

Tenancy by the entirety. In some states, this form of ownership exists when property is held jointly by a husband and wife only. It is similar to a joint tenancy, but there are some significant differences. First, tenancy by the entirety can exist only between husband and wife. Second, in many states the survivorship rights in it cannot be terminated except with the consent of both parties. Finally, depending on the law in the particular state, the husband may have full control over the property during their joint lives and be entitled to all the income from it.

It is a common error to assume that all the property owned by a husband or wife somehow is held "jointly" by them. This is not true. Except in community property states, where special rules apply, only property that is specifically titled or received as being held as joint tenants or tenants by the entirety is so held. Other property can be owned outright by the husband alone, by the wife alone, or even by either of them jointly with others. Survivorship rights apply only to joint tenants or tenants by the entirety. Thus, a wife may not automatically get all her husband's property at his death unless that is specifically planned for.

The mere fact that property is held as joint tenants or tenants by the entirety does not mean it has to stay that way. The joint owners can agree to split up their interests if they want. Sometimes splitting up joint ownership can save estate taxes, but again, it may not. It all depends on the circumstances. The advantages and disadvantages of joint ownership are discussed in Chapter 17.

Other joint interests. There are two common forms of joint ownership that involve the right of survivorship which are very similar to joint tenancy but are not quite the same.

1. Joint bank accounts. Many people have joint checking or savings accounts. Typically, either party can make deposits and either party can withdraw all or part of the account. When one party dies, the survivor becomes the sole owner of the account by operation of law. This is not exactly a joint tenancy because a joint tenant can get at only his or her share of the property.

2. Jointly owned government savings bonds. Many persons have purchased government savings bonds (such as Series E or H bonds) in a way that creates survivorship rights with another. Such bonds can be registered *in co-ownership form* and held in the name of "A or B." This means that either A or B can cash in the bonds during their lifetime, and if one of them dies the other becomes sole owner. Such bonds can also be registered *in the name of "A payable on his (or her) death to B."* In this case, only A can cash in the bonds while he (or her) is living, but B becomes sole owner if he (or her) survives A and A has not cashed them in previously.

The above forms of joint ownership—joint tenancy (WROS), tenancy by the entirety, joint bank accounts, and jointly owned government savings bonds—are common ways of holding property with family members. The survivorship feature makes this a natural and convenient method for transferring the property to the other owner(s) at one owner's death.

Tenancy in common. The main difference between this and the previous kinds of joint ownership is that tenants in common do not have the right of survivorship with respect to the property concerned. If John and his brother Frank own the investment real estate equally as tenants in common, and John dies, his half of the real estate goes to his heirs as if he had owned it outright. Frank, of course, retains his half-interest. Tenants in common can have different proportionate interests in property. John and Frank could have 75 and 25 percent interests in the real estate, for example. Joint tenants and tenants by the entirety always have equal interests.

Community Property. Some of the states (Arizona, California, Idaho, Louisiana, Nevada, New Mexico, Texas, and Washington) are community property states; the others are referred to as "common law states." In the so-called "common law states," the forms of property ownership discussed above apply. But in the eight community property states the situation is quite different with respect to property owned by husbands and wives.

In community property states, husbands and wives can own separate property and community property. While the laws of the community property states are not uniform, *separate property* generally consists of property that a husband or wife owns at the time of marriage, property that each individually inherits, and property purchased with individual funds. This property remains separate property after marriage and the owner-spouse can deal with it as he or she chooses. Income from separate property may remain separate property or become community property, depending on the community property state involved.

Community property, on the other hand, generally consists of property that either or both spouses acquire during marriage. Each spouse has an undivided one-half interest in their community property. While the husband and wife are both alive, the applicable state community property law would determine who has the rights of management and control over the community property. However, upon his or her death, each spouse can dispose of only his or her half of the community property by will.

Obviously, for those living in community property states, their state's community property law is very important to their estate planning. Since community property laws are not uniform, each person should be advised as to how his state's law operates with respect to his property. However, even those now living in non-community property states can have community property. This can happen if the person and his or her spouse once lived in a community property state and acquired property there that became community property. *Such property remains community property even after the owners move to a common law state.* However, property owned by a husband and/or wife in a common law state does not become community property when they move to a community property state. Considering how Americans move around the country, these rules can be important.

Other Property Interests

There are other interests in property that are commonly involved in estate planning. These include legal interests and equitable interests, life interests (or estates) and remainder interests, present interests and future interests, and powers of appointment. An example can help explain these concepts.

> By his will, A leaves his property to the XYZ Bank *in trust* to keep it invested and to distribute the net income from it to his wife, B, if she survives him, during her lifetime. At B's death, or at A's death if B does not survive him, the property is to go outright in equal shares to C and D (A's adult children) or their issue.

This example, incidentally, illustrates a will for the husband, with a trust for his wife for life and then distribution to his children—a reasonably common arrangement.

Legal Interests and Equitable Interests. In this example, upon A's death, the XYZ Bank technically becomes legal owner of the property that passes into the trust. But the bank must exercise this ownership, as trustee, according to the terms of the trust agreement. B, C, and D have equitable (or beneficial) interests in the property, since it is held for their benefit.

Life Interests and Remainder Interests. A *life interest in property* entitles the holder to the income from or the use of the property, or a portion of the property, for his or her lifetime. The *remainder interest* (or remainderman) is entitled to the property itself after a life interest has ended.

In the example above, B (A's wife) has a life interest in the trust property. But her interest will terminate upon her death, and then C and D (or their heirs if they are deceased) will get the property. Thus, C and D have remainder interests. Life interests often are created by trusts, but there can also be legal life estates without a trust.

Present Interests and Future Interests. A *present interest* exists in property when the holder has a present or immediate right to use or enjoy the property. In a *future interest,* on the other hand, the use or enjoyment of the property is postponed to some future time.

In the above example, upon A's death, B has a present interest in the trust property because she has the immediate right to the income from it. C and D, however, have future interests because their right to the property is postponed until B's death. As we shall see later, the concepts of present and future interests are important in connection with gift taxes.

Powers of Appointment. Powers of appointment are commonly used in estate planning. In general, a *power of appointment* is a power or right given to a person (called the "donee of the power") that enables the donee to designate, sometimes within certain limits, who is to get certain property that is made subject to the power. In a nutshell, a power is the right to "appoint" property to someone.

The basic nontax purpose of powers of appointment is to postpone and delegate the decision as to who is to get property until a later time when the circumstances about people can be better known. This can result in better decision making in estate planning. Powers also can be used to achieve estate tax advantages, as is explained later.

There are several kinds of powers of appointment, including: (1) general powers and special powers (or limited powers), and (2) powers exercised by deed, by will, and by deed or will.

The difference between general and special powers is important for tax-saving purposes. A *general power* is a power to appoint property to the person having the power (i.e., the donee), the donee's estate, his creditors, or the creditors of his estate. In other words, a general power really means the donee can appoint the property to anyone he wants, including himself or his estate. It is close to owning the property. If someone has a general power over property at his death, the property will be included in his estate for federal estate tax purposes.

A *special power* of appointment allows the donee to appoint the property only to certain persons who are not the donee himself, his estate, his creditors, or the creditors of his estate. The possession of a special power over property at a person's death does *not* result in the property's being included in his estate for federal estate taxation. This is the big tax advantage of special powers.

When the donee of either a general or special power can appoint the property only at his death, it is referred to as a power exercisable *by will* (or a *testamentary power*). A power exercisable *by deed* is one where the donee can appoint the property only during his lifetime. The broadest power in this respect is one exercisable *by deed or will*, which is one exercisable both ways.

All these forms of property ownership and property interests can apply to an almost endless variety of kinds of estate assets. The general objective, then, is to plan for the transfer of this property to your family so as to avoid the common pitfalls of estate planning.

WHAT IS YOUR ESTATE?

This sounds like a simple question, but there are several different ways of looking at your estate. There is the *probate estate*, the *gross estate for federal estate taxation*, the *estate for state death tax purposes*, and the *"net" estate* that actually is available to the heirs. These "estates" often are not the same.

Probate Estate

A person's *probate estate* is the property that is handled and distributed by his personal representative (executor if he has a will, or administrator if he does not) upon his death. Generally speaking, it is the property he can dispose of by will, including:

1. Property he owns outright in his own name
2. His interest in property held as a tenant in common with others
3. Life insurance (or similar proceeds) payable to his estate upon his death

It is sometimes argued that having property in your probate estate is bad. This is not necessarily true, and it really depends on the circumstances. There are, however, some disadvantages in leaving property so that it will be part of your probate estate, such as:

1. There will be *delay* in settling your estate and hence in the distribution of the property to your heirs.
2. The *costs* of administering your estate (executor's fees, attorney's fees, etc.) usually are based largely on the probate estate. These costs may not be levied, or at least not levied in the same amount, against assets passing outside the probate estate.
3. Your *creditors* can "get at" assets in the probate estate.
4. Your probate estate can be made *public knowledge*.
5. Disgruntled heirs may seek to *contest* a will and hence "get at" probate property.

6. Sometimes *death taxes* can be increased, depending on the property and/or the state involved.

Some common ways of arranging property so it will go outside your probate estate are:

1. Life insurance (or similar proceeds) made payable to a beneficiary other than the insured's estate (e.g., his wife, children, a trust, etc.)

2. Jointly owned property (WROS)

3. Joint bank accounts, government savings bonds, and the like

4. Living trusts with the trust property passing to the trust beneficiaries after the creator's death

5. Outright lifetime gifts

In all these cases, the property either goes, or has gone, directly to the beneficiary, joint owner, or other donee at the person's death without ever passing through his or her executor's hands.

But just having property bypass your probate estate is not an estate planning panacea. Most people have a probate estate. First of all, any property you own outright at death must pass through your probate estate. Many people do not want to part with ownership or control over property until they die. Also, estate owners usually want their executor to have adequate liquid assets to pay the claims, expenses, and taxes that will be owed by their estate.

Gross Estate for Federal Estate Tax Purposes

With the increased importance of the federal estate tax to more and more persons, this "estate" is of great importance in estate planning. The gross estate is defined by the tax law and is the starting point for calculating how much federal estate tax the estate must pay. It includes, among other items, the property in the probate estate; life insurance the insured owns on his own life; and jointly owned property, except to the extent that the survivor can show that he or she contributed to the purchase price of the property. Thus, a great deal of property can be in the gross estate that bypasses the probate estate.

Naturally, there are deductions and exemptions that can be taken from the gross estate to arrive at the taxable estate on which the federal estate tax is calculated. Credits also are available against the estate tax itself. The calculation of the federal estate tax is illustrated in Chapter 16.

State Death Tax Value

Another complication is introduced by the death taxes that exist in all states except one (Nevada). Most states have *inheritance taxes,* which are levied on the right to *receive* property by inheritance. This is different in concept from an *estate tax* (like the federal estate tax), which is levied on the right to *give* property. While both are *death taxes*, there are some practical differences between them.

Inheritance tax laws vary considerably among the states, so it is necessary to check your own state law to see how it will apply to your situation. Banks may have available brief pamphlets explaining the local inheritance tax law. Many states also have estate taxes, but these generally are less important than the inheritance tax.

Depending on the state, some property that will be included in a person's gross estate for federal estate tax purposes may not be taxable under the local inheritance tax. Some possible examples are: life insurance payable to someone other than the insured's estate, jointly owned property, and property subject to powers of appointment.

This means that generally both the federal estate tax and the state inheritance (and/or estate) tax must be considered in your estate planning. State death taxes can be significant, particularly as a percentage of the more moderate estates.

The "Net" Estate to One's Heirs

This is what most people really are concerned about. They want to know what will be available to support their family. Basically, this "net" estate consists of the assets going to one's heirs after the payment of the costs of dying (debts, claims, administration expenses, and taxes).

An illustration may be helpful at this point. Let us return to our friends George and Mary Able—whom we met first in Chapter 1. Briefly, their asset picture looks like this:

Property George owns outright in his own name:

Common stock	$ 6,000
Autos and other personal property	20,000
	$26,000

Property George and Mary own jointly (WROS):

Home	$50,000
Mutual fund shares	2,000
Bank accounts	2,000
	$54,000

Life insurance that George owns on his own life:

Individual life insurance, payable to Mary in a lump sum	$80,000
Group term life insurance, payable in a lump sum to George's estate	40,000
	$120,000

Other employee benefits:

Profit-sharing plan death benefit, payable
in one sum to George's estate $12,000

If George were to die today, his *probate estate would be $78,000*. This amount includes the $26,000 of property George owns in his own name and the $40,000 of group life insurance and $12,000 of profit-sharing funds payable to his estate. The rest of the assets pass to Mary or the children outside of George's probate estate.

Assuming Mary cannot show that she contributed to any of the jointly owned property, George's *gross estate for federal estate tax purposes would be $212,000*. This could be reduced by proper planning in this case; but as things now stand, all the property would be subject to federal estate taxation upon George's death.

Let us assume George and Mary live in a state whose inheritance tax does not apply to property held jointly by husband and wife and to life insurance payable to a beneficiary other than the insured's estate. Under these assumptions, the amount of this property for *state inheritance tax purposes would be $78,000*. Again, this might be reduced with proper planning.

Now let us see what George can transmit to his family—his net estate. This is estimated below.

Total assets		$212,000
Less:		
George's debts	$24,000	
Estimated funeral and estate administration expenses	8,000	
Estimated federal estate tax	3,000	
Estimated state inheritance tax	4,000	
Total estate "shrinkage"	$39,000	−39,000
Net estate to George's family		$173,000

Of this $173,000, probably about $127,000 could produce investment income for the family ($173,000 less a net equity of about $16,000 in the autos and personal property and $30,000 equity in the residence).

SETTLING THE ESTATE

When a person dies, what happens to his property (estate)? This depends on whether he dies *intestate*—that is, without having made a valid will—or whether he made a *valid will*. Most people can make a valid will to dispose of their property if they want to do so.

If someone dies intestate, his probate estate is distributed according to the applicable state intestate law. In this case, an administrator (or administratrix), who is appointed by a court, handles the estate settlement. The estate owner has no voice in who will receive his property or who will be administrator; this depends on state law and the court. In essence, the estate owner has an estate plan "created by the law," rather than himself, when he dies intestate.

A person who leaves a valid will, on the other hand, is the "captain" of his own estate plan. Through his will, he can determine who gets his property and can name his executor (or executrix). Almost without exception, *people with property should execute wills* if they can.

Intestate Distribution

The laws of intestate distribution vary among the states. The surviving spouse first is entitled to his or her statutory share of the estate or the comparable common law rights of a surviving wife (dower) or husband (courtesy), depending upon the particular state's law. Then, a typical order of intestate distribution to persons other than the surviving spouse would be: (1) lineal descendants (i.e., children, grandchildren, etc.), if any, then (2) parents, if any living, then (3) brothers and sisters and their descendants, if any, and then (4) other collateral kindred (e.g., grandparents, uncles, aunts, etc.). If, by chance, a person should leave no one capable of inheriting, his property goes (escheats) to the state.

To take a simple example of intestate distribution according to one state's law, assume a family consisting of Husband; Wife; Son, age 24, with two minor children of his own; Daughter, age 16; and Son, age 12. Husband dies without a will and leaves a net estate of $60,000 (consisting of property he owned outright) after the payment of all claims against his estate. The intestate distribution would be as follows:

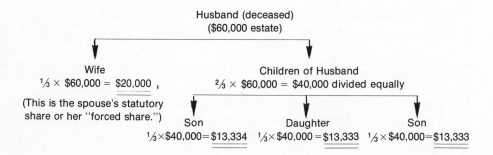

Husband (deceased)
($60,000 estate)

Wife
$\frac{1}{3} \times \$60,000 = \$20,000$

(This is the spouse's statutory share or her "forced share.")

Children of Husband
$\frac{2}{3} \times \$60,000 = \$40,000$ divided equally

Son
$\frac{1}{3} \times \$40,000 = \$13,334$

Daughter
$\frac{1}{3} \times \$40,000 = \$13,333$

Son
$\frac{1}{3} \times \$40,000 = \$13,333$

Suppose now that the 24-year-old son had died before his father. In this event, the deceased son's minor children would inherit their dead father's share equally ($6,667 each). Legal guardians would have to be appointed to manage property inherited by minor children.

Problems with Intestate Distribution

We noted above that people normally should make a will. The reason is that there are a number of problems that can arise when a person dies intestate.

1. Perhaps the most important is that intestate distribution is not specifically chosen by the estate owner. Thus, it may not be appropriate to his situation. For example, the wife's share often is inadequate (only one-third of the estate in the previous example). And other persons who may need support, such as daughters-in-law or stepchildren, are omitted completely.

2. Beneficiaries receive their inheritances outright, without regard to their individual capacities to manage the property. Guardians must be appointed for minor beneficiaries, and trusts cannot be used for the heirs.

3. The estate owner cannot select his or her executor. Also, in a will a person can excuse an executor from having to post bond with a commercial surety and thus save the estate the surety bond premiums.

4. Estate taxes may be increased because the surviving spouse's share may not be large enough to take full advantage of allowable estate tax deductions (see Chapter 16 for an explanation of the estate tax marital deduction).

5. The estate owner cannot delay distribution of property to his heirs even though they may be minors or otherwise not able to handle it, as he could through a trust under his will.

In view of these problems, it is indeed surprising the number of people who die intestate.

Distribution by Will

A *will* is a legally enforceable declaration of what a person wants done with his property and his instructions as to other matters when he dies. The will does not take effect until the person's (testator's) death and may be changed or revoked by him at any time up to his death. Thus, a will is referred to as "ambulatory" until the maker's death. To be effective, a will must be executed in accordance with the legal requirements of a valid will. Your attorney will see that these requirements are met.

With certain limitations, a person can leave his property by will to whomever he likes. One important limitation, however, is that in many states a husband or wife cannot deprive his or her surviving spouse of his or her statutory share (i.e., intestate share) of the estate by will. This is referred to as the *spouse's right to elect against the will*. Taking against the will does not deny the will's validity, but simply involves the spouse's taking his or her intestate share rather than what is left to him or her under the will.

The importance of the will in an estate plan depends upon how much of the estate is going to pass under the will (the probate estate) and how much will pass via lifetime-type transfers. In any event, however, it is important for both husband and wife to have wills for a complete estate plan.

Steps in Estate Settlement

What does a deceased's personal representative (executor under a will or administrator of a person dying intestate) do in settling the estate? After the executor's or administrator's appointment, the following are the basic functions the personal representative performs. Performing these functions can be rather routine or very complex, depending upon the circumstances of the estate.

1. Assembling the property belonging to the estate
2. Safekeeping, safeguarding, and insuring estate property during the period of estate settlement
3. Temporary management of estate property during the period of estate settlement, including carrying on or dealing with business interests
4. Payment of estate debts, taxes, and expenses
5. Accounting for the estate administration
6. Making distribution of the net estate to the proper heirs

In addition to these formal steps, we should also mention the valuable personal advice and services an executor can render to the deceased's family at this time which is particularly difficult for them. The estate owner should consider all these factors when selecting his executor(s).

For performing these functions, the executor is entitled to reasonable compensation, which is deducted from the estate. Executors' fees vary, but a reasonably typical schedule used by a commercial bank for normal services as an executor might be:

On principal:	
Estates under $50,000	5%
(Minimum fee, $1,000)	
Estates over $50,000:	
On the first $100,000	4%
(Minimum fee, $2,500)	
On the next $400,000	3%
On the next $500,000	2½%
On the next $1,000,000	2%
On gross income	5%

Sometimes lower percentage fees are also charged on property not passing under the will.

An executor can be an individual (the testator's spouse, brother or sister, an adult son or daughter, a trusted friend, etc.); or a corporate executor (a bank or trust company); or co-executors (such as the testator's spouse and a bank). An individual executor can waive any executor's compensation, or, if he or she is an heir anyway, can receive this compensation from the estate and thus save paying a fee to a corporate executor. However, remember that an executor's duties can be complex, difficult, and technical, and the executor can be held personally liable for mistakes or omissions. Therefore, many people decide to name corporate executors or co-executors and pay the fee involved. Also, executors' fees are deductible in computing any federal estate tax due, or the estate's (or beneficiaries') income tax, whichever the executor elects. In effect, then, the estate pays only the after-tax fee.

METHODS OF ESTATE TRANSFER

We mentioned earlier that one can pass his property on to others in a variety of ways. The estate owner must decide which methods of estate transfer he is going to use.

In making these decisions, however, the estate owner frequently must decide whether to give or leave his property outright or in trust. Therefore, we shall briefly review the nature of trusts at this point.

Trusts in Estate Planning

The famous jurist Oliver Wendell Holmes once said, "Don't put your trust in money; put your money in trust." Trusts have an important place in tax and estate planning today.

A *trust* is a fiduciary arrangement set up by someone, called the *grantor, creator,* or *settlor* of the trust, whereby a person, corporation, or other organization, called the *trustee,* has *legal* title to property placed in the trust by the grantor. The trustee holds and manages this property, which technically is called the trust *corpus* or *principal,* for the benefit of someone else, called the *beneficiary* of the trust, who has *equitable* title to the trust property. Thus, the essence of the trust relationship is the placing of legal title to property with a trustee who is to administer the property, as a *fiduciary,*[1] for the benefit of the trust beneficiary or beneficiaries.

Kinds of Trusts. There are various kinds of trusts; but as far as personal financial planning is concerned, the most important are: (1) living (or inter vivos) trusts, (2) trusts under will (or testamentary trusts), and (3) insurance trusts. A *living trust* is a personal trust created by an individual during his lifetime to benefit himself or someone else. A *testamentary trust* is a personal trust created under a person's will that, like the will, does not become effective until after the creator's death. An *insurance trust* is a particular kind of living trust whose corpus consists partly or wholly of life insurance policies during the insured's lifetime and/or life insurance proceeds after the insured's death.

Living trusts can be revocable or irrevocable. A *revocable trust* is one in which the creator reserves the right to revoke or amend the trust during his lifetime. In other words, he can change it or terminate it and get his property back. In an *irrevocable trust,* the creator does not reserve any such right to revoke or alter it.

Insurance trusts can be funded or unfunded. A *funded insurance trust* is

---

[1]A fiduciary is an individual or corporation that acts for the benefit of another with respect to things falling within the scope of the fiduciary relationship.

one where the trust corpus consists of life insurance and other assets. The income and/or principal from these other assets is used by the trustee to pay the premiums on the life insurance policy(ies) in the trust. An *unfunded insurance trust* is one containing only life insurance policies or one that is named as beneficiary of life insurance policies. The trust does not contain any other assets that can be used to pay the insurance premiums; these premiums must be paid by the creator or the trust or from some other source.

Reasons for Creating Trusts. There are a number of possible reasons for creating trusts. Some of the more common are:

1. To place the burdens of *property and investment management* in the hands of an experienced trustee, rather than leaving them to the creator, his or her family, or heirs.

2. To allow the trustee to use his, her, or its *discretion* (as a fiduciary) in handling trust property for the benefit of the creator, his or her family, or dependents.

3. To *protect the creator's family or dependents against demands* and entreaties made by well-meaning, or perhaps not so well-meaning, family members, friends, spouses, spouses-to-be, and the like.

4. To provide a *way of giving or leaving property to minors* so that the trustee can manage it for them until they are old enough to handle the property themselves. This avoids the legal rigidities and practical problems of having to have a legal guardian appointed for a minor.

5. In some cases, to *protect trust beneficiary(ies) against themselves* when they are physically, mentally, or emotionally unable to manage property themselves. Sometimes, for example, trusts are created to protect spendthrifts from themselves.

6. To provide *professional investment and property management for the creator himself or herself* during his or her lifetime. Also, investment diversification can be provided through the common trust funds set up by many banks.

7. To *manage a business interest* after the owner's death until it can be sold or one of his or her heirs can take over.

8. To provide an extremely useful device for *setting up tax-saving plans.* As a practical matter, tax saving is an important reason for creating trusts today.

Who Should Be Named Trustee? A trustee can be an individual, a corporation, or any other group or organization legally capable of owning property. There can be one trustee or two or more co-trustees. These co-trustees, for example, can be two or more individuals or a corporate trustee and one or more individual trustees. The creator of a trust, himself or herself, can be the trustee, but there may be tax problems in doing this.

Trustees, like executors, may receive compensation for their work. The fees charged by corporate trustees vary. It is common, however, for professional trustees to charge an annual fee based on the trust's gross income, or the value of the trust corpus, or both, with a minimum annual fee. As an example, the following is the annual compensation schedule for personal trusts of one trust company:

On the first $300,000 of trust corpus	$5 per $1,000	(or ½ of 1%)
On the next $400,000	$4 per $1,000	(or 0.4 of 1%)
On the next $300,000	$3 per $1,000	(or 0.3 of 1%)
On all over $1,000,000	$2 per $1,000	(or 0.2 of 1%)

Minimum annual fee:

For trusts invested entirely in the trust company's common trust funds	$125
For trusts invested otherwise	$250

But there usually is no fee charged by the trust company when a trust is created.

If we assume a trust with a $100,000 corpus and earning $6,000 per year, the annual trustee's fee under the above schedule would be $500 (0.005 × $100,000). This equals 8.3 percent of the current income from the trust property. However, trustee's fees generally are deductible for federal income tax purposes. Thus, the after-tax cost would be less, depending on the trust beneficiary's income tax bracket.

Since the trustee can be so important to the functioning of a trust, his, her, or its selection is an important decision. This choice often boils down to an individual or a corporate trustee.

An individual trustee (or trustees) may be the creator himself or herself, a member of the immediate family, a more distant relative, a trusted friend, an attorney, or someone else. The creator himself or herself may want to continue to administer the property as trustee, despite possible adverse tax results. An individual trustee may not charge any fee. It can also be argued that an individual trustee may be closer to the trust beneficiaries and more likely to be responsive to their needs than a corporate trustee. Finally, individual trustees can get professional help and guidance from attorneys, investment advisors, and the like, on the technical aspects of administering the trust.

On the other hand, strong arguments can be made for the use of corporate trustees:

1. Corporate trustees are professional money and property managers and hence can provide technical expertise in this area.

2. Individual trustees may die, resign, or otherwise become incapacitated, while corporate trustees provide continuity of trust management.

3. Corporate trustees are unbiased and independent of family pressures.

4. Corporate trustees normally are financially able to respond to damages in the event of trust mismanagement.

5. If an individual trustee is given discretionary powers over trust income or corpus, and the exercise of these powers may be beneficial to him or her personally (e.g., he or she is a trust beneficiary), he or she may be considered to be the owner of the trust corpus for federal estate and gift tax purposes and the

recipient of the trust income for income tax purposes. This would not be true of a corporate trustee.

6. A corporate trustee can serve as co-trustee with an individual trustee, thus combining at least some of the advantages of both. It should also be noted that it is possible to provide in a trust agreement that the corporate trustee can be removed and another corporate trustee substituted upon the demand of the trust beneficiaries (or someone else).

Estate Transfers at Death

We have already seen the problems of dying intestate and the desirability of having a will. When an estate owner leaves property to others by will, he must decide whether to leave it outright, under a testamentary trust, or perhaps some outright and some in trust.

To illustrate the use of a *will with a testamentary trust*, let us take the same family we did before in showing the intestate distribution of property. But this time let us assume the husband has made a will with a testamentary trust for his family. Here is one way his $60,000 (probate) estate could be handled under this kind of arrangement.

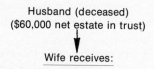

Husband (deceased)
($60,000 net estate in trust)

Wife receives:

1. Life income from $60,000
2. Limited right of withdrawal
3. Special power of appointment *
4. Trust principal for her or children's support or children's education at trustee's discretion

At Wife's Death

(Remaining trust principal divided into three equal shares, in trust, for the children or their issue)

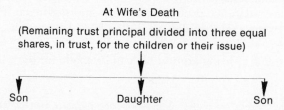

Son   Daughter   Son

Children receive:

1. Life income from his or her trust
2. Special power of appointment
3. Trust principal for his or her (or his or her issue's) support or education at trustee's discretion
4. Right to withdraw all or part of his or her trust at age 25 or 30

This kind of plan would meet virtually all the problems of intestate distribution. Of course, specific estate arrangements can take many different forms, depending upon the circumstances. (See Chapter 16, for example.)

Lifetime Transfers

As we saw before, there are many ways property can be transferred by an estate owner during his or her lifetime without passing under his or her will. In fact, in many cases lifetime transfers are more important than transfers by will. Thus, these lifetime transfers should be coordinated with an estate owner's will in a well-designed estate plan.

16
PLANNING FOR DEATH TAXES

It is said that "nothing is certain except death and taxes." Here we are dealing with both. A great deal of estate planning is concerned with saving and planning for death taxes.

DEATH TAXES AND ESTATE SETTLEMENT COSTS

A person's estate may be subject to a number of claims that must be paid in cash. These frequently are discussed in estate planning and might be referred to as "cash demands on the estate," "total claims, expenses, and taxes," "estate shrinkage," and "estate liquidity needs," among others. Estate planning first seeks to minimize and then to provide for the payment of these taxes and costs.

In an increasing number of estates, the federal estate tax represents an important part of this "shrinkage," and so we shall review this tax and how to plan for it below. We shall also consider state death taxes and other estate settlement costs.

How to Estimate Your Federal Estate Tax

The basic pattern for estimating your estate's federal estate tax liability is as follows:

Gross estate

Less: Deductions to arrive at adjusted gross estate (i.e., estate administration expenses, funeral expenses, and debts and claims against the estate), equals—

Adjusted gross estate

Less: Marital deduction (up to one-half the adjusted gross estate), charitable bequests, $60,000 specific exemption, equals—

Taxable estate, to which the estate tax rates are applied to produce the

Federal estate tax (before any credits)

Less: Credits, equals—

Federal estate tax payable

Gross Estate. The gross estate for federal estate tax purposes is the starting point for determining how much estate tax an estate must pay. In general, it includes the following items:

1. All property you own in your own name and your interest in property you hold as a tenant in common with someone else

2. Proceeds of life insurance policies on your life if you have any ownership rights in the policy (incidents of ownership) or if the policy is payable to your estate

3. The full value of property held jointly (WROS) with others, *except* to the extent the surviving owner(s) can show that he or she contributed to the purchase price of the property

4. Your share of any community property

5. Property over which you have a general power of appointment

6. Gifts made in contemplation of death (This applies only to gifts made within three years of death. Such gifts are presumed to have been made in contemplation of death, but this presumption can be rebutted by the facts.)

7. Benefits under employee benefit plans, with certain exceptions

8. Property you transferred by gift during your lifetime where you retained certain prohibited rights or powers in the gift property

Using this list of items, most people generally can estimate their gross estate by using a family balance sheet and some pertinent information about their life insurance policies and employee benefits (or perhaps by using an asset inventory or estate survey form) as basic data sources.

For purposes of estimating estate taxes, you normally need only approximate values for property in the estate. However, for some kinds of property the estate tax value may not be clear and valuation problems can arise. This can occur, for example, in the case of real estate, fine arts and collections, some kinds of tax-sheltered investments, and certain mortgages and loans. A particularly troublesome problem can be the valuation of closely held business interests, which may constitute a large portion of some estates. As we shall see in Chapter 18, this valuation problem can often be solved through a properly drafted buy-sell agreement for the business interest.

Deductions to Arrive at the Adjusted Gross Estate. These deductions also may be approximated for our purposes. Naturally, they vary among estates. The specific deductible items include:

1. Estate administration expenses, including executor's commissions, attorney's fees, court costs, accounting and appraiser's fees, brokerage fees, costs of maintaining estate assets, and the like. These may be estimated at between 6 and 8 percent of the probate estate for planning purposes.

2. Current debts of the estate owner and any claims against the estate.

3. Accrued taxes, including real estate and nonwithheld income taxes.

4. Unpaid mortgages on property included in the gross estate.

5. Funeral and last-illness expenses. Funeral expenses can be estimated, but last-illness expenses are entirely uncertain. If the estate owner has adequate medical expense insurance, however, it can be assumed that this coverage will reimburse most of these last-illness expenses.

Estate planners sometimes make a rough approximation of these deductions at, say, 8 to 10 percent of the gross estate for planning purposes.

Adjusted Gross Estate. This is used to determine the maximum permissible marital deduction—which is one-half the adjusted gross estate. Note, however, that this measures only the maximum permissible marital deduction. The deduction is not automatic, and whether this amount actually can be taken depends on how your estate is set up.

Federal Estate Tax Marital Deduction. This is normally a very important tax-saving device for married estate owners. An estate owner can leave his or her spouse up to one-half of his or her adjusted gross estate free of federal estate tax. Planning for the proper use of the marital deduction to achieve maximum estate tax savings in the estates of *both* the husband and wife will be considered in greater detail below.

Charitable Bequests. Bequests for public, charitable, and religious uses are deductible in calculating the federal estate tax. Thus, such gifts are not taxed.

Specific Exemption. Each estate is entitled to a $60,000 specific exemption. No estate tax return need be filed unless the gross estate exceeds this amount. The combination of this specific exemption and the marital deduction sometimes leads people to say that the federal estate tax is important only for estates over $120,000. This is so because approximately one-half of a $120,000 estate, or $60,000, could be left to a spouse and be taken as a marital deduction. The remaining $60,000 would be eliminated by the specific exemption, resulting in no estate tax. For estates over $120,000, the $60,000 specific exemption would not absorb the other half, so there would be some estate tax. This rule of thumb, however, assumes full use of the marital deduction, which may not be possible or desirable in some cases. Also, it does not consider what happens when the surviving spouse dies and the marital deduction is not available. Therefore, the estate tax still may be a factor to consider even in estates of less than $120,000.

Taxable Estate. The result of taking all these deductions from the gross estate is the taxable estate, to which the federal estate tax rates are applied. The estate tax rates are steeply progressive, ranging from 3 to 77 percent of the taxable estate. These rates, along with the rates of the state death tax credit, which is discussed below, are shown in Table 16-1. In this table, the taxable estate is shown before deducting the $60,000 specific exemption only for the sake of convenience in computations.

TABLE 16-1

FEDERAL ESTATE TAX RATES AND
RATES OF STATE DEATH TAX CREDIT

(1) Taxable Estate before Exemption	(2) Rate of Tax on Excess over Amount in Column 1	(3) Gross Tax on Amount in Column 1	(4) State Death Tax Credit Rate on Excess	(5) Credit for Column 1	(6) Net Tax
$ 60,000	3%	Exempt	No		$ 0
65,000	7	$ 150	Credit		150
70,000	11	500			500
80,000	14	1,600			1,600
90,000	18	3,000			3,000
100,000	22	4,800	.8%	$ 0	4,800
110,000	25	7,000	.8	80	6,920
120,000	28	9,500	.8	160	9,340
125,000	28	10,900	.8	200	10,700
150,000	28	17,900	1.6	400	17,500
160,000	30	20,700	1.6	560	20,140
175,000	30	25,200	1.6	800	24,400
200,000	30	32,700	2.4	1,200	31,500
225,000	30	40,200	2.4	1,800	38,400
250,000	30	47,700	2.4	2,400	45,300
275,000	30	55,200	2.4	3,000	52,200
300,000	30	62,700	3.2	3,600	59,100
310,000	32	65,700	3.2	3,920	61,780
350,000	32	78,500	3.2	5,200	73,300
400,000	32	94,500	3.2	6,800	87,700
450,000	32	110,500	3.2	8,400	102,100
500,000	32	126,500	4.	10,000	116,500
560,000	35	145,700	4.	12,400	133,300
600,000	35	159,700	4.	14,000	145,700
650,000	35	177,200	4.	16,000	161,200
700,000	35	194,700	4.8	18,000	176,700
750,000	35	212,200	4.8	20,400	191,800
810,000	37	233,200	4.8	23,280	209,920
850,000	37	248,000	4.8	25,200	222,800
900,000	37	266,500	5.6	27,600	238,900
1,060,000	39	325,700	5.6	36,560	289,140
1,100,000	39	341,300	6.4	38,800	302,500
1,250,000	39	399,800	6.4	48,400	351,400
1,310,000	42	423,200	6.4	52,240	370,960
1,560,000	45	528,200	6.4	68,240	459,960
1,600,000	45	546,200	7.2	70,800	475,400
2,060,000	49	753,200	7.2	103,920	649,280
2,100,000	49	772,800	8.	106,800	666,000
2,560,000	53	998,200	8.	143,600	854,600
2,600,000	53	1,019,400	8.8	146,800	872,600
3,060,000	56	1,263,200	8.8	187,230	1,075,920
3,100,000	56	1,285,600	9.6	190,800	1,094,800
3,560,000	59	1,543,200	9.6	234,960	1,308,240
3,600,000	59	1,566,800	10.4	238,800	1,328,000
4,060,000	63	1,838,200	10.4	286,640	1,551,560

TABLE 16-1 (Continued)

(1) Taxable Estate before Exemption	(2) Rate of Tax on Excess over Amount in Column 1	(3) Gross Tax on Amount in Column 1	(4) State Death Tax Credit Rate on Excess	(5) State Death Tax Credit Credit for Column 1	(6) Net Tax
$4,100,000	63%	$1,863,400	11.2%	$290,800	$1,572,600
4,500,000	63	2,115,400	11.2	335,600	1,779,800
5,000,000	63	2,430,400	11.2	391,600	2,038,800
5,060,000	67	2,468,200	11.2	398,320	2,069,880
5,100,000	67	2,495,000	12.	402,800	2,092,200
6,060,000	70	3,138,200	12.	518,000	2,620,200
6,100,000	70	3,166,200	12.8	522,800	2,643,400
7,060,000	73	3,838,200	12.8	645,680	3,192,520
7,100,000	73	3,867,400	13.6	650,800	3,216,600
8,060,000	76	4,568,200	13.6	781,360	3,786,840
8,100,000	76	4,598,600	14.4	786,800	3,811,800
9,100,000	76	5,358,600	15.2	930,800	4,427,800
10,060,000	77	6,088,200	15.2	1,076,720	5,011,480
10,100,000	77	6,119,000	16.	1,082,800	5,036,200

We can see from this table that the tax on a taxable estate of $40,000 ($100,000 before the specific exemption) is $4,800 or 12 percent of the taxable estate, while the tax on a $140,000 taxable estate ($200,000 before the exemption) is $32,700 or 23 percent of the taxable estate. Thus, the significance of the progressive federal estate tax is clear.

Credits. There may be several kinds of credits applied to reduce the federal estate tax as calculated above. Probably the most important is the credit for state death taxes paid, as shown in Table 16-1. This credit equals the *smaller of* (1) the amount determined by applying the increasing rates shown in Table 16-1 to the taxable estate, or (2) the amount of state death taxes actually paid. Because the state death taxes actually paid usually equal or exceed the rate of credit allowed by the law, in practice the rates shown in Table 16-1 often will determine the effective maximum credit.

Let us now illustrate an estimate of federal estate taxes by continuing to analyze the estate situation of George and Mary Able. We first met the Ables in Chapter 1 and calculated George's gross estate ($212,000) in Chapter 15. The rest of George's estate tax estimate is as follows[1]:

Gross estate		$212,000
Less deductions of:		
Estimated estate administration expenses	$6,000	
Current debts[2]	4,000	

[1]We also shall see later in this chapter what happens upon Mary's subsequent death.

[2]There would also be some income taxes due from George's estate because of the profit-sharing account which is payable to his estate.

Unpaid mortgages	20,000	
Estimated funeral expenses (last-illness expenses assumed covered by medical expense insurance)	2,000	−32,000
Adjusted gross estate		$180,000
Marital deduction (½ of $180,000, since more than this amount passes to Mary so as to "qualify" for the marital deduction)		−90,000
		$ 90,000
Less specific exemption		−60,000
Taxable estate		$ 30,000
Federal estate tax (on a taxable estate of $30,000, there is no state death tax credit —see Table 16-1)		$ 3,000

State Death Taxes

As noted in Chapter 15, state death taxes vary considerably among the states. State inheritance taxes, which are levied on the right to receive property, often have varying exemptions and rates for different classes of beneficiaries. One state, for example, levies a 6 percent inheritance tax on transfers to the spouse, children, grandchildren, other lineal descendants, adopted children and their descendants, stepchildren, spouse of a child, parents, and grand-parents. The tax rate on transfers to others is 15 percent. There are no exemptions in this state.

Many states also have a so-called "credit" estate tax designed to equal the difference, if any, between the tax payable under the state's inheritance tax law and the federal estate tax credit for state death taxes paid as shown in Table 16-1. This allows the state to tax at least up to the full federal credit.

Estimating Your Estate's Liquidity (Cash) Needs

As we saw above, there are a number of claims and taxes an estate must pay shortly after the estate owner's death. These can be summarized for George Able's estate as follows:

Current debts	$ 4,000
Estimated funeral expenses	2,000
Estimated last-illness expenses (assumed covered by medical expense insurance)	—
Estimated costs of estate administration	6,000

Unpaid mortgages (assume Mary will continue the $20,000 mortgage on their home after George's death)	—
State death tax	4,000
Federal estate tax	3,000
Any specific dollar bequests in the will (or widow's allowance)	—
Total cash needs	$19,000 (or 24% of George's 78,-000 probate estate and 9% of his $212,000 gross estate)

Providing Liquidity for Your Estate

Liquidity can be an extremely serious problem for some estates but of minor importance for others. Much depends on the composition of the estate and what previous planning has been done. Estate liquidity often is a major problem when a large part of an estate consists of relatively unmarketable assets such as closely held business interests, undeveloped real estate, or certain tax-sheltered investments.

Meeting the claims and taxes against an estate generally is the responsibility of the executor (or administrator) to do from the probate assets. These are the only assets directly available to the executor. However, other assets, such as jointly owned property or life insurance payable to a third-party beneficiary, that pass outside the probate estate, *may* be made available to the executor by the person receiving them (such as a surviving spouse) as a loan to the estate or by such person purchasing assets from the estate. The executor, however, cannot normally use assets passing outside the probate estate to meet estate liquidity needs without the consent of the person (or trustee) controlling such assets.

Proper planning for estate liquidity often is necessary. Here are some of the common *sources of liquidity* for an estate.

1. Cash and bank accounts—owned outright or jointly with someone who will make them available to the estate.

2. Life insurance proceeds—payable to the estate or to a person (or trust) who will make them available.

3. Stocks and bonds that are actively traded. These can be sold to meet estate cash needs. Of course, in a declining market such securities may produce less than the estate owner would have liked.

    There are some United States treasury bonds outstanding, called "flower bonds," that can be used at par to pay the owner's estate taxes. But such "flower bonds" are no longer being issued by the government.

4. United States government savings bonds—owned outright or jointly with someone who will make them available. These can be redeemed.

5. Mortgages or loans taken on estate assets.

6. Buy-sell agreements covering closely held business interests can produce substantial amounts of cash for the executor. In fact, a properly funded buy-sell agreement will usually solve the liquidity needs of an estate consisting largely of a closely held business interest (see Chapter 18).

7. Provisions of living trusts—by which the trustee is authorized to make loans to, and/or buy property from, the creator's estate. Thus, the trustee can provide liquidity to the estate from trust assets if necessary.

8. Redemption of stock by the estate from a closely held corporation. This is the so-called Section 303 redemption to pay death taxes and funeral and estate administration expenses, which is discussed in Chapter 18.

Let us now analyze the sources of liquidity in George Able's estate as presently constituted.

Probate Estate

Common stock	$ 6,000
Group life insurance	40,000
Profit-sharing plan death benefits	12,000
	$58,000

Passing Outside the Probate Estate

Mutual fund shares (owned jointly with Mary)	$ 2,000
Bank accounts (owned jointly with Mary)	2,000
Personal life insurance proceeds (payable in a lump sum to Mary)	80,000
	$84,000

It is clear that there is more than enough liquidity in George's estate as it now stands.

Determining What Is Left for Your Family (the "Net" Estate)

After estimated death taxes and estate settlement costs are paid, you want to know how much "net" estate will pass to your family and how much income it will provide for them.

Again using George Able's estate as an example, we saw in Chapter 15 that his "net" estate for his family would be $173,000. Of this amount, about $127,000 could be put in income-producing investments. If we assume, conservatively, that this amount can produce an average return of 6 percent before taxes. George's family would receive about $7,600 annually from this capital fund. When we add tax-free social security survivorship benefits of, say, about $700 per month (at least while the children are growing up) to this, George's family would appear to be in a reasonably good position as far as current income is concerned. Of course, this does not consider any possible invasion of the capital fund for purposes such as emergencies or the children's educations.

What Happens When the Other Spouse Dies?

What happens at George's death is only part of the story. We must also consider Mary's estate at her subsequent death. It is important to carry the analysis on through the estates of both spouses. This often discloses an unexpected estate tax liability.

Again using the estates of George and Mary Able as examples, let us assume that George leaves his "net estate" outright to Mary, she does not "consume" any of the capital or make any gifts during her lifetime, she does not remarry, and she receives the expected $50,000 inheritance outright from her parents. Then, on Mary's subsequent death we would have:

Property passing to Mary from George (through life insurance proceeds paid to her, jointly owned property, and under George's will)	$173,000*
Property Mary received by inheritance	50,000
Mary's gross estate	$223,000
Less: Estimated funeral and estate administration expenses and current debts	−10,000
Adjusted gross estate	$213,000
Marital deduction	-0-
	$213,000
Specific exemption	−60,000
Taxable estate	$153,000
Gross estate tax	$ 36,600
State death tax credit	−1,612
Final federal estate tax	$ 34,988 (or about $35,000)*

*These figures are slightly different from those on page 7 of chapter 1 because there we ignored state death taxes and the state death tax credit for purposes of simplicity.

Assuming Mary leaves her "net" estate to her children (and perhaps grandchildren), her state death taxes are assumed to be about $12,000, although this can vary considerably among the states.

Therefore, Mary's "net" estate for her family (assuming George's prior death) would be $166,000, computed as follows:

Total assets		$223,000
Less: Funeral and estate administration expenses and current debts	10,000	
Federal and state death taxes	47,000	
Total "estate shrinkage"	$57,000	57,000
"Net" estate to heirs		$166,000

Thus, after "shrinkage" in both estates ($39,000 in George's estate and $57,000 in Mary's estate) is considered, a "net" amount of $166,000 will end up going to their children and grandchildren or other heirs. In the next part of this chapter, we shall look at some ways this fearful "shrinkage" can be reduced by proper planning.

Reversing the Order of Deaths

A final step that can be taken is to assume a reversed order of deaths and do the analysis again. That is, in this case assume Mary dies first. This step may point up the problem of a wife with some assets of her own, or possibly with a potential inheritance as in the case of the Ables, leaving all her assets to her husband, who already has a sizable estate of his own. This problem is dealt with later in the section, "'Skipping Estates' to Save Federal Estate Taxes."

HOW TO SAVE ON DEATH TAXES AND SETTLEMENT COSTS

We have seen how death taxes and estate settlement costs can be important "estate shrinkage" items. It is no wonder, then, that estate planning often is much concerned with saving taxes and estate settlement costs.

Using the Marital Deduction to Save Federal Estate Taxes

The basic idea of the federal estate tax marital deduction is to allow a married estate owner to leave up to one-half of his or her estate to his or her surviving spouse free of federal estate tax. But this half (the so-called "marital" part) must be left to the surviving spouse in such a way that it would be included in his or her gross estate at the surviving spouse's subsequent death. In tax language, these are referred to as transfers to the surviving spouse that "qualify" for the marital deduction. Thus, use of the marital deduction is not automatic; there must be enough property in the gross estate that "qualifies" for the deduction to take full advantage of it.

The maximum allowable marital deduction is limited to one-half the adjusted gross estate, even though more than half may pass to the surviving spouse so as to "qualify." In George Able's case, for example, the maximum marital deduction would be $90,000 ($\frac{1}{2} \times$ $180,000), even though all his property now passes to Mary in a "qualifying" manner. In fact, as we shall see later, it is often disadvantageous to "qualify" more than one-half the estate for the marital deduction.

What Property "Qualifies" for the Deduction? Many kinds of transfers to a surviving spouse will "qualify." The spouse does not have to have outright ownership of the property, but, as a general principle, the spouse ultimately must have complete control over the disposition of the property at his or her death. In other words, the "price" of the tax saving through use of the marital deduction is giving the surviving spouse the power to decide who gets the property when he or she dies.

There are a number of kinds of transfers to a surviving spouse that will "qualify" for the federal estate tax marital deduction. The following are among the more common:

1. Outright bequests.

2. Property held jointly by the spouses (with right of survivorship) to the extent that the property is included in the deceased spouse's gross estate.

3. Property passing to the surviving spouse in trust with the trust income payable to him or her for his or her lifetime and with the surviving spouse having a general power of appointment over the trust corpus. This is the so-called "power of appointment trust" or "marital trust." It is so frequently used for qualifying property for the marital deduction that we shall discuss it in greater detail later in the chapter.

4. Life insurance proceeds payable to the surviving spouse in a lump sum or under a settlement arrangement that will "qualify" or to a life insurance trust which itself meets the requirements for "qualifying" its corpus.

Should You Use the Marital Deduction? Since using the marital deduction can cut the taxable estate in half, most married estate owners want to plan to use the maximum allowable deduction in their estate planning.

There may be cases, however, in which the estate owner does not want to use the marital deduction. For example, an estate owner may not want to give his or her spouse the power ultimately to dispose of half of his or her estate. In other cases, an estate may consist mainly of certain property, such as business interests or investment property, that the owner does not feel can conveniently be split up or left to the spouse. Finally, when both spouses each have a large estate, use of the marital deduction may actually increase total estate taxes on *both* estates. However, cases of this kind are relatively infrequent. And even when they occur, it still may be desirable to use the full marital deduction for various practical reasons.

Thus, in most cases the married estate owner will want to use the maximum allowable marital deduction. But this should not be taken for granted in all cases.

"Qualifying" the Right Amount (Avoid "Overqualifying" Your Estate). As we saw above, there is no particular tax advantage to an estate owner's qualifying more than one-half his adjusted gross estate for the marital deduction. However, when the surviving spouse dies (i.e., is the second spouse to die), there is a tax *disadvantage* if the previous estate owner (i.e., the first spouse to die) qualified more than one-half of his estate for the deduction. This results because, while the executor of the first spouse to die can deduct only one-half the adjusted gross estate (even if more property actually "qualifies"), *all* the property that passes to the surviving spouse in a qualifying manner will be included in her gross estate when she dies, unless she has given it away during her lifetime. Thus, more property will be included in both estates than is necessary to get the maximum allowable marital deduction upon the first spouse's death.

This is referred to as an estate's being "overqualified" for the marital deduction. It is a very common situation because so many husbands in their wills just routinely leave everything outright to their wives. Or, husbands and wives, probably in a spirit of togetherness, execute so-called reciprocal wills—he leaves everything to her and she leaves everything to him. While this may seem like the nice thing to do, it can be costly from an estate tax standpoint. Also, many husbands and wives hold property in joint names and/or have their life insurance payable to the other spouse.

The trick then is to qualify only enough property to equal the maximum allowable deduction and no more. Qualifying the estate either for less than the allowable deduction (being underqualified) or for more than the allowable deduction (being overqualified) does not result in the lowest possible estate taxes on both estates. Some examples will help illustrate this idea. The examples will be simplified for ease of illustration.

In each case below, assume Husband owns $200,000 of assets in his own name and his Wife has no property of her own. Also assume the Husband predeceases his Wife and she does not remarry.

Case No. 1. In his will, Husband leaves his entire estate outright to his Wife.

Husband's gross estate	$200,000
Deductible expenses and debts (estimated)	−20,000
Adjusted gross estate	180,000
Marital deduction (all property "qualifies" as an outright bequest)	−90,000
	90,000
Specific exemption	−60,000
Taxable estate	30,000
Federal estate tax (ignoring any credits) on Husband's death	$3,000

Now, on Wife's subsequent death:

Wife's gross estate (from Husband; $200,000 − $23,000)	$177,000
Deductible expenses and debts (estimated)	−7,000
	170,000
Marital deduction	-0-
Specific exemption	−60,000
Taxable estate	110,000
Federal estate tax (ignoring any credits) on Wife's death	$23,700
Total estate taxes on both estates	$26,700

Case No. 2. Husband in his will leaves to his Wife in a so-called "marital trust" (or outright) only enough property to equal the maximum allowable marital deduction. The remainder of his estate is left to his Wife for her lifetime in trust (a so-called "nonmarital trust" which does not "qualify" for the marital deduction), with the remainder interest to go to their children upon the Wife's death. (All death taxes are to be paid from the "nonmarital" trust.) Now, let us look at the result in this case.

Husband's gross estate	$200,000
Deductible expenses and debts (estimated)	−20,000
Adjusted gross estate	180,000
Marital deduction (just ½ of $180,000 qualifies)	−90,000
	90,000
Specific exemption	−60,000
Taxable estate	30,000
Federal estate tax (ignoring any credits) on Husband's death	$3,000

Now, on Wife's subsequent death:

Wife's gross estate (from Husband)	$90,000
Deductible expenses and debts (estimated)	−4,000
	86,000
Marital deduction	-0-
Specific exemption	−60,000
Taxable estate	26,000
Federal estate tax (ignoring any credits) on Wife's death	2,440
Total estate taxes on both estates	$5,440

The difference in the amount of estate taxes in Cases 1 and 2 is clear. The arrangement in Case 2 potentially saves $21,260 in estate taxes ($26,700 − $5,440), or an 80 percent reduction in estate taxes. Of course, in Case 2 the Wife does not have complete ownership of all the property as she would in Case 1. This is the "price" of the estate tax saving. However, as we shall see when we discuss "Methods of 'Qualifying' the Right Amount" below, the "marital" and "nonmarital" trusts assumed in Case 2 can be so arranged as to give the Wife almost the equivalent of outright ownership.

In the examples above, we illustrated the tax advantage of not overqualifying property for the estate tax marital deduction. In each case we assumed the Husband retained ownership of the assets until his death. Another possibility for achieving the same general tax result as in Case 2, however, would be for Husband and Wife to divide ownership of the property between them so as approximately to equalize their gross estates. Then, they each could leave their property in a way that would not result in its being included in the survivor's gross estate (a life income to the survivor with the remainder interest to their children, for example).

Methods of "Qualifying" the Right Amount. The approach shown in Case 2 above, using "marital" and "nonmarital" trusts (sometimes called "A" and "B" trusts) to qualify just the right amount (or portion) of the estate for the marital deduction, is commonly used in estate planning. It is perhaps the classical approach for handling this problem. Let us see what these trusts for the surviving spouse are like.

The property in the "marital trust," usually a "power of appointment trust," qualifies for the marital deduction. For the property in such a *power of appointment trust* (or portion of a trust) to qualify, the trust must meet certain minimum requirements. Among these are that all the trust income must be payable to the surviving spouse at least annually, and the surviving spouse must have a general power of appointment over the trust corpus. The property in this marital trust ultimately will go into the surviving spouse's gross estate at his or her death (because of his or her possession of the general power of appointment), unless he or she consumes or gives it away during his or her lifetime.

The "nonmarital trust" is so named because it is arranged so that its corpus does not qualify for the marital deduction and, hence, is not includable in the surviving spouse's estate when he or she dies. This trust can have a great variety of provisions for the estate owner's spouse, children, or other heirs, provided the estate owner does *not* give the surviving spouse such powers (as a general power of appointment, for example) that would cause the trust property to be included in the survivor's gross estate.

How can we know, before the estate owner's death, how much property should go into a marital trust (or gift) for the surviving spouse so as just to equal the maximum allowable marital deduction? This problem is difficult because the property and property values in an estate are changing constantly and because a good deal of property can pass outside the probate estate. A common solution to this problem is to use a *formula clause*. The effect of a formula clause is to cause such an amount (or share) of the estate to flow into the marital trust that, together with other estate assets that may go to the surviving spouse in other ways, will just equal one-half the adjusted gross estate and, thus, reduce estate taxes to a minimum. Thus, a formula clause automatically determines how much of your estate will go into a marital trust (or marital gift) and how much into a nonmarital trust.

Such a marital trust (or marital gift), formula clause, and nonmarital (or residuary) trust can be included in the estate owner's will as *testamentary trusts,* or in a *living life insurance trust* which would be the beneficiary of life insurance policies, or under the terms of a *revocable living trust,* depending upon the circumstances.

In the case of George and Mary Able, for example, the bulk of George's estate consists of $120,000 of life insurance proceeds and a $12,000 profit-sharing account. His estate also is overqualified for the marital deduction. Thus, George's estate plan could be rearranged so that most of his life insurance proceeds and perhaps the death benefits under his profit-sharing plan would be payable to a living life insurance trust. This trust would contain marital and nonmarital trust provisions and a formula clause. George's will could provide that his personal effects would go outright to Mary and then "pour over" any residuary estate into the life insurance trust. The jointly owned property could remain as it is.

"Skipping Estates" to Save Federal Estate Taxes

Some estate owners find themselves in the position where their natural instinct is to leave their property to a family member who already has, or will have, a sizable estate in his or her own right. Several examples come to mind—the widow or widower with successful and increasingly affluent children, the brother or sister with a well-to-do sibling, and the wife whose husband has a sizable estate. The estate owner, however, should think twice before leaving a substantial amount of property outright to such a family member, because by doing so he or she simply piles more property onto the family member's already sizable potential estate. This just unnecessarily increases federal estate taxes.

A technique for avoiding such an increase in taxes is to leave the relatively well-off loved one a life interest in the property in trust, rather than outright ownership. The property then can pass to someone else on the life tenant's death. If the trust arrangement is set up properly, nothing will be in the life tenant's estate at his or her death. Thus, the life tenant's estate is "skipped" for federal estate tax purposes. In addition, the life tenant can be given many rights and benefits in this trust without having its corpus included in his or her gross estate.

Returning to the case of the Ables, for example, it might be desirable for Mary (who is expecting a $50,000 inheritance in the future) to use this trust technique to "skip" George's estate if she should predecease him. At George's subsequent death, the trust corpus could go to their children, either outright or in trust for them.

Making Lifetime Gifts

Making completed lifetime gifts, either outright or in trust, generally removes the gift property from the donor's gross estate and, hence, saves estate (and inheritance) taxes on it. Of course, the gift property then will be owned by the donee (unless the gift is in trust) and upon the donee's death will be included in the donee's estate.

Lifetime gifts made within three years of the donor's death are presumed to have been made *in contemplation of death* and are included in the donor's gross estate. This normally is a major consideration only for older donors. Even for them, a possible contemplation-of-death problem normally should not deter an estate owner from making a gift he had otherwise planned to make to save estate taxes. First, the donor may well live the three years and then the contemplation-of-death question cannot be raised. Even if the donor dies within the three-year period, his estate may be able to rebut the presumption by showing living motives for the gift or may reach a compromise on the matter with the IRS. Finally, even if the whole gift is held to be in contemplation of death, the donor really is no worse off from a tax standpoint than if he had never made the gift, because there is a credit against the estate tax for any gift taxes paid at the time the lifetime gift was made.

Lifetime gifts can be an attractive estate tax-saving technique *under the right conditions.* For example, grandparents, after a lifetime of hard work, may be comfortably fixed and have a significant estate. They have a grown son or daughter who is married, and they now have several grandchildren. It is entirely logical for grandparents to consider embarking on a careful and planned program of lifetime gifts to their children and/or grandchildren, or perhaps others.

Such *lifetime gifts can have the following advantages* over bequeathing the property at death:

1. Federal estate taxes normally will be saved on the donor's estate.

2. If the gift is made in trust with the proper trust provisions, federal estate taxes can also be saved on the donee's estate.

3. Similarly, state death taxes can be saved.

4. Estate administration expenses, which generally are based on the probate estate, will be reduced.

5. Any income from the gift property will be transferred to the donee for income tax purposes.

6. Even if a lifetime gift results in a gift tax, which as we shall see later can often be

avoided by proper planning, the gift tax rates are progressive and, thus, a taxable gift almost certainly would be in a lower gift tax bracket than the donor's potential estate tax bracket. In addition, the gift tax rates are only 75 percent of the corresponding estate tax rates for the same brackets.

7. Finally, the donor can enjoy all the personal and family advantages of his or her generosity during his or her lifetime.

But there are *dangers in making lifetime gifts*, and the donor may want to consider the following warnings:

1. The donor should be very careful that he can do without the gift property. What if the donor's health deteriorates? What if the stock market plummets? What if interest rates decline, or some present source(s) of income dry up in the event of economic recession or depression?

2. If the donor is considering giving assets to his or her spouse, what would happen if they separated, divorced, or had marital difficulties?

3. A donor should be careful about giving away cash, life insurance, marketable securities, or other liquid assets, if his estate may have liquidity problems.

4. The owner of closely held corporation stock should be careful that he does not impair his interest in, or control over, the corporation's affairs through gifts of its stock.

5. Some family members actually may be harmed by having control of too much property too soon.

6. Some gift tax may have to be paid by the donor, although there are substantial gift tax exemptions, exclusions, and deductions available that frequently eliminate any actual gift tax.

It comes as a surprise to many people that there is a federal gift tax. This tax applies to the act of transferring ownership or ownership rights in property. It is levied against the donor, and a gift tax return must be filed when total gifts for a year to any *one* donee exceed $3,000.

However, there are several tax breaks available which, if properly used, can reduce or eliminate any gift tax on a donor's gifts. They are: the gift tax lifetime exemption, the gift tax annual exclusion, the privilege of "splitting" gifts between spouses, and the gift tax marital deduction.

The *gift tax lifetime exemption* permits every donor to make a total of $30,000 of gifts over his lifetime without incurring any gift tax. The lifetime exemption applies to any otherwise taxable gift—whether of a present interest or a future interest in property. It may be applied over a number of years; but once exhausted, it cannot be renewed.

Over and above the lifetime exemption, the *gift tax annual exclusion* allows every donor to make tax-free gifts *each year* of up to $3,000 each to however many persons the donor wishes. Gifts within the annual exclusion do not reduce the donor's lifetime exemption. To take a rather extreme example, a donor might give $3,000 in money or securities outright to each of, say, 12 persons (perhaps his children and grandchildren), or total gifts of

$36,000, in a given year without reducing his $30,000 lifetime exemption at all. For this reason, spacing out gifts to a single donee over several years sometimes can keep the amounts of the gift each year within the $3,000 annual exclusion.

The annual exclusion, however, applies only to gifts of a present interest in property (i.e., where the donee has the immediate use and enjoyment of the gift); it does not apply to gifts of future interests (i.e., where the donee does *not* have immediate use and enjoyment of the gift). Since donors generally want full use of the annual exclusion, this can be a complicating factor in making some lifetime gifts in trust.

We see, then, that by using the annual exclusion and lifetime exemption an unmarried (or widowed) person can give up to $33,000 in a year to one donee and still avoid any federal gift tax.

Furthermore, married persons, in effect, can double the annual exclusion and lifetime exemption by *"splitting"* any gifts either makes while they are married. Thus, if either spouse makes a gift to a third person, the gift can be treated for tax purposes as if it were made one-half by the donor-spouse and one-half by the other spouse, provided the other spouse consents to the gift. Suppose, for example, that Husband wants to give outright $6,000 of common stock he owns in his own name to his adult daughter in one year. If his Wife consents to the gift, the $6,000 gift is treated as a $3,000 gift by Husband and a $3,000 gift by Wife. Both these gifts would be within their $3,000 annual exclusions. Similarly, suppose Husband is wealthy and wants to give outright $66,000 of his stock to his daughter in one year. Again, if Wife consents, $33,000 would be considered a gift by Husband and $33,000 a gift by Wife. Both these gifts would be within their $3,000 annual exclusions and $30,000 life exemptions (assuming each had not used any of his or her lifetime exemption in prior gifts), and thus there would be no taxable gift.

Finally, when married persons make gifts to each other, the gift tax marital deduction applies. This parallels closely the federal estate tax marital deduction, and one-half of any gift made to a person's spouse is deductible in calculating his federal gift tax liability.

Suppose, for example, that Husband wants to give his Wife $100,000 at one time, perhaps to help equalize their estates to minimize federal estate taxes. Assume also that Husband has made no prior gifts. In this case, Husband's gift tax return for the year would show:

Gift to wife		$100,000
Less: Gift tax marital deduction		−50,000
		50,000
Less: Gift tax annual exclusion	$ 3,000	
Less: Gift tax lifetime exemption	30,000	−33,000
Taxable gift		$ 17,000
Federal gift tax on $17,000		$ 952

The federal gift tax is cumulative. Therefore, if Husband makes any future taxable gifts, the gift tax will be computed on his total taxable gifts to date, less a credit for prior gift taxes paid.

Gifts to charity are deductible in computing a person's federal gift tax. In effect, then, charitable gifts are not taxable.

Proper Arrangement of Death Payments under Pension and Profit-Sharing Plans

In Chapter 12, we saw that death benefits paid under a "qualified" retirement plan to a named personal beneficiary, *other than the employee's estate,* are not in the employee's gross estate for federal estate purposes (except to the extent attributable to the employee's own contributions, if any). Thus, estate taxes can be saved by making sure an employee's estate is not the beneficiary of such benefits.

In our case of the Ables, for example, George's estate is the beneficiary of his profit-sharing plan's death benefit. This causes this benefit (presently of $12,000) to be included in his gross estate, as well as in his probate estate. If George's profit-sharing plan death benefit were made payable to Mary, or perhaps to a trust, approximately $1,620 in estate taxes could be saved at George's death. Of course, as this benefit grows over time, this change could save much more.

How to Save State Death Taxes

State death taxes vary considerably, so no universal rules can be given here. Each state's law must be considered individually by the estate owner and his advisors.

Sometimes, however, state inheritance taxes can be saved by having life insurance proceeds payable to a named beneficiary other than the insured's estate. Also, jointly owned property may be favored for inheritance tax purposes—in some states only one-half the value is taxed regardless of who contributed the purchase price, and in others it is not taxed at all.

Saving Estate Settlement Costs

Estate administration expenses usually are based largely on the size of the decedent's probate estate. They also depend on the complexity of the particular estate situation. Thus, to a certain degree, these expenses can be reduced by minimizing the probate estate. The ways property can be arranged so as to go outside the probate estate are discussed above. However, this should not become "the tail that wags the dog." It may not be practical or desirable in many cases for additional property to pass outside the probate estate. But where this can conveniently be done, it often will save estate settlement costs.

17
WILL SUBSTITUTES
IN THE ESTATE PLAN

Jointly owned property, life insurance, and trusts that operate during a person's lifetime are so important in many estate plans that a separate chapter is devoted to them. As a practical matter, these are the major ways of transferring property to others at a person's death other than by his will (i.e., outside his probate estate). Hence they are referred to here as "will substitutes."

JOINT PROPERTY

The characteristics of jointly owned property (with right of survivorship) were described in Chapter 15. This form of property ownership, particularly between husband and wife, is very common and can offer some definite advantages for many people. There are, however, some pitfalls to joint ownership that you should understand.

Advantages of Jointly Owned Property

1. Joint ownership is a *convenient,* and perhaps natural, way to hold property among family members. At one joint owner's death, the property automatically passes to the other.

2. Jointly owned property passes outside the probate estate of the first owner to die and hence *avoids the costs and delays of probate.*

3. Holding property in joint names can *avoid or reduce inheritance taxes in some states.*

4. Jointly owned property generally passes to the survivor *free of any claims of creditors of the deceased joint owner.*

In many cases these are important advantages that justify holding at least some property jointly. But in other cases, particularly as estates grow larger, the estate owner should ask himself, "Is it really wise to hold so much property in joint names?"

Problems of Jointly Owned Property

1. Probably the biggest problem that may arise from too much jointly owned property is a potentially larger federal estate tax because of *overqualification of property for the marital deduction*. The extra estate taxes that can result from overqualification were explained in Chapter 16.

As we saw before, the *full value* of all property a person owns jointly with another with right of survivorship (including joint tenancies, tenancies by the entirety, joint bank accounts, jointly owned government savings bonds, and savings accounts where one person makes a deposit in trust for another person) will be included in his gross estate at his or her death, except to the extent the surviving joint owner can affirmatively demonstrate that he or she contributed to the purchase price of the property with his or her own funds. Note that the burden of proving contribution to jointly owned property by a surviving joint owner is on the deceased owner's estate. Sometimes, for example, when both spouses have separate assets and/or incomes, and both contribute to purchasing jointly owned property from their own funds, the *full value* of the joint property may wind up in the estate of the first spouse to die simply because the source(s) of the purchase price of the joint property cannot be traced and shown at that time, which may be many years later. Thus, in such situations, it may save tax dollars later if the spouses keep a record of their respective contributions to jointly owned property.

Now, let us see how too much jointly owned property can result in increased estate taxes on a husband's and wife's estates taken together. Assume Husband and Wife jointly own a residence worth $60,000, stocks and bonds worth $90,000, and a savings account of $30,000. Further assume Wife cannot show any contribution to the purchase price of this property. Husband also has $20,000 of life insurance payable to his estate. Husband's will leaves his probate estate outright to his Wife. In this situation, if Husband predeceases Wife and she does not remarry, the following will result:

Husband's gross estate	$200,000
Deductible expenses and debts (estimated)	−10,000
Adjusted gross estate	190,000
Marital deduction (all the jointly owned property "qualifies")	−95,000
	95,000
Specific exemption	−60,000
Taxable estate	35,000
Federal estate tax (ignoring any credits) on Husband's death	$3,900

Now, on Wife's subsequent death:

Wife's gross estate (from jointly owned property, $180,000; from Husband's probate estate, about $6,000)	$186,000
Deductible expenses and debts (estimated)	−16,000
	170,000
Marital deduction	-0-
Specific exemption	−60,000
Taxable estate	110,000
Federal estate tax (ignoring any credits) on Wife's death	$23,700
Total estate taxes on both deaths	$27,600

As we saw in Chapter 16, the total federal estate taxes on both estates could be reduced to about $6,000 if Husband could "qualify" only one-half of his adjusted gross estate and leave the remainder to his Wife in such a way that it would not be included in her gross estate upon her subsequent death. But in this case almost all their property is held jointly, and so the commonly used "marital" and "nonmarital" trusts (or gifts) with a formula clause will not solve the "overqualification" problem.[1] Thus, it would have saved estate taxes in this case if Husband and Wife had not put so much property in their joint names.

There are no cut-and-dried rules on how much property you should hold in joint names. In cases where the federal estate tax is not an important factor, the "overqualification" problem of joint ownership does not apply. Even where the federal estate tax is significant, the whole situation should be considered—perhaps joint ownership still is desirable. It may save state inheritance taxes, for example. Also, people often hold the family residence and perhaps small bank accounts in joint names for convenience. *As a general principle, however, when spouses begin to hold a sizable proportion (especially more than one-half) of their estates in jointly owned property, they should consider carefully the wisdom of this form of property ownership for estate tax reasons.*

2. When joint ownership in property is created, and one of the joint owners contributes all or more than his proportionate share of the purchase price, a gift for federal gift tax purposes is made *if* the transfer of joint ownership is irrevocable. Thus, if a Husband uses his earnings to buy common stock in his and his Wife's joint names, he will have made a gift to his Wife of half (or about half) of the value of the stock. Of course, he will also have surrendered some control over the stock to his wife. However, there is a special exception applying to the creation of joint ownership

---

[1] In such cases, it sometimes is desirable to split up the jointly owned property between the joint owners.

in *real estate as between a husband and wife*. In this case, any taxable gift may be postponed, at the election of the donor spouse, until the later sale of the real estate.

LIFE INSURANCE IN ESTATE PLANNING

Life insurance occupies an important place in many estates. It also has many uses in estate and business planning. Therefore, you should give careful consideration to how existing or any new life insurance should fit into your overall estate plan. Life insurance has some unique advantages in estate planning. However, before discussing the uses of life insurance in estate planning, we should say a few words about how life insurance benefits are taxed.

Taxation of Life Insurance

Life insurance has some interesting tax advantages. We shall consider these advantages in light of federal income, estate, and gift taxation.

Federal Income Taxation. The *face amount (or policy death benefit) of a life or accident insurance policy paid by reason of the insured's death* normally is not taxable income to the beneficiary. When life insurance proceeds are held by the insurance company under a settlement option, the proceeds themselves remain income tax–free, but any interest earnings on the proceeds may be taxable income. How this "interest element" is taxed depends upon the nature of the settlement option.[2]

When proceeds are left under the *interest only settlement option,* the total amount of the annual *interest* payable by the insurance company is taxable to the beneficiary as ordinary income. In essence, this is the same as interest from a bank account.

Payments to the beneficiary from life insurance proceeds left under the *fixed-amount, fixed-period,* or *life income settlement options* (the so-called "liquidating options") are partly a return of the tax-free death proceeds and partly an "interest element" on the proceeds held by the insurance company. Therefore, for income tax purposes, the periodic payments to the beneficiary are divided into two portions: (1) a portion of the death proceeds that is returned income tax–free, and (2) the interest earnings on the funds held by the insurance company (the "interest element"), which are taxable as ordinary income.

There is an added income tax break for a surviving spouse who receives life insurance death proceeds under one of the "liquidating options" (i.e., the fixed-amount, fixed-period, or life income options). This is the so-called *$1,000 "interest element exclusion,"* whereby the surviving spouse can exclude from his or her otherwise taxable income up to $1,000 per year of the

[2]The various life insurance settlement options are described in Chapter 4.

"interest element" arising from the periodic payments under these options. The exclusion gives the fixed-amount, fixed-period, and life income settlement options an income tax advantage over the interest-only option when the insured's husband or wife is the policy beneficiary. Thus, for example, if a wife is in a 22 percent federal income tax bracket, the full use of the exclusion could save her $220 per year in income taxes.

During the insured's lifetime, different tax rules apply. *Premiums paid for personally owned life or accident insurance*, or an employee's contribution to group life or accident insurance, normally are not deductible for income tax purposes. However, any *annual increases in the cash value* of a life insurance policy, which arise partly from the insured's premium payments and partly from interest earnings by the insurance company on the policy's "reserve," are not currently taxable to the policyowner. This is sometimes referred to as the "tax-free buildup" of life insurance cash values.

Similarly, *life insurance policy dividends* do not constitute taxable income to the policyowner. Furthermore, when policy dividends are used to buy accumulated paid-up additional amounts of life insurance (paid-up additions), there is also a "tax-free buildup" of the cash value of these accumulated additions. But if the policyowner elects to let his policy dividends accumulate with the insurance company at interest, the interest on the dividends, but not the dividends themselves, currently is taxable to the policyowner as ordinary income. Thus, a small tax advantage can be secured by using policy dividends to buy paid-up additions as compared with having them accumulate at interest.

If a life insurance or endowment contract is surrendered, is sold, or matures during the insured's lifetime, the policyowner will have taxable ordinary income to the extent that the amount he receives from the policy exceeds his "investment" in the policy. His investment in the policy normally is the sum of the net premiums he paid for it. Your life insurance company can supply the figures needed to compute any such gain.

Life insurance and endowment policies normally allow the policyowner to leave the policy surrender or maturity value with the insurance company under one or more policy settlement options. How any gain is taxed in this case depends on the circumstances. If at any time prior to 60 days after the date of maturity or surrender the policyowner elects to receive the policy amount under the fixed-period, fixed-amount, or life income options, any taxable gain will be spread out over the period of time during which payments will be made under the settlement option. The spreading out of taxable gain by the use of settlement options may be attractive, since it can avoid the realization of a large amount of ordinary income in one tax year. *But note that the settlement option must be elected before the 60-day deadline after the maturity or surrender of the policy*, or else the entire gain is considered taxable income in that year.

If the interest-only option is elected prior to maturity or surrender, and the policyowner does not reserve the right to invade the proceeds, any gain is again postponed, but the interest payments themselves are fully taxable.

However, if the policyowner does reserve the right to withdraw the proceeds, as he or she probably would want to do, the entire gain is taxable in the year of maturity or surrender.

A policyowner does not have to surrender a whole life insurance policy, before the insured's death. He or she can just continue it in force until the insured dies, at which time the death proceeds will be received by the beneficiary income tax–free. However, with an endowment insurance contract, if the insured does not die within the endowment period, the policy will mature and a day of tax reckoning will come.

But what if the policyowner does have an endowment that is approaching maturity? What can he do to reduce the tax impact in one year?

> As noted above, he can elect a fixed-period, fixed-amount, or even life income settlement option, within the 60-day time limit, and thus spread the gain over the settlement option period.
>
> He can simply accept the gain in the year the policy matures, and perhaps make use of the general income-averaging provisions of the tax law.
>
> He can exchange his endowment policy for an annuity (or for another endowment with payments beginning not later than under the present endowment). The annuity can be a fixed-dollar annuity or a variable annuity. No taxable gain is recognized at the time of making such an exchange, and it has the effect of spreading the taxable gain over the period of the annuity payments. Further, an exchange for a variable annuity gives the endowment owner a choice of an equity-type product. However, the exchange of an endowment contract for a life insurance contract or for another endowment of longer duration would be a taxable event.

Federal Estate Taxation. Life insurance can be favorable property as far as federal estate taxation (and also state inheritance taxation) is concerned. Not only can life insurance provide the liquidity an estate may need to pay death taxes and other costs, but also the proceeds can often be removed from the insured's gross estate.

Life insurance death proceeds will be included in the insured's gross estate for federal estate tax purposes if: (1) the insured's estate is named beneficiary, or another named beneficiary (such as a trust) is *required* to provide the proceeds to meet the estate's obligations; or (2) the insured at the time of his death owned *any* "incidents of ownership" (i.e., ownership rights) in the life insurance policy. However, merely paying the insurance premiums, in itself, will no longer result in the policy proceeds being taxable in the insured's estate.[3] Thus, estate tax savings can result if the insured policyowner is willing to absolutely give away, with no strings attached, his insurance policy (or coverage) to someone else.

The phrase "incidents of ownership" means any policy ownership rights, such as the right to change the beneficiary, borrow against the policy, surrender or assign the policy, elect settlement options, or receive policy dividends and other benefits. Therefore, the insured must not have *any* of

---

[3]There was at one time a "premium payment test" for including life insurance proceeds in the gross estate, but this rule is no longer in effect.

these policy rights and benefits at the time of his or her death in order for the proceeds to escape federal estate taxation.

However, life insurance policies, like any other kind of property, that are given away within three years of the insured's death are presumed to be gifts in contemplation of death. The main thing about life insurance in this regard is that, since it is so closely related in concept to thoughts of death, it is hard to rebut the presumption of a gift in contemplation of death. But if the policy is given away more than three years before the insured's death, the tax authorities cannot include *the proceeds* in the insured's estate as a gift in contemplation of death.

Suppose one person owns a life insurance policy on the life of another person and the policyowner (not the insured) dies. In this case, the then value of the insurance policy will be included in the deceased policyowner's gross estate, just like any other valuable property that he or she owns.

Federal Gift Taxation. The gift of a life insurance policy, like the gift of other property, may be subjected to federal gift taxation. Thus, if a policyowner absolutely assigns a life insurance policy on his life to someone else (his wife or a trust, for example), he has made a current gift to the donee of the then value of the insurance policy. The insurance company will supply you with this gift value upon request. If the insured continues to pay premiums on the gift policy, each such premium constitutes a gift to the new policyowner.

An unusual gift situation can arise when a life insurance policy on the life of one person is owned by another person and the beneficiary is still a third person. In this situation, upon the insured's death, the owner of the policy is considered to have made a taxable gift of the policy proceeds to the beneficiary. This sometimes is referred to as an "inadvertent gift" of the proceeds because the policyowner usually has no idea that he or she is making a taxable gift. Suppose, for example, that Husband absolutely assigns a $50,000 life insurance policy on his life to his Wife to avoid estate taxes in his estate. Their children (rather than the Wife) are named as beneficiaries. If the Husband then dies, the $50,000 of life insurance proceeds will be paid to his children as the policy beneficiaries, but his Wife will have made a $50,000 gift to the children. The situation that can produce this kind of taxable gift can easily arise when policies are being given away to save estate taxes, but fortunately such "inadvertent gifts" can be avoided by proper planning. *When the owner of a life insurance policy is other than the insured, the owner normally should name himself or herself as beneficiary.* In the above case, for example, this inadvertent gift could have been avoided if the Wife had been named as beneficiary. Of course, an insurance trust also could have been made the owner and beneficiary of the policy, which would have avoided this problem and perhaps offered other advantages as well.

How to Arrange Your Life Insurance

When life insurance is purchased for family protection purposes, the insured husband often names his wife as primary beneficiary and their children as contingent beneficiaries. This may be fine in many cases, but there are various other possibilities for arranging one's life insurance that should be considered. Since life insurance is an important part of many estates, particularly the more modest estates, decisions concerning how it is handled can be important.

A basic decision an insured needs to consider is whether he or she will be the owner of the insurance on his life, and thus have the proceeds included in his or her gross estate at death, or whether someone else, or a trust, will own the life insurance on his or her life and thus in most cases have the proceeds escape federal estate taxation at death. Another basic decision is whether to leave the insurance proceeds to his or her beneficiaries under the policy settlement options or to use an insurance trust. The pros and cons of both these questions will be covered here.

Now, let us briefly review the possibilities for arranging your life insurance.

Policy Owned by the Insured. First, let us assume the insured owns the policy, as is frequently the case. Individual life insurance policies customarily specify on their front page who owns the contract. The insured commonly is named as the owner. If this is the case, then the insured owns all rights and benefits (incidents of ownership) in the policy unless he takes specific steps to transfer ownership to another (such as absolutely assigning the policy to someone else, for example). Policies owned by the insured can be made payable in the following ways.

To the insured's estate. This usually is not done unless the insured wants to make sure that the proceeds will be available to his or her executor for estate settlement purposes.

To a third-party beneficiary or beneficiaries (i.e., other than the insured's estate) in a lump sum. As we noted above, this is a common arrangement, frequently with the insured's wife as primary beneficiary and the children as contingent (or secondary) beneficiaries. Upon the insured's death, however, this arrangement may leave the beneficiary with a sizable sum of money to manage, perhaps at the very time she or he is least able to manage it. True, the beneficiary, herself or himself, normally can elect to leave lump-sum proceeds under policy settlement options, but this also involves management decisions on the beneficiary's part. In addition, there are some advantages in the insured's at least initially electing settlement options for a beneficiary, as discussed below.

To a third-party beneficiary or beneficiaries under policy settlement options. The settlement options generally included in life insurance policies are described in Chapter 4. Most insurance companies give the insured wide latitude in the settlement arrangements he or she can make for the beneficiaries, or himself or herself for policy surrender values, under settlement options.

If an insured is not going to use an insurance trust, it generally is preferable for him or her to leave policy proceeds under settlement options for his or her named beneficiary(ies), rather than to them in a lump sum, even though some or all of the proceeds may not remain under the settlement options that he or she elects. First of all, the insured can generally give his or her beneficiary what amounts to complete control over the proceeds held under settlement options by electing to have the proceeds placed under the interest option, and by also giving the beneficiary full right of withdrawal and the right to change to other settlement options. This can be referred to as the "interest option—all privileges" arrangement; it gives the beneficiary the opportunity to withdraw the proceeds and invest them elsewhere, or to elect other settlement options, as she or he wishes. Of course, the insured can elect a more restrictive settlement arrangement for the beneficiary if he or she wishes.

In addition, settlement options have the following advantages over lump-sum payments: (1) the insurance company provides immediate management of the proceeds and relieves the beneficiary of worry and concern in this regard; (2) full provision can be made for the contingency that the insured and beneficiary may die in a so-called "common disaster" or within a short time of each other; (3) a settlement option elected by the insured extends to the policy proceeds the protection allowed by the applicable state law against claims by the beneficiary's creditors (i.e., the protection afforded by the "spendthrift provision" in a settlement agreement); and (4) the insurance company may be more liberal with respect to the settlement arrangements it will make with the policyowner-insured before his or her death than with a lump-sum beneficiary after the insured's death.

To a revocable unfunded life insurance trust. As we noted above, this often is a basic decision the policyowner-insured must make. It boils down to the question, "Should I leave my life insurance proceeds with the insurance company under a settlement option arrangement, or with a bank to be administered under a trust agreement?"

There are arguments on both sides, and insurance companies and banks compete with each other for this business. Here are the *main arguments made in favor of the use of settlement options:*

1. *Guarantee of principal and income.* A life insurance company *promises* to pay the full amount of the proceeds and at least a minimum rate of interest on proceeds left under settlement options. The insurance company legally owes the proceeds (and the guaranteed interest on them) to the beneficiary. A trustee, however, has only the duty to invest trust assets with due care under the terms of the trust. The trustee does not guarantee the security of, nor a minimum rate of return on, the trust principal. Of course, in the final analysis the real security and growth of your capital are much affected by the investment skill of both insurance companies and banks. However, the guarantees provided by insurance settlement options could become important in the face of economic recession or depression.

2. *$1,000 interest-element exclusion can be available to a surviving spouse.* This tax advantage is explained above in connection with the federal income taxation of life insurance.

3. *No direct fees for property management.* An insurance company charges no additional direct fees when policy proceeds are left under settlement options; this right is provided in the policy and its cost is covered by the general expense "loading" in the life insurance premium. As we saw in Chapter 15, corporate trustees charge an annual fee for administering trusts. The minimum annual fees for personal trusts (for example, $125 for trusts invested in the trust company's common trust funds and $250 for trusts invested otherwise, as illustrated in Chapter 15) tend to make the use of trusts uneconomical for smaller amounts of life insurance.

4. *"Excess interest" usually is payable.* This is interest paid by the insurance company on funds left under most settlement options in "excess" of the rate guaranteed in the policy. "Excess" interest is payable at the discretion of the insurance company and can be increased or decreased depending on the insurer's investment results.

5. *Life income (annuity) options can be used.* Only insurance companies can directly provide a life annuity for your beneficiary.

On the other hand, the following are the *main arguments made for revocable unfunded insurance trusts.*

1. *Great flexibility can be provided in paying out and managing trust assets.* A trustee can be given *discretion* with respect to paying out trust corpus and/or income to the beneficiaries, while an insurance company cannot exercise such discretion with respect to policy proceeds under settlement options. The trustee, for example, can be given such discretionary powers as to pay out or accumulate trust income; to "sprinkle" trust income in different amounts among trust beneficiaries, depending upon the beneficiaries' needs and perhaps their income tax brackets; to distribute trust principal to the trust beneficiary or beneficiaries as the trustee, in its discretion, thinks desirable for the beneficiary or beneficiaries; and other similar powers. Of course, a trustee can be given lesser discretionary powers in the trust agreement, as the creator of the trust desires. The exercise of discretion by a trustee can be desirable to meet changing family needs and circumstances; to help deal with emergencies; to respond to changing economic conditions (such as inflation or depression); to meet the special needs of certain beneficiaries, such as a physically or mentally handicapped child; and perhaps to save taxes.

Settlement options can be arranged to provide considerable flexibility by giving the beneficiary limited or unlimited rights of withdrawal, the right to change to other options, powers of appointment, and the like. But the insurance company cannot exercise its own discretion in paying out policy proceeds held under settlement options.

2. *Trustees can be given broad investment powers.* The trustee, for example, can be given the power "to invest in all forms of real and personal property." Naturally, the creator of the trust also can give the trustee lesser investment powers. In the past, as a practical matter, the availability of broad investment powers has meant that trustees could invest trust assets in common stocks, while life insurance companies remained largely fixed-dollar investors. During periods of business prosperity, this has favored trusts, but during a business depression the reverse could be true.

3. *Marital and nonmarital trusts can be set up under insurance trusts.* Thus, the insurance trust can become the main estate planning instrument. As we saw in Chapter 16, this may be desirable when life insurance and similar third-party beneficiary arrangements constitute the bulk of an estate.

Similarly, a trust can be used to unify the insured's estate. For example, a number of different life insurance policies can be made payable to one trust, and the estate owner's probate assets may be "poured over" into the insurance trust after his death. Thus, all or most of his estate assets can be administered for his heirs under the terms of one instrument—the life insurance trust.

4. *Trustees can administer assets for minors and in other special cases.* A trust can be used to administer assets for a minor when otherwise a guardian for the minor's property might have to be appointed. The same is true for other beneficiaries who may be physically or mentally incapacitated.

5. *Trust provisions can allow the trustees to save income taxes through proper planning of the distribution of trust income.* This can be done by giving the trustee the discretionary authority to pay out or accumulate trust income—to "sprinkle" trust income among beneficiaries with a view toward the income tax impact of the payments—and by creating multiple trusts.

Whether settlement options or a trust is used depends upon the estate owner's wishes, needs, and the particular situation. There may be a tendency to use trusts for larger amounts and settlement options for smaller amounts of proceeds. Since the end of World War II, there has been a general trend toward greater use of insurance trusts.

However, you do not have to "put all your eggs in one basket." You could leave a portion of your life insurance proceeds under settlement options, perhaps enough to take advantage of the interest-element exclusion, and have the remainder payable to an insurance trust. You can, in effect, diversify the handling of your life insurance proceeds. In this way, your beneficiaries will not be entirely dependent upon either an insurance company or a bank.

To a testamentary trust. Sometimes life insurance proceeds are made payable to the trustee of a testamentary trust, which is one set up at the insured's death under his will. Naming a testamentary trustee as beneficiary may be desirable in some estate situations. While some life insurance companies may not particularly like to have testamentary trustees named as beneficiaries, this normally can be done if proper safeguards are adopted.

Policy Owned by Someone Other Than the Insured. We now turn to the less usual, but increasingly important, situation where life insurance is owned by someone other than the insured (i.e., by a third-party owner). This usually is done to keep the policy proceeds out of the insured's gross estate and save on estate taxes. Also, premiums can sometimes be paid with lower after-income-tax dollars when they are paid by someone other than the insured.

Ownership can be placed in a third party at the inception of the policy or after it has been issued. The placing of policy ownership in another can be effected by an *absolute assignment of the policy* (with proper notice to the insurance company) or by *use of an ownership clause* in the insurance policy. When an ownership clause is used, successive owner(s) of the policy can be designated in the clause in the event of the first owner's death prior to the insured's.

Policies owned by others on the insured's life can be held in various ways. Here are some of the more common ways.

Owned by other individuals outright. Policies frequently are owned by various members of the insured's family—his or her spouse, adult children, parents, etc.

When policies are owned by others outright, the proceeds normally *will not be in the insured's gross estate upon his or her death,* and so there can be an estate tax saving for his estate. Also, any policy premiums paid by the insured during his or her lifetime will be considered gifts of a present interest to the policyowner, and thus the $3,000 gift tax annual exclusion will apply each year.

A disadvantage in this approach, however, is that, assuming the insured dies before the policyowner, the policy proceeds will be paid to the policyowner as beneficiary and will be included in the policyowner's gross estate upon his or her subsequent death. If, for example, Husband absolutely assigns a $50,000 life insurance policy on his life to his Wife, the $50,000 proceeds will not be in his gross estate upon his death, but they will be in the Wife's gross estate upon her subsequent death, unless she makes lifetime gifts of the proceeds and removes them from her estate.

Owned by unfunded irrevocable trusts. Rather than having life insurance owned by an individual other than the insured, the policies can be owned by and payable to an irrevocable insurance trust. Upon the insured's death, the policy proceeds are paid to the trustee named as beneficiary and are administered according to the terms of the trust, usually for the benefit of the insured's family. The trust owns and administers the life insurance policy(ies) during the insured's lifetime, but it is otherwise "unfunded" in that no income-producing assets are also placed in the trust, the income from which could be used to pay the life insurance premiums. The insured or someone else can pay the premiums as they come due or he or she can make periodic payments to the trustee, who then can pay the premiums.

An unfunded irrevocable trust as owner and beneficiary of your life insurance offers the advantage, in addition to the general advantages of trusts, of making it possible to avoid including the insurance proceeds in the trust beneficiary's gross estate. Thus, both the insured's estate and the trust beneficiary's estate can be "skipped" for federal estate tax purposes, provided the trust beneficiary is given only those powers over the trust that will *not* cause the corpus to be included in his or her gross estate.

But the tax "price" for this potential estate tax saving is that the gift of the policy, and any subsequent premiums paid by the insured to continue the policy in force, are not considered gifts of a present interest. Hence, you cannot use the $3,000 gift tax annual exclusion for such gifts. However, the $30,000 lifetime exemption and other gift tax privileges are still available. This means that the donor ultimately may have to pay some gift taxes if he or she uses up his or her lifetime exemption and other gift tax privileges. Thus, you must decide whether the possible gift tax "price" is worth the potential estate tax savings.

Owned by funded irrevocable trusts. This time the irrevocable trust not only owns and is the beneficiary of the life insurance, but also contains income-producing assets which are used to pay some or all of the life insurance premiums. Thus, if you create this kind of trust, you must give the trust income-producing assets to finance the life insurance owned by the trust.

Under the right kind of circumstances, the use of a funded irrevocable insurance trust can be quite attractive. However, the income tax rules as to who is to be taxed on the trust income that is used to pay the life insurance premiums are important. The tax law provides that any income from a trust that can be applied to pay premiums on insurance on the life of the creator of the trust, or on the life of the spouse of the creator of the trust, will be taxable income *to the creator* rather than to the trustee. Thus, for example, if you or your wife set up such a trust to buy life insurance on your life, the trust income will be taxable to *you,* rather than to the trustee and ultimately to the trust beneficiaries. This considerably reduces the attractiveness of *funded* irrevocable insurance trusts unless someone other than the insured or the insured's spouse can fund the trust. This income tax situation has given rise to an advantageous plan for funding these trusts that commonly is called the *grandparent-grandchild insurance trust.*

To take a specific example of a grandparent-grandchild insurance trust, let us change our facts with respect to the Ables a little and assume George's Father has a substantial estate and more than adequate income for himself and George's Mother to live on. Further assume George's Father and Mother want to do something meaningful for their Grandchildren (George's and Mary's children). As we have seen, George is beginning to accumulate an estate of his own (see Chapters 1 and 16) and also earns a good salary. Under these conditions, George's Father might want to create a funded irrevocable life insurance trust for the benefit of his Grandchildren by transferring some of his income-producing securities to an irrevocable trust and directing (or authorizing) the trustee to use the trust income to buy, own, and be the beneficiary of life insurance on George's life. The Grandchildren would be the trust beneficiaries, and upon George's death the trust corpus (insurance proceeds plus the original securities) would be used to pay income and/or corpus to the Grandchildren, or for their benefit, according to the terms of the trust.

Such an arrangement might have a number of advantages for the family as a whole. The original trust corpus (the income-producing securities George's Father gave in trust) would be out of George's Father's (Grandfather's) gross estate for federal estate tax purposes. Also, neither the insurance proceeds nor the original trust corpus would be in George's gross estate. Thus, George's estate would be "skipped" for estate tax purposes. The trust income would be taxed initially to the trust and ultimately to the Grandchildren when distributed to them. In any event, the trust income would be expected to be taxed in a lower income tax bracket than Grandfather's. Also, Grandfather would be making a truly meaningful gift to his Grandchildren and perhaps helping George meet some of his life insurance needs in the bargain. Further, the trust corpus could be made available to help meet any liquidity needs of George's estate by authorizing (but not directing) the trustee to make loans to, or purchase assets from, his estate. In addition, if George, or perhaps Mary, should ever be in need, the trustee could be authorized, in its discretion, to distribute corpus to them.

Of course, Grandfather would have to give up his income-producing securities. Also, such a gift would not be a gift of a present interest, and so Grandfather would have to use up some or all of his lifetime exemption and perhaps might have to pay a gift tax. But on balance, this often is an advantageous plan, given the proper circumstances (i.e., a well-to-do grandparent).

Should You Give Away Your Life Insurance?

This question is becoming increasingly common today, and many persons are making gifts of their life insurance policies.

Advantages of Gifts of Life Insurance. Life insurance is attractive as gift property since life insurance normally can be removed from the insured's gross estate by giving away all incidents of ownership in the policy. The potential estate tax savings make such gifts very tempting. Further, the insured can still continue to pay the premiums, *provided* he has made a *bona fide gift* of the policy. The gift tax value of insurance contracts normally is small, and in any event would be relatively less than the amount removed from the taxable estate (i.e., the policy face). In fact, there is normally little or no actual gift tax involved.

People also may be more willing to give away life insurance than, say, securities, because the life insurance usually is not producing income currently and is normally intended for the benefit of the policy beneficiaries anyway.

Pitfalls in Gifts of Life Insurance. Despite the potential attractions in gifts of life insurance, there are some problem areas to consider. First, the donor should be careful to divest himself completely of all his interest and rights in the policy. Otherwise, he may directly or indirectly retain incidents of ownership in the policy and, as a result, the estate tax-saving purpose of the gift will be defeated.

In addition, the gift of life insurance must be a *bona fide gift* and not merely a sham transaction intended for tax-saving purposes only. The donee of the policy should be, and act like, the owner. For example, the donee should have possession of and control over the policy contract, and probably also should receive the premium notices and make the actual premium payments to the insurance company, even though the donor may supply the donee with the necessary funds.

Where gifts of life insurance are made to individuals, care should be taken not to have the policies return to the donor by inheritance if the donee should predecease him. This normally can be handled by the donee's leaving the policy to someone else in his or her will, or by naming a successive owner in a policy ownership clause.

Finally, a life insurance policy normally is valuable property. Therefore, you should consider carefully whether you want to relinquish ownership and control over any of your insurance policies. You should also consider the effect of such gifts on the liquidity position of your estate.

Gifts of Group Life Insurance. Recent changes in the tax law have made it possible in most states for an employee to absolutely assign his group term life insurance to another and, thus, remove the proceeds from his gross estate for federal estate tax purposes. This can be an attractive tax benefit for many employees because the face amounts of group term life insurance on individual lives may be quite substantial today (for example, two, two and a half, or three times salary). Also, since it is term insurance, the employee himself really is not giving away much in the way of policy values during his lifetime. Thus, an employee's group term life insurance could be absolutely assigned, say, to his wife, his children, or a trust.

Historically, most group term life insurance policies (and certificates) prohibited assignment of the insurance by the covered employee. However, because the tax authorities now hold that group term life insurance can be removed from an employee's gross estate by a valid, irrevocable assignment of all his or her incidents of ownership in the insurance (i.e., by an absolute assignment), most states have enacted statutes that specifically authorize or permit the assignment of all rights, benefits, privileges, and incidents of ownership in a group life insurance policy. However, not all states have such authorizing statutes, and not all group life insurance master contracts permit such assignments, and so the estate owner should check into the situation in his own case with his professional advisors.

Wife Insurance

There is an increasing tendency to buy life insurance on women. Several reasons or advantages seem to account for this.

1. In our present social and economic framework, many women are active income earners and so may need life insurance protection to cover against the potential loss of their earned income in the event of their premature death. This is the traditional role of life insurance and is just as applicable to women as to men. Today, for example, many married women are working, and their earned income often contributes significantly to the family's financial well-being.

2. The loss of a wife's services in the home and to the children during their formative years can represent a sizable economic loss. Insurance on the wife can partially offset this loss. This probably is one reason for the popularity of the "Family Life Insurance Policy," which provides at least some life insurance on the wife and children as well as on the husband.

3. In estate planning, a wife's death before her husband's will deprive his estate of the use of the federal estate tax marital deduction, unless he should remarry. Depending upon the circumstances, this can be an important loss. Life insurance on the wife can help "hedge against" this potential loss of the federal estate tax marital deduction. In addition, other tax advantages, such as filing joint income tax returns, making "split gifts," and use of the federal gift tax marital deduction, will be lost upon a wife's death.

4. Life insurance companies now generally offer lower rates for insurance on women than on men at the same age.

Life insurance on the wife can be owned by the wife herself, her adult children, or a trust. If her husband owns, and is the beneficiary of, the life insurance on his wife's life, the proceeds ultimately would go into his gross estate if his wife predeceases him, and it generally is assumed that this will increase their federal estate taxes.

OTHER DEATH BENEFITS

Life insurance is a very common and important kind of death benefit. Therefore, we have devoted considerable attention to life insurance arrangements in the estate plan. However, depending on the circumstances, estate owners may also have other kinds of death benefits that can be quite significant in their overall estates. These may include death benefits under "qualified" pension and profit-sharing plans, death benefits under tax-sheltered annuity plans, survivors' benefits under nonqualified deferred compensation arrangements, and the like.

How these other benefits are to be arranged in an estate plan should be considered in the overall planning process. An estate owner may want to coordinate these death benefits with his life insurance arrangements, such as having them payable to a revocable unfunded life insurance trust. Naturally, the appropriate arrangement should depend upon the circumstances of each case.

REVOCABLE TRUSTS AS A WILL SUBSTITUTE

An interesting and often advantageous way of managing an estate owner's property during his or her lifetime, and then transmitting the property to others at the estate owner's death, is the *living revocable trust*.[4] The idea of a

---

[4]These are trusts that can be terminated or changed by the creator as he or she wishes during the creator's lifetime.

living revocable trust as a way to transfer property to your heirs outside of your probate estate is a novel one to many people. Yet, this inter vivos (i.e., during lifetime) method of estate transfer has many advantages when compared with leaving property by will.

The essence of the plan is that an estate owner during his lifetime creates a revocable trust into which he places some or the major part of his property. The trustee administers and invests the trust property and pays the income from the trust to the creator or as the creator directs. Since the creator can alter, amend, or revoke the trust at any time during his lifetime, he can get the trust property back whenever he wishes. Upon the creator's death, however, the trust becomes irrevocable and the trust property is administered according to its terms for the benefit of the creator's beneficiaries.

If desired, such a trust can contain marital and nonmarital trust provisions to make proper use of the federal estate tax marital deduction. Life insurance on the estate owner's life and other death benefits can be made payable to the trust. Also, where permitted by law, property can be "poured over" from the estate owner's will into such a trust. Thus, a revocable trust can unify an estate so that it can be administered under one instrument.

However, because a revocable trust can be terminated by its creator at will, the trust income will be taxable to the creator during his or her lifetime. Also, the trust corpus will be included in his or her gross estate at death. No taxable gift is made when the trust is created. Thus, tax savings by the creator are not the primary motivation for setting up such trusts.

Let us take a specific example of a revocable trust. Assume John Mature, age 55, owns in his own name securities and other income-producing property worth approximately $200,000. This property yields about $12,000 per year. John is a busy, successful business executive who also is active in church and civic affairs. He is married and has two married children and four grandchildren.

John decides to transfer the $200,000 of securities and income-producing property to a living revocable trust with the XYZ Bank and Trust Company as trustee. The income from the trust is to be paid to John during his lifetime, and following his death the trust is to be continued for the benefit of John's wife, children, and grandchildren. The trust agreement contains marital and nonmarital trust provisions so that at John's death his estate can make maximum use of the federal estate tax marital deduction without "overqualifying" his property for the deduction. John's will "pours over" the balance of his estate into this trust.

What might John hope to accomplish by the use of this revocable trust arrangement?

1. The XYZ Bank and Trust Company will manage and invest the trust property for John and pay him the income. John is relieved of these duties and has the benefit of the bank's expertise in these areas. However, if for any reason John becomes dissatisfied with the arrangement, he can revoke the trust and recover his property.

2. If John should become physically disabled or otherwise unable to manage his

own affairs, the trustee will continue to manage and invest the trust property for John's benefit without interruption.

3. If the trust property is invested in the bank's common trust fund(s), the advantages of investment diversification can be secured.

4. Upon John's death, the trustee will continue to manage and invest the trust property for the surviving beneficiaries (John's family) and pay the trust income to them without interruption. John can also make special provisions in the trust for any family members who may have unusual needs or special problems, such as a disabled or mentally retarded child or grandchild, for example. Ultimately, the property will be distributed to the trust beneficiaries according to the terms of the trust. The revocable trust thus acts as a will substitute for the transmission of John's estate at his death.

5. The use of a revocable trust may reduce the likelihood of a will's being contested with the attendant publicity. The importance of this factor, of course, depends upon the particular circumstances.

6. A revocable trust may provide protection against the creditors of John's estate.

7. In some states, a revocable trust may be used to avoid a surviving spouse's "intestate share" of the estate. Thus, a trust may be used in these cases to avoid the effect of a surviving spouse's electing to take against the will.

8. The revocable trust *may be* a less costly way for John to transfer his estate to his family, depending upon the circumstances. The XYZ Bank and Trust Company will charge an annual trustee's fee, which in this case might be $1,000 per year (say, $\frac{1}{2}$ of 1 percent of the $200,000). However, because such trustee's fees generally are income-tax deductible, the after-tax cost would be less, depending upon John's income tax bracket. On the other hand, John's estate would save all or a part of the executor's and other fees that otherwise would have been levied on the $200,000 had it passed as a part of John's probate estate under his will. These probate costs (which are deductible for estate tax purposes) might run, say, 6 to 8 percent of the $200,000 principal amount. Thus, this kind of revocable trust results in annual trustee's fees but saves on probate costs at the time of the creator's death.

18
PLANNING FOR YOUR
BUSINESS INTERESTS

When an individual has an interest in a closely held business, whether it be as a sole proprietor, partner, or stockholder in a close corporation, it is of great importance that proper financial planning take place to develop and maintain a coordinated and smoothly functioning financial plan for the continuation of the business in the event of the death or disability of an owner. In these cases, proper planning is especially important, since a closely held business interest often is one of the owner's most important assets. Building such a business often represents a person's major lifetime work. Protecting its value and earning power should be one of the main purposes in constructing the owner's personal financial plan.

Anyone who owns such a business interest should have a definite plan to provide for either the perpetuation or the disposition of the business. Business owners face the following kinds of questions:

1. Who will control the business when I die?
2. Will there be a market for the business if it has to be sold?
3. Will the business provide adequate income for my heirs?
4. How will the value of the business affect the taxes and liquidity needs of my estate?
5. Will I be able to continue in business if one of my associates dies?
6. How can working capital be kept intact?
7. How can a business be transferred to a new owner without shrinkage in value?
8. What would happen to the business in the event of my, or one of my associate's, disability?
9. What will become of my business interest if I retire?

To answer these questions, the business owner should understand the various forms of business organization, the risks affecting personal financial planning involved in each form, and how to solve the potential problems created by these risks.

SHOULD YOU SELL OR RETAIN YOUR BUSINESS INTEREST?

When a business owner is planning his or her estate, he or she has two initial alternatives regarding the fate of the business. The owner may plan to dispose of the business interest entirely upon his or her death or retirement or may plan for its retention in the family. Retention may be practical when the family owns a majority interest, when some member of the family is interested in the business and is capable of managing it successfully, when the future outlook for the business is promising, and when there are other assets in the owner's estate, including perhaps existing or new life insurance, so that the owner can arrange adequate liquidity for his or her estate and also equalize the distribution of the estate among those heirs who will receive a business interest and those who will not. If the above elements are missing, the business owner should carefully consider disposing of the interest in the most orderly and efficient way possible.

PARTNERSHIPS

A partnership can be looked upon as a business marriage—two or more people joined together to conduct a business for profit. The partners are the business.

The Business Continuation Problem

The death of a partner legally dissolves the partnership, and the deceased partner's interest in the business must be settled. The surviving partner or partners succeed to the ownership of the firm's assets *as a liquidating trustee.* The relationship between the surviving partner(s) and a deceased partner's estate is recognized as fiduciary in nature, particularly with respect to the remedies available if there is a breach of this trust. In this role, the surviving partner must make a fair and complete disclosure of all facts affecting those assets. Moreover, if anything goes wrong between the surviving partner and the heirs, who presumably are unfamiliar with partnership affairs, the surviving partner will have the burden of proving that his or her trusteeship was carried out in compliance with the high standards of responsibility required of trustees. Such a situation can abruptly bring the business to a standstill. It poses a dilemma both for the surviving partner(s) and for the heirs of a deceased partner that could result in severe financial loss to all concerned.

In the absence of an agreement entered into during the partners' lifetimes providing specifically for the continuation of the business, there are basically two alternatives at a partner's death: the business may be reorganized or it may be terminated (i.e., liquidated or wound up). Either choice usually is extremely costly for everyone involved.

There are various possible approaches for surviving partners to continue a partnership on a reorganized basis, but generally none are completely satisfactory. Three of the more popular ones are discussed below.

1. The surviving partners might take in the deceased partner's heirs as new partners and, in effect, form a new partnership. However, even if the surviving partners are willing to consider the heirs as new partners, the heirs in most cases will be inexperienced and incapable of joining actively in the conduct of the business. Also, lack of liquidity for estate settlement costs might force the heirs to demand cash for the deceased's interest rather than the interest itself.

2. The survivors might take in as a new partner an outside party to whom the deceased partner's estate would sell the deceased's interest. However, even if a party willing to assume the risk could be found, and a selling price could be agreed upon, the outsider might be personally unsuitable to the survivors, incompetent, or even a competitor seeking control of the business.

3. The survivors might buy the deceased's interest from his heirs or estate and assume full ownership. However, the survivors and heirs may not be able to agree on a satisfactory selling price. In addition, the survivors still have the problem of raising sufficient cash to buy the deceased's interest.

The general inadequacy of reorganizing and continuing the business generally leads to *forced liquidation,* which, as noted above, usually is very costly. Accounts receivable may be collected for less than half their value. At the same time, creditors press their demands for full payment. All business activity, except as necessary for winding up the partnership affairs, must cease. Credit tends to vanish, and goodwill typically is lost entirely. In the end, a valuable business may be liquidated (or sold) for a fraction of its worth as a going concern. Also, by liquidating the going concern, the survivors have liquidated their own jobs.

Clearly, what the partners usually need is a plan that allows the surviving partners to obtain full ownership of the business and pay a deceased partner's estate a fair price for his or her interest. The plan should establish a fair price and produce the necessary cash.

The Plan—A Buy-sell Agreement

This plan calls for a written agreement entered into during the partners' lifetimes, between the individual partners (cross-purchase type of agreement) or between the partnership and the partners (entity type of agreement), providing for the sale and purchase of a deceased partner's interest. The agreement establishes a mutually agreeable purchase price for each partner's interest and should contain a provision for adjusting the purchase price if the value of the business changes. Life insurance can be used to fund the agreement by providing, upon the death of a partner, the immediate cash necessary to purchase the deceased's interest.

As we said before, there are two main kinds of partnership buy-sell agreements—the *cross-purchase plan* and the *entity plan.* The partners, with the help and advice of their professional advisors, must make a choice as to which plan would be best for them considering their own circumstances and objectives. The factors involved in such a choice are complex and beyond the scope of this book. Figure 18-1 illustrates the results of both the cross-purchase type and the entity type of buy-sell agreement for a typical partnership of three equal partners and valued at $240,000.

FIGURE 18-1
PARTNERSHIP VALUE, $240,000

Partner A owns a ¹/₃ interest, $80,000	Partner B owns a ¹/₃ interest, $80,000	Partner C owns a ¹/₃ interest, $80,000

CROSS-PURCHASE AGREEMENT

The three partners agree in writing on: (1) the value of their interests, and (2) that in the event of the death of a partner, the estate of the deceased will sell, *and the surviving partners will buy,* the interest of the deceased.

Life Insurance to Fund Agreement

A insures:	B insures:	C insures:
B for $40,000	A for $40,000	A for $40,000
C for $40,000	C for $40,000	B for $40,000

Each partner is the applicant, owner, premium payor, and beneficiary of the policies on the other two partners.

At Death

Each surviving partner utilizes the insurance proceeds on the deceased partner's life that he or she receives as beneficiary to purchase one-half of the deceased partner's interest from his estate according to the terms of the buy-sell agreement. (There may also be a disability provision in the buy-sell agreement to meet this risk as well.)

ENTITY AGREEMENT

The three partners agree in writing on: (1) the value of their interests, and (2) that in the event of the death of a partner, the estate of the deceased will sell, *and the partnership will buy,* the interest of the deceased.

Life Insurance to Fund Agreement

Partnership insures A for $80,000, B for $80,000, and C for $80,000.

The Partnership is the applicant, owner, premium payor, and beneficiary of all policies.

At Death

The Partnership utilizes the insurance proceeds on the deceased partner's life that it receives as beneficiary to purchase the deceased partner's interest from his estate according to the terms of the buy-sell agreement. (There may also be a disability provision in the buy-sell agreement to meet this risk as well.)

Tax Aspects

The tax consequences of buy-sell arrangements are important and should be considered to evaluate their impact on the financial plans of the partners.

Income Taxation. The income tax aspects of partnership buy-sell agreements can be complicated and are only summarized here.

Insurance premiums. Whether paid by the individual partners or the partnership, life insurance premiums are not deductible for income tax purposes since the premium payor(s) are either directly or indirectly beneficiaries under the life insurance policies. Such payments are considered personal rather than business expenses.

Death proceeds. Life insurance death proceeds are received by the beneficiary(ies) income tax–free. This is true whether the beneficiary is the partnership or the partners.

Purchase payments. The proceeds received by the partnership or the partners are used as payments to purchase the deceased partner's interest from his estate. The tax treatment of these payments depends upon the particular partnership interest being purchased.

In typical commercial partnerships, tangible property, such as buildings, equipment and inventory, and perhaps goodwill, generally are the major items of value. These assets are considered capital assets.[1] Payments for capital assets are not deductible by the partnership or the partners and are not taxable as ordinary income to the estate of a deceased partner. Such purchase payments also usually will not result in a capital gain for the estate. This is so because if the buy-sell agreement has been drafted properly, the estate receives the deceased's interest in the business at the same value that it sells the interest to the surviving partners. In other words, its cost basis at death has been stepped up and equals the agreed-upon selling price.

In a professional or personal service partnership, tangible property normally represents only a portion of the total value of the partnership. A substantial portion of the firm's total value often consists of unrealized receivables and work in process.

In considering the total value of such a partnership, the value must be broken down into the portions allocable to tangible property and allocable to unrealized receivables, since different tax treatment is accorded to each. As in commercial partnerships, the payment(s) for capital assets (partnership property) is not deductible by the partnership and is not considered ordinary income to the decedent's estate. This amount generally is paid in a lump sum to the deceased partner's estate. On the other hand, payments of an agreed amount for unrealized receivables are deductible by the partnership when made and are taxable as ordinary income to the estate as income in respect of a decedent. The fact that these payments constitute ordinary income to the recipient usually makes it desirable to spread them over several years to cushion the tax impact.

Under an entity plan, the partners may elect to treat an amount paid for goodwill as either part of the purchase price for capital assets or as ordinary income.

Estate Taxation. Upon a partner's death, the value of his or her partnership interest normally would be included in the deceased's gross estate, like any

---

[1]This assumes that if an entity-type agreement is used, the agreement specifically provides for a payment for goodwill.

other asset he or she owns. A difficulty with closely held business interests, however, is that they may be difficult to value for estate tax purposes. There is, of course, no ready market for them. So the tax authorities may try to set a high value on such interests for tax purposes. But where there exists a properly drawn buy-sell agreement, only the purchase price actually paid for the interest will be included in the deceased partner's estate. This "freezing" of the business's value for federal estate tax purposes may be an important advantage of buy-sell agreements. To "freeze" the value for federal estate tax purposes, three conditions normally must be met. The buy-sell agreement must be an "arm's length" agreement among the parties. Second, there must be a first-offer commitment whereby a partner must first offer his or her interest during lifetime to the other partners upon dropping out of the partnership. And, third, there must be a provision that binds the estates of the partners to sell the interest of a deceased partner at the agreed-upon value.

Both a lump-sum payment for capital assets and the commuted value of income continuation payments will be included in a deceased partner's estate. However, since income continuation payments also are taxable as ordinary income, the estate, when reporting this income, may claim a deduction for any estate tax attributable to its inclusion in the estate.

CLOSE CORPORATIONS

In a close corporation, stock ownership is limited to a small group of individuals; the stockholders usually are employees of the corporation in a management role; and the stock is, of course, not publicly traded. Unlike a partnership, which must by law be dissolved upon a partner's death, a corporation continues in existence. However, in practice, the death of a close-corporation stockholder usually has important and far-reaching consequences for the other stockholders and the corporation itself.

Effects of a Stockholder's Death

The effects of the death of a close-corporation stockholder are discussed below in terms of their impact on the corporation, the surviving stockholders, and a deceased stockholder's heirs.

On the Corporation. The corporation itself may experience the following problems as the result of an executive stockholder's death:

1. Management disrupted
2. Credit impaired
3. Loss of business
4. Impairment of employee morale—employees may worry about the future of the business and their own financial security. A decline in efficiency and perhaps an increase in turnover may result.

On Surviving Stockholders. The following are some of the alternatives that may face the surviving stockholders:

1. They may continue in business with the heirs of the deceased stockholder as new stockholders. This often is undesirable, since the heirs frequently are not able or inclined to assume responsibility in management.

2. They may sell their stock. This often is undesirable or impractical, as they will sell themselves out of business, and there may be a real problem of finding an appropriate buyer who will pay a fair price for the stock.

3. They may buy the deceased's stock. Among the alternatives available after death, this probably is the best for all concerned. The surviving stockholders would acquire full control of the corporation, and the heirs could hope to receive a reasonable price for their stock interest. But there are several practical obstacles to this arrangement. Without a prior agreement, it is very difficult for all parties to agree on a selling price. Also, the surviving stockholders have the problem of raising the money needed for the purchase.

On the Deceased Stockholder's Heirs. On the other hand, here are some of the alternatives that may face the heirs of a deceased stockholder as they survey their new situation as stockholders in a close corporation:

1. The heirs may retain their inherited stock as active or inactive stockholders. This approach often does not work because of the divergent interests of the heirs and the surviving stockholders. The survivors frequently are interested primarily in maintaining business growth, while the heirs usually are interested mainly in income from the business.

2. The heirs may sell the stock to an outsider. However, it often is difficult for them to find a buyer who has the money, who will pay a fair price, and who will risk entering a close corporation with the remaining stockholders.

3. The heirs may sell their stock to the surviving stockholders. As we saw above, in the absence of a prior agreement, this probably is the best alternative for all concerned, if a fair price can be agreed upon and if the surviving stockholders can finance the purchase. But in practice these are big "ifs."

The Plan—A Buy-Sell Agreement

A prearranged written agreement between the individual stockholders (a cross-purchase agreement) or between the corporation and its stockholders (a stock retirement or stock redemption agreement) providing for the sale and purchase of the stock of a deceased stockholder often is the best solution to the problem of disposing of a business interest. The agreement would establish the purchase price for the stock and usually provides for periodic adjustments of the price as the value of the business changes over time.

Life insurance on the stockholders' lives is normally used to fund the agreement so that upon a stockholder's death the cash necessary to purchase his or her stock will be available. As in partnership situations, two types of agreements are available—a cross-purchase type and a stock retirement type.

Once again, as with a partnership, the choice of the type of agreement is of importance to the stockholders and should be made with the help of their professional advisors.

Figure 18-2 illustrates how a cross-purchase and a stock retirement buy-sell arrangement would operate for a typical close corporation with three equal stockholders.

FIGURE 18-2
CORPORATION VALUE, $300,000

Stockholder A owns $1/_3$ of the stock, $100,000	Stockholder B owns $1/_3$ of the stock, $100,000	Stockholder C owns $1/_3$ of the stock, $100,000

CROSS-PURCHASE AGREEMENT

The three stockholders agree in writing on: (1) the value of the stock, and (2) that in the event of the death of a stockholder, the estate of the deceased will sell, *and the surviving stockholders will buy,* the stock of the deceased.

Life Insurance to Fund Agreement

A insures:	B insures:	C insures:
B for $50,000	A for $50,000	A for $50,000
C for $50,000	C for $50,000	B for $50,000

Each stockholder is the applicant, owner, premium payor, and beneficiary of the policies on the other two stockholders.

At Death

Each surviving stockholder uses the insurance proceeds to purchase one-half of the deceased stockholder's stock from his or her estate according to the terms of the buy-sell agreement. (There may also be a disability provision in the buy-sell agreement to meet this risk as well.)

STOCK RETIREMENT AGREEMENT

The three stockholders and the Corporation agree in writing on: (1) the value of the stock, and (2) that in the event of the death of a stockholder, the estate of the deceased will sell, *and the Corporation will buy,* the stock of the deceased.

Life Insurance to Fund Agreement

Corporation insures:
  A for $100,000
  B for $100,000
  C for $100,000

The Corporation is the applicant, premium payor, owner, and beneficiary of all policies.

At Death

The Corporation uses the insurance proceeds to purchase the deceased stockholder's stock from his or her estate according to the terms of the buy-sell agreement. (There may also be a disability provision in the buy-sell agreement to meet this risk as well.)

Tax Aspects

Income Taxation. Here again, the income tax aspects of buy-sell agreements can be complex. The basic rules are only summarized here.

Insurance premiums. Whether paid by the stockholders or by the corporation, life insurance premiums are not deductible for income tax purposes, since the premium payor(s) is (are) either directly or indirectly a beneficiary (beneficiaries) under the policies.

Death proceeds. Life insurance death proceeds are received by the beneficiary(ies) free of federal income tax. This normally is true whether the beneficiary is the corporation or the individual stockholders.[2]

Purchase payment. A stock interest in a corporation is considered a capital asset. Thus, the purchase price for an interest is not deductible by the corporation or the stockholders, and it is not taxable income to the deceased stockholder's estate. Also, this payment will not usually result in a capital gain for the estate because the deceased's stock receives a stepped-up basis upon his or her death.

Estate Taxation

If the appropriate items are included in a buy-sell agreement as indicated above in the partnership discussion of estate taxation—namely, an arm's-length transaction, a first-offer commitment, and a provision binding the estate to sell the stock to the survivors—only the purchase price actually paid for the stock will be included in a deceased stockholder's estate for federal estate tax purposes.

SOLE PROPRIETORS

A sole proprietorship is not a separate entity apart from the individual proprietor (as is a partnership or a corporation). Consequently, special problems arise in planning for the orderly disposition of the business at the sole proprietor's death.

The sole proprietor, in an economic sense, is the business, and unless plans are made during his or her lifetime, the business often will die with its owner. Business assets and liabilities pass into the proprietor's estate along with his or her other personal assets and liabilities. The proprietor's executor, lacking specific authorization in the proprietor's will, cannot legally continue the business without personal liability. Thus, the executor normally must dispose of the business immediately, pay estate obligations as quickly as possible, and distribute the remaining property to the heirs. This often results in severe financial loss to the family because of the forced liquidation of the business.

[2]When the individual stockholders are the beneficiaries (in a cross-purchase plan), a special rule—the "transfer for value" rule—may apply under certain circumstances and cause a portion of the proceeds to be taxed as income.

The Problem for the Business

The success of a sole proprietorship usually depends upon the personal services and managerial ability of the proprietor. When the proprietor dies (or is totally and permanently disabled), and his or her family or a key employee is not capable of carrying on the business, the flow of income is cut off and, on forced liquidation, the business may end up worth only a fraction of the value of its assets as carried on the books. Further, the "going concern value" of the proprietorship is lost to the proprietor's family at his or her death. The executor, unable to operate the business without prior authorization, will be forced to liquidate it, probably at a loss.

The Estate's Problem

Estate settlement costs may be even more significant than normal in the case of a sole proprietor because in many cases the business has substantial debts. Since no distinction is made between the proprietorship and the proprietor, all the proprietor's assets would be available to meet all his or her debts—business and personal.

In paying estate debts and obligations, the executor often discovers a cash-poor estate, since much of the proprietor's personal funds and business profits were invested in the proprietorship during his or her lifetime and, thereby, were converted into often nonliquid business assets. This also may force the executor to sell the business as quickly as possible to raise the necessary cash.

Possible Solutions

Clearly, what is needed is a plan that will enable the proprietor *during his or her lifetime* to: (1) *set forth his or her objectives concerning the disposition of the business,* and (2) *make adequate financial plans to assure that these objectives can be carried out.*

The objectives set forth during the proprietor's lifetime will vary according to his or her desires and individual circumstances. However, three alternatives for disposing of the business generally are available: (1) orderly liquidation or sale, (2) family retention, and (3) sale to an employee.

Orderly Liquidation or Sale. Many sole proprietors do not have family members or employees to whom they can transfer the business at their death. So they must plan to convert the business into cash in the most beneficial manner. If possible, this normally means selling the proprietorship as a going concern.

If this course is to be followed, the proprietor's will should authorize his or her executor to continue the business without personal liability until an advantageous sale can be made—if possible, as a going concern. The will may also provide the executor with related discretionary powers that enable the executor to carry out its functions.

The executor's ability to avoid a forced liquidation of the business hinges on the availability of liquid assets in the estate to satisfy estate creditors so that liquidation of the business is not necessary. Life insurance on the sole proprietor can provide the cash needed to pay estate settlement costs, including business debts. Thus, the executor can be given enough time to look around for the best deal in disposing of the business. Life insurance on the proprietor can also offset the diminishing value of the business if liquidation becomes necessary.

Family Retention. In some cases, a sole proprietor will have a family member or members who can continue the business profitably. Perhaps it is a responsible son or daughter, or son-in-law or daughter-in-law, who has worked in the business and can retain the customers' goodwill. It may be the proprietor's wife or husband who has worked in the business. The proprietor in his or her will leaves the assets of the proprietorship, subject to its liabilities, to the family member, and then leaves the remainder of the estate to his or her other heirs. When a proprietorship is bequeathed to a family member in this manner, care must be taken to define carefully what is given as part of the business interest and what is to be considered as personal assets and liabilities apart from the business.

Life insurance on the sole proprietor can be used to supply cash to help pay estate settlement costs. The executor's ability to transfer the business as a going concern to the chosen heir depends on the ability to satisfy estate creditors from available liquid assets in the estate, rather than from the proceeds of liquidating the proprietorship. Thus, life insurance can be used to discharge estate obligations and help keep the business intact for the family member. Life insurance also can be used to provide those heirs who are not to inherit the business with equitable inheritances. Where a proprietor's estate consists of little property other than the business, as is so frequently the case, life insurance is an ideal means for creating such "inheritances."

Sale to an Employee. The proprietor may have a key employee who is capable of continuing the business. In this case, a logical solution would be to have the key employee buy the business at the proprietor's death. This would enable the proprietor's estate to realize the going-concern value of the business, rather than a deceased liquidated value.

Such a sale can be handled efficiently by having the proprietor and the key employee enter into a buy-sell agreement during their lifetimes providing for the sale by the proprietor's estate and the purchase by the key employee of the proprietor's business upon his or her death (and perhaps the proprietor's disability). Life insurance on the sole proprietor should be used to fund the agreement by providing, upon the proprietor's death, the immediate cash necessary for the employee to purchase the business.

Figure 18-3 illustrates how these three alternatives might operate in planning for a proprietorship. Naturally, the particular circumstances of each

FIGURE 18-3

ALTERNATE BUSINESS DISPOSITION PLANS—SOLE PROPRIETORSHIP
Assumed Business Value, $100,000
Assumed Estate Settlement Costs, $25,000

ORDERLY LIQUIDATION OR SALE

The proprietor designates in his or her will that in the event of his or her death: (1) the business will be liquidated or sold in the most favorable way possible, and (2) the executor can continue the business without personal liability until the best sale can be obtained.

LIFE INSURANCE TO FUND PLAN

Proprietor insures himself for $75,000.

Proprietor is applicant, owner, and premium payor of the policy on his own life, with the executor, a family member, or a trustee designated as beneficiary.

AT DEATH

Executor can utilize part of the insurance proceeds to pay the assumed $25,000 in settlement costs. The remainder of the proceeds, $50,000, passes to the heirs to offset the shrinkage in the business value, assuming the executor can sell it as a going concern and realize 50 percent of its current value. If not, additional life insurance could be purchased to compensate for this loss.

FAMILY RETENTION

The proprietor designates in his or her will that in the event of his or her death: (1) the business will pass to a designated family member as his or her share of the estate, and (2) the remainder of the property will be divided among the other heirs.

LIFE INSURANCE TO FUND PLAN

Proprietor insures himself for $125,000.

Proprietor is applicant, owner, and premium payor of the policy on his own life, with the executor, a family member, or a trustee designated as beneficiary.

AT DEATH

Executor can utilize part of the insurance proceeds to pay the assumed $25,000 in settlement costs. The remainder of the proceeds, $100,000, passes to the other heirs according to the proprietor's desires. Additional life insurance could be purchased if larger inheritances are desired.

SALE TO EMPLOYEE

The proprietor and a key employee agree in writing on: (1) the value of the business, and (2) that in the event of the proprietor's death, the employee will buy, and the proprietor's estate will sell, the business.

LIFE INSURANCE TO FUND PLAN

Employee insures proprietor for $100,000.

Proprietor insures himself for $25,000.

Employee is applicant, owner, premium payor, and beneficiary of the $100,000 policy on the proprietor.

Proprietor is applicant, owner, and premium payor of the $25,000 policy on his life, with his executor, a family member, or a trustee, designated beneficiary.

AT DEATH

Employee utilizes the insurance proceeds he receives to purchase the deceased proprietor's business from the estate.

Executor can utilize the $25,000 of proceeds to pay the assumed $25,000 of estate settlement costs.

business and estate situation would determine the particular plan appropriate for it. No "canned" solutions are possible in this field.

Tax Aspects

Income Taxation. Premiums paid by a key employee for life insurance to fund a sole proprietorship buy-sell agreement are not deductible by the employee. The death proceeds, however, are received by the beneficiary income tax–free.

Estate Taxation. Under the orderly liquidation or sale alternative discussed above, the life insurance proceeds would be included in the insured proprietor's gross estate if the proprietor has any incidents of ownership in the policy or names his or her estate as beneficiary. The liquidation value or sale price of the business also would be included in the proprietor's estate as assets he or she owns.

In the case of family retention of the business interest, the insurance proceeds also are included in the proprietor's estate if the proprietor retains incidents of ownership in the policy or names his or her estate as beneficiary. The value of the business also would be included.

When a properly drafted buy-sell agreement exists, only the value of the business as represented by the purchase price actually paid for it is included in the proprietor's estate.

ESTATE LIQUIDITY THROUGH SECTION 303 REDEMPTIONS

It has been said, "Section 303 of the Internal Revenue Code has been called the greatest tax boon ever made available to owners of closely held corporations." When certain conditions are met, Section 303 allows a corporation to redeem sufficient stock from a deceased stockholder's estate to pay death taxes, funeral costs, and estate administrative expenses without creating a taxable dividend to the estate.

Adding to the attractiveness of Section 303 is the fact that the proceeds received under a Section 303 redemption need not actually be used for meeting death expenses. Section 303 merely sets a limit on the amount that can be received from a partial redemption of stock before it may be considered a taxable dividend. Thus, if the executor already has sufficient liquid assets in an estate to pay death-related expenses, the proceeds of a Section 303 redemption still can be taken and used to meet other needs the decedent's family may have.

To qualify for a Section 303 redemption, the value of a deceased stockholder's stock in the corporation must comprise more than 35 percent of his gross estate or more than 50 percent of his net taxable estate. Assume, for example, the following estate situation.

Gross estate	$500,000
Less: Assumed funeral and estate administration expenses	−30,000
Adjusted gross estate	$470,000
Less: Marital deduction	−235,000
	$235,000
Less: Specific exemption	−60,000
Taxable estate	$175,000

In this case, if the deceased owned stock in the corporation valued at $100,000, the estate would fail to meet the 35 percent of the gross estate test, since $100,000 is only 20 percent of the $500,000 gross estate. However, by taking advantage of the marital deduction, the estate would be eligible for a Section 303 redemption under the 50-percent-of-the-taxable-estate test because 50 percent of the taxable estate in this case is $87,500, and so the $100,000 stock interest qualifies.

So if we assume $30,000 for funeral and estate administration expenses and combined federal and state death taxes of $44,000, this estate could sell a total of $74,000 of stock to the corporation without its being considered a taxable dividend.

SUBCHAPTER S CORPORATIONS

What Is a Subchapter S Corporation?

It is a corporation meeting certain qualification requirements that elects not to be taxed as a corporation. In every other aspect, except the areas of corporate taxation and limits on the use of qualified retirement plans, a Subchapter S corporation operates like a regular corporation.

A Subchapter S corporation is taxed essentially as a partnership rather than a corporation. The taxable income of the corporation is taxed directly to the stockholders, whether the stockholders actually receive the profits as dividends or whether the profits are left in the business. The net profits are reported and taxed to the stockholder(s) of a Subchapter S corporation as if they were distributed.

Subchapter S Qualification Requirements

In order to elect Subchapter S treatment, a corporation must meet the following conditions:

1. It must be a domestic corporation.

2. It must have no more than 10 stockholders.

3. It must have only individuals or estates as stockholders (not trusts, for example).

4. It must have only one class of stock.

5. It must not have a nonresident alien as a stockholder.

6. It must not be a member of an affiliated group of corporations entitled to file a consolidated return.

Additionally, all stockholders must consent to the election. In general, once revoked or terminated, an election cannot be made again for five taxable years.

As an example of how a Subchapter S election works, assume a sole stockholder of an incorporated drugstore whose annual income statement for the latest taxable year shows the following:

Gross sales		$500,000
Cost of sales		−300,000
Gross profit		$200,000
Expenses:		
Regular expenses	$130,000	
Stockholder employee's salary	40,000	−170,000
Net profit		$ 30,000

If the stockholder is considering making a Subchapter S election, and none of the financial data change, the comparison might appear as follows:

Regular Corporation Status	Subchapter S Corporation Status
Corporate income tax:	Corporate income tax: None

$$\frac{\$25,000}{\text{at } 22\%} + \frac{\$5,000}{\text{at } 48\%} = \$7,900 \text{ corporate tax}$$

Net corporate profits	$30,000
Corporate income tax	−7,900
Corporate after-tax income	$22,100

If the entire $22,100 is paid as a dividend to the stockholder (assuming a 48 percent individual income tax rate), his or her additional personal tax would be $10,608 ($22,100 × 0.48), and after-tax income would be $11,492. If this amount is retained by the corporation, retained earnings would increase by $22,100.	The $30,000 net profit is reported and taxed to the stockholder as an individual. His or her additional personal tax would be $14,400 ($30,000 × 0.48), and after-tax income would be $15,600.

In a Subchapter S corporation, the entire $30,000 of net corporate profits would be taxed directly to the stockholder. If these profits, or a portion of them, are paid to the stockholder, it is considered a dividend. If these profits, or a portion of them, are left in the business, this "undistributed taxable income" still is taxed to the stockholder. If "undistributed taxable income" is not paid out to the stockholder within 2½ months after the close of the corporation's taxable year, it becomes "income previously taxed" and increases the stockholder's cost basis of his or her stock. If "income previously taxed" is withdrawn in a subsequent year, it may be received as a tax-free distribution and reduces the stockholder's cost basis by that amount.

Why Should You Make a Subchapter S Election?

The previous example can help reveal the kind of situation where a Subchapter S election might be advantageous. The data for the two corporations were identical until the disposition of the $30,000 in net corporate profits. In the nonelecting corporation, the profits were subjected to the corporate income tax before they could be paid to the stockholder or, as is frequently the case in closely held corporations, retained and accumulated in the corporation. In the electing corporation, the profits passed through directly to the stockholder without first being reduced by corporate income taxation.

The desirability of a Subchapter S status generally depends on the nature of the business and the personal circumstances of the stockholder(s). For example, if there is a need for substantial amounts of new capital in the business, a regular corporation might be advantageous. The stockholder(s) could leave money in the business each year, at the tax cost of subjecting all or much of the profits to a low 22 percent corporate tax rate, instead of a personal tax rate which may be substantially higher. The corporation thus affords an economical means of accumulating surplus for investment in the business.

On the other hand, in a professional or personal service corporation, where the accumulation of surplus often is not important, the existence of a corporate taxpayer may work as a disadvantage. Although the stockholder(s) normally would not leave money in the business, the net profits would have to be taxed to the corporation before they could be distributed to the stockholder(s) personally and then taxed again. For the professional or personal service corporation stockholder, then, a Subchapter S election is a way to receive the profits directly and eliminate the corporate tax. Thus, if the stockholder(s) does (do) not need the corporation as a surplus accumulation vehicle, and wants (want) to receive all the net corporate income, the Subchapter S corporation provides a way to avoid the double taxation of profits and still enjoy the usual advantages of corporate status.

Another possible advantage associated with a Subchapter S corporation deserves brief mention. New corporations sometimes elect Subchapter S treatment and maintain this status during their early years in business. Normally, a net operating loss of a corporation for any taxable year is carried forward and used in subsequent profitable years to offset the corporation's taxable income. However, a net operating loss of a Subchapter S corporation would pass through the corporation directly to the stockholders, and can be used by them individually as a deduction from gross income. Thus, if a corporation sustains such losses during its early stages of growth, the Subchapter S election can provide a valuable personal tax-planning device for the stockholder-employees.

Other Aspects of a Subchapter S Election

Employee Benefit Plans. A great advantage of incorporating a closely held business is that the owner(s) who works (work) in the business is an *employee(s)* of the corporation. This includes the owner of a Subchapter S corporation who works in the business. When the owner is an employee, the corporation can deduct the contributions it makes for the owner for employee benefit plans along with its contributions for regular employees. These programs are available on a tax-favored basis only for employees; the owners of unincorporated businesses are not considered to be employees for tax purposes. However, Subchapter S corporations now have the disadvantage of a special limitation (that does not apply to regular corporations) on the amount of the tax deduction they can take for contributions to qualified pension and profit-sharing plans on behalf of stockholder-employees. This limitation is 15 percent of the stockholder-employee's compensation or $7,500, whichever is less.

Accumulated Earnings Tax. A regular corporation may have to pay a penalty tax, in addition to its regular corporate income tax, on any after-tax earnings that are retained and accumulated in the corporation beyond its reasonable business needs (in excess of a minimum amount of $100,000 per year). Subchapter S corporations are exempt from this problem, since the corporate profits have already been taxed each year to the stockholders.

Buy-Sell Plans. As in other corporations, the stockholders of Subchapter S corporations often need a buy-sell agreement to dispose of a deceased (or disabled) stockholder's interest. In fact, the need may be even greater than in nonelecting corporations. Without such a plan, for example, a deceased stockholder's interest could pass to a nonconsenting stockholder or to a nonqualified party (e.g., a trust, a corporation, or an eleventh stockholder). *One* stockholder who does not consent to a Subchapter S status can terminate the election and disqualify the corporation from further Subchapter S treatment.

PERSONAL FINANCIAL PLANNING CHECKLIST FOR DECISION MAKING

(You can use this checklist to evaluate your insurance, investment, retirement, tax, and estate planning programs. The book itself provides needed information on the points raised in the checklist. The checklist also contains cross-references to the appropriate parts of the book.)

I. OBJECTIVES

A. Generally identify your objectives in the following areas:

1. Protection for yourself and your family against the risks of death, disability, medical expenses, property losses, and liability losses

2. Capital accumulation and investments

3. Retirement

4. Estate planning

5. Other

B. What other special concerns do you have?

1. Children or other dependents with special problems or needs

2. Economic or investment uncertainties

3. Employment uncertainties

4. Other

II. USING INSURANCE EFFECTIVELY

A. Life insurance (See Chapter 4.)

1. What kinds of death benefits do you now have (other than social security)?

Kind of Plan	Amount
Group life insurance (employer-provided)	
Survivor's income benefits (employer-provided)	
Individual policies *you own* on your life	
Individual policies *others own* on your life	
Association group life insurance	
Death benefits under pension and profit-sharing plans	
Death benefits under tax-sheltered annuity and HR-10 plans	
Personal annuity contracts	
Death benefits under nonqualified deferred compensation plans and informal employer plans	
Other plans	

2. Do you have *enough life insurance,* along with other death benefits and assets available to your family, to meet your objectives? (Pages 73–77)

3. If you need *additional life insurance, how should you provide it?* (pp. 47–50)

4. Have you elected to take all the employer-provided group life insurance you are entitled to and want? (pp. 64–66)

5. If you need additional life insurance, *what kind of policy should you buy?* (pp. 50–53)

6. Should any new individual life insurance be on a *participating* or on a *nonparticipating basis?* (pp. 69–70)

7. Should you *surrender for cash* (or terminate) any of your existing life insurance policies? (pp. 55 and 57)

8. Should you place any of your existing life insurance policies under the *reduced paid-up* (or perhaps extended-term) nonforfeiture options and stop paying premiums on them? (pp. 57–58)

9. Check whether you have *waiver of premium benefits* on all your individual policies. If not, can you add this benefit? (p. 62)

10. Do you have *accidental death benefits* (double indemnity) on your individual policies? If so, do you want these benefits, or would you rather drop them and save the premium? (pp. 61–62)

11. Do you have *guaranteed insurability coverage* on your existing policies or any new policies? Do you need this coverage? (p. 61)

12. If you are carrying *decreasing term insurance* at a level annual premium, has the amount of insurance decreased to the point where you should consider dropping the insurance and saving the premium?

13. Do you have a *substandard premium rating* that the insurance company now will remove? Or, if the company will not remove it, can you now buy insurance at standard rates with another company? (pp. 62–64)

14. How are you using any *policy dividends?* Are you making the best use of your policy dividends for *your needs?* Can you get a better interest return on this money than the insurance company is paying with equal safety? (p. 58)

15. What are your *policy loan values (cash values)?* What is the policy loan interest rate(s) in your policies? Should you consider borrowing on your life insurance rather than elsewhere? (pp. 55 and 140–141)

16. Check your life insurance *beneficiary designations.* (pp. 56, 70–72 and 316–324)

a. Are your primary beneficiaries the ones you now want (up to date)?

b. Have you named contingent beneficiaries in all your policies? If not, why not? Are they up to date?

c. Is your estate named as primary beneficiary on any policy(ies)? If so, why?

d. Are minors named as beneficiaries? If so, have you made arrangements to avoid problems arising out of paying proceeds to minor beneficiaries?

e. If there are any children of a former marriage, are they included in any beneficiary designations of children, if this is your wish?

f. Are all your life insurance beneficiary designations consistent? If there are any differences among your policies, are they intentional?

17. Check the *beneficiary designations in any other plans* involving death benefits for your family. Are they consistent with those under your life insurance policies? If not, why not? (p. 324)

18. Check how your *life insurance proceeds are to be paid.* (Also see "Estate Planning" later.) (pp. 59–61 and 316–319)

a. *Lump sum*

b. Under *settlement options*

(1) Do the options used meet your present needs?

(2) Have you named second (or third, etc.) payees under the options where appropriate?

(3) What flexibility do your beneficiaries have under the options? If no flexibility, why not?

(4) Are any proceeds (other than National Service Life Insurance) payable under a life income option? Should this be changed?

c. To an *insurance trust* as primary beneficiary

19. Have you provided for the *common-disaster or short-term-survivorship situations* in your life insurance? (Also see "Estate Planning.") (pp. 72–73)

20. Do you own life insurance on others' lives? If so, you should be named beneficiary. (p. 315)

21. Do others (or a trust) own life insurance on your life? If so, the owner should be named beneficiary. (pp. 319–322)

22. Have you been told you are uninsurable? If so,

a. Have you checked with other insurance companies? (pp. 63–64)

b. Have you taken advantage of all the coverage you can get without having to show individual evidence of insurability? (pp. 65–66)

B. Disability Income Insurance (See Chapter 5.)

1. What kinds of disability income benefits do you now have (other than social security)?

Kind of Plan	Benefit Amount and Duration
Group short-term (employer-provided)	
Group long-term (employer-provided)	
Employer sick-pay plan (uninsured)	
Individual disability income policies	
Disability income riders added to life insurance policies	
Franchise (association group) plans	
Disability benefits under pension, profit-sharing, and group life plans	
Other plans	

2. Do you have *enough disability insurance,* along with other disability benefits available to you and your family, to meet your objectives? Presume the worst—*total and permanent disability.* (pp. 82–84)

3. If you need *additional disability insurance, how should you provide it?* (pp. 81–91)

4. Should you *terminate* any of your existing disability insurance and save the premium?

5. Check the *maximum benefit period(s)* of your disability income benefits. Are the periods (durations) long enough to protect you against *long-term disability* (i.e., to age 65)? (pp. 80 and 81–91)

6. Check the *elimination period(s)* of your disability income benefits. Should you increase the elimination period(s) to save premium and/or to coordinate your coverage with employer-provided or other ·benefits? (pp. 80 and 81–91)

7. Do all your policies cover against *disability caused by both accident and sickness?* If not, consider dropping the "accident only" coverage and save the premium. (p. 80)

8. If you have group long-term disability income coverage, check the *kinds of other disability benefits that will reduce the amount of insurance under the group plan.* In particular, will any individual disability policy you may buy serve to reduce your group plan benefits? (p. 84)

9. Does your employer have an uninsured sick-pay plan covering you (in addition to any group disability benefits)?

10. Check the *definition of disability* in existing or any new disability coverage you are considering. (pp. 80 and 81–91)

11. What rights do you have *to continue your individual disability coverage* (i.e., *continuance provisions*)? (pp. 101–102)

12. How much of your disability coverage is *franchise (association group) insurance* that can be discontinued if the franchise (group) plan is discontinued? (pp. 89–90)

13. If you are considering buying an individual disability policy, (pp. 85–89)

a. Does it provide both *occupational and nonoccupational coverage* (so-called "24-hour coverage")?

b. Does it contain a *relation of earnings to insurance provision?*

c. What *definition of disability* is used?

d. Is it *noncancelable and guaranteed renewable* ("noncan")?

e. Does it contain a *house confinement provision?*

f. Does it contain a *waiver of premium benefit?*

g. Does it have a *guaranteed insurability provision?*

h. Do you need any *supplementary disability income benefits* attached to it?

14. Check whether you have other *supplementary benefits* on your individual disability policies, such as: accidental death (AD) or accidental death and dismemberment (AD&D), accident medical reimbursement, and the like. If so, do you want these benefits, or would you rather drop them and save the premium? (pp. 87–88)

15. Do you have a *substandard premium rating* or *waiver of coverage* that the insurance company now may reconsider and perhaps remove? Or, if the company will not remove it, can you now buy insurance on a standard basis with another company?

16. Should you carry *at least some individual disability income insurance* (that you control) to supplement your group insurance? (But note No. 8 above in this regard.) (p. 85)

C. Medical expense insurance (See Chapter 5.)

1. What kinds of medical expense benefits do you or your family now have?

Kind of Plan	Brief Summary of Benefits
Group insurance (employer-provided)	
• Hospital, medical, surgical ("basic" coverages)	
• Major medical (supplementary to "basic" coverages)	
• Comprehensive medical expense	
• Health maintenance (HMO) coverage	
• Other	
Individual medical expense policies	
• Hospital, medical, surgical	
• Major medical	
• Comprehensive medical expense	
• Hospital income benefits	
• Other	
Medicare	
Other	

2. Do you have *enough medical expense benefits* available to you and your family to meet your objectives with respect to:

a. "Basic" hospital, medical, and surgical coverage

b. Major medical· coverage

c. Catastrophic (excess) medical expenses

3. For which family members (or others) are you, or might you be, responsible for paying medical bills?

a. Wife or husband

b. Children

c. Aged, dependent parents

d. Other dependents

Does your or any other medical expense coverage apply to them? Do they need coverage or supplementary coverage? (pp. 97 and 98–101)

4. If you have *major medical insurance,* do you need (or want) to *supplement this coverage—*

   a. With "basic" coverage to take care of uncovered expenses due to the major medical's deductible, "inside limits," and coinsurance limitations? (pp. 92–94)

   b. With "excess" coverage to take care of catastrophic losses over the major medical's maximum limit? (p. 96)

5. If you or your dependents are covered by *Medicare,* do you need (or want) to *supplement it?* (pp. 97 and 93)

6. If you or your dependents need *additional medical expense benefits, how should you provide them?* (pp. 99–101)

7. Should you *terminate* any of your existing medical expense benefits and save the premium?

8. Do you have any dependents who have, or soon will have, terminated their coverage under group or family medical expense coverage? If so, what *conversion rights* do they have? (pp. 99 and 101)

9. What rights do you have *to continue your individual medical expense coverage (i.e., continuance provisions)?* (pp. 101–102)

10. Does your medical expense insurance continue to protect your dependents in the event of your death? (p. 101)

11. Do you have a *substandard premium rating* or *waiver of coverage* that the insurance company now will reconsider and perhaps remove? Or, if the company will not remove it, can you now buy insurance on a standard basis with another company?

12. Do you have any *limited policies,* such as so-called "dread disease" policies, that you might want to drop and save the premium?

13. If you have any hospital income policies, do you need the supplementary coverage, or should you consider dropping it and saving the premium? (p. 93)

14. Do you have any *accident only* medical reimbursement coverage? If so, should you drop it and save the premium? (p. 101)

15. Do you have excess major medical coverage for catastrophic losses (1) under personal catastrophe (umbrella) liability insurance, or (2) as separate health insurance? (pp. 96 and 122)

D. Accidental death and dismemberment (AD&D) insurance

1. If you have such coverage (group and/or individual), check the beneficiary designations to see if they are consistent with your life insurance. If they are not, why not?

2. If you have the choice, consider whether to keep AD&D coverage or drop it and save the premium. This is a good place to cut costs if you want to?

E. Property and liability insurance (See Chapter 6.)

1. What property and liability coverages do you now have?

Kind	Limit(s) of Liability
Homeowners (or fire and related coverages)	
Personal liability (e.g., Section II of Homeowners)	
Automobile	
Workmen's compensation	
Watercraft	
Aircraft	
Professional liability	
Directors' and officers' liability	
Personal catastrophe (umbrella) liability	
Self-retained limit	
Excess major medical	
Personal articles coverage (or floater)	
Personal property floater (or Homeowners 5 coverage)	
Other	

2. Are you subject to the following *liability loss exposures* that may *not be covered* by your homeowners or automobile insurance? (p. 115)

   a. *Business or professional liability*

   b. *Watercraft liability*

   c. *Aircraft liability*

   d. *Recreational motor vehicles*

   e. *Workmen's compensation*

   f. Liability arising out of premises, other than an insured premises, that you may own, rent, or control

   g. Liability for property of others you have in your care, custody, or control

3. Are your *liability insurance limits high enough* and consistent in all coverages? (pp. 109–110, 119 and 120–121)

4. Do you have *personal catastrophe (umbrella) liability insurance?* Is its limit of liability high enough? Does it cover excess major medical? (pp. 120–122)

5. Do you have liability coverage for any *officerships and/or directorships* you may have? (p. 122)

6. Which *Homeowners form* should you buy (if applicable) for your property loss exposures? (pp. 110–112 and 115)

7. Do you have enough Homeowners insurance to get *full replacement cost coverage* on your dwelling and private structures? (pp. 112–114)

8. If you have Homeowners insurance, do you need *extra coverage* for:

   a. Money and *numismatic property* (coin collections)

   b. Securities, deeds, etc., and *philatelic property* (stamp collections)

   c. *Jewelry, furs,* and similar property

   d. *Watercraft*

   e. *Other high-value property* (e.g., fine arts, antiques, cameras, musical instruments, silverware, golfer's equipment, and the like) (pp. 114–115)

9. Do you have enough Homeowners (or other) insurance to cover your *personal property on and away from your premises?* (pp. 111 and 114–115)

10. Have you made an up-to-date *inventory of your personal property?* (p. 107)

11. Have you increased the hazard, or left your premises vacant, in a way that might possibly suspend your property insurance coverage? (p. 107)

12. Do you need *collision or comprehensive auto coverage,* or should you drop one or both and save the premium? (pp. 117–120)

13. Do you need *automobile medical payments* coverage, or should you drop it and save the premium?

14. Do you need *federal flood or crime insurance,* if you are eligible?

15. Have you shopped around with other insurers to see if you can buy your insurance at lower cost or with better coverage? (pp. 123–124)

III. HANDLING YOUR INVESTMENTS

A. What investments and assets do you now have?

1. Cash, bank accounts, etc.—include current balances and how owned (i.e., by yourself, your spouse, jointly, etc.)

   a. Cash on hand

   b. Checking accounts

   c. Savings accounts, credit union shares, etc.—yield

   d. Brokerage accounts, etc.

2. Bank savings certificates, etc.—yield, duration

3. United States savings bonds—maturity values

4. Life insurance and annuity cash values (net of policy loans)

5. Other liquid assets

6. Common stocks, including: the stock's description and investment goal (e.g., growth, cyclical, defensive, income, etc.); cost (tax basis) and how long held; current market value; annual dividend income; and how owned.

7. Mutual funds, including: the fund's description and investment goal (e.g., growth stock, diversified common stock, balanced, income, etc.); cost (tax basis) and how long held; current market or net asset value; annual distribution from income and capital gains; and how owned.

8. Real estate

   a. Residential, including: location and description; cost (including improvements); estimated market value; mortgage (including current balance, interest rate, prepayment privilege and termination date); and how owned.

   b. Income-producing, including: location and description; when acquired; cost (including improvements); estimated market value; mortgage (including current balance, interest rate, and monthly payment); estimated annual net income (or loss); estimated annual cash flow; and how owned.

9. Bonds, including: par value; coupon rate (annual income); cost (tax basis) and how long held; current market value; maturity date; investment rating; and how owned.

   a. Corporate

   b. Convertible

   c. Municipal

   d. United States government

10. Preferred stocks

11. Tax-sheltered investments (other than real estate)

12. Business interests (sole proprietorships, partnership interests, and close corporation stock)

13. Other investments and interests

B. How should you deal with your new and existing investments?

1. Review your *investment objectives.* Is your present program consistent with them? If not, what changes should be made? (pp. 143–144)

2. Have you decided upon an *investment strategy (policies)* to follow? (pp. 144–148)

3. Have you analyzed the *composition of your investment portfolio?* Is it right for you? (pp. 146–147)

4. Do you depend on your investment income for part or all of your livelihood? (pp. 142–143)

5. Do you want, now or someday, an investment income to supplement your job earnings (to provide a *"second income"*)? How much?

6. Are you earning as high an *after-tax total return* on your investments as you can in your circumstances? What can you do to improve your after-tax yield—current income and/or capital gains? (pp. 133–137)

7. How large an *emergency fund* do you want? (pp. 23–24)

8. How much capital do you need for your children's education, and how much time do you have to accumulate it? (pp. 24–25)

9. What other personal or family capital needs—travel, weddings, gifts, etc.—do you have? (pp. 23–27)

10. Do you have enough *liquidity and marketability* in your investment portfolio? (pp. 138–139)

11. Is your portfolio adequately *diversified*? In what ways? (pp. 139–140)

12. Do you have enough *security of principal and income* in your portfolio? (pp. 129–133)

13. To what extent, if at all, do you want to *speculate*? In what ways? Can you afford to speculate? (pp. 128 and 194)

14. In your investment planning, *are you ready for prosperity*? *Recession*? *Depression*?

15. What amount do you presently have available for investment?

16. How much do you have available annually for discretionary investments?

17. Which of the following *kinds of investment media* or speculations would you consider for your program? (See Chapters 7, 8, 9, 10, and 11 for descriptions of these investment media.)

   • Bank savings certificates

   • Certificates of deposit (or "money market" funds)

   • Corporate bonds

   • "Deep-discount" bonds

   • Corporate bond funds

   • Convertible bonds

   • United States government securities

     Treasury bills

     Treasury notes

     Treasury bonds

     United States government agency securities

   • Ginnie Mae pass-throughs

   • Municipal bonds

   • Municipal bond funds

   • Preferred stocks

   • Convertible preferreds

   • Common stocks

   • Mutual funds

   • Writing options

   • Investment real estate

     Direct ownership (sole or joint)

Limited partnership interests

Real estate investment trusts (REITs)

- Variable annuities
- Tax-sheltered investments
- Common stock warrants
- Selling stock short
- Buying puts and calls
- Trading in commodity futures
- Buying new issues

18. Have your *common stocks lived up to your investment expectations* for them? (Chapter 8)

If not, should you sell and invest elsewhere, switch to other stocks, or hold?

If so, should you buy more or hold?

19. Do you have stocks with *short-term capital losses* you could sell? (pp. 249–252 and 255–257)

20. Do you have stocks with *long-term capital losses* you could sell? (249–252 and 255–257)

21. Do you want to use *dollar cost averaging* or *formula plans* in buying common stocks? (pp. 147 and 157–158)

22. Do you own stock acquired under stock option or stock purchase plans? (pp. 243–244)

23. Do you have any *unexercised stock options* or *rights under stock purchase plans*? (pp. 243–244)

24. Have your mutual funds lived up to your investment expectations for them? If not, what action should you take? (Chapter 9, particularly pp. 178–182)

25. If you are going to buy funds (investment company shares), *should they be closed-end or open-end (mutual) funds*? (pp. 170–171)

26. If you are going to buy mutual funds (open-end), should they be *load or no-load funds*? (pp. 172–173 and 175–176)

27. If you are going to buy a load-type mutual fund, *how can you save money on the sales load*? (pp. 174–175)

28. How should you buy mutual fund shares? (pp. 176–178)

29. If you are going to liquidate mutual fund shares, should you use a *mutual fund systematic withdrawal plan*? (pp. 177–178)

30. In your income tax bracket, *would municipal bonds be attractive to you*? (pp. 199–200)

31. In your income tax bracket, *would tax-sheltered investments (including real estate) be attractive to you*? (pp. 183–185)

32. If you are investing in fixed-income securities, do you have an investment strategy? Short-term? Long-term? (pp. 205–206)

33. Are you taking steps to *protect yourself against bond and preferred stock callability*? (pp. 141 and 198)

34. If you believe a recession or depression is coming, are you ready for the *contracyclical price movement of high-grade bonds*? (p. 139)

35. Should you consider *professional investment advisory services or other professional management* of your investments? (pp. 30–32 and 324–326)

IV. PLANNING FOR YOUR RETIREMENT (In general, see Chapters 12 and 13.)

A. What retirement benefits do you now have?

Kind of Plan	Estimate of Benefits (at Retirement)
1. Social security retirement benefits (for yourself and your spouse)	
2. Pension plan (employer-provided)	
3. Profit-sharing plan (employer-provided)	
4. Nonqualified deferred compensation	
5. Other employee benefits	
6. HR-10 plan	
7. Tax-sheltered annuity (TSA) plan	
8. Life insurance cash values	
9. Individual annuities (fixed-dollar and variable)	
10. IRA plan	
11. Projected general investment fund	

B. How should you plan for your retirement?

1. At *what age* would you like to retire? How old will your spouse be?

2. What *after-tax retirement income do you want*:

a. While both you and your spouse are alive?

b. For your spouse if you die first?

3. Do you have enough retirement benefits, along with social security and your general investment fund, to meet your objectives? Too much?

4. If you need *additional retirement income*, how should you provide it?

5. How have you *provided for your surviving spouse* if you should die first? (pp. 214–215 and 216–219)

6. What annuity form should you select for your pension and/or other retirement benefits? (pp. 216–218)

7. Can you afford to retire early (before age 65) if you desire?

8. Are any qualified pension and profit-sharing plan death benefits payable to your estate? (pp. 225 and 308)

9. To what extent are your employer-provided *pension benefits vested*? (pp. 215–216)

10. How, if at all, are your pension benefits protected against inflation after your retirement? (pp. 225–226)

11. What *vested rights* do you have under any *deferred profit-sharing plan*? (p. 227)

12. Do you have any *withdrawal or loan privileges* under a deferred profit-sharing plan? (pp. 227–228)

13. Are you eligible to adopt an *HR-10 plan? IRA plan*? If you are, should you do so? (pp. 234–237)

14. Are you eligible to participate in a *tax-sheltered annuity (TSA) plan*? If so, should you? (pp. 237–239)

15. Should you consider entering into a *nonqualified deferred compensation plan* with your employer (if offered) to defer income until your retirement? (pp. 240–241)

16. Should you adopt a *professional corporation* (if appropriate) to help provide you with qualified retirement and other employee benefits? (pp. 239–240)

17. Should you use life insurance settlement options (for cash values) to provide retirement benefits? (p. 233)

18. Should you buy a commercial single-premium annuity? (pp. 229–230)

19. How secure are your retirement benefits? How much is

guaranteed? Are you ready for prosperity? Recession? Depression?

V. TAX AND ESTATE PLANNING

A. Income tax planning (In general, see Chapter 14.)

1. What *top income tax bracket* (rate) are you and your spouse now in (federal, state, and local)?

2. Are you taking all the income tax exemptions, deductions, and credits to which you are now entitled (e.g., expenses of an office at home, club dues and fees, costs of a professional library, etc.)? (pp. 247–248 and 253–254)

3. Should you file an *amended return* for deductions not taken in the past?

4. What is the *relative advantage* for you and your spouse [considering your top income tax brackets(s)] of *tax-exempt income versus taxable income*?

5. Is *tax-deferred income* attractive to you?

6. Is your present *taxpayer status* (joint return, separate return, etc.) best for you?

7. Check your securities portfolio for possible *tax-loss sale candidates*. Should you use a *tax exchange* to maintain your investment position? (pp. 255–257)

8. How can you plan for returns in the form of long-term capital gains rather than ordinary income? (pp. 265–266)

9. How can you postpone the income tax bite? (pp. 266–269)

10. If you are selling stock you have purchased over a period of time, which certificates are best to sell from a tax viewpoint? (p. 268)

11. How can you arrange your life insurance for best income tax savings? (pp. 312–314)

12. If you have a sizable long-term capital gain in securities you own, do you have a "capital gains tax lock-in problem"? If so, how should you deal with it? (pp. 269–270)

13. Which of the following specific tax-saving techniques should you consider (or perhaps are now using)?

   a. Buying *municipal bonds* (Also see "Handling Your Investments.")

   b. Making *other tax-sheltered investments* (Also see "Handling Your Investments.")

   c. *Income averaging*

   d. Adoption of *tax-favored employee benefits or HR-10 plans* (Also see "Planning for Your Retirement.")

   e. Giving *appreciated long-term capital gain property to charity*

   f. Use of a *charitable remainder trust*

   g. Making gifts of income-producing property (Consider what property and to whom.)

   h. Creation of *short-term reversionary ("Clifford"-type) trusts*

   i. Taking a *lump-sum distribution from a "qualified" retirement plan*

   j. *Incorporating* for tax reasons (Consider a *Subchapter S Corporation* or a *Professional Corporation,* if applicable.)

   k. Using United States government savings bonds to best tax advantage

14. What tax-planning warnings (caveats) should you consider? (pp. 270–271)

B. Estate planning (In general, see Chapters 15, 16, 17, and 18.)

1. How large, and what is the nature of, *your estate,* including your *gross estate for federal estate tax purposes,* your *probate estate,* and the *"net"* estate going to your heirs? (pp. 278–281)

2. How large is, and what is the nature of, *your spouse's estate,* assuming (a) your spouse survives you, and (b) you survive your spouse? (pp. 298–299)

3. Do *other family members* have sizable estates?

4. What financial obligations will your estate have, including *potential federal estate taxes and state death taxes?* (pp. 295–296)

5. What will be your *estate transfer costs* (a) at your death, and (b) at your spouse's subsequent death? Can they be reduced by better planning? (pp. 295–308)

6. How *liquid* is your estate? Can it meet its liquidity needs? (pp. 296–297)

7. What *inheritances* (if any) do you, your spouse, or other family members expect in the future?

   a. Can you estimate the amount?

   b. Will it be outright, in trust, or both?

   c. Will any inheritance become part of your or your spouse's gross estate for federal estate tax purposes? (If so, should your estate be "skipped" for federal estate tax purposes?)

8. Are you, your spouse, or your children presently the *beneficiary(ies) of any trusts?*

9. Are you or your spouse presently the donee of any *unexercised powers of appointment?* General powers? Special powers?

10. Do you live or have you ever lived in a *community property* state?

11. Who do you want to be the *primary beneficiaries of your estate?* How should they share in it, and in what amounts? Will it be adequate for their needs? (pp. 272–273)

12. Do any of your *dependents have special problems* you should consider in your estate planning? (pp. 272–273)

13. Do you have *dependent parents* (or others) to consider? (pp. 272–273)

14. Are you interested in making any *charitable bequests?*

15. Have you or has your spouse a *closely held business interest* for which you should plan? (pp. 327–328)

16. What *methods of estate transfer*—lifetime and/or at death—are you and your spouse now using? Should you consider others? (pp. 273 and 285–289)

17. Have you had an estate planning conference with your lawyer? Banker? Life insurance agent? Accountant? Investment advisor? Others? (*Note:* You must have an attorney to give legal advice.)

18. Review your *estate planning objectives.* Is your present plan consistent with them? If not, what changes should be made? (pp. 272–273)

19. *Do you have a will?* If not, why not? (pp. 281–283)

20. *Does your spouse have a will?* If not, why not? Are your wills properly coordinated? (pp. 281–283)

21. Who is *named executor (executrix)* in your and your spouse's wills? (pp. 284–285)

22. Have you made specific provision for your personal effects?

23. Are *specific bequests in percentages* of your estate, or limited by percentages, rather than in absolute amounts?

24. Are you making full *use of the federal estate tax marital deduction* to save estate taxes on your estate? Why or why not? Should you plan on using the marital deduction at all in your estate? (pp. 299–300)

25. Is *your estate "overqualified"* for the estate tax marital deduction? Do you have *too much property held in joint names* with right of survivorship? (pp. 301–303 and 310–311)

26. What method(s) are you now using to *qualify the right amount of property for the marital deduction*? Is a *formula provision* desirable? (pp. 303–304)

27. If you are using *marital* and *nonmarital trusts*, what *rights or powers* should you give your *surviving spouse* (or perhaps others) in one or both of these trusts? (p. 303)

28. In general, how much latitude do you want your spouse (or others) to have in dealing with your estate after your death?

29. What provisions (or other considerations), *if any*, do you want to have in the event of *your spouse's remarriage*?

30. When should your *children* (or grandchildren, etc.) *have final control* over their share of your estate?

31. Can you *coordinate* your estate planning with that of *other family members* (parents, grandparents, grown successful children, etc.) who will or do have sizable estates?

32. Are there family members (or others) who may try to unduly influence your spouse or other heirs? How can you deal with this?

33. Do you need any *trusts* in your estate planning? If so, *who should be named trustee* or co-trustees? Should you use *individual or corporate trustees*, or both? (pp. 286–288)

34. Will the trust(s) have enough assets to make naming a corporate trustee economical? (pp. 286–287)

35. Is there a provision in the trust agreement *allowing the beneficiaries to change a corporate trustee*? Should there be one? (p. 288)

36. How have you provided for property that may go to *minor heirs*? (Also see "Life Insurance" above.)

37. Should you leave property to some individuals for their lifetime only (life estate) rather than outright?

38. Have you or your spouse made any *taxable gifts*? Filed a *federal gift tax return*? (pp. 306–308)

39. Should you consider *making some gifts during your lifetime* (inter vivos gifts)? What factors should you consider? Should any *gifts be outright or in trust*? (pp. 305–308)

40. If you want to do so, how can you make *lifetime gifts to minors* (children, grandchildren, nieces, nephews, etc.)? (pp. 262–264)

41. What part of your estate goes to your heirs under your will (probate estate) and what part goes outside of your probate estate? How? Should this be changed? (pp. 278–279)

42. Can you *reduce federal estate taxes, state death taxes,* and *estate settlement costs*? Are these important considerations in your case? (pp. 299–308)

43. Should you provide *more liquidity for your estate*? *How* can this be done? (pp. 296–297)

44. Should you attempt to *"skip the estate"* of one or more of your heirs to save estate taxes? Should your spouse

attempt to "skip" your estate for the same reason? (Also see No. 7 above.) (pp. 304–305)

45. Are any *death benefits under a "qualified" retirement plan payable to your estate*? (Also see "Planning for Your Retirement," No. 8 above.) If so, should this be changed?

46. How should you hold title to your property? In your own name? Jointly? Other? Should any of your present property arrangements be changed? (pp. 273–276)

47. How can you deal with the tax impact of a *maturing endowment insurance policy*? Of a policy you are surrendering? Are you taking the necessary actions in time? (pp. 313–314)

48. Will your spouse be able to take advantage of *the $1,000 interest-element exclusion* with respect to your life insurance proceeds? (pp. 312–313)

49. *Should you own the life insurance on your life*, or should someone else or a trust be the owner? (pp. 316–323)

50. *Should you own the life insurance on another's life*, or should someone else or a trust be the owner? (pp. 319–320)

51. *Should you give away any of your existing life insurance*? What factors should you consider in deciding? (pp. 322–323)

52. *Should you give away your group life insurance*? (p. 323)

53. How should your life insurance (or other death benefits) be made payable? Should you use *settlement options, an insurance trust, or both*? (pp. 316–319 and 324)

54. Should you, your parents, or other relatives consider establishing a so-called *"grandparent-grandchild insurance trust"*? (pp. 321–322)

55. Do you carry *life insurance on your spouse (wife insurance)*? Should you? (pp. 323–324)

56. Is a *revocable living trust* advisable for you and your family? Can it be used to serve as a will substitute in your case? (pp. 324–326)

57. Have you made provision for the *common disaster* or short-term-survivorship situation in your estate plan? How would this affect your decision on the use of the marital deduction?

58. If you own a closely held business interest, do you *plan to sell (or liquidate) it, or to retain it, in the event of your death, disability, or retirement*? (p. 328)

59. If you plan to sell your interest, do you have a legally enforceable *buy-sell agreement*? Is it *insured*? Does it deal with both death and disability? (pp. 328–339)

60. If you plan to retain your interest, should you consider a *partial stock redemption (Section 303 redemption)* if your estate would be eligible? (pp. 339–340)

VI. COORDINATION AND REVIEW

A. Do you *regularly review and update* your personal financial planning?

B. Who are your *professional and financial advisors*? Accountant? Attorney? Banker? Broker or investment advisor? Life insurance agent? Property and liability (general) insurance agent or broker? Other?

C. Do you have *adequate and accessible personal financial records*?

D. Do you have a *safe deposit box* or other safekeeping system?

PERSONAL FINANCIAL PLANNING REVIEW FORMS

INCLUDING THE FOLLOWING FORMS:

1. Your Family Balance Sheet
2. Your Family Income Statement
3. Your Insurance Coverages Worksheets
4. Analysis of Your Investment Portfolio
5. Your Estimated Retirement Income
6. Tax and Estate Planning Worksheets

HOW YOU CAN USE THESE FORMS

You can use these forms in many ways. First, you can use them in conjunction with Personal Financial Planning to review your entire personal financial situation in an organized, coordinated manner. By reading the book and then filling out the information that is appropriate for you in these six forms, you can identify the areas in which your previous planning has met your and your family's financial needs as well as the areas in which there may be gaps, problems, or weaknesses in your present planning.

The information developed in the forms along with the explanations in the book also may suggest some possible solutions for these gaps, problems, or weaknesses that you can discuss with your professional and financial advisors. Of course, any specific solutions or financial plans should be developed with the aid and advice of your professional and financial advisors. The book and these forms are not intended to be a substitute for their services and professional advice.

On the other hand, you may not wish to complete all the forms at once. Instead, at that time you may be interested in reviewing only one or a few areas, such as your investments, pension and retirement benefits, or life insurance coverage, for example. In this case, you can review in detail only those forms, or parts of forms, that apply to your particular interests, and then relate the information developed in the form or forms to the specific parts or chapters of the book that explain the area or areas in which you are interested.

The forms also may provide you with much useful, organized information about your personal financial affairs that you may need in dealing with your professional and financial advisors. The more you can tell them about your affairs, the better they can serve you. Again, of course, these forms are not intended to be a substitute for the more detailed and extensive information that your professional advisors may seek in making specific recommendations to you in the area of their specialty.

An effort has been made to design these forms to cover as many situations and areas as reasonably possible. Therefore, certain items or areas will not apply to everyone. Also, some items deliberately call for estimates or approximations. In most cases, however, a great deal of the information needed to complete these forms is readily available.

FORM 1

YOUR FAMILY BALANCE SHEET (as of present date)

ASSETS

Liquid Assets

Cash and checking account(s) $ _____

Savings account(s)   _____

Life insurance cash values   _____

U.S. Savings Bonds   _____

Brokerage accounts   _____

Other   _____

    Total liquid assets $ _____

Marketable Investments

Common stocks   _____

Mutual funds   _____

Bonds (corporate, municipal, etc.)   _____

Other   _____

    Total marketable investments   _____

"Nonmarketable" Investments

Business interests   _____

Investment real estate   _____

Pension, profit-sharing, etc.,
accounts   _____

Tax-sheltered investments   _____

Other   _____

    Total "nonmarketable"
    investments   _____

Personal Real Estate

Residence   _____

Vacation home   _____

    Total personal real estate   _____

Other Personal Assets

Auto(s)   _____

Boat(s)   _____

Furs and jewelry   _____

Collections, hobbies, etc.   _____

Furniture and household
accessories   _____

Other personal property   _____

   Total other personal assets   _____

      Total assets $_____

LIABILITIES AND NET WORTH

Current Liabilities

Charge accounts, credit card
charges, and other bills payable $_____

Installment credit and other short-
term loans   _____

Unusual tax liabilities   _____

   Total current liabilities $_____

Long-term Liabilities

Mortgage(s) on personal real
estate   _____

Mortgage(s) on investment real
estate   _____

Bank loans   _____

Margin loans   _____

Life insurance policy loans   _____

Other   _____

   Total long-term liabilities   _____

      Total liabilities $_____

      Family net worth $_____

      Total liabilities and family net
      worth $_____

FORM 2
YOUR FAMILY INCOME STATEMENT (for the most recent year)

INCOME

Salary(ies)

You $ _____

Your spouse _____

Others _____

Total salaries $ _____

Investment Income

Interest (taxable) _____

Interest (nontaxable) _____

Dividends _____

Real estate _____

Realized capital gains _____

Other investment income _____

Total investment income _____

Bonuses, Profit-sharing payments, etc. _____

Other income _____

Total income $ _____

EXPENSES AND FIXED OBLIGATIONS

Ordinary living expenses $ _____

Interest expense

Consumer loans $ _____

Bank loans _____

Mortgage(s) _____

Insurance policy loans _____

Other interest _____

Total interest expense _____

Debt amortization (mortgages, consumer debt, etc.) _____

Insurance Premiums

Life insurance _____

Health insurance _____

Property and liability insurance _____

Total insurance premiums _____

Charitable Contributions   _____

Taxes

   Federal income tax   _____

   State (and City) income tax(es)   _____

   Social Security Tax(es)   _____

   Local property taxes   _____

   Other taxes   _____

     Total taxes   _____

      Total expenses and fixed
      obligations $ _____

Balance available for discretionary
   investment $ _____

FORM 3

YOUR INSURANCE COVERAGES WORKSHEETS (How Much Do You Have and Need?)

I. Life Insurance and Other Death Benefits

A. Individual life insurance policies you own on your own life:

Kind of policy (including any life insurance riders)	Net annual premium (gross premium –any policy dividends)	Latest annual increase in cash value	Total cash value	Policy loans out-standing	Net amount of protection (face of policy & additional death benefits– policy loans
	$	$	$	$	$

B. Individual life insurance policies that others own on your life:

Kind of policy (including any life insurance riders)	Net annual premium (gross premium –any policy dividends)	Latest annual increase in cash value	Total cash value	Policy loans out-standing	Net amount of protection (face of policy & additional death benefits– policy loans
	$	$	$	$	$

C. Group life insurance: **Face amount**

   1. Employer provided group term life $

   2. Other employer provided group life $

   3. Association group life $

D. Death benefits under: **Lump sum**

   1. Pension and profit-sharing plans $

   2. Other employer provided plans $

   3. HR–10, IRA, and tax-sheltered annuity (TSA) plans $

   4. Personal annuity contracts $

E. Other death benefits $

F. Total of other income producing assets you own that would pass to your heirs (include property you own in your own name, jointly owned property, and community property) $ _____

G. Total available assets to your family (insurance, employee benefits, and others—Sum of A, B, C, D, E, and F) $ _____

H. Less estimated estate transfer costs (i.e., total estate "shrinkage" because of taxes, expenses, debts, and claims against the estate) (See Chapter 16) $ _____

I. Net income producing assets available to your family $ _____

J. Estimated annual (or monthly) income available to your family:

   1. Net income producing assets (I above) × a reasonable, aftertax investment rate of return (such as 5–7 percent per year) $ _____

   2. Estimated social security survivorship benefits (See Chapter 4) $ _____

   3. Other possible sources of income to your family (e.g., nonqualified deferred compensation plan, survivors' income benefit insurance, pension benefits under a joint and last survivor annuity form, income from a likely inheritance, etc.) $ _____

   4. Total estimated income available to your family (Compare this amount with your family's current budget to note any deficiency (or surplus) in the amount they would need) $ _____

      Estimate from your budget of how much current aftertax income your family would need $ _____

K. The approach, used in I and J above, is a simplified one that most people can just apply for themselves. However, it does not allow for many of the variables that are considered in the more sophisticated *life insurance programming approach* as described in Chapter 4. For example, it does not allow for changing income objectives for your family over time; for family lump sum objectives, such as education, emergency, and mortgage redemption needs; for the fact that Social Security survivorship benefits will change for your family as your children and spouse reach certain ages; and that your life insurance, and perhaps other death benefits, can be liquidated in installments or otherwise to increase the current income available to your family.

Therefore, you also should get an estimate of how much life insurance (and other death benefits) you need according to the *life insurance programming approach* (and perhaps also the human life value approach). Both are described in Chapter 4. For this, most people need the services of their life insurance agent or advisor. These amounts can be shown below:

   1. Total death benefits needed to meet your stated objectives according to your *life insurance program* $ _____

   2. Net income producing assets now available to your family (Item I. above) $ _____

   3. Amount, if any, of additional death protection needed to meet your stated objectives $ _____

   4. For additional reference, if desired, your present human life value: $ _____

II. Disability Income Insurance and Other Disability Benefits

Sources of Monthly Income Available to You and Your Family During Your Total Disability

Source	1st month of disability	Next 4 months of disability (i.e., up to 5 months)	After 5 months until your youngest child reaches age 18 or 22	From when your youngest child reaches age 18 or 22 until you reach age 65 (retirement)
A. Social security disability benefits	$ -0-	$ -0-	$	$
B. Other government disability benefits	$	$	$	$
C. Employer provided "sick-pay"	$	$	$	$
D. Group disability income insurance				
1. Employer provided *short-term* disability insurance	$	$	$	$
2. Employer provided *long-term* disability insurance	$	$	$	$
3. Association group disability insurance	$	$	$	$
E. Individual disability income policies	$	$	$	$
F. Disability income riders added to life insurance policies	$	$	$	$
G. Disability income benefits from pension and profit-sharing, group life insurance, nonqualified deferred compensation, HR-10, and TSA plans	$	$	$	$
H. Other disability benefits	$	$	$	$
I. Estimated monthly investment income	$	$	$	$
J. Total estimated monthly income during disability (sum of A through I)	$	$	$	$

Your Objectives for Monthly Income Available to You and Your Family During Total Disability

Objectives $ ____ $ _____ $ _____ $ _____

Amounts, If Any, of Additional Disability Income Benefits Needed to Meet Your Stated Objectives

Amounts $ ____ $ _____ $ _____ $ _____

III. Medical Expense Insurance and Other Benefits

A. Medical expense insurance and benefits available for you and your family (include maximum limits and any coinsurance and deductible provisions)

Persons Covered   Type of Need (Objective)

	"Basic" hospital, surgical, and medical	"Major medical" (or comprehensive)	"Excess" or catastrophe medical	Health maintenance (HMO)	Medicare (or coverage over age 65)
Yourself	_____	_____	_____	_____	_____
Your spouse and children	_____	_____	_____	_____	_____
	_____	_____	_____	_____	_____
	_____	_____	_____	_____	_____
Other dependents	_____	_____	_____	_____	_____

B. Unmet needs for medical expense insurance or duplicate medical expense insurance

     _____   _____   _____   _____   _____

IV. Property and Liability Insurance

Need (or exposure to loss)	Present protection (including limits of liability)	Unmet needs
A. Property risks (exposures)		
1. Real estate		
a. Residence—estimated replacement cost new is $ _____	_____	_____
b. Vacation or other home-estimated replacement cost new is $ _____	_____	_____
c. Investment real estate	_____	_____

       d. Other real estate (e.g.,
rented, leased, under
construction, etc.)   _____   _____

2. Personal property

   a. Regular (or "unscheduled")
types of personal property

      (1) Owned on your
premises (i.e., your
residence contents)—
estimated current value
$_____   _____   _____

      (2) Owned away from your
premises—estimated
current value $_____   _____   _____

   b. Special personal property
(or "scheduled" types of
personal property)

      (1) Automobiles—
estimated current
values

          $_____   _____   _____

          $_____   _____   _____

          $_____   _____   _____

      (2) Watercraft—estimated
current value $_____   _____   _____

      (3) Jewelry, furs, etc.—
estimated current
values $_____   _____   _____

      (4) Money and coin
collections—estimated
current values $_____   _____   _____

      (5) Stamp collections,
securities, etc.—
estimated current
values $_____   _____   _____

      (6) Other high-value
property (e.g., fine arts,
antiques, cameras,
musical instruments,
etc.—estimated current
values $_____   _____   _____

      (7) Aircraft   _____   _____

B. Liability risks (exposures)

  1. Real estate (premises
exposures)

    a. Residence   _____   _____

b. Vacation or other home   _____   _____

c. Investment real estate   _____   _____

d. Other premises (e.g., rental, leased, under your care, custody, or control)   _____   _____

2. Automobiles   _____   _____

3. Watercraft   _____   _____

4. Aircraft   _____   _____

5. Snowmobiles or other recreational motor vehicles   _____   _____

6. Business or professional liability   _____   _____

7. Workmen's compensation   _____   _____

FORM 4

ANALYSIS OF YOUR INVESTMENT PORTFOLIO

I. Your Present Investment Portfolio (Include Assets You Own Individually or Jointly)

Kinds of assets	Descriptions and amounts of assets	Cost (basis for income tax purposes)	Current market value	Percentage of portfolio (based on current market value)	Net annual income	Current yield	Current yield after taxes	Has asset increased or decreased in value in last year? 5 years?
A. Cash, checking accounts, and brokerage accounts			$					
Subtotal			$	%				
B. Savings accounts and savings certificates			$		$	%	%	
Subtotal			$	%	$			
C. Life insurance cash values (See Forms 1 and 3)			$	%				

Kinds of assets	Descriptions and amounts of assets	Cost (basis for income tax purposes)	Current market value	Percentage of portfolio (based on current market value)	Net annual income	Current yield	Current yield after taxes	Has asset increased or decreased in value in last year? 5 years?
D. Common stocks		$	$		$	%	%	
Total common stocks		$	$	%	$			
E. Mutual funds			$		$	%	%	
Total mutual funds			$	%	$			
F. Corporate bonds		$	$		$	%	%	
Total corporate bonds		$	$	%	$			
G. Municipal bonds			$		$	%	%	
Total municipal bonds			$	%	$			

H. U.S. government
securities: _____ $_____ $_____ % $_____ %

I. U.S. savings bonds _____ $_____ % $_____ % $_____ %

J. Preferred stocks _____ $_____ % $_____ % $_____ %

K. Investment real
estate (show
mortgages,
depreciation, cash
flow, etc., if
desired) _____ $_____ % $_____ % $_____ %

L. Tax-sheltered
investments _____ $_____ % $_____ % $_____ %

M. Profit-sharing,
thrift, tax-
sheltered _____ $_____
annuity, HR-10, IRA, _____
and similar _____
accounts _____

Subtotal _____ $_____ % _____

N. Business interests
you own _____ $_____ % $_____ % $_____ %

O. Other investment
type assets _____ $_____ % $_____ %

Totals _____ $_____ 100% $_____

II. Your Spouse's Present Investment Portfolio (Include Assets Your Spouse Owns Individually or Jointly with Someone Other Than Yourself)

Kinds of assets	Descriptions and amounts of assets	Cost (basis for income tax purposes)	Current market value	Percentage of portfolio (based on current market value)	Net annual income	Current yield	Current yield after taxes	Has asset increased or decreased in value in last year? 5 years?

III. Breakdown of Your (and Your Spouse's) Current Annual Investment Income (Use Current or Latest Year as Desired) (Also see Form 2)

Investment source	Ordinary income	Realized long-term capital gains	Tax-free income	Tax deferred income
A. Savings accounts				
B. Savings certificates				
C. Common stocks				
D. Mutual funds				
E. Corporate bonds				
F. Municipal bonds				
G. U.S. government securities				
H. U.S. Savings Bonds				
I. Preferred stocks				

J. Investment real estate

K. Other

_____

_____

_____

Totals $ _____ $ _____ $ _____ $ _____

IV. How Attractive Is Tax-exempt Investment Income
(e.g., from Municipal Bonds) to You?

A. Current tax-exempt yield available to you _____ %

B. Current fully-taxable yield (on securities of comparable quality) available
to you _____ %

C. Your highest federal tax rate (and state, etc., if yield in A above also is tax-
exempt with respect to these other income taxes) _____ %

D. Subtract your highest tax rate (from C above) from 100% _____ %

E. Multiply the fully-taxable yield (from B above) by 100% — your highest tax
rate (i.e., D above), and compare the resulting aftertax yield with the
current tax-exempt yield (from A above).

V. Your Investment Objectives

A. Rank the following investment goals in their order of importance to you (1 through 9).

1. Long-term capital growth primarily _____

2. Conservative long-term capital growth with some current income _____

3. Intermediate-term appreciation (up to, say, 12 months) primarily _____

4. Intermediate-term appreciation with some current income _____

5. Maximum current income, accepting the appropriate investment risks _____

6. Safety of capital with as high an aftertax current return as possible (consistent with safety) _____

7. Aggressive, rapid capital growth _____

8. Tax-sheltered investments _____

9. Other _____

B. How much annual income should your investment portfolio provide?
$ _____   Yield _____ %

C. Does your present investment portfolio meet your stated objectives? _____
If not, why not? _____

D. Can you increase the yield from your portfolio, consistent with your other objectives?
If so, how _____

VI. Composition of Your Portfolio

A. Diversification

1. From I and II above of Form 4, what kind of asset (e.g., stocks, bonds, etc.) represents the largest percentage of your present investment portfolio?
Asset _____   Percentage _____

2. Also, what single security is most important?
Security _____   Percentage _____

3. What other concentrations of assets do you have?
_____
_____
_____

4. Is your portfolio sufficiently diversified to meet your objectives? If not, why not?
_____

(See Chapter 7 for the factors you should consider on diversification.)

B. Liquidity position (emergency fund)

   1. Present liquid assets (See Form 1 for total)

     $ _____

   2. Your liquidity (emergency fund) objective is

     $ _____

VII. Analysis of Your Debts

Obligation (kind and amount)	Maturity date	Interest rate	Periodic payments	Prepayment privileges
		%	$	

A. Considering your aftertax interest cost, would it be advantageous for you to liquidate any of your present investments and use the proceeds to pay off debt? If so, which ones? _____

B. Considering available yields, security, and your tax position, should you consider borrowing to acquire any investments (i.e., using leverage)? If so, what obligations should you incur for which investments? _____

FORM 5

YOUR ESTIMATED RETIREMENT INCOME

I. Planned Retirement Age: You _____ Your Spouse _____

II. Estimated Monthly Retirement Income Desired

   1. For you (and your spouse) $ _____

   2. For your surviving spouse $ _____

III. Sources of Estimated Monthly Retirement Income Available to You (and your spouse)

Source	Age when the income is to begin	Income for you (and your spouse) —amount and duration (if not for life)	Continuing income for your surviving spouse —amount and duration (if not for life)
A. Social security retirement benefits	_____	$ _____	$ _____
B. Other government benefits	_____	_____	_____
C. Pension plan	_____	_____	_____
D. Profit-sharing plan	_____	_____	_____
E. Nonqualified deferred compensation	_____	_____	_____
F. Other employee benefits	_____	_____	_____
G. HR-10 plans	_____	_____	_____
H. Individual retirement annuity or account (IRA)	_____	_____	_____
I. Tax-sheltered annuity (TSA) plan	_____	_____	_____
J. Life insurance cash values and the estimated value of any accumulated dividends	_____	_____	_____
K. Other individual annuities (fixed-dollar and variable)	_____	_____	_____
L. Estimated investment income from your (and your spouse's) general investment fund, projected at a reasonable rate of return to your planned retirement age	_____	_____	_____
M. Estimated investment income from any expected inheritances	_____	_____	_____
N. Proceeds from any sale or liquidation of a business interest at or during retirement	_____	_____	_____

O. Proceeds from any other
planned liquidation of
assets during retirement   _____   _____   _____

P. Other sources of
retirement income

_____   _____   _____   _____

_____   _____   _____   _____

_____   _____   _____   _____

_____   _____   _____   _____

Totals $_____ $_____

IV. Control of Your Estimated Retirement Income

How much of the above sources of retirement income would you retain (control) if you
took an action such as changing jobs (e.g., social security, vested rights in pension and
profit-sharing plans, etc.)?

For you (and your spouse) $_____

For your surviving spouse $_____

V. What, If Any, Additional Retirement Income (Or Guarantees) Do You (Or Your Spouse)
Need to Meet Your Objectives?

Possible sources	Amounts
_____	$_____
_____	$_____
_____	$_____

FORM 6

TAX AND ESTATE PLANNING WORKSHEETS

I. Income Tax Planning

   A. Your top income-tax-bracket or rate (consider federal, state, and local income taxes)
     _____ %

    (Also see Item IV. C of Form 4)

   B. Tax planning for capital gains and losses (See Chapter 14 for tax-saving techniques regarding such gains and losses)

     1. *Realized* capital gains and losses for the current year

Capital asset	Short-term (on assets held 6 months or less)		Long-term (on assets held more than 6 months)	
	Short-term capital gains	Short-term capital losses	Long-term capital gains	Long-term capital losses
_____	$ _____	$ _____	$ _____	$ _____
_____	_____	_____	_____	_____
_____	_____	_____	_____	_____
_____	_____	_____	_____	_____
_____	_____	_____	_____	_____
Totals	$ _____	$ _____	$ _____	$ _____

     2. *Unrealized* capital gains and losses

Capital asset	Short-term (on assets held 6 months or less)		Long-term (on assets held more than 6 months)	
	Short-term capital gains	Short-term capital losses	Long-term capital gains	Long-term capital losses
_____	$ _____	$ _____	$ _____	$ _____
_____	_____	_____	_____	_____
_____	_____	_____	_____	_____
_____	_____	_____	_____	_____
_____	_____	_____	_____	_____
Totals	$ _____	$ _____	$ _____	$ _____

C. Consideration of specific tax-saving techniques, for example:
(See Chapters 13, 14, and 18 for discussions of these techniques)

Technique	Presently used	Not applicable	Would consider	Would not consider
Taking tax-losses on securities	_____	_____	_____	_____
Deduction of expenses for an office at home	_____	_____	_____	_____
Deduction of the costs of a professional library	_____	_____	_____	_____
Income averaging	_____	_____	_____	_____
Buying municipal bonds	_____	_____	_____	_____
Making other tax-sheltered investments	_____	_____	_____	_____
Giving appreciated long-term capital gain property to charity	_____	_____	_____	_____
Use of short-term "Clifford-type" trusts	_____	_____	_____	_____
Gifts to minors under uniform gifts to minors acts	_____	_____	_____	_____
Other gifts	_____	_____	_____	_____
HR-10 plans	_____	_____	_____	_____
Individual retirement annuities or accounts (IRAs)	_____	_____	_____	_____
Tax-sheltered annuity (TSA) plan	_____	_____	_____	_____
Election of subchapter S corporation status	_____	_____	_____	_____
Other				
_____	_____	_____	_____	_____
_____	_____	_____	_____	_____
_____	_____	_____	_____	_____

II. Estate Planning

A. Estimating your estate for federal estate tax purposes (See Chapter 16 for the calculation of the federal estate tax)

Gross estate $ _____

Less: deductions from the gross estate   − $ _____

Adjusted gross estate $ _____

Less:

    Marital deduction $ _____

    Charitable bequests _____

    Specific exemption + 60,000 _____   – $ _____

Taxable estate $ _____

Federal estate tax (ignoring possible credits for simplicity) $ _____

B. Your top federal-estate-tax bracket or rate (if any)   _____ %

C. Estimate of state death taxes payable (if available) $ _____

D. Estimate of your estate's liquidity needs (transfer costs):

    1. Federal estate tax $ _____

    2. State death tax   _____

    3. Debts   _____

    4. Estimated funeral and estate administration expenses   _____

    5. Other needs   _____

    Total liquidity needs $ _____

E. What part (if any) of your gross estate potentially "qualifies" for the federal estate tax marital deduction? (See Chapter 16 for an explanation of the marital deduction.)

    1. Property passing outright to your surviving spouse $ _____

    2. Property passing to your surviving spouse in trust so as to "qualify" for the deduction   _____

    3. Jointly owned property that "qualifies"   _____

    4. Life insurance and other death benefits payable to your spouse so as to "qualify" for the deduction   _____

    5. Other ways

    _____   _____

    _____   _____

    _____   _____

    Total that potentially "qualifies" (ignoring, for simplicity, amounts that may have to be used to pay estate debts, expenses, and taxes.) $ _____

F. Maximum allowable federal estate tax marital deduction (½ × adjusted gross estate) $ _____

G. For purposes of the marital deduction, is your estate at present potentially:

   1. "Overqualified?" Approximate amount $ _____

   2. "Underqualified?" Approximate amount $ _____

H. What part of your estate now must pass through probate?

   1. Property you own in your own name (i.e., individually) $ _____

   2. Life insurance proceeds and other death benefits payable to your estate   _____

   3. Your share of property you own as tenants in common   _____

   4. Separate property in community property states   _____

   5. Other   _____

   Total probate estate $ _____

I. Who will receive your net estate under your present estate arrangements? (Include any special arrangements, such as trusts)

_____

_____

_____

_____

_____

J. Methods of estate transfer—check the methods you are now using and would consider (See Chapters 15, 16, and 17 for discussions of these methods)

Method	Presently used	Would consider	Not applicable
Outright bequests in your will	_____	_____	_____
Bequests in trust under your will (testamentary trusts)	_____	_____	_____
Jointly owned property	_____	_____	_____
Community property	_____	_____	_____
Life insurance and other beneficiary designations	_____	_____	_____
Revocable lifetime trusts	_____	_____	_____
Irrevocable lifetime trusts	_____	_____	_____
Outright lifetime gifts	_____	_____	_____
Other			
_____	_____	_____	_____

K. Arrangement of life insurance in your estate plan

1. Life insurance (and other death benefits) that you own on your life

| | | | Settlement arrangements | | |
Policy or plan	Amount	Beneficiary designations	Lump sum	Settlement options(s)	Life insurance trust
_____	$ _____	_____	_____	_____	_____
_____	_____	_____	_____	_____	_____
_____	_____	_____	_____	_____	_____
_____	_____	_____	_____	_____	_____
_____	_____	_____	_____	_____	_____
_____	_____	_____	_____	_____	_____
_____	_____	_____	_____	_____	_____

2. Life insurance that others own on your life

Policy	Amount	Owner	Beneficiary designations	Settlement arrangements
_____	$ _____	_____	_____	_____
_____	_____	_____	_____	_____
_____	_____	_____	_____	_____

3. Life insurance that you own on the life of another

Policy	Amount	Insured	Beneficiary designations	Settlement arrangements
_____	$ _____	_____	_____	_____
_____	_____	_____	_____	_____
_____	_____	_____	_____	_____

L. Lifetime gifts

1. What, if any, significant lifetime gifts have you made? What property, to whom, and how?

_____

_____

_____

2. Have you made gifts that are subject to federal gift taxation?

_____

If so, what is your top federal-gift-tax rate? _____

INDEX

INDEX